CLARENDON LIBRARY OF LOGIC AND PHILOSOPHY

General Editor: L. Jonathan Cohen, The Queen's College, Oxford

METAPHOR

The Clarendon Library of Logic and Philosophy brings together books, by new as well as by established authors, that combine originality of theme with rigour of statement. Its aim is to encourage new research of a professional standard into problems that are of current or perennial interest.

General Editor: L. Jonathan Cohen, The Queen's College, Oxford.

Also published in this series

METAPHOR

ITS COGNITIVE FORCE AND
LINGUISTIC STRUCTURE

EVA FEDER KITTAY

CLARENDON PRESS · OXFORD

Oxford University Press, Walton Street, Oxford OX2 6DP

Oxford New York
Athens Auckland Bangkok Bombay
Calcutta Cape Town Dar es Salaam Delhi
Florence Hong Kong Istanbul Karachi
Kuala Lumpur Madras Madrid Melbourne
Mexico City Nairobi Paris Singapore
Taipei Tokyo Toronto

and associated companies in
Berlin Ibadan

Oxford is a trade mark of Oxford University Press

Published in the United States by
Oxford University Press Inc., New York

© Eva Feder Kittay 1987

First issued in paperback 1989

British Library Cataloguing in Publication Data
Kittay, Eva Feder
Metaphor: its cognitive force and
linguistic structure.—(Clarendon library
of logic and philosophy).
1. Metaphor. I. Title
808 PN228.M4
ISBN 0-19-824246-8 (Pbk.)

Library of Congress Cataloging in Publication Data
Kittay, Eva Feder.
Metaphor: its cognitive force and linguistic
structure.
(Clarendon library of logic and philosophy)
1. Metaphor. 2. Semantics. 3. Field theory
(Linguistics). 4. Cognition. I. Title. II. Series.
P301.5.M48K58 1987 169 87-1596
ISBN 0-19-824246-8 (Pbk.)

5 7 9 10 8 6

Printed in Hong Kong

TO MY PARENTS,
SARA AND LEO

ACKNOWLEDGEMENTS

THIS work has been a long time in the making, and there have been numerous persons who have offered extensive and invaluable help. The one individual who read and commented on the manuscript in its entirety—and read most parts of it many times over—whose generous encouragement and unstinting criticisms have made this a far better book than it would otherwise have been is Richard Grandy. I owe him a great debt of gratitude. Adrienne Lehrer is importantly responsible for a portion of the book. The specific employment of the theory of semantic fields for the analysis of metaphor would not have been possible without her collaboration. I am indebted to Malgorzata Askanas for her help in formulating the formal representations in Chapters 2 and 4 and for the many hours of discussion we have had on the issues dealt with in this book. I want to thank L. Jonathan Cohen for his interest in this work and for his useful comments. Colleagues and friends who have read the manuscript in part or in its entirety and have offered useful criticisms include Patricia Athay, Dan Hausman, Jeffrey Kittay, Keith Lehrer, William Lycan, Rita Nolan, Michael Simon, Neil Tennant, Mark Aronoff, Donn Welton, and an anonymous reviewer for the Oxford University Press; I also wish to thank Leofranc Holford-Strevens and the OUP Desk-editing Department, for their care in editing the manuscript. I owe profound gratitude to Lindsay Waters for his early and steadfast interest in and encouragement of my work.

Since my thinking about the question of metaphor began in the prehistory of my professional career in philosophy, I must express my gratitude to my friend and former teacher, Elfie Raymond. In her classes I first became aware of the importance of metaphor. I want to thank Peter Caws, who directed the dissertation that eventuated in this book, as well as Arnold Koslow, Charles Landesman, and Samuel Levin, who offered valuable suggestions which in time became incorporated in the present work.

A number of graduate students have been instrumental in this project. The graduate students in seminars in which I treated metaphor stimulated my thinking on a number of issues. For help in the preparation of this volume I want to thank Judy Russell for her assistance in collecting bibliographical material, and James Hatley and James Carmine for their thoughtful and diligent editorial assistance on various drafts of the manuscript. My thanks to the staff at the Department of Philosophy at SUNY, Stony Brook, especially Mary Bruno and Virginia Massaro for their support in various aspects of this project. Lorna Malloy, typist and friend, helped with putting the finishing touches to the manuscript.

Portions of the book have appeared elsewhere. Chapter 2 originated as 'The Identification of Metaphor', *Synthese*, vol. 58, No. 2 1984. Copyright ©1984 by D. Reidel Publishing Company. Reprinted by permission. Chapter 7 Section 1 is a revised version of an article co-authored with Adrienne Lehrer, 'Semantic Fields and the Structure of Metaphor', *Studies in Language*, vol. 5, 1981. Finally, portions of Chapter 3, Section 1 and Chapter 8, Section 2 are taken from 'A Reply to Davidson's "What Metaphors Mean"—Or Rearranging the Furniture of Our Minds' in *The Philosophy of Language*, edited by Max Freund (Costa Rica, University of Costa Rica Press, forthcoming). I should like to thank the editors and publishers for permission to reprint the materials here.

Financial assistance for the preparation of Chapters 2 and 4 was provided by a SUNY Awards Grant. The manuscript would have taken still longer to complete had the Department of Philosophy at SUNY, Stony Brook, not been so gracious in granting me time on leave.

To my family, Jeffrey, Leo, Sesha, and Margaret Grennan, I owe the greatest gratitude. Without their patience and support in all areas, truly, this work would not have been possible.

CONTENTS

INTRODUCTION

Philosophy and Metaphor

THE study of metaphor has long been with us, and throughout its history it has had a stormy, tenuous, but tenacious affair with philosophy. Philosophy has, by turns, rejected and embraced metaphor, its suppliant. We can tell the tale from its inception in Greek philosophy. Plato, himself a master of metaphor, disdained the finery of eloquence. Aristotle, the more prosaic writer, gave metaphor its due—in his writings both on poetics and on rhetoric. Aristotle's treatment found its way into the classical and Renaissance texts on rhetoric. Plato's disapproval prevailed in the more strictly philosophical texts. Locke's denunciations of figurative language set the tone for the philosophical disregard for metaphor—a position in which rationalist and empiricist were united. Only those philosophers associated with the Romantic tradition paid much heed to its importance.

With the notable exception of the Romantics, thinkers regarded metaphor primarily as an enhancement of language, one in which either a substitution or an implicit comparison took place. To its detractors it was a mere embellishment, swaying the passions, 'seducing the Reason', as Gaston Bachelard wrote—while he himself used the figure, seductively, to damn it. To its champions, its lack of utility, its sheer capacity to delight, was the reason for its privileged place in language. Quintilian wrote: 'The ornate is something that goes beyond what is merely lucid and acceptable' (*De Institutione Oratoria*, 803. 61, trans. H. E. Butler). And Cicero relates that metaphor was first invented out of necessity ('it sprang from necessity due to the pressure of poverty'), but in the affluence of a mature language it became decorative and noble:

> As clothes were first invented to protect us against cold, and afterwards began to be used for the sake of adornment and dignity, so the metaphorical employment of words began because of poverty, but was brought into common use for the sake of entertainment. (*De Oratore*, 3. 155, E. W. Sutton and H. Rackham.)

Cicero might have remarked that dress, no matter how elaborate it becomes, still serves basic needs and desires for warmth, protection, etc.—so metaphor might serve a basic need even in the midst of an affluent language. Yet for Cicero, the remnant of utility would only tarnish the brilliance provided by metaphor: 'there is another somewhat bolder kind that do not indicate poverty but convey some degree of boldness to the style' (*De Oratore*, 3. 156). The society of metaphors is not classless, but aristocratic, mirroring the society from which this view sprang forth, where what is most valued is furthest removed from utility and need.

Today, metaphor is experiencing a revitalized interest within philosophy. If we cannot claim that ours is a period of blissful reunion, we can say that there are attempted reconciliation and compensation for centuries of neglect. The articles on the subject in professional philosophical journals and books bear testimony to something more than a mere dalliance. And the fervour, curiously, is most pronounced among analytic philosophers.

The new closer relation brings a new focus to the study of metaphor. Metaphor is plumbed not for its affective and rhetorical efficacy, but for its cognitive contribution. From our own work-centred perspective, if metaphor is to be prized, it must do work, and the work that most interests philosophers is that which is cognitively meaningful.

A Bow to Aristotle

> But the greatest thing, by far, is to be a master of metaphor. It is the one thing that cannot be learnt from others; and it is also a sign of genius since a good metaphor implies an intuitive perception of similarity of dissimilars. Through resemblance, metaphor makes things clearer. (Aristotle, *Poetics*, trans. W. D. Ross, 1459[a] 5–7.)

The argument can be made that Aristotle had already pointed out the cognitive importance of metaphor, particularly metaphor based on analogy. As an example, Aristotle chooses the phrase 'sowing around a god-created flame'. The casting forth of seed-corn, he says, is called sowing, but the act of the sun casting forth its flames has no special name. The phrase emerges through an analogical transfer of meaning: 'This nameless act (B), however, stands in just the same relation to its object, sunlight (A), as sowing (D) to the seed-corn (C). Hence the expression in the poet 'sowing around a god-created flame (D + A)'. (1457[b] 26–30.)

This act is nameless because it was not conceived as an act until the perception was so formulated by the metaphor. The metaphor was itself instrumental in having identified a *something* to be named. The metaphor thereby provides us with a way of learning something new about the world, or about how the world may be perceived and understood. Where metaphor is used when a 'proper' name exists, Aristotle indicated yet another cognitive feature: it is a means of remarking on a previously unrecognized similarity. Aristotle speaks of the usefulness of an examination of likeness: ' . . . it is by induction of particulars on the basis of similarities that we infer the universal.' (Topica 108^b 7–10 trans. by E.S. Forster. Harvard UP 1966) 'Examining likeness' is useful for hypothetical reasoning because 'it is a general opinion that among similars what is true of one is also true of the rest'. Aristotle, believing similarity to be the basis of metaphorical transference, and granting to the perception of similarity an important cognitive role, saw in metaphor a conceptual tool of much power.

Aristotle most valued metaphor based on analogy, because he regarded analogy as important for reasoning. If two things bear an analogous relationship to one another, the analogy can be a basis for classification and selection different from those applied when two things possess a common generic name. This is applicable to the various fields of inquiry: to ethics as well as to science. In the latter, for example, it allows us to classify together such anatomically related things as 'a squid's pounce, a fish's spine, and an animal's bone'. Aristotle writes: 'It is impossible to find a single name which should be applied to pounce, spine and bone; yet the fact that these too have <common> properties implies, that there is a single natural substance of this kind.' (Posterior Analytica 98a 20–25, trans. by H. Tredennick, Harvard UP, 1966). In ethics, it allows us to produce arguments of the following sort: as sight is good in the body, so intelligence is good in the soul. Presumably, those metaphors that are based on analogy partake of the intellectual virtues Aristotle affords to analogy itself. None the less he warned against metaphorical argument.

Aristotle and the scholastic tradition relied on the coincidence of language and reality: distinctions in language were seen as capturing ontological distinctions (Ross 1981). Discerning analogical uses of language can help us to discern analogical states of reality. If we can perceive the analogical relations between intelligence and sight, then we can argue that the relations between sight and the body hold for relations between the intelligence and the soul.

If we insist that the analogical relations pertain to language and not to the things named, then analogical argumentation fails to rest on adequate grounds. In the chapters that follow, I shall argue for the indispensability of analogical thinking for diverse areas of cognition, seeing it as importantly related to metaphorical thought. But I shall see the justification of the analogical and metaphorical in a validity tied not to ontological commitments but to their role in the formation of predictive and explanatory hypotheses. The hypotheses are, at once, generated metaphorically and analogically from current conceptualizations of the world. Through such metaphorical generation, current conceptualizations undergo transformations.

But the modern interest in the cognitive role of metaphor is one that Aristotle *almost* hit upon. In a negative appraisal,[1] he wrote that, as argumentation, metaphorical expression is always obscure because metaphor results in the same object being placed in two different genera, neither of which includes the other (*Topics*, 139^b 32–140^a2). If a genus is regarded as a perspective upon an object, metaphor results in the placing of an object in two perspectives simultaneously. From this juxtaposition results a reconceptualization, sometimes permanent, more frequently transient, in which properties are made salient which may not previously have been regarded as salient and in which concepts are reorganized both to accommodate and to help shape experience.

While we have credited Aristotle with an appreciation of the cognitive importance of metaphor, most developments of the Aristotelian tradition have treated metaphor as decoration or comparison. In either case metaphor is dispensable in favour of a plainer expression or an explicit statement of similarity.

The Romantic Heritage

> Language is vitally metaphorical; that is, it marks the before unapprehended relations of things and perpetuates their apprehension, until words, which represent them, become, through time, signs for portions or classes of thought instead of pictures of integral thoughts: and then, if no new poets should arise to create afresh the associations which have been thus disorganized, language will be dead to all the nobler purposes of human intercourse. (P. B. Shelley, *A Defence of Poetry*, quoted in Richards, 1936, 90–1.)

The view of language and thought according to which metaphor appears as ornament or comparison requires a conception of mind as a passive receptacle of perceptions. These perceptions, when tidily

---

[1] This appraisal conflicts with what can be inferred from statements he makes regarding analogy and metaphor based on analogy.

brought together through proper rules of inference and logical deduction, result in knowledge only when not adulterated by the imperfect but indispensable vehicle of language. Instead, we need to understand language as an expressive medium, which as Ross (1981) points out, allows us to say that we think *in language*, just as the artist expresses herself *in paint*; that we understand that language is not merely a conduit (see Reddy 1979) for our thoughts. But it is the view of language as conduit that has prevailed—certainly within the philosophical tradition. Without acknowledging his complicity in the use of figurative language, Locke speaks of language as a 'conduit' that may 'corrupt the fountains of knowledge which are in things themselves' and even 'break or stop the pipes whereby it is distributed to public use'.[2] Through the eighteenth and early nineteenth centuries, the view that metaphor was decorative, to be carefully and judiciously administered, dominated the texts of rhetoric. These were largely taxonomies of various stylistic modes, along with principles and precepts admonishing readers on the appropriate use of ornament.[3]

In a short treatise, *Essay on the Origin of Languages* (1781), Jean-Jacques Rousseau speculates that the first time a person sees a stranger in the distance his fear and awe of the stranger compel him to regard the stranger as a giant. Similarly, thought Rousseau, we invest our first perceptions with a magical and metaphorical nature whereby that which is perceived appears to incorporate a multitude of feelings and perceptions. All language originated in metaphor. Literal language is a pruning away and a rationalization of our figurative thought. Rousseau's arguments may be naïve. Nonetheless, they foreshadow a view of language according to which metaphor could be treated as more than mere ornament.

The conception of thought and language necessary to move beyond a restricted view of metaphor requires an understanding of mind as active and creatively engaged in the forming of percepts and concepts

[2] Quoted in de Man 1979, 14. The accompanying view of figurative language can be gleaned from the following excerpted passage: 'If we would speak of things as they are we must allow that . . . all the artificial and figurative application of words eloquence hath invented, are for nothing else but to insinuate wrong *ideas*, move the passions, and thereby mislead the judgment . . . they . . . cannot but be thought a great fault either of the language or person that makes use of them'. (*An Essay on Human Understanding* (1689) bk. 3, ch. 10, quoted in de Man 1979, 13).

[3] Accounts of exemplary English and French studies are given respectively by I. A. Richards and Paul Ricœur. Richards (1936) criticizes Lord Kames's *Elements of Style*. Ricœur (1978*b*) discusses the 19th-cent. French rhetorician Pierre Fontanier.

and in unifying the diversity of the given. For Coleridge, language is not a conduit but an expressive medium for artist and thinker alike, the ground for the work of the imagination. For Coleridge, the imagination is: 'The power by which one image or feeling is made to modify many others and by a sort of fusion to force many into one . . . combining many circumstances into one moment of thought to produce that ultimate end of human thought and human feeling, unity' (*Biographia Literaria* (1817), ch. 2). Metaphor is the linguistic realization of this unity. Metaphor or, at least, metaphor shaped through the imagination, does not record pre-existing similarities in things; rather, it is the linguistic means by which we bring together and fuse into a unity diverse thoughts and thereby re-form our perceptions of the world. Symbols such as a national flag, a crest, an object with ritualistic significance, an iconic and conventionally used representation, also involve such fusion. A unification is also achieved, in a different way though, through the dreamwork Freud calls 'condensation'. What we call metaphor achieves this fusion in a characteristic manner, one which I hope to describe in later chapters.

The conception that rejects the position that metaphor is ornamental, or an implicit comparison, entered contemporary analytic philosophy through the discussions of Max Black. Black put forward the interaction theory of metaphor, which asserted that metaphors have an irreducible meaning and a distinct cognitive content. Black borrowed heavily from I. A. Richards, who in turn was a student of Coleridge. Hence the lineage of current discussions of the cognitive import of metaphor is traced back to that Romanticism, tempered with Kantianism, epitomized by Coleridge.

From Romanticism to contemporary analytic philosophy appears to be a leap across an abyss.[4] The logical positivism to which analytic philosophy is the legitimate, if rebellious, heir had little use or interest in metaphor. Why this new happy union of philosophy and metaphor?

Metaphor and Analytic Philosophy

In turning away from logical positivism, analytic philosophers have become impressed with the importance of metaphor. Curiously those

---

[4] Nietzsche has been an important figure in reviving the interest in metaphor in the continent. His work, especially 'Über Wahrheit und Lüge im außermoralischen Sinne' taken from his Notebooks of the early 1870s (translated into English in Nietzsche, 1979), is central to Derrida's (1975) treatment. But Nietzsche's work has had a limited impact on analytic philosophers.

areas most closely aligned with positivism, philosophy of language and philosophy of science have been most struck. According to the verificationist principle of meaning, the cognitive meaning of a sentence was its method of verification. The doctrine condemned metaphysics and much traditional philosophy to live outside the borders of cognitive significance. Metaphorical language was, of necessity, similarly excluded. If we wanted to ascertain the meaning of Romeo's 'Juliet is the sun' (*Romeo and Juliet*, I. ii. 3), we should determine its truth by checking if Juliet was a celestial body around which planets orbit—the sentence would obviously be false. But, of course, Shakespeare had no such thing in mind when he wrote the line. Some metaphors would fare still worse. It is not clear that there would even be a method of determining the truth or falsity of Wallace Stevens's line 'Moisture and heat have swollen the garden into a slum of bloom'. ('Banal Sojourn', l. 4). Without a procedure to determine its truth, the sentence would be judged to be not false but meaningless. This is not to say that it might not be decorative or evocative and have some sort of *emotive meaning* but it could have no *cognitive meaning*. It could in no way enhance our knowledge of the world. The exemplars of verifiable statements were to be the statements of scientific discourse, the paradigms of cognitive activity. The object of philosophy was to be the systematic presentation of the logical syntax of science. The object of philosophy of language was the construction and investigation of formal languages in which the pristine verifiable statements of science could be stated and studied.

However, it was clear that science made use of 'models'. These models must be understood as extended metaphors—not literally true, but useful representations of the phenomena which often led to fruitful theoretic conceptions and new empirical discoveries. Examples such as the billiard-ball model of gases or the wave models of sound and light were cited as demonstrating the importance of models in the construction of scientific theories. The positivists' response was to say, in a fashion analogous to granting metaphors an emotive meaning distinct from a cognitive one, that models had a merely heuristic value for science. That is, they were valuable for guiding discoveries in science—but then discoveries could be guided by almost anything: dreams, fortuitous findings, a random remark. Models contributed nothing essential to the activity of science itself—an activity to be characterized by the justificatory procedures which uniquely characterized it. Hesse (1966), however, argued persuasively that models were crucial to give theories real predictive power. They figured not just incidently in the context of discovery, but also in the context of justification. Models appeared to play a cognitive role in science, and yet they, like the metaphors of our language, were obviously false or unverifiable.

We now recognize that the verificationist principle sins against itself—that it cannot itself be verified. And positivists' efforts to show that the statements of science were verifiable led to the unproductive programme of reducing theoretical statements to observation statements. In philosophy of science, the thrust was to look at the activities that scientists were engaged in, to examine the history of science and to look at the 'context of discovery'. In philosophy of language the first turning away from positivism was an interest in the ordinary languages people actually spoke rather than in the formal languages of logic and 'reconstructed science'. The very notion of meaning itself became suspect, and the later views of Wittgenstein were condensed in the motto, 'Don't look for the meaning, look for the use'. The move toward the analysis of ordinary language and its various uses, the questioning of the notion of the 'given', the breakdown of the synthetic–analytic distinction, the insistence on the theory-ladenness of observation terms, and progress in linguistics in formulating precise ways of representing the underlying structure and processes of natural language have all created a favourable climate for an inquiry into metaphor.

In addition, metaphor has a bearing on related issues which have begun to occupy philosophers of language and science: creativity in language and science; paradigm-shifts in the history of science; and change of meaning. In language studies, transformational grammar as formulated by Chomsky challenged the view of language as a set of sentences and sought instead to see it as a rule-governed activity in which each speaker exhibited creativity in the production and comprehension of ever new sentences. At first transformational grammar ignored one of the most creative aspects of language use, the use of metaphor. That is now changing and there is great interest among linguists to account for metaphor. The Kuhnian revolution in the philosophy of science provides further incentive to study metaphor, for the notion of a paradigm seems itself, tantalizingly, to be a root metaphor. The interests of linguistic philosophers and philosophers of science converge again on the question of change of meaning. When one theory replaces another in a paradigm-shift, do the terms of the second theory which are carried over from the first theory change in meaning? Because metaphor is itself a kind of change of meaning, some of the interest in metaphor has been generated by the interest in change of meaning. Furthermore, if, as Hesse (1966, 1974, 1980), Wartofsky (1979), and others have argued, models are integral to scientific theories and to the construction of theories, then the philosophy of science calls for an adequate theory of metaphor. We need such a theory to understand the source and the status of scientific concepts and theories.

A final, but vitally important, consideration has come from the joint attempts by philosophers and cognitive scientists to develop models of mind which can be tested by, and can guide, the development of artificial intelligence. The creative functioning of the human mind—its active sorting of informational input such that it can influence and alter its environment in new, unexpected, and yet suitable ways—poses some of the major challenges to philosophers of mind interested in the capacities and limits of artificial intelligence. Can we construct models of mind that allow for the use of metaphor? Is it possible to understand metaphor so that it becomes amenable to the development of artificial intelligence? To what extent can metaphor be given a computational realization? The answers to these questions require a theory of metaphor. Such a theory will advance our understanding of cognitive and creative processes.

The demise of positivism and the concerns raised today provide a climate favourable to the investigation of the cognitive efficacy of metaphor. The criteria by which metaphor was dismissed as meaningless or non-cognitive are themselves now thought questionable. Moreover, new efforts to articulate a semantics and a philosophy of science are committed to providing theories of language as ordinarily encountered, and science as generally practised. That is, there now exists a recognition of the importance of explaining the prima-facie meaningfulness of metaphorical language and the prima-facie importance of models for science. But theories of language which have gained currency have not as yet been able to accommodate metaphor. Today the intellectual atmosphere is attentive to the importance of metaphor; metaphor continues to present a challenging problem for current semantic theories and theories of cognition.

When science is seen as a human activity rather than as the repository of ultimate truths, and cognition generally is seen as the creative shaping of our conceptions of the world, the creative imaginative play of metaphor is seen as characteristic not only of poetry, but also of science. When language is seen not only as the medium of making

picture-like true statements about the world but as a tool for communicating, expressing and creating—a chief element in 'worldmaking'—the role of metaphor must be accounted for in a theory of
language. Consequently, as analytic philosophy turns away from its
vision of the mind as primarily a recorder of empirical data—collected
and ordered in the ratified statements of empirical science—the need
for the development of an adequate theory of metaphor becomes
urgent. By illuminating the creative contribution of mind and language
to knowledge, the study of metaphor will, in turn, force revisions of our
basic views of language and thought.

Some Remarks to the Reader

This book is an attempt to provide a theory of metaphor. In particular,
it is a theory of linguistic metaphor. I do not attempt to answer all the
many questions and concerns for which a theory of metaphor is
needed; nor do I do justice to all aspects of metaphorical thought. It
has seemed to me that the first step in an account of metaphor is to
provide a full understanding of the metaphorical utterance. (For a justification of this strategy see the introductory remarks in Chapter 1.)
Once we have probed the microstructure of the linguistic metaphor,
we shall be in a better position to understand the functioning of metaphor in our daily thought and in the systematic thought of science.
Furthermore, attention to the linguistic metaphor forces us to recon-
sider many strongly held views concerning the nature of language
itself. And an understanding of language has itself come to be seen as
crucial for understanding the nature of thought.

   While many contemporary theories of metaphor have invoked the
semantic–pragmatic divide, insisting that metaphor falls squarely
within one division, my account refuses to stay within the putatively
well-drawn boundaries. Metaphors, I argue, have meaning and they
therefore require a semantic account. But I also hold that a semantic
account does not give us a full comprehension of the ways in which we
understand metaphor and must be supplemented by pragmatic considerations. It is arguable that metaphor does not differ in this regard
from at least some literal language, for example, sentences with
semantically ambiguous terms, indexicals, demonstratives. It is further
arguable that all language is understood contextually and that the
semantic–pragmatic divide is therefore ill drawn. My intent is to give a
full understanding of the linguistic phenomenon that is metaphor, not
to engage in the polemics of defending or denying a sometimes useful

distinction. I therefore use both semantic and pragmatic considerations in my account of metaphor.

A last note to the reader. Detailing a theory of metaphorical meaning has at times required the use of formal notation to represent notions with the desired precision. I have attempted throughout the text to paraphrase all symbolic notation so that the ideas are accessible to readers who are unaccustomed to such formalisms. To readers who are uneasy with formalisms, I suggest that they simply skip these passages. Although some of the aimed-for precision may be lost, the text ought to be quite comprehensible without them.

I

Towards Perspectival Theory of Metaphor

> We cannot get through three sentences of ordinary fluid discourse
> [without the use of metaphor] . . . We think increasingly by means of
> metaphors that we profess *not* to be relying on. The metaphors we
> are avoiding steer our thought as much as those we accept.
> (Richards, 1936, 92.)

A Perspectival Stance; A Linguistic Approach

SINCE writers began to concern themselves with the topic, it has been
recognized that a metaphor is a displaced sign. Aristotle identified the
displacement as a transference and the sign as a name. But why
transfer the name of one thing to another? Words have their meanings,
names name what they name; why displace words and names from
their usual designations? Few writers today take metaphors to be
names; most identify the metaphorical unit as the sentence (and I shall
insist that sometimes still longer strings serve as units). Some writers
have objected to the notion of metaphor as a displacement on the
ground that it makes metaphor appear to be anomalous when instead
we need to recognize it as an integral feature of natural language. But
even these writers find it hard to avoid speaking of metaphor as some
sort of transference of meaning. Thus the question remains: why
engage in such nominal or conceptual detours? Most pertinent to a
philosophical inquiry is whether such transference of meaning serves a
cognitive end.

Black's (1962) essay on metaphor has engendered a literature committed to developing and exploring the thesis that metaphor has an
irreducible cognitive force. The theory to be developed here grows out
of, and sometimes in opposition to, the views of I. A. Richards,
Monroe Beardsley, Paul Henle, Nelson Goodman, and others who
have variously contributed to the interactionist theory articulated by
Black. I prefer to call the account a *perspectival theory*. To call our
theory perspectival is to name it for the function metaphor serves: to
provide a perspective from which to gain an understanding of that

which is metaphorically portrayed. This is a distinctively cognitive role. Since *perspectival* implies a subject who observes from a stance, we can say that metaphor provides the linguistic realization for the cognitive activity by which a language speaker makes use of one linguistically articulated domain to gain an understanding of another experiential or conceptual domain, and similarly, by which a hearer grasps such an understanding. In the theory I shall present, I shall examine the resources and rules in language which enable the subject to take such a perspectival stance. My aim is to stress the linguistic realization, as objectively available given the resources of the language rather than the subjective stance of the observer, for unless language were structured in certain specifiable ways, metaphor would not be possible. I shall say little about individual speakers' intentions in making metaphor. Such intentions are neither necessary nor sufficient for determining that an utterance is metaphorical. On the one hand, we may intend but fail to make metaphor—we may not be sufficiently competent in the language. On the other hand, we may interpret as metaphorical statements which were never so intended. (A favourite pastime of some linguists and philosophers appears to be finding metaphorical interpretations for putative examples of literal or meaningless strings.)

In exploring metaphor as a phenomenon of language, I do not mean to claim that metaphor is found only in language nor that metaphor is *merely* linguistic. We can have metaphor in dance, in painting, in music, in film, or in any other expressive medium. Nor is all language conducive to metaphor—some artificial languages and the notational systems described by Goodman (1968) may not support metaphor.[1]

From Richards to Lakoff and Johnson (1980), theorists have insisted that metaphor is conceptual and that many of our actions are based on metaphorical conceptions. I take this to be implicit in the claim that metaphors have cognitive significance. Lakoff and Johnson, and a number of linguists and psychologists inspired by their work,[2] have begun to study some conceptual structures which are metaphori-

---

[1] What is required of an expressive medium is that there should be some implicit or explicit categorial scheme such that an *x* is subsumed under a class or category A, and that there is another category B ≠ A such that it is possible, but not necessary, that A includes B or B includes A, and that it is possible that A and B intersect. In a notational scheme the classes must be disjoint. In a notational scheme it is not possible that A and B include or intersect one another. I offer an argument that this is a precondition of metaphor and that a notational system cannot support metaphor in Kittay 1978.

[2] e.g. Quinn (1985), Gentner and Gentner (1982), and Carbonell (1981). See also Johnson, forthcoming, and Lakoff and Kovecses, (1983).

cal in character and from which flows metaphorical utterance. That our metaphors are conceptual and have a systematic structure is a position I endorse and do not mean to challenge when I provide an analysis of metaphor based on its utterance. But the linguistic utterance of metaphor exists in relation to a language whose organization reflects and helps shape a conceptual system. And I insist that the conceptual requires an expressive medium. As I shall argue, a conceptual organization itself requires an expressive medium for the articulation of concepts. Concepts, as I understand them, are not free-floating, but emerge from the articulation of a domain by a set of contrasts and affinities available in an expressive medium. Without an expressive medium we most likely should not be able to form metaphors or even think metaphorically. Certainly we should have no access to metaphor. My motivation for dealing with metaphor as linguistic utterance is therefore that only through its expression in some representational system can we grasp the structure of metaphor, and the most elaborated representational system available to us is linguistic. Since our present understanding of language exceeds our understanding of any other expressive medium, an explication of metaphor in linguistic terms will do most to advance our understanding of the conceptual and cognitive significance of metaphor. I aim to understand the cognitive force of metaphor through the elucidation of metaphoric meaning.

The view that metaphors provide a distinct cognitive function has not gone unchallenged. But the challenge can indeed be met if we have a sufficiently sound theory. The theory I present is to be understood not as an absolute and unqualified characterization of metaphor but as provisional: revisable given a more adequate characterization of literal meaning, and revisable given an available representation of an extra-linguistic conceptual structure—if such were indeed possible. The more modest ambition of this book is to further the project of theory construction.

Interactionism as a First Approximation

> As for metaphorical expression, that is a great excellence in style . . .
> for it gives you two ideas in one. (Samuel Johnson, in *Boswell's Life*,
> ed. G. B. Hill, rev. L. F. Powell, iii. 174; quoted in Richards
> (1936), 93.)

The key notion in seeing metaphor as cognitive is the recognition that in metaphor two concepts are operative simultaneously. But unless the two ideas brought together in metaphor work on each other in some significant way, then apart from being merely ambiguous, metaphor would be either a succinct way of speaking, or, conversely, an elaborate way of speaking, since an extra (extraneous?) idea is brought in where a single thought would do just as well.[3] The Romantic and Kantian insistence on unity directs attention to the nature of the relation between these two ideas.

Richards was the first to baptize the two ideas active together in metaphor. He called them *tenor* and *vehicle*. Unfortunately he offered no explicit definitions. None the less, we can say that the *vehicle* is the idea conveyed by the literal meanings of the words used metaphorically. The *tenor* is the idea conveyed by the vehicle.

Indeed, explicit definitions seem difficult to formulate. Like Richards, we too shall proceed by example. Consider a metaphor from Shakespeare's sonnet 73 (1.4):

1.1 Bare ruin'd choirs, where late the sweet birds sang.

The vehicle is the idea conveyed by the words 'bare ruin'd choirs', and the tenor the idea of autumnal boughs. The metaphor, then, is neither the vehicle nor the tenor but the two conjoined. The difficulty with these terms becomes evident when we try to make precise the inter-action between them. This will lead to some terminological changes in later formulations.

Black, in his celebrated article on metaphor, makes a number of significant contributions and emendations to Richards. A metaphor is not an isolated term, Black claims, but a sentence. He calls the metaphorical sentence the *frame* and the word or words used metaphorically the *focus*: the frame imposes 'extension of meaning upon the focal word' (1962, 39). In his use of 'vehicle', Richards does not make clear whether the term is to apply to the idea signified by the focal word or to the contextual and conceptual inferences relating to the focal word. Black uses *subsidiary subject* to indicate the former and introduces 'a system of associated commonplaces' for the latter. By separating out the latter, Black makes explicit what Richards only hints at, namely

---

[3] In ambiguity, two meanings are supported by a single term. Some writers have indeed made metaphor a species of ambiguity (notably Empson (1966) and Scheffler (1979)). Provisionally let us say that, in the case of ambiguity, the two (or more) thoughts expressed are independent of each other and each reflects conventional uses of the term, while, in metaphor the thoughts depend on and are motivated by each other. As we develop the conception of metaphor outlined here, we shall have more to say about relationship between metaphor and ambiguity. See, for example, Chapter 2, p. 78 ff., below.

that a metaphor not merely invokes two subjects but, in the case of the vehicle (or subsidiary subject), involves a 'system of associated commonplaces'. Such a system will serve as a 'lens' or 'filter' by which to organize our view of the principal subject. (1962, 39–40).

It was Richards's aim to portray metaphor not as 'an *added* power of language' but as its 'constitutive form', as 'the omnipresent principle of language'. The theoretical ground for holding that metaphor is the omnipresent principle of language lies in Richards's contextual conception of meaning: signs are efficacious as they 'bring together into new unities the abstracts, or aspects, which are the missing parts of their various contexts'. (1936, 93.) Black's emphasis on 'systems' can best be elaborated by an understanding of all language as contextually and systematically related. Like Richards, I shall argue for a contextual concept of meaning, presented as a *relational theory of meaning*. Language itself is a bringing together of diversities into a unity of meaning which is contextually supported.

Metaphor enhances and distills this process by juxtaposing ideas which are distinct and incongruent, given the conceptual frame relative to which the expression is metaphorical. Metaphor is both continuous with, and distinct from, literal language. The distinction is salient in the difference between metaphor and literal comparison.

Metaphor, Comparison, and Simile

Black argued that the claim that metaphors are comparisons 'suffers from a vagueness that borders upon vacuity' and that to presume that metaphors simply record pre-existing similarities among things is at best naïve. Rather than the similarities being 'objectively given', he wrote, 'it would be more illuminating in some of these cases to say that the metaphor creates the similarity than to say that it formulates some similarity antecedently existing'. (1962, 37.) A metaphor such as 1.2, based on the line from Wallace Stevens's, quoted above, illustrates the point:

1.2 The garden was a slum of bloom.

What objectively given similarity is there between a garden and a slum prior to the formation of the metaphor itself?

The argument against the comparative view of metaphor is often expressed by denying that metaphors are implicit similes. Although there are important distinctions to be drawn between metaphor and simile, a point frequently missed is that similes are not mere comparisons any more than metaphors are. T. S. Eliot's simile provides an example:

> 1.3 When the evening is spread out against the sky
>   Like a patient etherized upon a table;

The opening to 'The Love Song of J. Alfred Prufrock', as much as any metaphor, creates a similarity rather than records an antecedent one. Contrary to Black and others, disclaiming the comparison view does not entail drawing a sharp distinction between metaphor and figurative simile in regard to their cognitive import.[4]

If the substitution theory—the view that a metaphorical term is a more decorative (or interesting, or lively, etc.) substitute for the literal term—has lost favour in recent times, the comparison theory continues to hold sway, if in newer versions. A number of current psychological and linguistic studies purport that metaphor should be studied as comparison, and in the course of this essay, we shall critically examine some of these views. One view, in particular, deserves attention in the context of the discussion concerning the cognitive content of metaphor. Donald Davidson, while dissociating himself from the older view that metaphors are elliptical similes, none the less argues that 'metaphor and simile are merely two among endless devices that serve to alert us to aspects of the world by inviting us to make comparisons' (1981, 211). He cites several stanzas from T. S. Eliot's poem 'The Hippopotamus' to make the point that the poem neither explicitly tells us that the Church resembles a hippopotamus nor uses metaphor to 'bully us' into making the comparison. Descriptions of the Church and the hippopotamus are merely juxtaposed, and the poet thereby 'intimates much that goes beyond the literal meanings of the words' (1981, 211).

While we may grant that Davidson is right that metaphor and simile are among many ways in which we are invited to make comparisons, we must see that comparing the Church to a hippopotamus is not like comparing the Church to the State—nor is it like comparing an elephant to a hippopotamus. Literal comparison takes place within fixed, common, or given categories, for example, when hippopotami are

---

[4] Ortony (1979c) has introduced a helpful distinction between literal and figurative similes. The former are mere comparisons: 'a wolf is like a dog'; 'having a word processor is like having a private secretary'; 'a bicycle is like a car'; etc. The latter are closer to metaphor: 'a man is like a wolf'; 'a word processor is like a dear friend'; 'a woman without a man is like a fish without a bicycle'.

compared to elephants—a comparison within the category of large mammals—or when the Church and the State are compared—a comparison within the category of authoritative and powerful institutions. But comparisons in metaphor and simile cross categorial boundaries, for example, when a large mammal is compared to an authoritative powerful institution.[5] The special nature of this comparison is epitomized by metaphor. Seeing metaphors this way, and recognizing that they are not limited to phrases or sentences but can take the form of a larger text, we can say that Eliot's poem, as a whole, is the metaphor.

In simile, the 'like' is itself a metaphor. Thus metaphor is not merely one 'among endless devices'; it is the paradigmatic device for pointing out analogies and making comparisons which cross the bounds of our usual categories and concepts. This is what gives import to Black's contention that metaphors do not describe pre-given similarities, but rather create the similarities which they bespeak.[6]

The Literal/Metaphorical Distinction

In this regard, it is important to note that an expression is not metaphorical in an absolute sense. It is metaphorical only relative to a given conceptual organization in which certain categorizations capture similarities and differences taken to be salient for that language community. For the contemporary reader the Homeric phrase 'the rosy-fingered dawn' is metaphorical. But for the ancient Greek who believed the dawn to be a goddess, human-like in form, do we say that the expression was figurative or literal? Although the term 'wave' was first applied to sound in a metaphorical sense, is it still appropriate to say that it is meant as a metaphor? Do we not actually take sound to have the essential properties of a wave and to have those properties in a way not true of light, to which the application of 'wave' is more likely to

---

[5] Note that we can have figurative comparisons among large mammals as well. Samuel Wheeler III (in a personal communication) has suggested the sentence: 'My overweight cow is the hippopotamus of the herd'. Here I would suggest that the comparison is again cross-categorial since we are literally comparing the different cows of the herd, on the one hand, and metaphorically comparing (one of) the largest of these to a member of the category of extremely large mammals. Terms belong to different categories, and it is the categorical placement within a given context which will determine the literality or figurativeness of the comparison. There will be further discussion of this point in Chapter 7.

[6] See Kittay 1982 for a discussion of the sense in which we can speak of metaphors as creating similarity.

be metaphorical? I mean to say that metaphors are always relative to a set of beliefs and to linguistic usage which may change through time and place—they are relative to a given linguistic community.

In their zeal to insist on the cognitive and conceptual importance of metaphor, some writers have claimed that we need to break down the distinction between literal and metaphorical language. Most recently, Lakoff and Johnson sometimes appear to take this position, especially in their notion of a 'literal metaphor'. But the notion of a literal metaphor is a confusion between what is conventional and what is literal. I shall argue that metaphors exhibit a structure which is distinguishable from language that is at once literal and conventional. Lakoff and Johnson's 'literal metaphors' will turn out to be conventional metaphors. Ultimately, Lakoff and Johnson do posit a distinction that separates literal from metaphorical use of language: language which is literal speaks of how 'we understand our experience directly when we see it as being structured directly from interaction with and in our environment'. In contrast, 'we understand experience metaphorically when we use a gestalt from one domain of experience to structure experience in another domain'. (Lakoff and Johnson 1980, 230.) Such a distinction is necessary if the discussion of metaphor is not to reduce to incoherence. If we deny the literal in language, we deny the possibility of metaphor as well.

The desire on the part of some theorists to obliterate the distinction between the literal and the metaphorical is motivated by the thought that cognitive priority will inevitably be granted to literal language. Metaphor then appears to be a deviant, marginal, or reducible use of language. Rather than erase the distinction, we ought to relativize it. If we relativize the distinction, then the cognitive efficacy of the literal cannot be withheld from the metaphorical—literal and metaphorical language are, so to speak, made of the same stuff. Maintaining the literal/metaphorical distinction need not conflict with Lakoff and Johnson's claims that our conceptual system is largely structured metaphorically, for past metaphors—now taken as literal—can generally be retrieved as metaphors. Retrieving their metaphorical origins may sometimes enhance our understanding of the concept; at other times it obscures the current literal meaning.

The way that literal language appropriates metaphorical meaning can be brought out by an archaeological analogy. During the current excavations of the Old City of Jerusalem, a site that has been continuously inhabited for 2,000 years, archaeologists have found that uncovering the structure of one synchronic period threatens to destroy the archaeological record of subsequent periods. For the city has time and again been conquered, destroyed, and built anew upon the wreckage of the old. The very foundations of some of the structures depend on the previous, destroyed dwellings, and these newly erected structures have their own integrity and character—a character which derives less from the foundational structures and more from the period in which they were built. Language, similarly, has an archaeological, layered quality. We must decide at a given point whether we take a diachronic stand or a synchronic stand. Whether we characterize a term as metaphorical or literal may well depend on which stance we take.

A particularly interesting case of layering that has not even required excavation is presented by the Mosque of the Dome of the Rock, in Jerusalem. At the centre of the mosque, which is covered by a glorious golden dome, is the rock said to be the one upon which Abraham was to sacrifice Isaac. This rock was itself a site of religious significance in Abraham's time: it was a place where sacrifices took place, as is evidenced by a small hole in the rock into which flowed the blood of the sacrificial creature. The rock is the very one under which Christ preached to his disciples. And Muhammad chose this spot as the place from which to begin his flight to Mecca. The mosque now situated there is one of the three holiest places for Muslims. Because of its history, this site is holy to all three major monotheistic religions. It functions, however, not as a synagogue, nor as a church, but as a mosque. The latter and latest utilization is the primary one, and yet its special character results from an appropriation of its significance for Judaism and Christianity, since Islam also venerates Abraham and Christ.

Similarly, there is language that we now understand as literal but whose origins are metaphorical, whose meaning still carries some of the import of its metaphorical beginnings. The originating metaphorical sense has not been destroyed. Instead it subsists in the new sense just as the ruins of former cities persist in the foundations of the new city. The metaphorical origins have been carefully preserved and acknowledged, like the history of the sacred rock under the dome of the mosque. Still, in its current usage, the language functions literally, and the metaphorical origins are only a resonance. This is comparable to the fact that the site of the rock functions as a mosque—its current use—not as a synagogue nor a church although its history has significance for Judaism and Christianity. The term 'en*light*enment' is a case in point. Its metaphorical origin is easily retrieved. The visual domain resonates and continues partially to structure the domain of intellectual terms.

One can and ought to draw the literal/metaphorical distinction, while agreeing that metaphors are central to our understanding and acting in the world. One need only make the distinction relative to a given synchronic moment in a given language community. If this involves a certain amount of abstraction, such abstraction is inherent in the enterprise of understanding. In addition, this relativization allows us to see the dynamic inherent in language by which the metaphorical becomes literal (as in the case of sound 'waves') and the literal becomes metaphorical (as in the case of dawn's 'rosy fingers'). That dynamic displays an important relation between meaning of language, conventions of usage, and belief (or conceptual) systems.

From an Interactionist Theory to a Perspectival Theory

While Richards (and Black after him) spoke of interaction, it is Burke (1941) who discusses metaphor as 'perspectival incongruity'. Burke assimilates metaphorizing to categorizing, emphasizing the choice of category in which we place objects as a choice of perspective governed by distinct interests and conventions. Metaphorizing is distinguished from categorizing by the incongruity we find in metaphor. This incongruity is related to the fact that when we categorize metaphorically we are guided by special interests—interests different from those which guide our usual classifications. (The conventionalism and interest-bound nature of our categorial decisions allies Burke with Nietzsche and Nelson Goodman.) As classification and categorization are both orderings, the intrusion of an incongruity is a disordering—one that forces a reordering if the structure of our conceptual organization is to retain a coherency. A new perspective is achieved—a new, if tenuous, point of view on the issues in hand. I favour the term *perspective* because it is more precise in regard to the sort of interaction that occurs between what Richards called tenor and vehicle.

In putting forth the tenets of a perspectival account, I shall begin by outlining the salient features of interactionism. They are summarized as follows:

    (1) That metaphors are sentences, not isolated words.
    (2) That a metaphor consists of two components.
    (3) That there is a tension between these two components.

(4) That these components need to be understood as systems.
(5) That the meaning of a metaphor arises from an interplay of these components.
(6) That the meaning of a metaphor is irreducible and cognitive.

The first four theses specify the structure of metaphor. The latter two pertain to the interpretation of metaphor. Each claim, when modified and elaborated, serves as an important element of the *perspectival theory*. Below I shall discuss each of these six tenets and provide a sketch of the theory to be developed in the succeeding pages.

That metaphors are sentences, not isolated words. The claim that only sentences are metaphors is justified on the ground that only in a sentence can we tell whether a given word is used literally or metaphorically. Yet, on the one hand, the linguistic setting of words used metaphorically need not be as full as a sentence: without a context to indicate the contrary, we generally recognize the phrase 'slum of bloom' to be a metaphorical expression, although it is not necessarily apparent, without some further contextual information, which term in the expression should be understood metaphorically.[7] On the other hand, we may have an entire sentence that may be interpretable either literally or metaphorically, and only a given context can render one interpretation rather than the other appropriate.

Consider the following example from Reddy, (1969, 242):

---

[7] This point is made in Kittay 1984. The referee of that article called to my attention that we may be wrong in supposing that this phrase is metaphorical. The referee suggested the following passage in which both 'slum' and 'bloom' are to be understood literally, if we take the definition of 'bloom' to be 'a lump of puddled iron' (*New Webster Dictionary of the English Language*): 'The rioting in the South Bronx went out of control. The rioters set fires everywhere, and the conflagration was beyond imagining. Automobiles and even the metal girders which had formed the framework of some of the tenements melted. Through the flames one could see that the South Bronx had been reduced to nothing more than a *slum of bloom* and ash.'
My point in citing the phrase 'slum of bloom' is that, even in the absence of a wider context, the phrase suggests the incongruity characteristic of metaphor, but the incongruity supposes that we are implicitly working with a commonly understood meaning of 'bloom', e.g., 'the flowering state'. When a wider context is not specified, we tend to assume that the meanings of the words employed are those most commonly known and that the context is a situation easily conceived of by speakers of the language and members of that particular language community. On such an assumption, 'slum of bloom' defies a simple literal interpretation and hence is generally identified, minimally, as nonliteral.

1.4 The rock is becoming brittle with age.[8]

While the sentence might be literal in the context of a geological exposition, it is metaphorical when spoken of a professor emeritus. Thus the sentence may be too large or too small a unit to determine whether some expression is to be identified as a metaphor. In order to understand how we recognize that an utterance is metaphorical we must consider the unit of metaphor to be independent of any particular grammatical unit. My claim, developed in Chapter 2, is that a unit of metaphor is any unit of discourse in which some conceptual or conversational incongruity emerges. The incongruously used term(s), the vehicle of the metaphor, will be the *focus* of the metaphorical utterance. The *frame* will be that minimal unit which establishes the incongruity.

The incongruity indicates that metaphors involve some sort of rule-breaking. I draw a distinction between first-order meaning, that is, the literal and conventional senses of an utterance, and second-order meaning, which is a function of first-order meaning (see Chapter 2). Metaphor breaks certain rules of language, rules governing the literal and conventional senses of the terms. The rule-breaking takes place not in any arbitrary way but in certain specifiable ways. Hence we can tell the difference between metaphors and mistakes, and the difference between metaphors and new, technical uses. In interpreting metaphors, we assign to the grammatical string a second-order meaning. In Chapter 4 I shall specify the function that distinguishes that second-order meaning which is metaphorical meaning.

That a metaphor consists of two components. We want to say that in metaphor one expression supports two contents: one is a content the expression supports literally, the other is a content the expression supports only in the given metaphor. In

1.5 Man is a wolf,

the metaphorically used term is 'wolf', and the term 'wolf', along with its usual sense, is used to talk about man.

---

[8] Reddy uses this example to dispute the view that metaphors could be identified as semantically deviant simply in so far as they violate selection restrictions. He adduces this example to demonstrate that we can form metaphors that violate no selection restrictions. I agree that the example accomplishes this goal. The argument I present in Chapter 2 below is that the deviance—or incongruity, as I prefer to call it—is not to be sought at the grammatical level of the sentence.

We have noted that Richards's original formulation, *tenor* (man) and *vehicle* (wolf), present difficulties. First, it is not always clear how to identify tenor and vehicle.[9] There is an inherent ambiguity in meta-phorical utterances such that we sometimes do not know which terms ought to be understood metaphorically and which are to be taken liter-ally. A sentence such as

1.6 This man is my mother[10]

may be understood to mean that a certain man has behaved to me as I might expect a mother to act toward me, in which case 'mother' is the *vehicle*, or it may mean that I am remarking on the presumed masculine characteristics of a woman who is literally my mother. The sentence can only be resolved contextually, and, although Richards stresses the importance of context, he provides no guides for determining how we use context to distinguish tenor and vehicle in a given metaphor.[11] This may not be a problem inherent in the terms themselves, but we should like a terminology which reflected the relation of a metaphor to its context.

Secondly, as we have noted, Richards is not clear whether the terms are to be understood as applying to the ideas signified, the actual words used, or the contextual or conceptual frame of the words of the meta-phor. Black's modification, *principal subject* and *subsidiary subject* (corre-sponding to *tenor* and *vehicle* respectively), is less helpful than it could be. Are we to understand *subsidiary subject* as naming the idea expressed by the focal word(s) or the actual term itself? Furthermore, Black's terms have not been much used in the literature. Instead I shall

---

[9] The vehicle is more or less equivalent to what critics and rhetoricians have often called the 'image'. But, as Richards and others have pointed out, 'image' suggests that metaphor is primarily visual. Adducing evidence that there need be nothing visual in metaphor, Richards (1936, 129) quotes the following lines from Shakespeare: 'If thou didst ever hold me in thy heart / Absent thee from felicity awhile / And in this harsh world draw thy breath in pain / To tell my story' (Hamlet, v. ii). This is not to say that images are not a feature of metaphors nor never accompany metaphors. They may even do so with greater frequency than they do non-metaphorical language. And it is for a psychology of metaphor to explore this. But imaging is not essential to metaphor. Some persons claim never to have images, and yet have no difficulty comprehending meta-phors. However, the persistent claim that metaphors are images may have the truth which can be brought out using information-theoretical notions—see Chapter 3 below.

[10] This example is due to Sanders 1973.

[11] There may be literary works in which the author has constructed a text so that both alternative interpretations are entirely consistent within the text, and thus the metaphor cannot be disambiguated.

retain *vehicle* with its suggestion of transport, to denote the focal term—that is, the label itself *and* the content that label conveys literally. The second content, carried by the metaphorical expression, will be called the *topic*. *Topic* suggests not an expression in a text, but rather what a text is speaking about. The ambiguity of 1.5 is resolved in a context which makes the vehicle appear incongruous and the topic cohere with the contextual discourse. This way of putting matters brings into relief the 'double semantic relationship' (Henle 1965) of metaphor.[12]

It is important to see that the *topic* is not the meaning of a metaphor. In the simple metaphorical sentence 1.5, the vehicle is 'wolf' while the topic is man (or the idea of man). Were man (or the idea of man) the meaning of the metaphorically used term 'wolf', we could substitute the term 'man', (which has man as its meaning) in 1.5. Then we should arrive at the tautology 'Man is a man'. Metaphors do not reduce to such tautologies, because the topic is *not* the same as the meaning.

The argument presented here parallels Frege's question why an identity statement such as 'The morning star is the evening star' is not simply a tautology equivalent to 'A = A'. Out of this query emerged the celebrated distinction between sense and reference. The parallel suggests that a confusion of topic with meaning is parallel to the conflation of sense and reference in theories of meaning of non-figurative language. Richards's naming of the two components has played a role analogous to Frege's distinction between sense and reference. When

---

[12] Henle writes: 'Metaphor, then, is analyzable into a double sort of semantic relationship. First, using symbols in Pierce's sense, directions are given for finding an object or situation. Thus [far], use of language is quite ordinary. Second, it is implied that any object or situation fitting the direction may serve as an icon of what one wishes to describe. The icon is never actually present; rather, through the rule, one understands what it must be and, through his understanding, what it signifies' (1965, 178). According to Pierce, a sign which is a *symbol* signifies by means of an arbitrary connection between itself and the object it signifies. An *icon* is a sign which signifies by virtue of some resemblance between itself and the object it signifies. See Pierce 1931, vol. 2, pp. 247 ff.

The iconic relation, however, is problematic, built as it is upon poorly analysed notions of similarity and resemblance. Goodman (1968) provides good evidence for the difficulty, indeed the futility, of distinguishing conventional signs (*symbols*) from those which signify by virtue of similarity (*icons*). The relevant distinction, claims Goodman, lies elsewhere, namely in the relative density or relative differentiation of marks or utterances and their applications. In seeking a satisfactory account of the relation between topic and vehicle, the understanding of which will yield insight into the interpretation of metaphors, I shall search for a means by which to characterize the double semantic relation of which Henle speaks without depending on the unspecified concept of an icon.

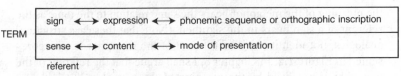

FIG. 1.1

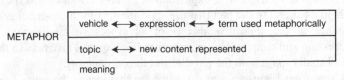

FIG. 1.2

metaphor is no longer conceived as an image conveying a meaning, and meaning is no longer confused with one of its components, metaphor can be more adequately conceptualized.

Ferdinand de Saussure (1966) enunciated another duality in language which is serviceable here. Generalizing upon linguistic entities such as words, Saussure spoke of *un signe*, a sign, as a duality of expression and content, which he called respectively *le significant* and *le signifié*. We can again generalize: not only the linguistic sign but any sign may be said to have a *level of expression* and a *level of content*.[13] Frege used the terms *sign* to refer to a 'name, combination of words, letter', *sense* to designate that which indicates 'wherein the mode of presentation is contained', and *reference* to designate that which is denoted by the sign (1970, 57). In at least some regards, the Saussurean sign consists of the Fregean sign and sense. I shall drop the Saussurean use of 'sign' and adopt *term* to designate a content, or 'mode of presentation', and the means of expression (which in the case of natural language consists of a sequence of sounds (a phonemic sequence) or letters (an orthographic inscription), or more precisely tokens of types of such sequences). A schema of a literally used term could be represented as in Figure 1.1; and a schema of metaphor could be represented as in Figure 1.2.

We see that the meaning of the metaphor bears the same structural relation to the metaphor as the referent of a sign bears to the sign; and

---

[13] These terms, *level of expression and level of content*, are due to the Danish semiotician and linguist Louis Hjelmslev, to whom I am also indebted for the notion of a *connotative semiotic* (see below).

the meaning of the metaphor bears the same relation to the topic as the referent of a sign bears to the signified. (Note that these are structural analogies, not identities.) The referent of the metaphor is not represented in Figure 1.2. In Chapter 8, I shall argue that the referent of the metaphor is not fixed by the meaning of the metaphor but is determined by means of an anaphoric chain of which the metaphorical expression is a part. The juxtaposition of Figures 1.1 and 1.2 is meant to help us attend to the fact that the apposition[14] of vehicle–tenor is an instance of the appositive duality of all expressive media, that of expression and content. But in metaphor it is a special instance. In this text, I shall exploit both the parallel and the particularity.

Comparing Figures 1.1 and 1.2, we see that just as the sense fixes, but is not identical to, the referent of the term, so the topic fixes, but is not identical to, the meaning of the term. But in the case of the non-metaphorical term, it is only the content level that fixes reference. The means of expression does not contribute to fixing the reference. In the case of metaphor, what occupies the level of expression contributes to fixing the meaning of the metaphor. This disanalogy occurs because, as will be evident below (see Figure 1.4), the expression level of the metaphor itself contains a level of content. In metaphor both the expression level and the content level bear content, and thus the new meaning of the metaphor emerges from some interrelation between the vehicle and the topic.

That there is a tension between these two components. To explicate the idea of a double semantic content, I use the notion of a *connotative semiotic*, which permits the two components not to be conflated but to be held in a tensive relation. In a connotative semiotic, the expression level itself consists of an expression and a content.[15]

Consider Shelley's metaphor 'Bees of England' in his poem 'Song to the Men of England', (11. 9–12):

1.7   Wherefore, Bees of England forge
        Many a weapon, chain and scourge,
        That these stingless drones may spoil
        The forced produce of your toil?

---

[14] This term is due to Peter Caws (personal communication).
[15] This notion, borrowed from Hjelmslev, was never used by him to speak of metaphor. See Chapter 4 below. However, I find its adoption to be quite natural.

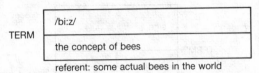

TERM	/bi:z/
	the concept of bees

referent: some actual bees in the world

FIG. 1.3

the TERM 'bees'	/bi:z/
	idea of bees and their social hierarchy
the idea of workers (and their social and economic hierarchy)	

meaning (one approximation): the workers of England considered within an exploitative socio-economic hierarchy parallel to one between worker bees (and queen) and drones

FIG. 1.4

Let us apply the schemes discussed above to the example of the vehicle 'Bees'. In Figure 1.3 it is used literally to refer to the sort of honey-producing creatures that buzz about flowers, etc., and in Figure 1.4 to illustrate its metaphorical use in the lines by Shelley.

On this view, the perspectival nature of metaphor becomes more evident for we can see that one component of the metaphor can be used as a way of organizing or conceptualizing the other. The meaning of the metaphor is the result of the perspectival juxtaposing of two ideas. More precisely, we can say that if there exists a topic, which is a conceptual content and not the meaning, and if the vehicle has a conceptual content as well, distinct from the meaning, then every metaphor involves two conceptual contents which function as two simultaneous perspectives or categories in which some entity is viewed. Remaining within a Fregean framework, we can say that the entity is usually the referent of some term for which the topic serves as a conceptual content. The topic, then, picks out that which is named or spoken of in the metaphor. If a metaphor can be said to have a referent, then it has a referent only in an indirect fashion: the topic can direct us to the referent by providing the category in which we normally classify the referent. (Cf. Figure 1.5, schematizing a term in an oblique context, indicated by quotation marks.) The category may be

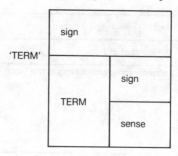

F𝗂𝗀. 1.5

thought of as the (or a) habitual perspective through which we grasp or comprehend the referent, given the wide set of classifications according to which we organize experience.[16]

I have drawn a number of parallels between Frege's inquiries into sense and reference and Richards's distinction between the tenor and vehicle of metaphor. Another occurs to us if we consider an identity statement.

1.8 The evening star is the morning star.

This states that an entity, the referent of the definite description on the left, is the same entity which is the referent of the definite description on the right. This statement is not a tautology such as A = A, because we can learn something by finding that the referent which is described as the evening star is the same referent which is described as the morning star. The identity statement informs us that these are *two modes of presentation* of the same object. The dual content of metaphor is strikingly analogous. But in the case of metaphor a single term car-

---

[16] We may remark that this conception of metaphor justifies a perception of Davidson's, one which he himself briefly entertains but then dismisses. Davidson (1981) suggests that metaphors may have a meaning systematically related to their literal sense, just as words and sentences used in oblique contexts have a meaning systematically related to their usual meaning. Frege says that the designation of words used in oblique contexts is their sense rather than their referent.

In oblique context, the sense of the term (relative to direct discourse) occupies the position of the referent of a designating term and the position of the meaning of a metaphor. In Figure 1.5, as in Figure 1.4, we no longer have the simple configuration of Figures 1.1 and 1.2. Instead, one of the two levels contains an entire term. Thus both the use of a term in an oblique context and the metaphorical use of a term have what we may call an 'iterated structure'. I shall make use of this notion when I introduce the idea of second-order discourse.

ries the two modes of presentation by virtue of certain linguistically recognizable features which I have yet to describe and which license the interpreter to interpret the term as a metaphor. The cognitive value inherent in regarding a single object (understood broadly here) under two modes of presentation is similarly inherent in a metaphor's dual content. But in the case of literal identity statements, unlike that of metaphors and similes, there is no incongruity, no tension between these modes of presentation. Metaphors, even when they have the apparent form of an identity statement, are rather categorical statements in which a given entity is placed under two (or more) concepts or in two (or more) categories which are incompatible. Thus the metaphorical A = B, unlike the literal A = B, does not state that a given entity may, in fact be picked out by either definite description A or definite description B, but that an entity normally classified as a kind of A is being described here as a kind of B.

That these components need to be understood as systems. Richards spoke of metaphor as 'a transaction between contexts' (1936, 94). Black (1962) specifies the 'transaction between contexts' as an interaction between the principal subject and the system of associated commonplaces of the subsidiary subject. Illustrating his point with 1.5, he remarks that the reader or listener must know not only a dictionary definition of 'wolf', but more importantly, must possess a layman's beliefs, regardless of their truth, concerning wolves:

Literal uses of the word normally commit the speaker to acceptance of a set of standard beliefs about wolves (current platitudes) that are the common possession of the members of some speech community . . . The idea of a wolf is part of a system of ideas, not sharply delineated and yet sufficiently definite to admit of detailed enumeration. (1962, 40–1)

In a later essay, Black notes 'in retrospect, the intended emphasis upon "systems" rather than upon "things" or "ideas" . . . looks like one of the chief novelties in the earlier study' (1979, 28).

I have two modifications of Black's account: first, the systems are not 'associated commonplaces' but *semantic fields*; secondly, both the vehicle and the topic belong to systems, not only the vehicle (the subsidiary subject).

The use of a system of *associated commonplaces* and the indifference to the meaning of the term appear to be a new version of the old saw that metaphor depends on a word's associations—on its connotation rather than its denotation.[17] That commonplace associations are prominent in metaphorical interpretation appears so when we consider banal metaphors dislodged from context.

As Black himself saw in the later essay (1979), the system of implications need not be the associated commonplaces. When a sentence is out of context we have only commonplace associations and background knowledge to rely on, while in metaphors lodged in rich contexts the linguistic and situational environs will supplement or override background assumptions. These, together with our understanding of the meaning of the terms, supply what is generally sufficient for us to interpret a metaphor. In response to criticism, Black, in the later essay, shifts his ground and suggests that we speak of an 'implication complex'. In defence of his former notion, Black writes:

> My notion was that the secondary subject, in a way partly dependent upon the context of metaphorical use, determines a set of what Aristotle called *endoxa*, current opinions shared by members of a certain speech-community. But I also emphasized, as I should certainly wish to do now, that a metaphor producer may introduce a novel and non-platitudinous 'implication-complex'. (1979, 29.)

It is, however, when using metaphors which are dislodged from their originating discourse that we are guided solely by such *endoxa*. Whenever we have a sufficiently rich context, we construct a system of implications guided in part by *endoxa* and in part by the specificity of the contextual constraints and leads.

Perhaps more than any other writer, Goodman (1968), has recognized the importance of seeing metaphor as the interaction of two systems. In attempting to distinguish literal falsehood from metaphoric truth, he remarks that to say of a grey picture that it is yellow is not metaphorical but simply false; whereas to say of that picture that it is sad is metaphorically true, but literally false. But to say of it that it is gay is both metaphorically and literally false: 'Just as the picture clearly belongs under the label "gray" rather than under the label "yellow," it also clearly belongs under the label "sad" rather than the label "gay" ' (1968, 70).

Implicit here is the recognition that a label is applied by virtue of its

---

[17] I am using 'connotation' and 'denotation' as they are used by the literary critic, not the logician. That metaphor is based on these connotations and not on denotation is a position we learn to adopt in school English lessons.

opposition or affinity to another label and that the appropriateness of its application—in this case its metaphorical truth—will depend on its relative appropriateness in regard to the alternative label. This point, he recognizes, is generalizable to language as a whole:[18]

> An understanding of metaphor further requires the recognition that a label functions not in isolation but as belonging to a family. We categorize by sets of alternatives. Even constancy of literal application is usually relative to a set of labels; what counts as red, for example, will vary somewhat depending upon whether objects are being classified as red or non-red, or as red or orange or yellow or green or blue or violet. (1968, 71–72)

The system Goodman evokes, a 'family' of labels, is different from either the 'system of associated commonplaces' or the 'implicative complexes' of Black. Black considers systems of predicates applicable to the given term—whether these predicates are drawn from our commonplace beliefs concerning the entity designated by the term or whether they are predicates suggested through implication from contextual considerations. Goodman's *schemes*, the sets of alternative labels, are related through affinities and oppositions and are not predicated of one another, for example, sad is not predicated of gay, but both can be predicated of persons, literally, and pictures, metaphorically.

Unfortunately, Goodman's excessive extensionalism will create problems when we attempt to explain how we interpret metaphors. And Goodman himself has never given an account of how literal application is relative to a set of alternatives.

The idea of a set of alternatives which is not wedded to Goodmanian nominalism is captured in the notion of a *semantic field*. When a set of words, a *lexical set*, is applied to a domain unified by some content, a *content domain*, we have a *semantic field*. The semantic fields are comprised of terms which cover some specifiable conceptual ground and which bear certain relations of affinity and contrast to one another.

---

[18] Goodman's terminology is somewhat idiosyncratic and therefore it will be useful to provide a short glossary. A *label* is a means by which we classify objects or their labels. A label has an *application* to the object or aggregate of objects to which it applies. What the label applies to is its *extension*. A *schema* consists of a set of labels. The aggregate of the *range of extension* of the labels in a schema is called a *realm*. Goodman points out that even a label with a unique range of extension rarely operates in a unique realm since realms depend on the schema invoked and a label is to be found in a number of different schema, as is evident by the relatively simple example Goodman provides above.

Any experiential, phenomenal, or conceptual domain may be a content domain, for example, colour, fishing, electricity, etc. In other words, anything we may want to talk about, and which would require a set of related terms to talk about it, could serve as a content domain. The terms 'red', 'blue', 'green', 'yellow', etc. would be contrasts in the semantic field of colour. Terms such as 'fishing', 'fish', 'trout', 'fisherman' exhibit various contrasts and affinities within the semantic field of fishing. Examples of relations in a semantic field include synonymy: big, large; graded antonymy: hot, warm, cool, cold; hyponymy: bird, robin; cyclical series: summer, winter, autumn, spring; noncyclical series: birth, childhood, adolescence, etc.; ranks: general, colonel, sergeant, private. The relational concept of meaning I set forth in Chapter 3 has as a premiss the proposition that the meaning of a term is determined in part by other related words available in the lexicon—words bearing relations of affinity and opposition to one another. That is, a word's meaning is partially determined by its position in a semantic field.

Both vehicle and topic are elements of semantic fields—or more precisely the vehicle is an element of a semantic field while the topic is part of some content domain that may not be articulated by a set of lexical items. *Contra* Black, not only ought the topic to be considered as a part of a system (a content domain or a semantic field), the vehicle ought to be understood as being part of its own system as well. If it is not, then the distinction between the topic and the meaning of the metaphor becomes more difficult to maintain. In some metaphorical utterances the topic is named in the text, while in others it must be inferred. Indeed, sometimes it is extracted only with a difficulty equivalent to that of arriving at the very meaning of the metaphor. In some metaphors, there is no single idea to which the vehicle may be said to apply. Consider these lines from T. S. Eliot ('Prufrock' ll. 59–60; my emphasis):

1.9 Then how should I begin
     To spit out all *the butt-ends of my days and ways*?

Are 'the butt-ends of my days and ways' the latter part of each day, or the end of my life, or the discarded, unusable part of my days and actions, or . . . ? And how do these various interpretations, simple as they may be, differ from the meaning of the metaphor? In 1.9, the topic itself seems to be a product of a process of interaction with the vehicle rather than a component of the interaction. The difficulty of identifying the topic suggests that the ideas involved are not so easily resolved into two separable ideas. Rather the topic is also a part of a system of ideas. From the imposition of one system upon another system, we arrive at a meaning.

But the primary reason why both the vehicle and the topic must be considered in relation to systems is not particular to metaphor. It is the systematic nature of lexical structure and word meaning and the nature and structure of the information which serves to form the content domain. According to what we may call 'atomistic theories',[19] the meaning (or reference or semantic role) of a term can be given by specifying an idea, concept, or referent for a *label*, where a label is a type of sound sequence or a type of inscription. The specification is carried out relatively independently of similar specifications for other sound sequences or inscriptions.

No one subscribes to such a rough and general picture—but it embodies the general principle I want to contest, namely, that we have, ready at hand, delineated and individuated acoustic (or inscriptional) types and individuated concepts to fit the sounds or inscriptions. Instead, I shall argue a point first made by Saussure, that we do not identify a sound (for the purpose of language) outside a system of sound differentials. Moreover, it is through the apposition of such a system of sound differentials with a system of differentials of a conceptual sort that the relevant acoustic differences (and simultaneously, the relevant conceptual differentials) are established. To expand Saussure's insight, we may add that any language, natural or artificial, requires some appositive system which can be calibrated into disjoint and differentiated units in order to have a measure by which to consider certain sounds as the same and others as different. This is a point I shall make some effort to justify in Chapter 6. If this view is correct, then the isolated meaning of 'wolf' cannot figure in an interactionist theory of meaning of metaphor, because a single term with its isolated meaning does not exist in language, and thus cannot function in any theory describing linguistic phenomena. It should be possible to draw a specification of the systems operative in metaphor within a general account of meaning, where the general theory identifies the meaning of a term as systematically involving relations to the meaning of other terms in a language. Semantic field theory will provide for us just such a ground on which to build a theory of metaphorical meaning.

---

[19] See Kittay 1978, Cohen 1986, and Chapter 5 below.

In discussing the first four tenets of interactionism, I have attempted to introduce the notions central to my conception of the nature of metaphor: the distinction between first- and second-order meaning; the notion of a connotative structure; the notions of semantic fields and a relational concept of meaning. Having introduced these concepts, I can embark on the task of theory building, aiming for a theory of the identification and interpretation of metaphor that will account for its meaningfulness and cognitive significance. The discussion of the other two tenets will be relatively brief, since their import and validity are best realized as the theory is presented.

That the meaning of a metaphor arises from an interplay of these components. The interaction of which Black speaks reconceives the Aristotelian view that in metaphor we have a transference of meaning. On Black's view, we project on to the topic predicates appropriate to the vehicle. Given associative systems of commonplaces or implication-complexes, we are prone to regard metaphorical transfers of meaning as transfers or 'projections' of a set of predicates—those pertaining to the vehicle—on to the topic. This, I argue in Chapter 5, is a mistake. Given Goodman's family of labels, we are more likely to regard metaphorical transfers of meaning as transfers of relations across different domains. Goodman writes:

Now metaphor typically involves a change not merely of range but also of realm. A label along with others constituting a schema is in effect detached from the home realm of that schema and applied for the sorting and organizing of an alien realm . . . the shifts in range that occur in metaphor, then, usually amount to no mere distribution of family goods but an expedition abroad. A whole set of alternative labels, a whole apparatus of organization, takes over a new territory. (1968, 72–3)

In metaphor we do not simply extend the range of application of a given label; that label, together with the labels with which it forms a schema of classification, is shifted to a new realm of application.

Semantic field theory permits us to specify the nature of the 'expedition abroad'. Metaphorical transfers of meaning are transfers from the field of the vehicle to the field of the topic of the relations of affinity and opposition that the vehicle term(s) bears to other terms in its field. More precisely, in metaphor what is transferred are the relations which pertain within one semantic field to a second, distinct content domain. That, in short, is how I characterize metaphor.

If, for example, I say of a basketball player that her playing is 'hot' in this game, 'hot' is the vehicle, and its semantic field is the field of temperature terms; the domain of the topic is athletics. *Hot* and *cold* are graded antonyms in the temperature field; when they are transferred to sports, we can construe a *hot* player as one who plays well and scores, while a *cold* player does not. The antonymy of the pair is preserved. Moreover, if a player scores only moderately well, we can say 'she was lukewarm in the third quarter'. Since 'hot' and 'cold' are not absolute but graded antonyms, we can capture all sorts of performances in between, and even on the outer extremes, for example: 'Her performance on the court today is sizzling'. In this way metaphor can, through a transposition of relations, structure an as yet unstructured conceptual domain or reorder another semantic field, thereby altering, sometimes transiently, sometimes permanently, our ways of regarding our world.

That the meaning of a metaphor is irreducible and cognitive. The cognitive significance of metaphor arises from its capacity to restructure or to induce a structure on a given content domain. Such structuring or restructuring will yield many implicated propositions, some literal, some metaphorical. But no one statement from this explication will capture the full meaning of the metaphor. We can give an exposition of a metaphor, but not a paraphrase—not if the metaphor is still a live metaphor and has not collapsed into literality. The irreducibility of metaphor is importantly tied to the incongruity between the domains of the topic and vehicle. That incongruity guarantees that a metaphorical predication cannot easily accommodate itself in the conceptual scheme which lies behind literal and conventional language. Without such accommodation it cannot be paraphrased. In Chapter 4, I give an account of how we interpret metaphors. We will see the linguistic representation of metaphors that accounts for their irreducibility. In my concluding chapter, I shall use a metaphor for metaphor to suggest how metaphors clash with and force accommodations in our conceptual systems. Such conflict and accommodation is again the source of their cognitive power.

In Chapter 7, I shall use the apparatus of semantic fields to show how metaphors structure distant domains. In one example I cite Socrates' figure of himself as midwife. When Socrates calls himself a 'midwife' he sets up an incongruity: not only is philosophizing not midwifery, but, in ancient Greece, men would not be midwives just as virtually no women would be philosophers. Yet if Socrates wants to explain his role as educator to Theaetetus it will not do simply to liken himself to an educator of a more paradigmatic sort such as Protagoras, for instance. There is no paradigm within the field of education or philosophy for the sort of educating Socrates performs, which is, at least in part, distinguished by the sort of relationship Socrates bears to his students. Hence no literal statement of similarity will do the job of highlighting the distinctive features of Socrates' capacity as an educator. To describe and justify his activities, Socrates moves to a distant field, that of human procreation and speaks of himself as a midwife and of his student as one who is in labour.[20]

The fields of philosophical education and of human procreation certainly share some common features—for example, both are fields involving human agents. Since this shared feature does not distinguish them from other groupings within the larger class of human beings, it will not be a feature which figures in the salient similarity. Since these two fields, understood in their historical setting, are completely differentiated along sexual lines,[21] there are few other substantive features which they may share. What the two domains do share are a set of relational features, features that are brought to the fore precisely by virtue of the otherwise scarce and purely general similarity shared by the two fields. These relational features primarily concern the relations of the mother to her baby and to the midwife and that of the student to his ideas and to Socrates. By elaborating on these relations, the metaphor can serve its mediational role—the relations which pertain to the field of procreation are borrowed and used to order and reorder suitable relations within the field of philosophical education.

In my concluding chapter I address the question of the reference of a metaphor. If metaphors are to have cognitive import, then presumably they should be able to refer. Expressions understood metaphorically may be said to have a *metaphorical referent*, just as such expressions understood literally may have a *literal referent*. But the metaphorical referent will turn out to be just the literal referent of some term in the

---

[20] It is doubtless significant that Socrates' mother was in fact a midwife. Elsewhere (Kittay unpublished) I have argued that the relation of the mother to the child serves as a model and source of metaphors for subsequent activities of the adult.

[21] Today not only are there some women philosophers but the exclusively female role of midwife has largely been usurped by male physicians. When we understand the metaphor, we set aside those contemporary facts which we know to be at odds with the sexual differentiation of the two domains presupposed by the metaphor. Our comprehension is facilitated by the scarcity of women philosophers and the female associations of the term 'mid*wife*'.

topic domain. The cognitive force of metaphor comes, not from providing new information about the world, rather from a (re)conceptualization of information that is already available to us. Information which is not articulated and conceptualized is of little cognitive importance. Metaphor is a primary way in which we accommodate and assimilate information and experience to our conceptual organization of the world. In particular, it is the primary way we accommodate *new* experience. Hence it is at the source of our capacity to learn and at the centre of our creative thought. In the process of accommodation and assimilation through metaphor, we gain a needed *epistemic access* to the metaphorical referent.

2

The Identification of Metaphor

IF we adopt the position that metaphorical meaning is not reducible to a literal paraphrase, we need to be able to specify how metaphorical meanings emerge. Although analyses of metaphor in the past few years have surpassed previous ones in subtlety and sophistication, we still lack an adequate understanding of metaphorical meaning. The present chapter begins to address the question by discussing an issue that has received little attention, namely, the identification of an utterance as metaphorical.

How do we recognize that an utterance is metaphorical rather than literal or inept and mistaken? Generally, we have little difficulty making such distinctions. But what are the criteria we use in so identifying utterances which ought to be metaphorically interpreted? In asking how we recognize metaphors, I am posing not a psychological but a conceptual question; that is I am not asking for the pyschological processes we undergo when we opt for a metaphorical interpretation. I am asking what conditions pertain when the appropriate interpretation of an utterance is metaphorical rather than literal, technical, fanciful, figurative but not metaphorical, or simply mistaken. In so far as the conditions taken individually are only necessary and not sufficient, some will not rule out interpretations other than metaphorical ones. None the less, the set of necessary conditions taken conjointly are meant to pick out just those utterances for which it would be appropriate to give a metaphorical interpretation.

I LITERAL AND CONVENTIONAL MEANING

The Unit of Discourse of a Metaphorical Utterance

The question of how we identify a metaphor has never been adequately treated, in part, I believe, because writers have not correctly identified the unit of discourse that constitutes a metaphor. Language can only be identified as metaphorical by virtue of linguistic and contextual conditions that require that we interpret it differently from its surrounding discourse; therefore, we cannot give the conditions by which we recognize metaphors without identifying that unit of discourse which constitutes a metaphor. In Chapter 1 we saw that a metaphor need not be a full sentence—it may be a phrase. Nor is a sentence always sufficient to distinguish a metaphorical from a literal use of a term.

If we want to contrast literal and metaphorical meaning, we need to be able to span linguistic units which range from a word to a group of coherently organized sentences. Some linguists have attempted to formulate explicit rules of cohesiveness by which to explain why sentences hang together in a text. Such rules of cohesiveness will prove to be useful in articulating the considerations which are operative when we identify and interpret a bit of discourse as metaphor.[1]

First-order and Second-order Meaning

Some people may claim that the fact that metaphors are identifiable neither as single words (which would thus have meanings in some way similar to or analogous to word meaning) nor as sentences (which would thus have meanings by virtue of rules concatenating single words into sentences) constitutes an argument against a semantics of metaphor; that the difficulty I point to indicates that metaphor is not a unit of discourse, but a use of discourse, and as such belongs to pragmatics.[2] If we are to hold the view that metaphors are not reducible to literal paraphrase, then we have to demonstrate that an understanding of metaphor belongs, at least in part, to semantics. If metaphor belonged only to pragmatics, then the question of how we understand a metaphor

[1] Linguists and philosophers of language have as a rule limited their investigations of meaning to word meanings and sentence meanings. Talk of 'texts', has, within the canon, been viewed with suspicion. See, e.g., Dascal and Margalit 1974. The argument against a text grammar is that, in theory, any group of sentences can be written as a single sentence connected by conjunctions, thus rendering extra-sentential grammars superfluous. Those favouring text grammars have pointed to the difficulty of conjoining non-declarative sentences, such as imperatives and questions, and of grasping the point of sentences beyond certain conventionally accepted lengths (though such accepted conventions differ from language to language and even within a language from one group of speakers to another). Furthermore, there exists a literature which is, at least prima facie, interesting in what it reveals about how sentences cohere in a text. Even if we grant that ultimately we need only a sentence grammar, we may still want to explain why some sets of sentential conjuncts (or disjuncts) have a cohesive character, while others do not. It is here that the work of 'text grammarians' would be able to illuminate the work of 'sentence grammarians', even if the latter were to insist on the primacy of the sentence.

[2] For some arguments that metaphor is not a matter of semantics at all, but strictly a matter for pragmatics, see Sadock 1979 and Davidson 1981.

would simply be a question of how we pick out the appropriate proposition intended by the utterer of the expression, a proposition which could then be treated as identical to the propositional content of some literal expression, and so be equivalent to literal paraphrase.

As I develop the criteria for identifying metaphors, the value of treating metaphor semantically, as well as pragmatically, will become evident.[3] I want to posit and utilize a distinction that cuts across the semantic–pragmatic divide and is more useful in delineating metaphor, that is, a distinction between a first-order meaning and a second-order meaning.

As a first approximation, we can say that first-order meaning is what we have in mind when we ask about 'the meaning' of the word 'rock', or some concatenation of 'the meanings' of the individual words (as is an account given according to some version of transformational grammar), in the sentence:

2.1 The rock is becoming brittle with age.

A second-order meaning is obtained when features of the utterance and its context indicate to the hearer or reader that the first-order meaning of the expression is either unavailable or inappropriate. For example, in the case of 2.1, the first-order meaning of the word 'rock' is a naturally occurring solid material matter, and the first-order meaning of the sentence is a comment on the brittle quality of such matter given the passage of time. If 2.1 were uttered in the absence of any talk about geology or rocks, but in the context of the ageing of a professor emeritus, we could reasonably assume that any meaning the sentence might have would not be a first-order meaning. Instead we could assume that the professor was being spoken of as a rock which was becoming brittle—that is, the first-order interpretation, while not the appropriate meaning in this context, would none the less be pertinent to the meaning intended. The distinction as put forward here is necessarily rough; it will be refined as we develop the required technical apparatus and conceptual precision.

Grice (1969) makes a number of relevant distinctions between 'timeless meaning', 'applied timeless meaning', 'occasion meaning' and 'utterer's occasion meaning'. If we apply his distinctions to the term 'rock', they may be explicated as follows:

---

[3] I shall none the less grapple with a particularly virulent form of the argument, one posed by Davidson, in Chapter 3.

(a) *The timeless meaning(s) of an utterance-type*:[4] this includes some specification of one or more meaning that an utterance-type *x* has in a chosen version of given language, for example, the various senses of 'rock' in English, as a noun—solid mineral matter; as a verb—to move back and forth, etc.

(b) *The applied timeless meaning*: this is the specification of which timeless meaning is connected to a particular utterance of *x*, for example, the sense of 'rock' in sentence 2.1 that is, the noun—solid mineral matter.

(c) *The occasion meaning of an utterance-type*: this involves a consideration of what an utterer meant by *x*, for example, if *x* is 'rock' in sentence 2.1, the occasion meaning of the time-worn 'rock' would be the ageing professor.

(d) *The utterer's occasion meaning*: this is what an utterer meant by uttering *x*. The specification of (a)–(c) would be given in quotation marks or italics, while that of (d) would be given as indirect speech, for example, the utterer meant the ageing professor by uttering 'the rock' in sentence 2.1.

We can say, provisionally, that timeless meaning and applied timeless meaning depend on conventional assignments of meaning to utterance-types. When I discuss a relational theory of meaning (Chapter 3), I shall modify this account somewhat. The utterance-type's occasion meaning and the utterer's occasion meaning are often, but need not be, identical to some applied timeless meaning. If, for example, 2.1 were uttered with reference to some actual geological specimen then our examples for (c) and (d) would coincide with that for (b). I shall say that when both the utterance-type's occasion meaning and the utterer's occasion meaning are identical to the *appropriate* applied timeless meaning, then we have first-order meaning.[5] When

---

[4] Grice distinguishes between an utterance-type and token, analogous to the type-token distinction made for words and sentences. When 'utterance' is used alone, I depend (as does Grice) on the context disambiguating between type and token.

[5] What is deemed appropriate is the meaning that coheres with the linguistic and situational context of the utterance. If I were to look at my watch and mutter something to the effect that I had not realized how late it was, and then say, 'Time flies,' it would be obtuse of some listener to respond by taking out a stop-watch so as to time the speed of a fly buzzing overhead. See sentence 3.5 below. To assume that I was issuing an imperative to clock the speed of the fly would be to assign the inappropriate timeless meanings to the words 'time' and 'fly' as well as to their concatenation in the sentence 'Time flies.' Notice that these applied timeless meanings would be inappropriate even though what would, in fact, be the appropriate timeless meanings of the words 'time' and 'flies' yields what is, literally speaking, a nonsensical sentence, i.e., time, in the sense of the substantive noun, does not in any literal sense move through the air with wings.

there is a divergence between either the utterance-type's occasion meaning or the utterer's occasion meaning and the appropriate applied timeless meaning of the utterance, then I shall say that this is a case of second-order meaning.

This is not simply a distinction between literal and figurative language, for there is non-figurative language that has a second-order meaning. Searle's case of indirect speech acts are of this sort—for example, 'Excuse me, you are stepping on my toe.' Taken at its first-order meaning, such a statement requires, at best the response: 'I know,' or 'I didn't know.' It is an indirect speech act because there is a further message connected to the first, namely, 'Get off my toe.' (1979, 30–57, 76–117.) I want to assimilate the latter to a second-order meaning.

First- and second-order meanings are related in that second-order meaning is some function of first-order meaning. Whether we have metaphor, indirect speech acts, or some other form of second-order meaning depends on the function which operates on first-order meaning. In this chapter, I shall speak of what constitutes first- and second-order meaning generally and what conditions, taken conjointly, are necessary (but not sufficient) to identify metaphors as opposed both to other manifestations of first-order meaning and to some other forms of second-order meaning. The attempt to specify a particular function for metaphor requires a full discussion of how we interpret metaphor, and will be treated in a later chapter.

It may appear that the distinction between first- and second-order meaning simply replicates the distinction between sentence meaning and speaker meaning, but takes into account linguistic units that range from words to sentences to texts and discourses. However, if 'speaker's meaning' is a term which designates the actual intentions of actual speakers, then it is arguable that speaker's meaning is not pertinent either to metaphor or to indirect speech acts—though it may still be relevant to direct speech acts.[6]

---

[6] Certain philosophers and linguists, for example, Searle (1979), Loewenberg (1973), and Mack (1975), regard metaphor as a speech act. Cohen (1979) argues that metaphor is not a speech act because, when we move from *oratio recta* to *oratio obliqua* in the case of a speech act, the sentence loses its status as that given speech act, while in the case of metaphor the metaphorical nature of the sentence remains constant under the conversion. Contrast the pairs of sentences below:

    (*a*) I am sorry.
    (*b*) Tom said he was sorry.
    (*a*) The boy next door is a ball of fire.
    (*b*) Tom said that the boy next door was a ball of fire.

However, I believe that it may none the less be appropriate to say that there are

Grice's four-fold distinction sublates the speaker/sentence meaning difference. Between the *timeless meaning of an utterance-type* and the *applied timeless meaning of an utterance-type*, which generalizes and refines the notion of sentence meaning, and the *utterer's occasion meaning*, which correlates with speaker meaning, Grice interposes the *occasion meaning of the utterance-type*. And while Grice believes that ultimately the latter can be assimilated to the utterer's occasion meaning, I want to argue that it is necessary to maintain the distinction between the occasion meaning of the utterance-type and the utterer's occasion meaning. In this matter, I believe Chomsky is correct when he writes:

> Though consideration of intended effects avoids some problems, it seems to me that no matter how fully elaborated, it will at best provide an analysis of successful communication, but not of meaning or of the use of language, which need not involve communication or even the attempt to communicate. If I use language to express or clarify my thoughts, with the intent to deceive, to avoid an embarrassing silence, or in a dozen other ways, my words have a strict meaning and I can very well mean what I say, but the fullest understanding of what I intend my audience (if any) to believe or to do might give little or no indication of the meaning of my discourse. (1971*b*, 19.)

To see why this is so and to see what is wrong with the dependence on the actual intentions of an actual speaker, let us consider an example of Grice's (1969, 147–8), the sentence S:

> (*S*) If I shall then be helping the grass to grow, I shall have no time for reading.

Grice suggests two possible timeless meanings for S:

(i) If I shall then be assisting the kind of thing of which lawns are composed to mature, I shall have no time for reading.
(ii) If I shall be assisting the marijuana to mature, I shall have no time for reading.

Although either (i) or (ii) could be an applied timeless meaning for S, someone might mean by S something like:

important analogous features between metaphor and speech acts and that it may even be correct to posit some 'force' of metaphor which is analogous to the illocutionary force of assertions, commands, or questions. Cohen's argument, rather, points out that, whatever dependence metaphor may have on something like speaker meaning or some sort of speech act 'force', it cannot be of the same nature as the 'force' of a speech act like apologizing. As a result, speech act theory can only be auxilliary to an account of metaphor.

(iii) If I am then dead, I shall not know what is going on in the world.

Grice points out that it will not do to say that (iii) is yet another time-less meaning of S, for it is not an accepted idiom for being dead, as is the phrase 'pushing up the daisies'. Although it is the case that the words 'I shall be helping the grass to grow', as Grice says, 'neither means nor means here that "I shall be dead",' we can say of some utterer of S that when the utterer uttered S, he meant by S (iii).

If (iii) is the occasion meaning of the utterance-type, then the speci-fication of the utterer's occasion meaning is given by:

    (iv) the utterer of S meant by uttering S that if he would then be dead, he would not know what was going on in the world.

Here the occasion meaning of the utterance-type is very closely tied to the utterer's occasion meaning and only loosely connected to either of the applied timeless meanings of the utterance-type. And this may seem only right, especially in the case of metaphor, for how else are we to ascertain the occasion meaning of the sentence when it diverges from timeless meanings except by reference to the utterer's occasion meaning. None the less, we need to establish *that metaphors, while diverging from the timeless meanings of the utterance-types, need not be dependent on utterer's occasion meaning.* Instead in the chapters that fol-low, I shall show that the metaphorical use of language depends on systematic semantic features of language. It is this which allows them to be understood independently of speakers' intentions.

The first and critical step in building this argument depends on showing that the occasion meaning of an utterance-type can be inde-pendent of the utterer's intentions, even when it diverges from the applied timeless meanings of the utterance-type. To demonstrate this, let us say that S is uttered by an editor for a publishing firm in a country undergoing severe political repression and that the editor, whom we shall call E, believes that her life would be seriously endan-gered if she were to take on the assignment given to her by her employer. She responds by uttering S. It seems that in such a situation, we could say that the utterer's occasion meaning could be specified by (iv'):

    (iv') E (the utterer of S) meant by uttering S that, if E were to take the assignment, her life would be endangered.

It appears that (iv') meets the conditions Grice gives for utterer's occasion meaning. These are given below:

'U meant something by uttering x' is true iff:

(1) U intended, by uttering x, to induce a certain response in A

(2) U intended A to recognize, *at least in part from the utterance of x*, that U intended to produce that response

(3) U intended the fulfilment of the intention mentioned in (2) to be at least in part A's reason for fulfilling the intention mentioned in (1). (1969, 153.)

Furthermore, not only is it the case that (iv′) is as adequate a characterization of the utterer's occasion meaning for S as (iv), it is perhaps even more adequate; (iv′) specifies what E really meant to communicate to her employer.

Yet from these intentions alone, we could not arrive at (iii). If we did not understand the expression 'helping the grass to grow' as a way of euphemistically and metaphorically suggesting death, then knowing (iv′) would not help us to understand how E could mean, by uttering S, that were she to take the assignment her life would be endangered. My point is that, while the utterer's intention, that is, the utterer's occasion meaning, often coincides with the occasion meaning of the utterance-type, it need not do so.

A class of cases in which the occasion meaning of the utterance-type diverges from utterer's occasion meaning are easily found if we look at utterances produced on stage. Here it is the actor who appears to be the utterer. However, whatever meaning these utterances may have is quite independent of any intentions on the part of the actor doing the speaking. And if the language used on stage is indirect speech, metaphor, or irony, that is, speech in which we distinguish between the (applied) timeless meaning of the utterance-type and the occasion meaning of the utterance-type, we would further see that, in understanding the utterance meaning, we make no recourse to the intentions of the actual speaker, namely, the actor. If an actor utters, 'Sir, you are stepping on my toe!', we need not appeal to the actor's actual intentions to understand that this is not merely an assertion but an imperative. To this one may reply that the actor on stage is not, in some sense, a genuine speaker. The actor is only the mouthpiece of the playwright, and it is the latter's intentions that matter. But an author's intentions in writing any given line may be to achieve a particular effect or to inform the audience of a character's 'nature' or ulterior motives, and may be significantly different from either the applied timeless meaning or the utterance's occasion meaning. In addition, the play may have been written by an author whose identity has been lost or never revealed, and hence whose intentions are inaccessible to the spectator or reader of the play. It seems odd to have to appeal to intentions to which we could not possibly have access.

Should we say that it is the intentions of the character in the play that are at issue? But the character has no reality outside the words with which she is construed. If we try to ascertain the intentions of the character, we are, in fact, simply attempting to understand the utterance in the light of the contextual features of the discourse. These features include the social and literary conventions governing the discourse, as well as the immediate linguistic environs. The fictional case allows us to see with particular clarity that the situational and linguistic context of the utterance provides us with enough information to understand (most of the time, that is) the proper construal of the words uttered—so much so that even without having an actual speaker to whom to ascribe intentions we can recognize when the meanings properly attributed to the words are not simply their literal meanings.

Contrary to Davidson's (1986) claims that we understand a malapropism by reference to the speaker's intentions, if we consider Sheridan's creation Mrs Malaprop, we see that the 'intentions' we so cleverly construe in spite of the misuses are within the text in which we locate the malapropism and its situational context.[7] The expectations we form by virtue of the discourse itself lead us to interpret other terms so that we can make meaningful what does not, at first glance, appear meaningful. We need not rely on any actual intentions for meaningfulness; rather what we do is impute intentions, and the imputed intentions derive from the regular and systematic interrelations of terms within a language.

And this is just what we do in non-fictional cases as well. If I absent-mindedly or emphatically utter, 'Would you mind passing the salt?', you generally presume that I am making a request, and not inquiring into what you do or do not mind; at the same time you need not be at all concerned with what I am thinking about or otherwise intending at the time. I may care less about making the request and more about informing my host that he has once more overdone his fetish of providing salt-free food; or I may care little about food seasoning, and be making

---

[7] Davidson (1986), in speaking of malapropisms and other linguistic mistakes which, in spite of the misuses, are none the less understood as the utterer intended them to be understood, sees here a case to be made for the view that meanings have something to do with the intentions behind the use of words. Yet, interestingly enough, the paradigm case of Mrs Malaprop's amusing errors is a case in which there are no actual intentions of an actual utterer. Mrs Malaprop is a fictional entity and her 'intentions' are inferences from a linguistically constructed 'person' (like a paper moon in a paper sky).

the remark only to catch the attention of an appealing dinner guest. My actual intentions matter little for the successful execution of the indirect speech act, assuming that it is uttered in the appropriate linguistic and situational setting.

Of course, we want our communications to convey what we intend them to convey. But whether or not they do so depends on how successfully we manipulate semantic and pragmatic rules governing linguistic and communicative situations so that our actual intentions are conveyed. And, similarly, we can manipulate these rules so that our actual intentions are not conveyed but concealed. That is why lying is a paradigmatic case of language use as opposed to language meaning.[8]

In speaking of metaphor, indirect speech, irony, and those cases in which we can distinguish what is said from what is meant in some systematic fashion, and in which what is meant is dependent on, though not coincident with, what is said, we ought to distinguish the occasion meaning of the utterance-type from any applied timeless meaning *and* from the utterer's occasion meaning, that is, from *actual* intentions of an actual utterer. These considerations indicate the need for a linguistic theory not only to account for how we get conventional meanings, whether or not we want to insist (cum a meaning nominalism) that these are ultimately explicable in terms of utterer's intentions, but also to account for how we can have meaning distinct both from the conventional senses of words and from the particular actual intentions an utterer has when producing the utterance.

This need becomes imperative if we give due consideration to the insights first that metaphor has properties that qualify it for a semantic account and a cognitive content distinct from a literal paraphrase, and second that speaker meaning, understood in terms of speaker's intentions, is inadequate as an account. Positing the distinction and describing the relation between a first-order meaning and a second-order meaning will facilitate the project in hand.

Metaphor and Deviance

Distinguishing the two orders of discourse can be of immediate help in resolving a debate as to whether or not metaphors are to be regarded as deviant expressions. If they are a form of deviant language then it may be futile to attempt any sort of systematic inquiry into the meaning of metaphors. And yet to view metaphors as deviant appears to condemn

---

[8] See the discussion of this point in Chapter 3.

a substantial portion of both daily and specialized discourse as deviant, since metaphors pervade ordinary and even specialized languages.[9]

The position to be worked out in this book is that metaphors necessarily break some semantic rules, however subtly, but only to be subject to a new set of conditions whereby they are metaphors as opposed to mistakes or other deviant language. The semantic rules which metaphors break are the ones governing first-order discourse. These are rules governing discourse in which we are to assume that the applied timeless meanings are coincident with the utterance-type's occasion meaning. Where there is an indication (the nature of which will be discussed below) that there is a divergence between the two, we no longer have first-order discourse, for second-order meaning emerges just when there is a divergence between some applied timeless meaning and an utterance occasion meaning. The utterance is then governed by second-order rules.

My attempts here are directed at integrating metaphorical meaning into a general theory of meaning and simultaneously accounting for the distinctive character of metaphor. Most discussions of meaning have dealt only with what I call first-order signification, in which word meaning and sentence meaning figure prominently. In the remainder of this chapter, I shall supply a sufficiently general way of discussing the meaning of utterance-types which will be useful to second-order as well as first-order signification. Thereafter, I shall determine the significant first-order rules whose violation both signals and is a condition of a second-order meaning of metaphor. The accomplishment of these two goals will yield the set of necessary conditions for the recognition of a metaphorical utterance.

Literal and Conventional Meaning: First-order Meaning

To accomplish these tasks, it will be helpful to develop a linguistic frame and a formalism by which to represent a theory of metaphorical meaning. I have said that the unit of metaphor need not be coincident with the grammatical units of the single word or the sentence. Words combine to form phrases, which in turn combine to form sentences.

---

[9] See Lakoff and Johnson 1980 for a persuasive discussion of the prevalence of metaphor in daily discourse and thought. However, I differ in some of my intuitions about what constitutes an example of metaphor. It appears that, at times, Lakoff and Johnson have completely conflated the distinction between literal and metaphorical language—a distinction upon which their own discussion nevertheless hinges, as I have pointed out in Chapter 1.

Sentences relate to one another to form texts, and texts cohere into discourses. We can say that these progressive combinations produce increasing orders of *grammatical complexity*. Therefore, let us consider a language to be comprised of classes of utterances of increasing grammatical complexity, from a single word to an entire text or discourse. These classes will be indicated by U^0, U^1, ... U^m, ... U^n, $n > 0$, such that U^0 is a class of simplest utterance-types, e.g. uncombined single words (monolexemes), and elements of U^{m+1} are obtained by concatenations of utterances belonging to U^0, U^1, ... U^m according to some combinatory rules analogous (and sometimes identical) to the syntactic rules which govern the formation of sentences. The reason for introducing classes of utterances so ordered is to avoid the necessity of specifying whether one is dealing with a single word, a phrase, a sentence or a coherent group of sentences (a text or discourse) except in so far as these stand in relation to one another in degrees of grammatical complexity.

I shall speak of each utterance-type, u, as 'an element' of some U^n, that is, $u \in U^n$. Each u will have an expression, $E(u)$, and a content $C(u)$. The ordered pair $<E(u), C(u)>$ will be a 'term'. At each level of complexity we assign meanings to the elements which belong to the class. That is, there is some way in which we assign meanings to uncombined words, as there are rules for assigning meanings to phrases, sentences, and groups of sentences. More formally, we shall say that each unit in U^n which we call the element $u \in U^n$, is assigned a first-order meaning at each level of complexity n. First-order meaning is the most literal yet still conventional meaning of an expression. The use of both *literal* and *conventional* here is not a redundancy. If we were speaking only of the class of monolexemes, that is, of utterances of null complexity, U^0, then we could not draw a distinction between a conventional and literal meaning. However, as soon as we speak of combined terms, that is, utterances for which $n > 0$, we find that the conventional meaning is not necessarily the literal meaning. Witness idioms and very conventionalized metaphors, for example, 'Hold your tongue'. For the present analysis of first-order meaning, I want to consider only the case in which the literal and conventional meanings coincide. This will henceforth be designated as meaning$_{LC}$.

In Chapter 3, I elaborate a *relational* theory of meaning in which I criticize many aspects of standard theories of meaning. The standard theories, I claim, cannot give us an adequate understanding of metaphor. The account I give of first-order meaning in this chapter must therefore be provisional. For the sake of intelligibility, I shall need to depend more on standard theories than a complete understanding of my view entails.

Let us say that if we are to use a term in the language in a literal and conventional manner, then when we use it in a particular sense, we understand it to have a certain content and certain constraints on the permissible possible semantic combinations. For example, if I use the term 'rock' in the sense of a concreted mass of stony matter, we understand the utterance to carry just a content representable by the concepts *inanimate, material, mineral, solid,* and so on. We also understand that if we are to interpret a sentence literally, we cannot speak of a rock spilling, or splashing or running, etc. If we designate the *meaning* of a term as consisting of all the literal/conventional *senses* of that term, then the meaning of a term consists of a content, represented as a set of concepts, and a set of conditions which relate to the permissible semantic combinations of the term. For an utterance-type, call it 'u', the first-order meaning, $M(u)$, can be regarded as the set of all possible literal and conventional senses of u, $s(u)$, that is, $M(u) = \{s_1(u), s_2(u) \ldots s(u)\}$. This formulation does not yet differ, in form, from standard models of the semantic component of a transformational grammar, such as that given by Katz and Fodor (1963),[10]

---

[10] The theory sketched in Katz and Fodor (1963) provides the basis for a *componential semantics*. Although many different versions have been put forward, when I refer to a componential semantics I refer to one that incorporates the following claims: (*a*) That the meaning of a word consists of several *senses*, each of which is represented by an ordered set of components, usually called *semantic features* or *semantic markers*. For example, 'woman' may be represented as [adult] [human] [female]. (In some accounts these are accompanied by a '+' or '−', e.g. [+ animate], [− animate]—although the negative sign is problematic since it is sometimes used to convey the presence of a contrary feature [− masculine], and at other times the absence of the feature). (*b*) That these 'features' are either linguistic, conceptual, or (according to some accounts) empirical in nature, and represent our knowledge of the sense of the word. (*c*) That some of these features have the special task of representing a set of conditions which relate to the permissible semantic combinations of the lexical item. These are usually called *selection restrictions*. They codify the restrictions concerning the sorts of words with which a given word can collocate. If a term has a selection restriction, <R>, then it can combine with terms which have among their semantic features, [R]. (*d*) That the meaning of a sentence is arrived at through a recursive application of rules combining the senses of the constituent words of the sentence. As such, combinations eliminate all but the relevant senses of the constituent words which allow for semantically permissible combinations. (*e*) That sentences which are formed of constituent lexical items that do not allow for semantically permissible combinations are called *semantically anomalous* or *semantically deviant*.

The account outlined in this chapter adheres to a number of these tenets, but in a substantially modified version.

(henceforth KF).[11] Models such as KF give a representation of the meaning of words and provide rules for concatenating words into sentences. They do not take semantic considerations to pertain to units larger than the sentence. We need a model which will accommodate the generalization of meaning to classes of utterance-types U^0, U^1 . . . U^n, including pertinent considerations from discourse grammars. Beyond this, I require a model which will incorporate the insights of semantic field theory.

On my view, a literal, conventional sense (sense$_{LC}$) has three components. The first component, α, is *a set of semantic features* or *semantic descriptors*, representing the conceptual (informative) content of the term, along with syntactic markers indicating a syntactic category (for example, noun, transitive verb, adjective, etc.). Another component, β, is *a set of conditions and restrictions on the semantic combination of utterances* (in KF the inter-sentential restrictions are called 'selection-restriction rules'). These will be known as *semantic combination rules*, or *sc-rules*. These two components may be illustrated with the term 'rock' as understood in 2.1 above: the α-component includes a grammatical descriptor [noun], and a number of semantic descriptors [inanimate], [object], [mineral], [solid], etc.; the β-component contains specifications of semantic restrictions on the sorts of terms with which 'rock' might combine—for example, 'rock' in the sense understood here cannot combine with verbs whose subject must include the concept [animate]. Although the β-component is meant to capture semantic as opposed to syntactic restrictions on the combinatory possibilities of a term, I do not exclude the possibility (again in contrast to the KF model) that it may include certain empirical considerations. This point will be relevant later in our discussion.

A final component, γ, is *a semantic field indicator and includes the relations of contrast and affinity*[12] by which the conceptual content in α is

---

[11] There have been important modifications in the original projection rules postulated by Katz and Fodor. And the notion of projection rules has been criticized for its inability to account for anaphora, opacity, quantification, and other problems that result from the gap between word meaning and sentence meaning. Whatever turns out to be the best theory accounting for compositionality would be the theory to be employed here.

[12] In contrast to my previous position (Kittay 1978; Lehrer and Kittay 1981), it seems to me preferable not to speak of the relations among terms as 'sense-relations'. This expression appears to tie these relations too closely to analytic truths about the meanings of the term. In their formulations of semantic field theory, Lyons (1968; 1977) and Lehrer (1974) speak of 'sense-relations', but they do not intend these relations to express analytic truths. Lyons (1968), for example, explicates sense-relations in terms of empirical criteria of what speakers actually take to be similarity and difference in

related to other concepts within a content domain.[13] In a later chapter I shall give a full account of semantic field theory. For now, we note that the notion of a semantic field is based on the empirically supported belief that words in a language may be grouped according to their conceptual content so that they may be said to apply to distinct, although interconnected, domains.

The notion of a semantic field provides a basis for maintaining that the meaning of a term in a language is, in part, dependent on relations of affinity and contrast that its elements, i.e. terms, bear to other terms in the language.[14] For example, since 'hot' and 'cold' are gradable antonyms, if we are to understand the meaning of the term 'hot', we need to know that it applies to the thermal state of an entity, *and also* that if a thing to which thermal states may be attributed is not hot it may, but need not, be cold. It may be warm or cool. That is, we need to know that, at least in those cases in which terms such as 'warm' and 'cool' are admitted, 'x is not hot' $\neq$ 'x is cold'. The permissibility or impermissibility of such entailments suggests that we ignore semantic fields and the contrastive and affinitive relations at serious peril to an understanding of a term's meaning—particularly since such entailments have notoriously failed to yield to other analyses of a term's meaning (see Lehrer 1974). The significance of these relations is most

meaning. Noting the philosophical problems with analyticity, Lyons suggests that the linguist developing a semantic analysis of language requires only a '*pragmatic* concept of analyticity: . . . one which gives theoretical recognition to the tacit presuppositions and assumptions in the speech community and takes no account of their validity within some other frame of reference assumed to be absolute or linguistically and culturally neutral' (1968, 445) and Grandy 1987*a*. None the less, I am persuaded that the expression itself is misleading.

[13] The application of a set of lexical items to such areas or domains allows us to speak of distinct concepts which stand in certain specifiable relations to one another. It ought to be understood, however, that I do not presume a pre-existent set of concepts which need only to be named by labels. Whether or not we must have some language or sign in order to have concepts, we can say that the differentiations made possible through an expressive system such as language makes possible the formation of concepts that may not have been possible otherwise. In later chapters, I shall say more about the relation between concepts and their linguistic articulation.

[14] It is useful to consider the relation between the α-, β-, and γ-components. If the descriptors in the α-component of u also indicate concepts belonging to terms that have relations of affinity and contrast with u, then it may appear that the semantic field can be generated from the α-element alone. What are not capable of being so generated are the particular sense-relations which characterize the way in which the elements in a group relate. See Chapter 6, Section 3, below. I want our sense representation to reflect these relations, i.e. the term's 'position' in a semantic field. Although it is by no means obvious how this should be done, the inclusion of a γ-component is intended to capture the import of these considerations.

obvious in the interpretation of metaphor. I shall later demonstrate that when we interpret a metaphor we transfer the relations a term bears to other terms in a semantic field to a second semantic field, forcing a reorganization of the latter.

Default Assumptions

Thus far, in speaking of meanings$_{LC}$ and senses$_{LC}$ I have been speaking of what Grice would call 'timeless meaning'. What I must now do is establish a way of speaking of the applied timeless meaning of an utterance(-type). For this purpose I shall speak of an interpretation$_{LC}$ of an utterance-type *u*.

For reasons that I make explicit and argue for in Chapter 3 the interpretation of an utterance-type is dependent upon the context. There I argue that we cannot intelligibly speak of the meaning of a context-free sentence. That we seem to be able to speak of the meaning of an expression as independent of context is, in large measure, the result of the supposition of assumptions which are shared by all or some of the members of a language community and which form an implicit context for utterances which are explicitly set in a context. Dictionary entries are frequently couched in terms which, in a sketchy manner, provide the appropriate assumptions for different senses of a word. Therefore, before I proceed to discuss first-order interpretation, it will be useful to introduce and discuss the notion of a *default assumption*.[15]

By default assumptions I mean those assumptions upon which speakers rely, in both verbal and non-verbal behaviour, in the absence of any contextual evidence cancelling or questioning such assumptions. Because speakers are scarcely conscious of employing such assumptions, they presume, again with little consciousness of making such presumptions, that their audience has the same assumptions. They are *default* assumptions because they are what we assume in the absence of any contradictory evidence. Therefore, they only become conscious when something occurs which jars, such as the use of 'she' rather than 'he' when the context does not indicate the gender of the subject. When attempts to communicate fail because the interlocutors each proceed from different (default) assumptions, or when the world as normally experienced is altered by social, economic, political, or natural (gradual or cataclysmic) forces, our assumptions may be jarred.

---

[15] See Hofstadter (1985), Chapter 7, pp. 136–59.

As we become conscious of a presumption which has been a default assumption, we may simply affirm it; or we may revise it in accordance with the modified conditions, with the needs of the discourse, or with the speech habits and beliefs of a given group; or we may temporarily adopt other assumptions suitable for the immediate situation without permanently revising our default assumptions.

A word-processing model will be helpful. We may generally use a certain format (margins and spacing) for most of our writing needs. Thus we set that format as the default setting for almost all of our discs. However, we prefer different margins and line spacing for our correspondence, and thus we set a different default setting for our correspondence discs. But even while working on a manuscript we occasionally need to employ different formats, for example, for verse quotations, listed points, etc. To accommodate these we do not alter the default settings; we simply format for the portion of text in question, and then return to the default setting.

Variations in our default assumptions are continuous. They range from those which are shared by virtually all who employ a given language and exist within a given cultural tradition, for example, that 'down' is relative to the gravitational pull of the earth; to those shared by subcultures (for example, that 'American' is an adjective referring to something or someone from the United States of America—an assumption by people from the United States not shared by Canadians and South Americans), specific professions (for example, that an 'argument' is not something to be avoided but something to be offered when making a claim—an assumption specific to philosophers), religions, etc.; to those specific to a particular genre (that the laws of nature may be violated—an assumption prevalent in literary fantasies); to those which are shared by a few speakers whose lives are so intimately entwined that a single word conveys to one another what would require sentences to communicate to a stranger; and finally to those, estabished *ad hoc*, for the purpose of a given discourse or conversation. While recognizing this continuity, I want to distinguish between general background default assumptions and special background default assumptions:

(i) *General background default assumptions.* These are the ordinary background assumptions shared by speakers of a given language within a given culture (or cultural tradition), assumptions and presuppositions about what the world (in both its natural and social aspects) is like as circumscribed within an historical period. When Searle (1979d) points to the context-dependence of 'The cat is on the mat', he is alluding to the fact that we generally understand the sentence against such general background default assumptions.

(ii) *Special background default assumptions.* Different conditions give rise to these. We can group them roughly into those which arise to meet the demands of a given situation, endeavour, or discourse, and those which arise by virtue of shared experiences of groups which, because of geographical proximity and common interests, develop common background assumptions.

(a) *Discourse-specific default assumptions.* These are alterations in or specifications of the general background default assumptions which are meant to encompass the requirements of a specific discourse. The discourse may be *craftbound*,[16] or it may be bound by a text, an author, or an extended conversation. The assumptions may be ones which encapsulate presuppositions or knowledge or general understanding needed for persons to engage in an enterprise. These assumptions may become part of the meaning of terms—often a technical meaning. For example, when physicists today speak of the atom, they do not *mean* atom in the sense understood by Democritus. Similarly, in legal discourse, 'person' has a technical meaning distinct from its ordinary meaning. Within a given craftbound discourse, we can speak of *subdiscourses*. Various subdiscourses will alter meanings of terms in accordance with requirements, practical and theoretical, so that not only do these diverge from the ordinary meanings of the terms but they diverge from the sense in which the same term is applied by another subdivision of the same general discourse. For example, different traditions in philosophy will use the same term with distinct senses— compare 'interpretation' as used by Donald Davidson and by Jacques Derrida. But discourse-specific default assumptions do not necessarily alter the meanings of terms in the way I have just suggested.

Fairy-tales alter our general background assumptions that animals do not speak. But it is not clear that we are to understand the term 'speak' differently when it is used in fairy-tales in which animals speak. Of course, considerations such as these once again bring to the fore questions of analyticity in language and the validity of the distinction

---

[16] For the notion of a 'craft' as used here, see Ross 1981.

between a dictionary and an encyclopedia. But notice that the discourse-specific default assumptions suggest that these questions ought to be raised not merely at the level of the language generally but with regard to the language as it is employed relative to a specific discourse and, as will emerge below, relative to the speakers involved. What is suggested here is that to ask questions of analyticity *simpliciter* is to ask the wrong questions.[17]

(*b*) *Group-specific default assumptions.* General background default assumptions may be modified not only by the demands of the discourse but also by virtue of a proximity and shared experience of certain language speakers. At one end of the spectrum, we may have fairly large groups in geographical proximity that produce specific dialects. Dialects are not discourse-specific but they are group-specific. At the other end of the spectrum we have the default assumptions shared by friends, cohabitants, or family members. For members of a family who have spent the years, let us say 1976–80, in a town in Connecticut, a response such as 'That was Connecticut' may be a perfectly adequate answer to a question dating a certain event, regardless of whether the event occurred in Connecticut. The locution simply indicates the time period between 1976 and 1980. Yet to a stranger such a response would seem uninformative or anomalous.[18] Default assumptions which are group-specific suggest issues of analyticity and semantic anomaly similar to those suggested by default assumptions which are discourse-specific.

First-order Interpretation

We denote an interpretation$_{LC}$ of an utterance-type u by $I(u)$. An interpretation$_{LC}$ of an utterance u is any one of the senses which appear in the meaning of u. For each uncombined word, that is, $u \in U^0$, the meaning$_{LC}$ is assigned through the use of a lexicon or dictionary. Again, I leave open the question as to whether some empirical information, particularly of a well-entrenched sort, may be included in such a dictionary representation.

Where $n > 0$, the meaning$_{LC}$ of u will be a function of the constituent parts of u, as they are set within a given context. But a context may

---

[17] The fact that certain terms do not alter their meaning when they exist in a particular discourse, unless they are explicitly defined in a special way, may be related to how entrenched these terms are in relation to our general background assumptions.

[18] I owe this perception to Leo Kittay, aged 9.

not always be available, or may be very sparse. In the absence of a sufficiently explicit differentiating context, the *default assumptions* provide an implicit context I call the *default frame*, against which we interpret the utterance. The default frame differentiates among the timeless meanings of a term the most entrenched meaning which is compatible with the most entrenched meanings of the terms in the frame and with general background default assumptions or, when appropriate, with discourse- or group-specific default assumptions. (Group- or discourse-specific default assumptions are sometimes listed in a dictionary with a keyed word identifying the group or discourse to which a given sense of a term belongs, for example, 'will: (law) the legal declaration of a person's mind as to the manner in which he would have his estate disposed of after his death', etc.)

Where *u* is a sentence, we can apply rules that are the equivalent of the *projection rules* in the KF model: these are a 'set of rules that reconstruct the speaker's ability to project sentence meanings from morpheme meanings [i.e. the meaning representations that are given in the dictionary]' (Katz 1972, 36). In my more generalized scheme, projection rules will serve as the combinatory mechanism for all utterances of a grammatical complexity greater than zero. In formulating projection rules applicable to combinations of sentences, I shall have recourse to work in the theory of cohesion.

I have already indicated what the meaning of an utterance *u* would look like. In order to speak of the semantic interpretation of $u \in U^0$ we would need to select one sense$_{LC}$ of *u*. In order to speak of the semantic interpretation of some $u \in U^n$, where $n > 0$, we need to appeal to rules by which speakers of the language combine terms to form grammatical units of greater complexity; that is, we require some specification of projection rules.

Projection rules operate at a level at which some senses of the terms' meanings will have been eliminated from consideration by syntactic considerations. More technically (Katz 1972, 298), they operate on underlying phrase-markers in which the lowest-level constituents are already partially interpreted. They will 'bracket together' these senses, that is, combine their senses according to appropriate syntactic rules. We arrive at an interpretation of an utterance by choosing a given sense of a constituent of an utterance which can combine with the sense of another constituent in accordance with the sc-rules of these senses.

A *constituent* of an utterance is an utterance of a lower degree of grammatical complexity which, together with other terms with a degree of complexity lower than the utterance, comprises the utterance in question. If the utterance in question is 2.1 above, then 'the rock', 'is' 'is becoming brittle', 'age', 'with age', etc. are all constituents of the utterance 2.1. Similarly, 'age' is a constituent of the utterance 'with age'. More formally we can say, if we have an utterance a which belongs to the class of utterances U^m and an utterance b which belongs to the U^n, and a is a constituent of b then $m < n$. We can speak of an utterance being a constituent of itself, in which case, $m = n$. If a and b are both constituents of an utterance c, then either both a and b may be on the same level of complexity, one which is lower than that of c, or they may themselves be hierarchically ordered but each must be of a lower order than c. In our example both 'with' and 'with age' are constitutents of 2.1, but 'with' is also a constituent of 'with age'; both, however, are of a lower order than 2.1. (Notice that this formulation requires that we treat sentences which contain no logical connectives as belonging to a lower order than sentences with connectives, and the latter are in turn hierarchically ordered with respect to the number of connectives. Similarly, we would have to consider embedded sentences in opaque contexts as being of a lower order than the utterance containing the embedded sentence.) We see that the constituent relation is transitive—if a is a constituent of b, and b is a constituent of c, then a is a constituent of c; asymmetrical—if a is a constituent of b, then b is not a constituent of a; and reflexive—a may be a constituent of itself.

We are now in a position to define our projection rules. The projection rule provides for the combination of utterances of a lower degree into ones of a higher degree.

Definition of projection rules. We represent the process of obtaining an interpretation of $u_x \in U^n$ where $n \neq 0$: Some projection rule, φ, operates on the lowest-level constituents of u_x, $u_a \in U^0$, $u_b \in U^0$, etc., bracketing these together, according to the appropriate syntactic rules. We select some interpretation for each lower-level constituent which the appropriate projection rule combines so that the conditions of the sc-rules are met with respect to all $u \in U^m$ ($m < n$)—which are constituents of u_x. We proceed similarly with all $u \in U^{m+1}$ which are constituents of u_x until we arrive at an interpretation of $u_x \in U^n$.

We can say that the first-order interpretation of an expression $u \in U^n$ is got by proceeding from the bottom up, from the lowest-level to the highest-level constituents. But interpretations at the lower levels are only partial until the projection rules have operated so as to combine the units properly. By this process various possible interpretations of lower-level units are rejected as not combinable with certain possible interpretations of other lower-level constituents. One can say, then, that the particular senses given to lower-level constituents in a given interpretation of the discourse of which they are elements are also determined from the top down. This is especially important in determining to which semantic field a word—in a particular applied timeless meaning—may be said to belong. This decision is constrained, hence partially determined, by the dictionary assignment of the lexical item, but is progressively more constrained by the higher-level utterance into which the term enters.

If all lower-level units comprising $u \in U^n$ ($n \neq 0$) have been interpreted$_{LC}$ successfully (preserving the literal and conventional senses of the words), we get the set of concepts, α, that comprises the first element in the ordered triple $<\alpha, \beta, \gamma>$; a β-component which includes the sc-rules for u and which is some function of the sc-rules for the constituent elements of u; and a specification of the semantic fields of the constituents of u, that is, a specified γ-component.

In an interpretation$_{LC}$, γ will assign the same (or adjacent) semantic fields to all the terms—this will already provide constraints on the nature of the sc-rules and the semantic descriptors. In so far as projection rules and sc-rules play a critical role in the interpretation of higher-level units and since metaphors are properly such only at the higher levels, we can see that rules for combining terms play a significant role in the identification and interpretation of metaphors. We need, therefore to consider these in further detail. As I have pointed out earlier, we must often consider an utterance in its linguistic or situational context to identify it as a metaphor. Our projection rules must characterize not only how a word combines within a sentence but also how a sentence coheres with its context. Our projection rules must govern permissible linguistic combinations which are both intra- and inter-sentential.

For the purposes of this discussion, I want to presume the truth of the *expressibility principle*: that the salient elements of a situational context can be expressed in linguistic terms.[19] I shall generally speak only

---

[19] I do not assume that the expressibility principle demands one unique, correct, linguistic rendering of such a non-linguistic context, only that there should be at least one adequate linguistic rendering of non-linguistic salient features which participants in

of an utterance's context, presuming either that this context is given as linguistic or that, if it is non-linguistic, then at least part of the relevant situation, namely its most salient features, together with the utterance in question, can be rendered linguistically as an utterance of a level of complexity higher than that of the given expression.

What might projection rules look like for inter-sentential cases, for example, for a group of coherent sentences which appear to form (part of) a text? A sentence has clearly defined grammatical features. These serve to provide a structure which makes possible a cohesiveness between its constituents. When we consider a group of sentences which we judge to cohere as a text, we need to look for those features of the text that serve to bind the sentences together into a semantic whole.[20] The use of demonstratives and pronouns, the repetition of key words, the use of elliptical phrases requiring information in other sentences for their interpretation, the use of conjunctives and the use of lexically related words dispersed through the text are examples of the sort of cohesive elements we find in texts.

These cohesive relations may be classified (Halliday and Hasan 1976) as reference, substitution, ellipsis, conjunction, and lexical cohesion. The two sentences below, which comprise a 'text', illustrate several sorts of cohesive relation.

2.2(i)   Put the blueberry tart on your best platter.
2.2(ii)   It deserves to be beautifully presented.

'It' is *co-referential* with 'blueberry tart'. Had we used an expression such as 'the pastry', we should have had a co-referential relation with a

---

the discourse could agree to, given their good faith and essential rationality. Using some information-theoretic notions (which I develop in greater detail in Chapter 3), we might want to say that the information we receive from the non-linguistic situation is in analogue form while linguistic information is mostly in digital form (see Dretske 1983). In that case, one could object that no linguistic expression could be an adequate representation of the situational context. But notice that I say that the *salient* elements of the situation are expressible. The cognitive gain of the semantic encoding of information is precisely the distinguishing of some features as relevant, with an inevitable loss of information. Hence, even if a linguistic representation of *all* aspects of the situation may not be possible, the salient and relevant features should be expressible in linguistic terms.

[20] That groups of sentences cohere as a text is generally, though not always, intuitively apparent. Such a group may be more or less recognizable as a text, or may be a text only by virtue of some 'external' requirement, e.g. exercises in an English grammar textbook. See Dascal and Margalit 1974. Our interest here is only in questions of coherence, and hence we are not concerned with texts which might not be recognizable as such solely through their appeal to our intuitive sense of their coherence.

substitue term which also exhibited *lexical cohesion*. The terms 'your best platter' and 'beautifully presented' exhibit lexical cohesion both in that 'best' coheres with 'beautifully' and in that 'platter' coheres with 'presented'. 'Best' also coheres with 'deserves'. I shall view these relations as one of two types of relation. When terms may be substituted for one another in their respective sentences, preserving the sentences' syntactic well-formedness, I shall say that they stand in a *substitutive relation* to one another. When terms may potentially collocate within a single sentence, or in a syntactically well-formed utterance, I shall say that they stand in a *collocative relation* to one another. In addition to preserving well-formedness, substitutive and collocative relations, in so far as they are cohesive relations, must preserve the cohesive character of the text. For example, all referring terms which are *cohesively substitutable* should co-refer (in our example, 'blueberry tart', 'it' 'the pastry'); cohesively substitutable predicates should all be predicable of the same referent (with appropriate modifications for the tense, manner, mood, etc.). The cohesive feature of substitutable modifiers seems harder to specify. I must leave it to cohesion theorists to work out how cohesive factors work in all cases. Furthermore, collocative relations would need, as a minimum constraint, to respect the semantic combination conditions of the terms related. For example, 'best' could collocate with 'deserves' because 'deserves' involves an evaluative sc-rule and 'best' is an evaluative term, hence the possibility of forming the sentence:

2.2(iii)   It deserves the best.

Cohesiveness requires attention to the field indicator of the terms related. To say that 'your best platter' and 'beautifully presented' are lexically cohesive (a collocative relation) is to say that the terms belong to the same or to adjacent semantic fields.

The object of projection rules which function inter-sententially is to bracket together the elements of the sentences which enter into cohesive relations with one another. Hence, in our example, the projection rule would bracket together the pronoun 'it' and 'the blueberry tart', since they are in a *cohesive substitutive relation*. Since these are referring terms, they must both co-refer. The sc-rules governing 'the blueberry tart' in sentence 2.2(i) would similarly apply to 'it' in sentences 2.2(ii) and 2.2(iii). If two terms are in a *cohesive collocative relation*, such as 'your best platter' in 2.2(i) and 'deserves' in 2.2(ii) then the sc-rules for 'your best platter' must conform to the sc-rules for 'deserves' so that it is possible to form a sentence comprised of the terms which preserves the original sense and reference of these terms. In this case we can form a sentence, which I shall call a *conversion sentence*, 'It deserves your best platter'. Or by nominalizing 'best' we can form 2.2(iii). Below I give a more precise and formal definition of the cohesive projection rules.

Definition of cohesive projection rules. For terms u_a and u_x, where u_a is a constituent of u_b and u_x is a constituent of u_y, $u_y \neq u_b$, and both u_b and u_y are constituents of an utterance u_z, the cohesive projection rules bracket together u_a and u_x as follows:

(*a*) In the case that u_a and u_x are in a *cohesive substitutive relation*, both u_a and u_x must conform to the sc-rules operating on either u_a or u_x, in their respective utterances u_b and u_y; and in the case that u_a and u_x are referring terms, they must preserve co-reference.

(*b*) In the case that u_a and u_x are in a *cohesive collocative relation*, u_a must conform to the sc-rules governing u_x, and u_x must conform to the sc-rules governing u_a.

(*c*) In the case of (*a*), we treat u_a and u_x as if there were a sentence formed that the constituents of u_z, in which u_x replaced u_a or u_a replaced u_x. (For example, if we take u_z to be text 2.2, u_b to be 2.2(i) and u_y to be 2.2(ii), we could substitute for u_a 'It' in 2.2(ii), and for u_x 'blueberry tart' in 2.2(i).) In the case of (*b*), we treat u_a and u_x as if there were a sentence formable from the constituents of u_z in which u_a collocates with u_x. (For example, if we take u_a = 'best' in u_b, and u_x = 'deserves' in u_y then we can form sentence 2.2.(iii).)

(*d*) These hypothetical sentences, called *conversion sentences*, are then subject to the projection rules which operate intra-sententially.

In my analysis I shall find it useful to work with the conversion sentences permitted by the cohesive projection rules; where necessary to enhance readability, I shall allow for trivial modifications of the substituted and collocated terms.

2 LOCATING INCONGRUITY

A Metaphorical Utterance: Focus and Frame

Now that I have given a sketch of first-order meaning, sense, and interpretation, as well as the cohesive projection rules, I am ready to talk about how these enter into the identification of utterances as meta-phorical. I shall adopt the general position that in a metaphor there is some constituent of the utterance which is incongruous when that utterance is given an interpretation$_{LC}$. As I remarked in Chapter 1, the incongruent constituent I shall call the *focus*, while the remaining con-stituents will be part of the *frame*.[21] The focus alone is incomplete as a metaphorical utterance, whereas the frame and focus together indicate the incongruity which appears requisite for a complete metaphorical utterance.[22]

In the sentence 2.3 (quoted above (1.2)) the incongruity between 'slum' and the remaining sentence is readily apparent.

2.3 The garden was a slum of bloom.

The frame/focus distinction is not always so unproblematic. First, the incongruity may be concealed in implications of the linguistic or situational context, so that a linguistically expanded frame is necessary to capture the particular violation in question. This is the case in sen-tences like 2.1 above. Furthermore, sometimes it is difficult to identify a frame and a focus because a given utterance is not simply composed of one part which is to be understood metaphorically while the remain-ing terms are to be understood literally: we have constructions in which the metaphors are far more complex, in which two or more metaphors, or figures other than metaphor, are operative in a single utterance. For example, a metaphorical verb may be predicated of a different metaphorical subject, or some other figure may modify or be

---

[21] Black 1962. In this seminal work, Black took the frame to be a complete sentence of which the focus was a constituent word or phrase. In keeping with my rejection of the sentence as the metaphorical unit, I am generalizing the notions of focus and frame.

[22] Grice (1969) calls an utterance-type 'complete' if it is a sentence or, in the case of non-linguistic utterances, something which is 'sentence-like' such as a hand-signal. An 'incomplete' utterance-type is a non-sentential word or phrase, or a non-linguistic ana-logue. Grice does not justify his use of the terms 'complete' and 'incomplete', but I gather that by complete he must mean something like syntactically or semantically self-sufficient. Sentences are always syntactically complete in this sense. In the case of non-linguistic utterances not ruled by any recognizable syntactic considerations, we should have to look for a sense of semantic self-sufficiency such that the utterance could be understood in and of itself. I extend the notion of a complete and incomplete utterance-type to metaphorical utterances, so that a complete metaphorical utterance is one which is recognizable as such. Since the units of metaphorical discourse are not necessarily coincident with grammatical units, metaphorical completeness need not be coincident with syntactic completeness.

modified by a metaphorically used term. Consider the line quoted above (1.1) from Shakespeare's sonnet 73:

2.4(i)   Bare ruin'd choirs, where late the sweet birds sang.

We cannot tell whether the line is literal, unlikely but possible, or metaphorical. If it is metaphorical, is it the case that 'choirs' is used metaphorically for tree branches or that 'sweet birds' is used metaphorically for children who sing in choirs? That is, we cannot establish whether there is a focus/frame distinction to be made or what the focus would be, if the frame/focus distinction did apply. Looking at the two previous lines in the sonnet we see that the focus is indeed 'choirs'.

2.4(ii)   When yellow leaves, or none, or few, do hang
          Upon those boughs which shake against the cold,
          Bare ruin'd choirs, where late the sweet birds sang.

But when we consider the poem as a whole we learn that the autumnal boughs are themselves metonyms for the autumn which serves as a metaphor for the ageing of the poet-lover and the dying of a love affair:

2.4(iii)   In me thou see'st the twilight of such day
           As after sunset fadeth in the west;

Shakespeare's is a complexly structured metaphor in which the focus and frame do not remain constant through the poem and in which metaphors become metonyms for more encompassing constructions which are themselves metaphorical. The examples 2.4(*i*)–(*iii*) do not invalidate the focus/frame distinction. Instead they exhibit its usefulness in articulating the complexity of such metaphors.

A somewhat different problem arises in the line:

2.5   The heart is a lonely hunter.

As that sentence is understood in the title of Carson McCuller's book, the sentence employs the term 'heart' with a conventional metonymic use for the emotions, particularly love, and the term 'hunter' metaphorically to speak of what 'heart' metonymically signifies. Normally the frame helps us to identify the incongruity of the focus and directs us to the appropriate interpretation. But how are we to identify the focus when there are apparently two foci and little else in the utterance? Moreover, as a title the sentence has little linguistically renderable context, outside the book itself, into which we could embed the line and distinguish frame and focus. Titles, like newspaper headlines, aphorisms, and similar utterances, are meant to be understood, or at least to suggest possible meanings, as they stand. (Though, of course, many a writer will pack more into a title than at first meets the mind's eye, and a knowledge of the article or book will make possible many other readings as well.)

First we need to recognize that the focus/frame distinction pertains to other figurative language, such as metonomy. Consider the following:

2.6 The Crown has not withheld its assent to a Bill since 1707.

We have a conventional metonym, 'Crown', which is used to speak of the monarch. In 2.6 the incongruity is the result of a metonym rather than a metaphor. The frame/focus distinction can be maintained on the basis of different sorts of first-order meaning incongruities. The nature of the incongruity as well as other additional constraints will distinguish the metaphorical focus.

In 2.5 I suggest that there are two distinct foci, one metonymic, the other metaphorical. The use of two figures in a single utterance such as 2.5 will, most likely, render an utterance intelligible if the reader can identify conventional, albeit non-literal meanings, for at least one of the terms. And when dealing with phrases or sentences meant to be understood without a specified context, we reasonably draw upon the common background knowledge, both linguistic and non-linguistic, which serves competent, mature speakers of the language as an *implicit context*, or *default frame*. Like other default mechanisms, this can be overridden by a more highly specified context. In interpreting 2.5 we must rely on a default frame to identify the metonymic use of 'heart' for love. That which the heart then signifies is, through synecdoche, the person in love—this again is a familiar linguistic convention. 'The heart' thus interpreted serves as a frame for the phrase 'the lonely hunter'. But it is a *minimal frame*, in that we must, in fact, evoke a far-ranging understanding of certain linguistic and literary conventions in order to make out what the metaphor is. An idea of a minimal frame may be used to mark an apparent incongruity in the light of the default frame, and is to be taken as a tentative indication that we may be dealing with a metaphor, although we may not yet know what the metaphor is. In the phrase from 2.3 above, 'slum of bloom', given the generally known senses of 'bloom' (see Chapter 1, n. 7, for a contrary instance) and 'slum', the terms are incongruous. Thus if we take 'bloom' as the focus, and '*the slum of* bloom' as the *minimal frame*, the utterance that sufficiently disambiguates the embedded utterance is the sentence 2.3 which is the frame (*simpliciter*).

Incongruity

I posited an incongruity in the metaphorical utterance such that the frame and focus reflected this incongruity, and noted that the distinction and indeed an incongruity were not necessarily confined to metaphors. In dealing with a metaphor we need to ask the following questions: is it always the case that there is an incongruity in a metaphorical utterance, and, if so, is there an incongruity distinctive to metaphor? And what is its significance?

The general position, that metaphor involves some incongruity (be it semantic deviation, a conceptual anomaly, or a category mistake), a position as old as Aristotle's treatment of the subject, has been seriously questioned in a number of its more specific versions. Those who attack this view are sometimes critical of the particular mechanism used to specify the anomaly. Others, as I have pointed out earlier, object to the thesis in its more general form, because they believe it is inimical to the view that metaphors have an irreducible cognitive content. The reasoning goes as follows: if metaphor is semantically anomalous, then it cannot be subject to linguistic rules; hence we cannot speak of metaphorical meaning, for the production and interpretation of meaningful utterances is rule-governed; but if there is no distinctive metaphorical meaning, then there is no irreducible conceptual content which may have cognitive efficacy. I hope to show that this set of inferences is not justified, even if we grant that metaphors involve what are anomalies according to first-order meaning rules. To say a thing is not subject to a given set of rules is not to say that it is subject to no rules. In my treatment, therefore, I want to be sufficiently precise about the rules of discourse violated by metaphor, for us to be able to see what rules metaphor does indeed follow. Moreover, I want to show how the violations are systematically connected to the proper interpretations of metaphorical utterances.

First, we must acknowledge the justifiable criticism the anomaly view has received. Critics have pointed out completely non-deviant sentences which can be used metaphorically. We have already encountered one such example, the sentence 2.1 above. Proverbs and colloquial expressions are a rich source of illustrations:

2.7 I shall kill two birds with one stone.

2.8 He is up against the wall.

Another interesting non-deviant sentence is

2.9 Smith is a plumber.

which is metaphorical when both speaker and hearer know that Smith is not a plumber but a surgeon.

But this criticism is founded on the belief that the unit of a metaphorical utterance is a sentence. Although 2.1, 2.7, 2.8, and 2.9 are sentences and hence complete as grammatical utterances, they are not complete as metaphorical utterances. Their completeness as metaphor requires a setting which renders them metaphorical. That setting, I contend, will yield a first-order incongruity of a conceptual sort.

The nature of the deviance attributed to metaphorical sentences has often been couched in terms of a selection-restriction violation, avowedly a semantic rendering of Ryle's category mistake (Katz 1972, 91–2). Yet clearly, none of the above sentences contains within it a selection-restriction violation. Any incongruities resulting from embedding the sentences in units of a high level of complexity could not be captured by the KF notion of a selection-restriction violation since these are only operative within a sentence (not so, of course, the Rylean category mistake).

But consider the following sentence:

2.10 The seal dragged himself out of the office.

If 'seal' is taken to mean the animal, sentence 2.10 does not violate any selection restrictions. But unlike sentences 2.1, 2.7, 2.8, and 2.9 sentence 2.10 is odd. It is, none the less, conceptually possible. The oddity appears empirical: seals of the animal variety are rarely found in offices. Thus whether 2.10 is metaphorical or not depends on a context which will clarify the nature of the oddity of 2.10.

Some writers, wary of the synthetic–analytic distinction, have criticized both the view that there are rules for the concatenation of words in a sentence which are purely linguistic and the notion of selection-restriction rules of the Katzian sort. These writers want to speak of degrees of semantic deviance.[23] On this view, 2.10 would be less

---

[23] See e.g. Weinreich 1966.

deviant than 2.3, for example. Yet without a suitable context, we cannot claim that 2.10 is deviant; it may even be literally true. But such concerns arise when we take the unit of metaphor to be the sentence. When the sentence is conceived of as the semantic and metaphorical unit, then we are led to distinguish between a degree of semantic deviance and absolute semantic deviance, as given in the confines of the sentence. The problem dissolves when we see that a metaphorical utterance, that is, focus and frame, need not be a sentence, but may be any utterance of some non-null degree of grammatical complexity, and when we recognize that there are semantic strictures governing the combination of units from the first level of complexity upwards. We can then begin to ask the right sorts of question concerning the nature of the incongruity inherent in metaphorical discourse.

The nature of the incongruity is related to the violation of the first-order restrictions and conditions on the semantic combination of elements bracketed together by projection rules. The incongruity is a direct result of the bringing together of semantic fields which are kept distinct in first-order discourse, and which I shall call *incompatible*. A more precise formulation is given below.

The Incongruity Principle. Consider a complete metaphorical utterance u_C, with a focus u_A and frame u_B. Let us say that one tries to give an interpretation$_{LC}$ of u_C. Once the projection rules have operated on the lowest-level constituents of u_C, bracketing them according to their syntactic (for intra-sentential) and cohesive (for extra-sentential) relations, there will be at least some u_a and some u_b, constituents of u_A and u_B respectively, such that u_a has been bracketed with u_b. However, given some preferred sense$_{LC}$[24] of u_b: (*a*) there is no sense$_{LC}$ of u_a which would not violate some sc-rule governing u_a and u_b, and (*b*) the γ-component of the preferred sense$_{LC}$ of u_b is incompatible with each sense$_{LC}$ of u_a. In the case that there is some sentence in which u_a and u_b are both constituents, there would be no first-order interpretation of that sentence. In the case that u_a and u_b belong to two different sentences, both of which are constituents of u_C, there is a conversion sentence formable through the cohesive projection rule which would not have a first-order interpretation.

---

[24] A preferred sense would be determined by some utterance of which u_b is a constituent.

To illustrate the functioning of the Incongruity Principle (henceforth IP) let us consider sentence 2.3. If we take the focus of the metaphor to be the word 'slum', then the minimal frame is the phrase 'slum of bloom'. 'Slum' and 'bloom' will have γ-component that are incompatible, for the terms come from two distinct semantic fields, let us say the fields of urban life and gardening (or vegetation), respectively. Further, we can suppose that the sc-rule for 'bloom' includes a condition that in a prepositional phrase it concatenates with terms that have the descriptors [living], [vegetative].[25]

In the case of a sentence such as 2.1, where the context concerns an ageing professor emeritus, 2.1 would itself be the focus and the sentences with which it combines to form a text would constitute the frame. If 2.1 occurs as a sentence in an otherwise rambling conversation and is said as an aside, accompanied perhaps by a gesture, for example, a nod in the direction of the professor, we must take the relevant gesture as the situational context which can, at least in part, be rendered linguistically, thus providing the frame of the metaphor. For the purposes of illustration, consider the text below:

2.11 (i)   The rock is becoming brittle with age.
   (ii) He responds to his students' questions with none of his former subtlety.
   (iii) His lectures also lack the verve which was characteristic of them.

From 2.11 we see that if we take sentences 2.11(i)–(iii) as cohering to form a discourse, then 'he' in 2.11(ii) would have 'the rock' in 2.11(i) as an anaphoric referent. Presumably, a cohesive projection rule would bracket 'the rock' and 'he' as well as the possessive pronouns 'his' in 2.11(ii) and 'his' in 2.11(iii). The possessive pronouns would be possessive pronominalizations of 'the rock'. According to our definition of cohesive projection rules, 'the rock' should be substitutable for 'he' in 2.11(ii) and 'the rock's' should be substitutable for 'his' in 2.11(ii) and 2.11(iii). But 'rock' has none of the descriptions, that is, [human], [animal], [animate], which would make it satisfy the sc-rule for the subject

---

[25] Alternatively we can speak of the metaphorical sentence 'the garden was a slum of bloom', in which case we can speak of a similar type of violation of sc-rules governing 'garden' and 'slum'. If we consider only the phrase 'slum of bloom', its actual grammatical analysis is, as Adrienne Lehrer has pointed out (in a personal communication), 'tricky, since it is not completely clear what the head is—*bloom*, in which case *a slum of* is similar to a quantifier expression (e.g. a cup of coffee), or *slum*, in which case *of bloom* is a prepositional phrase modifying it.'

of 'responds', and this is especially so when we consider the phrase 'responds to his student's questions'—only humans, particularly instructors of some sort, have students to respond to. The remainder of the sentence, 'with none of his former subtlety', further restricts the choice of subject to satisfy certain presuppositions, in particular, that the subject was at one time subtle in his response. A similar analysis can, I believe, be undertaken with regard to other elements of the text. Note that although the term 'professor' is never mentioned, there is a lexical cohesion which comes from a choice of words appropriate to a semantic field of higher learning, of which 'professor' is an important and central member. There is an implicit invocation of this field and with it of 'professor'.

In both 2.3 and 2.11 the violations in the sc-rules appear to be simply violations of selection-restriction rules. In KF, selection restrictions are those semantic markers in the semantic representation of a term which indicate which markers must be possessed by terms with which the word collocates in a sentence. Within the semantic representation of a word, these restrictions are specified for the different categories of terms a word might combine with, so that we shall have one set of restrictions for the subject, another for a transitive verb, another for the direct object, still another for the indirect object, etc. The selection restrictions pertain only intra-sententially and provide what Katz, Fodor, Chomsky, and others take to be linguistic and conceptual information possessed as part of the linguistic competence of speakers of the language.

I questioned earlier whether linguistic information of this sort was sufficient, or whether we must not also include knowledge about the world in determining what terms can concatenate meaningfully$_{\text{L.C.}}$. Metaphorical utterances which suggested this were cases such as 2.9, in which Smith is known to be a surgeon, and 2.10, in which the context indicates that no real seal entered the office. In the case of 2.9, there is no selection-restriction violation in the combination of 'Smith', as the name of a person, and 'plumber', as in the predicate 'is a plumber'. The verb phrase would simply require the marker—or descriptor—[human] in its subject. The oddity of sentence 2.10 is surely due not to any linguistic facts but to our empirical knowledge of seals and offices.

Yet if we construct linguistic contexts for 2.9 and 2.10 which contain, explicitly, the information required to give these sentences a metaphorical interpretation, we find that we rely far less substantially on what seems to be empirical knowledge than on linguistic or conceptual knowledge. (Here, as elsewhere, I presume that the distinction is relative to a common language and its default assumptions.)

Consider 2.12, a text in which the situational context, that both speaker and hearer know that Smith is a surgeon and not a plumber, is given expression in the discourse.

2.12(i) Don't let Smith perform such a delicate surgical procedure.
   (ii) Smith is a plumber.
   (iii) His last two patients died.

The cohesive projection rules would bring 'plumber' in 2.12(ii), together with both the occurrences of Smith, in 2.12(i) and 2.12(ii), and the pronominalized possessive in 2.12(iii), while preserving co-reference. Both 2.12′ and 2.12″ are plausible candidates for texts which preserve the propositional content of sentence 2.12(i)–(iii) taken together.

2.12′(i) Don't let that plumber perform such a delicate surgical procedure.
    (ii) Smith's last two patients died.
2.12″(i) Don't let Smith perform such a delicate surgical procedure.
    (ii) That plumber's last two patients died.[26]

While it is true that none of the sentences in 2.12 violates selection-restriction rules, the substitutions made possible by the cohesive co-referential relations yield structures which are contrary not just to empirical but also to linguistic facts. This is particularly evident in 2.12′(ii), for the sense of the term 'patient' is here sufficiently disambiguated by the lexical field indicated by terms such as 'surgical procedure' and 'died' to recognize that we are speaking of that sense captured in the representation ([Human], [under the care of a physician]). A plumber, however, operates only on inanimate, non-human things. Although the cohesive projection rules can substitute 'plumber' for nominal phrases whose verb phrases include terms from the field of surgical medicine in texts 2.12, 2.12′, and 2.12″, phrases such as 'plumber's patient' cannot be given a first-order interpretation.[27]

---

[26] In 2.12′ the categorical identification of 2.12(ii) is captured in the metaphorical reference relation between 'that plumber' in 2.12′(i) and 'Smith' in 2.12′(ii); in 2.12′ the two phrases have an anaphoric relation.

[27] One example, suggested by Rita Nolan (in a personal communication), needs consideration. Let us say that, during a war, medics in US submarines are permitted to do surgery in emergency cases and that aboard one submarine there are two such medics, one a plumber, the other a mechanic. We can imagine some of the crew referring to these

At this point I want to put forward what I take to be only a conjecture but one which, if true, turns out to have significant consequences. The conjecture is that whenever we decide, on the basis of some oddity in an utterance, to give that utterance a metaphorical interpretation, if we construct or reconstruct a sufficiently rich context, we shall find that the sc-rules violated turn out to be the familiar selection restrictions of the KF model, either in the sentence or phrase which is the metaphorical utterance, or in some conversion permitted by our cohesive projection rules. Moreover, with one important qualification which I shall discuss below, if there is no possible conversion which yields a selection-restriction violation between the focus and frame of the metaphor (or of the related metaphor generated by the conversion) the oddity is such that it would be a misunderstanding of the utterance to interpret it metaphorically.

Because this is merely a conjecture, I want to maintain a distinction between the sc-rules and the selection-restriction violations, for, if the hypothesis turns out to be false, it may be that there are other linguistic or non-linguistic considerations which affect the way in which terms

---

different medics by their non-military occupations. In so doing, they give the phrases 'the mechanic's patient' and 'the plumber's patient' a first-order interpretation. Counter to the statement made above, within this context there appears to be no incongruity in speaking of 'the plumber's patient'. None the less, in the story I propose in the text, speakers and audience alike know, or at least can presume, given ordinary circumstances in which surgeons rarely moonlight as plumbers and vice versa, that the person referred to is *not* a plumber but a surgeon. In the former context, in which the usual circumstances do not prevail, 'plumber' is used to pick out or identify one individual among others who might be similarly characterized, for example, as medical officer cum surgeon. But notice it is not through the attribute of Smith as a plumber that he possesses patients. If a hearer was so to interpret 'the plumber's patients', he would incorrectly construe the phrase in this context. This situation seems to parallel, though it does not quite coincide with, the distinction Donnellan makes between the attributive and the referential use of a definite description. According to Donnellan (1977), a definite description serving a referential function need not be bound by the meaning of the terms in the description any more than proper names are so bound. Similarly, when we use 'plumber' simply to designate a particular individual by a distinctive property, but one which bears no relation to the relevant properties which belong to him as a surgeon, the meaning of the distinctive property by which we gain referential access to the individual plays no role in these predications—it serves as a quasi-proper name. While Donnellan's distinction is a pragmatic and not a semantic one, the point being made here is semantic: it is *qua* plumber, i.e., given the concept of what it is to be a plumber, that one cannot have patients in the first-order sense of plumber and patient. Thus when it appears that the context indicates that we can give the phrase 'the plumber's patient' a first-order meaning, it is only by virtue of the same linguistic function that permits us to continue to call a grey-haired, but formerly red-haired, person 'Red', i.e., it is by treating the term as a quasi-proper name or a *rigid designator* which does not refer by means of its descriptive content.

may be combined.[28] If true, the significance of the conjecture lies in the fact that it places the identification of metaphors squarely within the province of semantics, or at least, of a semantics broad enough to include the consideration of inter-sentential connections in discourse. If the hypothesis is correct, then it is a necessary condition for the identification of an utterance as metaphorical that the utterance should involve a violation of first-order *linguistic* rules, and not merely that the utterance should be empirically implausible though otherwise linguistically (first-order) sound.

Furthermore, there is an even more important consideration regarding the cognitive import of metaphor. The selection restrictions, along with other semantic descriptors, are meant to capture the conceptual content of the terms of the language, and if metaphor is to be capable of forcing a conceptual reorientation it is plausible that only a conceptual incongruity, and not merely an empirical unlikelihood, would warrant a metaphorical interpretation. For if someone says something which challenges our beliefs concerning empirical matters, and it turns out that what was said was true, we may have gained some new empirical information. But if metaphors are cognitive it is not because they add to our store of factual data. It is because a metaphor causes us to think about something in a new way, to reorganize the concepts we already have, and to form new conceptualizations. For it to accomplish this conceptual task, it seems reasonable to expect that a conceptual incongruity be inherent in anything which is indeed a metaphor. This is because the conceptual incongruity, when the appropriate pragmatic considerations are operative, requires a conceptual resolution (an at least tentative conceptual reorganization)—just as the empirical novelty requires an empirical resolution (the acceptance or rejection of some unexpected empirical information).

At this point a caveat is required, for the distinction between the empirical and the conceptual is not as neat as the last sentence implies. I ought to have said that an empirical novelty *generally* requires an empirical resolution. But empirical novelty may eventuate in a conceptual reform or revolution, for it may raise the issue of the adequacy of current conceptual constructs and contrariwise current conceptual constructs may importantly influence what is taken as empirical

---

[28] The fact that definite descriptions can be used in the manner discussed in n. 27 may influence such considerations. Also, once Ross's (1981) notions of 'dominance' and 'resistance' are spelled out, we might better understand the constraints and directions of the sc-rules.

novelty. One is forced to be humble about making assertions such as those in the previous paragraph when one considers, first, the general consensus among contemporary philosophers of science that observation terms are theory-laden, and, secondly, the general puzzlement over the interaction of the theoretical, that is, conceptual, and the empirical. None the less, these distinctions, still have value within relativized contexts.

Explicit Cues for Metaphor

Early in this chapter, I distinguished the psychological from the logical question of identifying metaphors, claiming that an incongruity within the utterance itself or between the utterance and its situational context was a necessary condition for the identification of a metaphorical expression. However, when explicit cues are given, such incongruity does not appear to be necessary, logically or psychologically. We might say 'speaking metaphorically . . . ', where the ellipsis is replaced by a remark exhibiting no apparent incongruity. In what follows I hope to show that an incongruity of a conceptual sort is ultimately involved if such explicit cues are being correctly used.

Consider the case exemplified by the following:

2.13 The thieves ordered him against the wall and tied his hands. There was no escape. He realized that both literally and metaphorically (i) he was up against the wall, and (ii) his hands were tied.

In 2.13 there is no apparent textual incongruity: no selection restrictions are violated, there is no empirical falsity or oddity, no violations of sc-rules. Yet notice that we could aptly (or even truthfully, if we want to accept the idea of metaphorical truth) describe a person's predicament as 2.13(i) or 2.13(ii) where the truth conditions for the expressions' literal applications were not met. Similarly, a person might literally be up against a wall, or have his or her own hands tied, and yet metaphorically not be in such an uncomfortable position. The embedded sentences 2.13(i) and 2.13(ii) as meant metaphorically, do not indeed refer back to the circumstances portrayed in the first sentence of 2.13 in the immediate and direct way in which they so refer when they are meant literally. Rather, they refer back to the second sentence, 'There was no escape.' Furthermore, the set of implications to be drawn from 2.13(i) and 2.13(ii) understood literally, would fail to coincide with the implications to be drawn were these to be understood metaphorically. An explicit elaboration of this analysis in textual terms would most likely produce the conditions required to satisfy the Incongruity Principle.

Such an elaboration, however, is unnecessary if we supplement the Incongruity Principle with another principle, which I shall call the Independence of Applicability Conditions Principle (henceforth IAC). In text 2.13, we have sentences which may be sensible, even true, whether interpreted literally or metaphorically. It is one of many examples that neither grammatical deviance nor literal falsity is required for an utterance to be metaphorical.[29] The introduction of the IAC is intended to acknowledge this phenomenon and yet show how an incongruity is, none the less, introduced into the discourse by such utterances (utterances generally preceded by an explicit cueing of the metaphor), an incongruity these share with utterances to which the Incongruity Principle applies. The principle is based on the observation made above that in texts such as 2.13 the sentence can have different truth conditions on a literal interpretation and on a metaphorical (or other second-order interpretation).

Truth conditions are only one type among what I call *conditions of applicability*. If the utterance is a statement, the conditions result in truth-values for its literal interpretation. If the utterance is a performative, the conditions for its correct literal application are felicity conditions. If the utterance is a descriptive phrase, the conditions of applicability of a literal reading are the conditions for its correct referential or attributive use. I believe we can fashion analogous conditions of applicability for second-order discourse—for example, some statements or descriptions are metaphorically 'apt' while others are not. Conditions for applicability, then, are to be understand as broadly as necessary to include as many diverse forms of utterance as metaphors come in, and metaphors come in many forms: assertions, questions, imperatives, performatives, promises, definite descriptions, etc.

In order to formulate the IAC, I need to remark first that what I call a second-order interpretation of an utterance involves some function either of a first-order interpretation of the utterance, if one exists, or of a first-order interpretation of the constituents of the utterance. In addition, I need to specify what I mean by the *context* of an utterance.

---

[29] See Stern 1983. Goodman (1968) provides another example by pointing out that a painting may both be literally and figuratively 'blue'. An entire class of examples are provided by 'negative' metaphors, metaphors which assert that an *x* is *not* a *y*, e.g. Mao's remark 'A revolution is not a dinner party'. Understood literally, these are trivially true. But understood metaphorically they carry a particular set of implications that do not follow from the statement understood literally.

The context of an utterance is another utterance of greater complexity of which the first is a constituent. That is, if one utterance $u_x \in U^k$ is contained as a constituent of a more complex utterance, $u_y \in U^m$ ($k < m$), we can say that the latter is the context for the former. In keeping with the expressibility principle enunciated earlier, whereby we assimilate the situational context to a linguistic one, the context may be the linguistic environs of u_x or it may be a linguistic rendering of the salient features of the situation in which u_x is uttered.[30]

The General Independence of Applicability Conditions Principle. Given some u_x, in a given context u_y, that is $u_x \in U^k$ is a constituent of $u_y \in U^m$ (where $m > k > 0$), which has more than one interpretation, and there is no $u_z \in U^{m+n}$ ($k < m < m+n$) which will disambiguate the two interpretations, the satisfaction of the applicability of one interpretation is different from and independent of that of some other interpretation.

The Special Independence of Applicability Conditions Principle (for metaphor and other second-order significations). In the case that the IAC applies to u in a given context so that one interpretation is first-order and a second interpretation is a function of that first-order interpretation, that is, a second-order interpretation of the specified first-order interpretation, the latter may be a metaphorical interpretation.

There are a number of important points we need to note in regard to the General IAC. It would appear to pertain in the case of all forms of ambiguity. However, in most types of ambiguity there is a supposition that given a sufficiently rich context (see n. 30) the utterance may be disambiguated. The IAC applies only when such disambiguation is not achieved by the choice of a sufficiently rich context. Note that there are particular forms of second-order interpretation which are not metaphorical and to which the (Special) IAC does not apply—but not because their meaning cannot be disambiguated. As I have claimed and discussed more explicitly above, all utterances are potentially ambiguous between literal and metaphorical interpretations if the con-

---

[30] The utterance $u_y \in U^m$ which serves as the context for $u_x \in U^k$ may itself be embedded in a context, $u_z \in U^n$ ($k < m < n$). In that case, u_z is also a context for u_x, but a richer one.

text is not rich enough to permit such a disambiguation. But the metaphorical cases to which the Special IAC pertains are those in which no context can disambiguate between the literal and the metaphorical, that is, where both interpretations properly apply.

Second-order significations that are not subject to the Special IAC are exemplified by Searle's indirect speech act. When Jones says to Brown, 'Pardon me, but you're stepping on my toe,' the truth-value of the informative first-order interpretation (that is, the fact that Brown is stepping on Jones's toe) directly influences the appropriateness of the request which is the second-order interpretation (that is, Jones's request to Brown that Brown stop stepping on Jones's toe). Were the first-order statement not true, the second-order interpretation would fail to be appropriate.

Quite serendipitously, the General IAC provides the conditions necessary for a pun. A pun is just a use of language in which there is more than one possible interpretation of the phonetic or orthographic label, and the conditions of applicability which are independent for each interpretation of at least two such interpretations are, in this particular instance, both fulfilled. The semantic cleverness required to bring about such a confluence often tickles our fancy. The observations concerning puns are of some significance, for although the IAC was formulated with the intent of explaining a certain feature of some metaphors, it has a range of application which is considerably broader. This at once legitimates the principle, removing some of its *ad hoc* character, and demonstrates the way in which the exploration of the phenomenon of metaphor helps us uncover general features of language.

The IAC draws our attention to yet another point. In much, if not most of our speech, we attempt to avoid overt ambiguity. (Incidently, we do not as regularly avoid vagueness—not because of sloppiness, but because what we intend to communicate, express, or refer to *is* vague or general.) In the figure zeugma[31], for example, 'In New York City, actresses spend most of their time waiting at tables and for their big chance', or in puns, ambiguity is exploited—generally for humour. In rhetorical modes such as advertising and political slogans, ambiguity is exploited for its attention-drawing quality. As comprehenders of

---

[31] Zeugma is defined by Lanham: 'One verb governs several congruent words or clauses, each one in a different way' (1969, 143).

language, we aim at *specifying meaning*, at selecting, out of the many possible interpretations, one interpretation that coheres with our background default assumptions and other contextual considerations. (Note that *specificity* here contrasts with *multiplicity* of meaning, not with *generality*. We may very specifically want to convey something very general, for example, that I shall be coming round at *approximately* six o'clock, that is, expect me shortly before six but don't assume I'm late until well after six. The relation between specificity as I am using the term and generality is related to information-theoretic notions developed and discussed in Chapter 3.)

An utterance in which a single meaning cannot be specified (for example, in which the IAC is operative) draws attention to itself and thereby captures our attention. In literature, and especially poetry, many specifiable and interrelated senses are supported by a given expression. The different layers of meaning are often sustained for an entire text. The blatant form is allegory; but all literary craft requires skill in constructing language having such purposive multiplicity of meaning. And while we may be unintentionally ambiguous through carelessness or inattention, purposive and sustained ambiguity requires skill in manipulating language. Such purposive ambiguity must work against a basic strategy we employ in understanding language: to interpret the linguistic utterance and its contextual setting so that we can arrive at a specified meaning. Skill in purposive ambiguity can lend its purposes to potent ends: the increase of wealth, the acquisition of political power, the enjoyment and enhancement of art. We remark that advertisement-writers are richly rewarded; political speech- and slogan-writers much sought after; and literary writers, when successful, highly esteemed. The strategy for specifying meaning is not easily thwarted.[32]

The Strong Thesis

What underlies the IAC for metaphor is that the first- and second-order interpretations represent, presuppose, or in some way allude to distinct semantic fields. In text 2.13 we can recognize that talking about the actual binding of human hands is different, semantically and conceptually, from talking about possibilities of escape, even though an

---

[32] There is a contrary pull to that of meaning specification, which is manifest in what psychologists have called 'spreading activation' (see Motley 1985).

understanding of the metaphor as metaphor (and not just as an idiomatic expression) requires an understanding of the literal meaning.

It is likely that the IP and IAC are ultimately reducible to the same principle, but I shall take them as two principles which can serve either alternatively or conjointly as a necessary condition for metaphor. When there is no first-order interpretation then the Incongruity Principle is appropriate. When u has at least one possible but implausible interpretation$_{LC}$ both principles may serve conjointly. When u has at least one possible and plausible interpretation$_{LC}$ as well as at least one plausible metaphorical interpretation, which would need to be signalled through a direct statement of an intent to have u metaphorically interpreted, then the IAC serves as the necessary condition.

In formulating the notion that an incongruity between a focus and a frame constituted a necessary condition for metaphor, I added a conjecture that, given the operation of the cohesive projection rules, the incongruity could be identified as a violation of a selection restriction within the metaphorical utterance itself or of some conversion sentence permissible from the utterance and its context. This view had to be modified in the light of cases in which there was an explicit signalling of metaphor and no semantic incongruity. In such cases, I suggest that the conditions for the correct applicability of the utterance when interpreted literally are independent of similar conditions for an appropriate metaphorical interpretation. When there are independent conditions of applicability for first- and second-order interpretations, there is an implicit logical incongruity in the way in which such metaphors as those contained in example 2.13 conflate the two independent sets of conditions. To show this best, I can change the example somewhat to:

2.13′   My hands were tied (literally), but my hands were not tied (metaphorically).

On a first-order reading of 2.13′ with the parenthetical remarks omitted, we should have a contradictory sentence. If we assimilate logical and semantic (or linguistic) incongruity to conceptual incongruity, we can state a strong version of our thesis: that all metaphors must have as a necessary condition some kind of conceptual incongruity on a first-order interpretation. But our necessary condition would not be sufficient. For it is not the case that whenever we have such conceptual incongruity we also have metaphor. We could say that this necessary condition is semantic. And while I have argued that metaphor requires a semantic analysis, a semantic analysis alone will not suffice. There are important pragmatic considerations which figure in the understanding of metaphor as well.

The Role of Context

Before we go on to consider the necessary pragmatic conditions for metaphor, we need to consider that in specifying the semantic necessary conditions I have frequently appealed to context.

The degree to which I have stressed the context-dependence of metaphor may appear to threaten efforts at establishing a semantics of metaphor which is also a *rule of metaphor*. Contextual matters have traditionally lain outside the scope of semantic inquiry for two reasons: first the semantic unit has been regarded as either the word or the sentence; secondly, each context is unique, while each rule, which is to reflect the lawlike propositions of a semantic theory, must be general. In regard to the first point, I shall argue in Chapter 3 that a context-free sentence is an abstraction which at best has methodological usefulness. I shall argue that literal sentences are also highly context-dependent, and that for any given literal interpretation of an utterance we make implicit or explicit use of context. We have already seen that many sentences can be interpreted metaphorically or literally, depending on context. If we are to speak of a semantics of natural language, we cannot ultimately ignore dependence on context for the interpretation of literal as well as metaphorical sentences.

In regard to the second point, I have developed a set of formulations which will permit us, given the plausibility of the expressibility principle, to regard a term's context as yet another (though higher-level) utterance-type. In this way, the original term or expression plus its context may be treated as the expression itself would be, namely, as an utterance-type, and not an utterance-token, which may itself be situated in a particular context.

Pragmatic Considerations: The Co-operative Principle

Among our assumptions and expectations concerning an utterance are some that pertain to a speaker's reasons for saying what he or she says. Grice is undoubtedly correct in suggesting that the participants in a conversation, if they are to carry on a conversation in good faith, need to adhere to what he calls the Co-operative Principle (henceforth CP), which he describes as some 'rough general principle' along the following lines:

Make your conversational contribution such as is required, at the stage at which it occurs, by the accepted purpose or direction of the talk exchange in which you are engaged. (1975, 44.)

Talk which follows along the lines of what Grice specifies as four maxims, Quantity, Quality, Relation, and Manner, will in general result in discourse which accords with the Co-operative Principle. We can briefly characterize these maxims as follows:

Quantity: Give neither less nor more information than is required.
Quality: Try to make your contribution truthful.
Relation: Be relevant.
Manner: Be perspicuous (by avoiding obscurity, ambiguity, etc.).

Occasionally we cannot follow one maxim because doing so interferes with following another. Sometimes we want to mislead and will knowingly violate one maxim, assuming that our audience assumes we are following it. At other times we might not obey one or more maxims because we intend not to respect the Co-operative Principle. When it seems clear that a speaker is attempting to abide by the CP and yet appears to be flouting one of the maxims for none of the above reasons, then Grice maintains, we must ask what is being *implicated* by the blatant violation of a maxim. Grice calls such a situation a case of *conversational implicature*. Humour is often generated when a question asked is answered with the background information that is obvious to all. Humour depends on foiling the expectations of our default assumptions. A story of an infamous bank robber tells of his being asked, 'Why do you rob banks?' He replied, 'Because that's where the money is.' But we presume that if one chose to commit a robbery, one would only choose to rob where one believed the money was, and so no one would reasonably ask the question with that in mind. Thus the question normally asks why the bank robber engages in this unsanctioned behaviour. But the answer makes the question appear ridiculous because it takes what is contravened as the norm.

Similarly, the jokes below illustrate that we do not normally answer a question with background information that is obvious to all and this is because we presume that a question is asked because there is some problem to be addressed.

Q. On which side of the house should you plant a tree?

    A. On the outside.
    Q. Why does a crane stand on one foot?
    A. Because if it picked up the other it would fall.

The person who puts forward the riddle exploits one of the maxims (probably Manner) for the purpose of humour.

I have claimed that the conceptual incongruity embodied in the IP and motivating the Special IAC is a necessary condition which an utterance must fulfill to warrant a metaphorical interpretation. It is not a sufficient condition, in part because we must also decide whether the speaker is adhering to the Co-operative Principle and (a point not mentioned by Grice but significant in the case that what is implicated is a metaphor) whether a term is simply being misused. In the latter case, an utterance made by a sufficiently non-proficient speaker may have a metaphorical appearance or quality but may be a mistake none the less.

Percy (1958) recollects a childhood memory of a hunting trip on which he saw the breathtaking flight of a fascinating bird. The guide identified the bird with an appropriately wonderful name, 'blue-dollar hawk'. The boy learned later, to his great disappointment, that the guide was mistaken—the bird was called a blue darter hawk.

Children tend to make the most poetic mistakes. While sitting in a good Italian restaurant, I overheard a seven-year-old boy, seemingly boarding-school educated, complain that unlike the spaghetti sauce served here, the one at school was always 'blunt'. His mother corrected him: 'bland'. 'No,' he insisted, 'blunt, the way a knife is blunt.' The difference between a food critic and this young boy assessing a tomato sauce as 'blunt' is the difference between using the term metaphorically and using it (however charmingly) literally, but incorrectly.

Finally, there are the amusing errors of that winningly pretentious fool Mrs Malaprop. In a remark which ought to be about prodigies, she states, 'I would by no means wish a daughter of mine to be a *progeny* of learning' (Sheridan, *The Rivals*, Act 1 Scene 2).[33] These are all instances of utterances in which the speaker was not intending to violate a conversational co-operative principle, and the utter-

---

[33] This self-referential error draws our attraction to the fact that there is no chance of Mrs Malaprop's stated wish going unheeded.

ance was intended as meaningful and literal speech but simply failed as such.[34]

A speaker may want to 'opt out' of the conversation, that is, refuse to be bound by the CP. This can be done by some version of 'I can say nothing more', or by speaking nonsense: putting together words and sentences which are perhaps syntactically well-formed, but by which one means to say nothing at all.

When the speaker is not sufficiently competent in salient regards, or when she or he has opted out of the conversation, no conversational implicature can arise and, in particular, no metaphor can be implicated. Therefore, the identification of an utterance as a metaphor also supposes, as a necessary condition, that we have the circumstances in which a conversational implicature can arise; this is the situation in which, as Grice says, the speaker appears to flout some maxim of the CP. We then have some of the necessary conditions for an utterance to be identified as metaphorical in either of two cases:

(1) A maxim of Quality, Relation, or Manner is so flouted that an incongruity arises within an utterance. The utterance then satisfies the Incongruity Principle (and, in the strong thesis, satisfies the IP so that the violated sc-rules are, in fact, based on violated selection restriction rules).

(2) The utterance is lacking this incongruity but is subject to two interpretations satisfying the IAC.

Reinterpreting Language—Reinterpreting our World

However, the satisfaction of the above conditions is not yet sufficient to warrant a metaphorical identification. An utterance may fulfill these conditions, and the correct interpretation may still be a literal one. When a maxim appears to have been violated, but we decide that the speaker is still adhering to the CP, we still have to decide whether we ought to construe the speaker's words in other than their literal sense or whether we are required to suppose that the world (actual or poss-

---

[34] Davidson (1986) asks how it is that we none the less manage to understand the intended meaning of malapropisms. I believe that the somewhat nihilistic conclusions about language that Davidson draws are not warranted. We have enough experience of error and of attempts to approximate to the best possible explanation of an utterance to make our understanding of malapropisms and other mistakes quite explicable. Malapropisms, particularly, unlike many other linguistic errors, are rather systematic sorts of mistakes for which the corrective moves on the part of the interpreter are easily forseen. In this regard, they are not so unlike metaphors.

ible or perhaps even impossible) to which the statements apply (or which they presuppose) is significantly different from the world as we ordinarily take it to be. For example, although we remarked that sentence 2.10 ('The seal dragged himself out of his office') was odd, it was none the less possible to interpret it (and possible that it was intended to be interpreted) as a literal statement.

There are possible situations in which we could correctly interpret 2.10 so that the senses$_{LC}$ of each of the constituents was preserved. We might suppose the following:

(*a*) The sentence occurs in an actual or fictionalized account of an unusual occurrence in which the mammal, for some reason, appears in an office, and 2.10 is a purported description of its exit.

(*b*) The sentence occurs in a fairy-tale in which

   (i) a seal, in the sense of an animal, is portrayed as carrying on an anthropomorphic existence, on the model of Westernized, industrialized society, putting in a day's work at the office;

   (ii) a seal, in the sense of an imprinting device, is made animate (Walt Disney style) and drags itself (or perhaps him/herself) out of the office in which it (or he/she) is stored.

In case (*a*) we have neither a radical reconstrual of the world nor any change of meaning at all. However, our normal expectations of the sorts of beings found in offices are not met—instead we have a rare and unexpected event in the world we are familiar with. Notice that all the words in 2.10 retain their literal senses.[35]

In case (*b*), as in fairy-tales generally, we have to suspend disbelief and accept a world picture substantially different from our usual one. We allow for a suspension of physical and biological laws so that sea-lions function in offices or medallion seals are animated and move about. For us to be able to speak of such a mixture of the alien and the familiar, the familiar must maintain its resemblance to what we know and yet take on some features of what is normally alien to it. The meaning of certain key terms must be modified in the light of their new

---

[35] Curiously, my intuitions tell me that this interpretation is the least likely people would give if asked to interpret 2.10 out of any given context. Perhaps, if we are forced to construe the world contrary to our expectations, we prefer to construe it as radically different so that it becomes possible only as a fantasy world. Maybe it is most difficult to imagine the actual world not meeting our expectations.

setting. For example, we would implicitly add some human-like descriptor to 'seal' in (i), or delete a restriction <human> for office worker in (i). But these reinterpretations are not metaphorical. In fairy-tales and other accounts, in which the world is presumed to be quite different from our own, the reinterpretation of language is limited to the incorporation of necessary modifications in the special background default assumptions—those that are discourse-specific.

Within this modified conception of our world, language is used quite literally, and metaphor, when present, contrasts with literal language within that modified world view. Allegories, in this regard, should probably be classed with fairy-tales rather than with metaphor, and both should be viewed as within the scope of first-order meaning. When allegories get reinterpreted for their allegorical message, then we must consider them as having a second-order meaning. In Chapter 4, I shall give an account of the interpretation of metaphors in which we shall be able to distinguish metaphor from the modified though still literal meaning found in fairy-tale language.

A metaphorical interpretation, I want to suggest, involves a more radical reinterpretation of the language used than is the case when we revise or suspend our empirical beliefs with some concomitant semantic change. The incongruity which signals a metaphor must be captured in the metaphorical reading which we give to an utterance. The reinterpretation that 2.10 receives in (*b*) above is still within a first-order meaning—the conventions of the language used have been somewhat modified in a way understandable to the hearer, and the language is used literally within the new conventions. This is similar to a technical adoption of terms—for example, the legal sense of 'person' whereby a corporation may be said to be a person, or the mathematical use of terms like 'ring' and 'chain'. These are governed by specific conventions which are different from those governing their more common uses but which employ certain elements of their literal use (some features are deleted, others are added). Once we adopt the conventions specific to the terminology of law or mathematics there is no incongruity involved in the use of these terms. Compare the technical use of such a term as 'chain' in set theory with its use in Rousseau's exclamation 'Man was born free but is everywhere in chains'. In the latter case the very incongruity is put to service.

What I have said then is that when we are faced with a syntactically well-formed unit which appears conversationally odd, we must decide whether to keep our expectations of the world fixed and change the meanings of the words or whether to change our expectations of the world and keep the meanings fixed. Sometimes a third choice seems appropriate: to modify our expectation of the world and alter the meanings of words, but only in so far as the modified conception of the world demands. We choose the third option when we read fairy-tales—though we do not take the modified conception to be applicable to the actual world. It may be that in periods of scientific change we also choose the third option, only then the revisions concern our theories about the actual world. The second choice involves the assimilation of new information that may surprise us but does not force a conceptual change. Such conceptual change is appropriate when the oddity is one which, in suitable circumstances, yields metaphor: we utilize first-order meanings incongruously strung together to guide us to a second-order meaning. My conjecture is that this choice is appropriate only when there is a genuine conceptual oddity. The reorganization of meaning that the conceptual oddity forces may also, in the end, direct us to a new conception of the world, either to new theories about the actual world or to a new vision of the world as reflected in a poem or novel. I shall return to the conjecture and to this point in Chapter 8.

Conventional Metaphors

Notice that when I defined meaning$_{LC}$, I said that first-order meaning was both the literal and the conventional meaning of the utterance, and while the two coincided in the case of utterances belonging to the class U^o, they did not necessarily coincide in utterances that belonged to U^n where $n > 0$. Since we can only speak of metaphorical meanings in utterances u^n where $n > 0$, conventionalized metaphors do not have a first-order meaning, although a dictionary entry for a given term may include a metaphorical sense which a given word has attained through repeated usage in related metaphorical utterances. And yet to claim that conventionalized metaphors require an analysis such as the one extracted above and summarized below, seems otiose. Moreover, in so far as much of our language is the repository of worn-out metaphors, as Nietzsche, Derrida (1975), and most recently Lakoff and Johnson (1980) have well demonstrated, the elaborated second-order interpretation would appear to be required for a major part of our language. What would have second-order meaning, logically speaking, would then have a certain linguistic priority. Furthermore, for the practical purposes of everyday speech, conventional metaphors seem to require an analysis suited for first-order signification.

Conventionalized metaphors, rather than simply having second-order meaning, seem instead to be hybrids in the schema I have outlined. With Goodman's (1968, 1978a) metaphor of conventional metaphors as 'naturalized citizens', we can view language as a sort of New World in which natives are no longer more plentiful than the naturalized citizens. For all practical purposes of citizenship, the naturalized citizen and the native are not to be distinguished. But the cultural character of the land with a heterogeneous population is distinct from that of those with homogenized populations. Similarly, a logical analysis of language with its normative rules of inference can seem to ignore the diverse origins of the language which functions well according to first-order rules. But such an analysis fails to capture the texture and richness of the language and fails to account for the range of inferences possible through metaphor. A logical point remains, however, for the very idea of citizenship requires the concept of a prior homeland for the population of varied origins. Out of this consideration comes the fact that, no matter how 'dead', or conventionalized, metaphors are metaphors none the less. Consider the ease with which their metaphorical origins may be called forth. Few metaphors seem as dead and worn-out to us as the 'leg of a table'. Yet, reputedly, within the purview of Victorian sexual prudery this phrase was revivified, replete with salacious meaning: Victorians regarded it as necessary to cover tables with long table-cloths to avoid the indecency of viewing exposed 'limbs'. The most sexually modest Victorian who attended only to logically valid rules of inference would not be moved to invoke such measures. But the abductive-like nature of metaphorical inference makes the extension of sexual prudery to merely metaphorical limbs virtually inevitable.

The conventional metaphor may, then, be viewed as falling within first-order analysis when its dormant double semantic import is either fully forgotten by the generally competent speaker (a genuinely dead metaphor) or for practical linguistic purposes safely disregarded.[36] It requires a second-order analysis when it carries the burden of its double semantic import, that is, when it is placed in a setting in which its original literal meaning is highlighted and may be seen as incongruous in the context of the utterance.

We see that an important element of its metaphorical origins

---

[36] Perhaps this is what lies behind the puzzling notion of a 'literal metaphor' in Lakoff and Johnson 1980.

remains. This concerns the inferences and implications that structure the topic of the metaphor. Lakoff and Johnson (1980) convincingly demonstrate that such structuring need not be limited to a particular text or discourse, but can pervade the language. They offer examples of such metaphors as 'language is a conduit'; 'love is a physical force'; 'death is a journey'. As I have said elsewhere (Kittay unpublished), of special note are a host of metaphors (not mentioned by Lakoff and Johnson) in which woman, or a decidedly female activity serves as a vehicle: nature as woman; creativity as birth-giving; cities as women; artifice as woman; etc. (Note that these metaphors need not be consistent with one another. Both nature and artifice are topics for the vehicle 'woman'.) The interconnections and systematicity of these metaphors is, I believe, nicely accounted for by the use of semantic field theory. In Chapter 7, I speak of metaphor extended through a text—but the resources available can be exploited for the expanded metaphors that are not confined to a single text. Whether we deal with textual metaphors or language-pervasive metaphors, we encounter the significance of the metaphorical move. Metaphor is the linguistic realization of a leap of thought from one domain to another—in which the springboard is a structure-preserving mapping. The more we investigate metaphor, the more we become aware of how basic the movement is in language and in thought.

Conclusion

When we can judge from the contextual features of an utterance that the utterer adequately executed her or his intentions in making the utterance (that is, did not make any mistakes) and was adhering to the CP, then, if one of the maxims is flouted (or, what amounts to the semantic realization of this pragmatic principle, if the IP or the IAC is fulfilled) and the context gives us no reason to suspect that our normal expectations and conception of the world should not remain intact, we can perhaps best make sense of the utterance by abandoning the meaning$_{LC}$ of some of the terms of the utterance. If 2.10 occurs in a context such that the movements of a human office worker are being discussed and there is no other reference to any large mammal or animated medallion seal about, then we are required to presume that, if the speaker is adhering to the CP and is a competent speaker of the language, we must take some term, presumably 'seal', to be understood in a non-literal, non-conventional sense, and to see the IP as operative in this discourse.

To reiterate, the following conditions, some of which are semantic and some of which are pragmatic, must be met if we are to decide whether an utterance (in a given language) should be metaphorically interpreted:

(A) *Conditions on the presumed utterer*: that she or he is a competent speaker of the language, is not in this utterance making an error, and is adhering to the CP, so that, if the utterer flouts a maxim, the audience is warranted in concluding that a conversational implicature has arisen.

(B) *Conditions on the context*: that there is nothing in the context to persuade us that the world to which the utterance applies is substantially different from our own or that the usual expectations we have are not to be met; that there is nothing in the context to persuade us that the conventions of our discourse have been altered in specifiable ways (for example, to include technical language).

(C) *Conditions on the utterance*: that the utterance, taken with its context, displays a conversational oddity or (an inclusive *or*) is announced to be metaphorical so that

   (i) if there is an oddity, it arises from the incongruity of a term which is a constituent of an utterance of a higher order of complexity;

   (ii) a first-order interpretation of the utterance yields violations expressed in the IP and/or the IAC is operative;

   (iii) where the IP is effective, the incongruent elements belong to at least two distinct semantic fields; where the IAC holds, the independence of applicability conditions is related to the divergent semantic fields appropriate to the different things talked about.

(D) *Conditions for the strong thesis*: That where the IP is effective, the sc-rules violated are based on or are selection restrictions.

Clearly, in our practices, we do not examine each term to see if conditions A–D obtain. As I pointed out above, in the case of conventionalized metaphors the process of metaphorical identification and interpretation is short-circuited and they generally function as first-order discourse, although they retain their metaphorical potential. The process of identification of metaphors also involves a less complex procedure if any of the conditions are met in a particularly strong fashion. For example, in a newspaper article, written during the Nixon administration, discussing 'Nixon's plumbers', condition B would be so strongly fulfilled that a simple first-order interpretation would clearly be inadequate. This is apparent to any adult English-speaker who is even poorly acquainted with American politics and the contents of political news coverage. None the less, even when a competent speaker announces that his utterance is metaphorical or when the utterance appears to be a conventionalized metaphor or when some of the conditions are met with special force, if it turns out that the utterance, viewed in a sufficiently rich context, does not meet all three (or four) sets of conditions, we must revise our identification of that utterance as metaphorical.

The last point is crucial to an understanding of my insistence that the aim of this chapter is conceptual and not psychological. Conditions A–D are not to be understood as a description of actual psychological processes speakers undergo when they identify an utterance as metaphorical, but rather as a conceptual analysis of what is required of the utterance and its accompanying circumstances for us *correctly* to characterize an utterance as a candidate for a metaphorical reading. Psychologists, basing their views on time studies which indicate that the processing of metaphorical utterances does not require any more time than the processing of comparable literal utterances, have criticized theories proposing that metaphorical language involves extra identifying and interpreting procedures.[37] But these criticisms do not apply to my position since the 'extra' identifying 'procedures' I delineate above, and 'extra' interpreting 'procedures' I espouse with the view that metaphor is a second-order signification, are not put forward as psychological procedures capable of being measured in such studies. They are not procedures at all, but criteria for the identification of a certain sort of utterance.[38]

The studies in question do not undertake to examine the time required for less common and more complex metaphors. It may well

---

[37] See Ortony *et al.* 1978b; Glucksberg *et al.* 1982, and Gildea and Glucksberg (1984).

[38] Intuitively it appears to me that Lakoff and Johnson's views on the systematicity of metaphors may be able to account for the fact, observed in these time studies, that there is no discernible difference between the time taken to process commonly found metaphors and relatively simple metaphors and that needed to process comparable literal utterances, especially when the former are cued by a context. The systematic relationship between metaphors doubtless facilitates our comprehension of metaphor in ways comparable to that in which the systematic relationship between literal terms facilitates our choice of the proper interpretation of a given term in a given context.

be that these do require additional processing time. While questions concerning the psychological procedures are ones philosophers must pay attention to if they are not to make false claims for their own theories, one can still separate out a conceptual issue here which is independent of such findings.

Given the subtlety of linguistic circumstances surrounding discourse which exhibits oddity (when the oddity is construed within the scope of a first-order signification), I think it unwise to claim that the above summary gives us both the necessary and sufficient conditions for identifying a metaphor. What, for example, do we make of the surrealist André Breton's (1972, 57) title of a series of poems on automatic writing, poems which accompany his *Manifestes du surréalisme*:

2.14 'Poisson soluble' (soluble fish)?

The phrase, as a title, shares the apparent contextlessness of other titles, and more so than most since the poems do little to elucidate the phrase. Is it a metaphor? If it is not a metaphor and if A–D are conjointly sufficient conditions, 2.14 would have to fail at least one such condition. I do not believe 2.14 is a metaphor, and yet it is hardly clear which of these conditions it fails to meet. Let us presume that A is met. Conditions B and Ci, ii seem easily fulfilled. Only Ciii and D are questionable. Are 'soluble' and 'fish' from two different semantic fields? Are there selection restrictions on 'soluble' and 'fish' so that D is fulfilled? If we presume 'fish' to be live swimming fish, rather than dead fish, fish-shaped sweets, fish tattoos, etc. (ambiguities to which animate nouns are generally subject), it cannot properly collocate with 'soluble' for the obvious reason that what we understand by fish is a species which lives in water, something not possible of what is both animate and soluble. Of course we can play on the ambiguities cited and use 'fish' in 2.14 to mean fish in some other sense than live and swimming fish, and we can use the sense of 'being able to be solved' rather than 'that which dissolves in liquid' and arrive at wonderful texts in which both terms are used sometimes literally, sometimes metaphorically or otherwise figuratively.[39] If we eschew such interpret-

---

[39] I am grateful to the referee of *Synthese*, who reviewed the paper on which this chapter is based. The referee called my attention to the fact that the phrase 'soluble fish' 'by itself is not much of anything', and supplied a set of imaginative interpretations of the phrase that are too delightful to remain within the obscure confines of a referee report. I cite some of these interpretations below. In the light of them, I have amended the earlier discussion with the two settings in which the phrase is found, that is, the bare title of

ations for the moment and rely on the sort of implicit context which titles force us to adopt, the phrase has an incongruity which is still more radical than that of metaphors generally. As real live fish cannot both be fish and be soluble it is closer to the oxymoron: it is a self-destructing incongruity. Can we identify the phrase, then, as metaphor? Here our intuitions are still too weak. The phrase, in spite of the necessary conditions A–D, leaves us puzzled as to its status as a metaphor.

In the *Manifestes* itself 2.14 appears in the text:

Poisson soluble, n'est-ce pas moi le poisson soluble, je suis né sous le signe des Poissons et l'homme est soluble dans ses pensées! La faune et flore du surréalisme sont inavouables.
[*Soluble fish*, am I not the soluble fish, I was born under the sign of the Fish and man is soluble in his thoughts! The fauna and flora of surrealism ought not to be spoken of.] (Breton 1972, 49)

In the line 'am I not the soluble fish', we readily identify 'soluble fish' as metaphorically used to speak of the self-referential I—the writer of the essay cannot literally be a fish, whether soluble or insoluble. The attribution of soluble to fish appears to be mediated by a sym-

---

2.14 and the passage in the *Manifestes* itself. A careful look at the latter yields interesting but still inconclusive results as to how to identify this phrase within its surrealistic context. This difficulty may say more about surrealism than metaphor, but it demonstrates the subtlety and seemingly infinitely protean nature of meaning which will force itself on to nearly any string of words. This is demonstrated as well by the following passages invented by the referee:

(i) 'My friend, an unskilled cook, had some frozen fish which he wished to eat. Since he knew nothing of preparing food, he placed the frozen fish pieces in boiling water to cook. When he returned to the simmering pot an hour later, he could find no pieces of fish in the water, which had become cloudy and slightly thick. My friend drank the 'fish soup' as he called it, and assumed he had discovered a product he had not known the existence of previously: he thought he had purchased some *soluble fish*. [Both "soluble" and "fish" meant literally.]'

(ii) 'The writer speaks of a sailor who, after a night of drunken carousing, gets himself a tattoo of a fish. In the morning he showers and finds that the fish tattoo is gone. He exclaims that his had been a *soluble fish* tattoo. [Again, both "soluble" and "fish" used literally.]'

(iii) 'None of the ichthyologists could figure out the origins of the very odd fish which had been found in a stream in New Guinea. The problem was quite baffling and seemed to have no solution. But Kingsley solved the mystery and entitled her essay explaining the matter "the case of the *soluble fish*".'

A more clearly metaphorical use was suggested by my graduate assistant, James Carmine: 'The trout is a wild game fish whose colour is quite like the pebbles in the river bed; once he strikes your fly, either you hook him or he vanishes like sugar in tea—the trout is a *soluble fish*.'

bolic (though not metaphorical) identification of 'I' with the astrological sign of the Fish (Pisces), and by a conception of man as 'soluble in his thoughts' (soluble as 'dissolvable' or as an enigma which is to be 'solved'?). The two notions join in the attribution of 'soluble' to fish. We might say that the conception of man as 'soluble in his thoughts' is literal if we think of man solely in the attribute of thought—the Cartesian thinking thing, the unavowable thinking thing revealed in automatic writing. If we take soluble as 'able to be solved', then the view that man is 'soluble in his thoughts' may be seen to embody a sort of enthymeme to be filled in as follows: man, as such, is a mystery, an enigma, that which has not been avowed or voiced but reveals itself in his thoughts, and thus through the process of automatic writing—an uninhibited revelation of his thoughts—the mystery can be solved or, again, be dissolved. Thus although the text quoted is clearly a metaphor, the status of the phrase, even as it appears there remains problematical.

Whether or not conditions A–D are jointly sufficient, they do, as necessary conditions, focus on the crucial considerations, and at the very least delimit the class of phenomena to which metaphor may belong.

Furthermore, I suspect that no sufficient conditions can be given for metaphor as long as we confine ourselves to a discussion of first-order meaning, for the comprehension of a metaphor requires a function of the first-order meanings of the constituents of an utterance. A sufficient condition would need to posit the availability of just such a function for a given utterance in a given context. But within first-order meaning, we have no way to represent such a function. Therefore, the best we can hope for at this point in the inquiry, is a list of conditions which are necessary to identify an utterance as a candidate for such second-order interpretation as will result in metaphor. That is what conditions A–C (with D in the strong version) are meant to supply.

3

An Interlude concerning Context:
A Relational Theory of Meaning

> Language well used, is a *completion* and does what the intuitions of
> sensation by themselves cannot do. Words are the meeting points at
> which regions of experience which can never combine in sensation
> or intuition, come together. They are the occasion and the means of
> that growth which is the mind's endless endeavor to order itself . . .
> Language is no mere signalling system. (Richards, 1936, 130–1.)

In the previous chapter, I said that if we take metaphors to have cognitive efficacy, we require an account of metaphorical meaning. What I
have thus far exhibited is that semantic aspects enter into the very
determination that an utterance be interpreted metaphorically. Therefore, at the very least, some aspects of language meaning as well as
aspects of language use, are at work in our comprehension and production of metaphor. But, one may argue, the considerations which are
said to be semantic are so only in virtue of an extention of semantics by
a questionable inclusion of contextual features. The received view is
that to speak of meaning requires that the semantic unit should be
context-free.

When we say that meaning is context-free, we may mean:

(1) that the meaning of a word is independent of its context; or
(2) that the meaning of a sentence is independent of its context; or
(3) that features of the context figure in the meaning of a sentence
    in a rule-governed way, such that we may bracket these con-
    textual features in order to consider the meaning of the sen-
    tence to be context-free.

I shall argue against all three positions, although my own view is
closest to the third. I hold that both word and sentence meaning
depend on context in systematic and rule-governed ways. But if a
theory of meaning is to be a theory of understanding, then we cannot
bracket all these dependences and still speak of meaning being con-

text-free. The ways in which words and sentences depend on contextual considerations are crucial to what we understand when we
understand their meaning.

Using as my foil Davidson's (1981) argument that metaphor is a
matter of language use not language meaning, I shall argue that both
literal and metaphorical language are context-dependent, although the
dependence takes different forms. If the argument is successful, it
should remove the objection to the idea of metaphorical meaning. In
addition, I shall argue that a truth-theoretic semantics such as Davidson's is not hospitable to a theory of metaphor. In its stead, I shall propose a *relation theory of meaning* in which contextual features are
constitutive of meaning, a theory which is well suited to situate metaphorical meaning.

The task of this chapter, then, is threefold. I wish, first, to remove
the objection to metaphorical meaning; secondly, to argue for the context-dependence of both literal and metaphorical meaning; and thirdly,
to argue for a relational theory of meaning.

I ON THE VERY IDEA OF METAPHORICAL MEANING

Davidson on Metaphorical Meaning

Davidson (1981) tries to demonstrate that both the idea of metaphorical meaning and the concomitant belief that metaphors possess a
special cognitive content are mistaken. At the same time he wants to
assert that: 'Metaphor is a legitimate device not only in literature but in
science, philosophy, and the law: it is effective in praise and abuse,
prayer and promotion, description and prescription' (1981, 202). His
argument runs as follows:

(1) Meaning in language is context-free.
(2) Aspects of language which are not context-free are not ques-
    tions of language meaning but of language use.
(3) Metaphorical interpretation is context-bound, hence it is not a
    question of meaning but a question of use.
(4) Therefore there is no meaning of metaphorical utterances
    beyond their literal meaning.
(5) If there is only literal meaning of metaphorical utterances, then
    any cognitive content they possess must be expressible in a
    literal utterance.
(6) Whatever is interesting about metaphor must therefore lie in a

use of language and cannot be a question of an unparaphraseable cognitive content.

The positive corollary is that metaphors serve to intimate similarities—and as such are among the endless devices we use to draw attention to similarities in things.

In Davidson's project of tying meaning to Tarski-like truth conditions the importance of sentence meaning and word meaning being context-free becomes evident. According to Davidson, a satisfactory semantic theory must give an account of the truth conditions of every sentence and a modified version of Tarski's (1959) semantic theory of truth can provide such an account. The theory says that 'for each sentence *s*, a statement of the form "*s* is true if and only if *p*", where in the simplest case '*p*' is replaced by *s*.' (Davidson 1974b, 248.) That is, a theory of truth will entail an appropriate *T-sentence* for each sentence in the language. So for the sentence 'Snow is white', we assign the T-sentence

'Snow is white' is true if and only if snow is white.

Our theory ought then to entail all true sentences of the language. To accommodate Tarski's theory to natural language, we must recognize that the same sentence may be true for one speaker at one time at one place, and false at another time or for another speaker or at a different place. Furthermore a sentence may not be in its correct logical form (Davidson 1968); for example, it may be ambiguous such that it is true on one reading but false on another. In Davidson's account, for each sentence in the object language, we need to identify its correct logical form, and relativize it to a given speaker, time, and place. The assignments are given all at once for the totality of sentences in the language for which we have a correct canonical form—they are not assigned to sentences one at a time. In learning to interpret a language, we ascertain a pattern from among those sentences to which speakers of a language assent (Davidson 1974a); and we will abstract the word's meaning from its role in these sentences. For any particular word, we can state what role it plays in a given sentence (Davidson 1969).

For this procedure to be effective, sentences (relativized to speaker, time, and place) must not vary in meaning from context to context but must remain relatively stable. If metaphorical sentences had distinct metaphorical meanings and were included among literal sentences, they could have truth-values different from those assigned to them on a literal reading. Abstracting word meaning from a totality of sentences which included metaphorical meanings along with literal meanings would yield terms having odd and inconsistent extensions. That is, the truth conditions for the totality of sentences would fail to yield consistent patterns of word and sentence meaning. As long as we insist, as Davidson does, that metaphors have no meaning apart from the literal meanings of the words that constitute them, the meaning of metaphors poses no difficulty. While some metaphorical sentences will turn out to be trivially true—for example, Mao's remark quoted above, 'A revolution is not a dinner party'—most will be obviously false. For the sentence (1.5 above) 'Man is a wolf', we can formulate a T-sentence which will provide the truth conditions for the sentence understood literally:

'Man is a wolf' is true if and only if man is a wolf.

Evidently man is not a wolf and thus the sentence is simply false. From these truth conditions, taken together with other sentences in the language for which we formulate T-sentences, we can speak of the meanings of the words in the sentence 'Man is a wolf'.

Davidson's is but one way of formulating the interdependence of the theses that language is governed by a set of recursive rules which permit us to generate an infinite supply of sentences from a finite stock of words and a finite set of rules; that literal language is context-free; and that metaphor lies outside the bounds of a semantics of natural language. In Davidson's scheme, Tarski's T-convention serves to provide a semantics which binds these theses to the requirement that a semantics be truth-conditional.

An important implicit supposition here is that the rule-governed production and comprehension of meaning requires a context-free meaning for sentences, since each context is unique, while each rule must be general. That language is rule-governed and that metaphor is context-dependent would not, I believe, pose an insurmountable obstacle to the inclusion of metaphor in a semantics even if it were indeed the case that literal language is context-free. What is required is that we are able to specify salient and regular features of context which influence, again in a specifiable manner, the way in which we assign readings to metaphorical utterances. While each context may be unique, there is no a priori reason to assume that there are no general rules for the way in which context interacts with the meaning of the words in an utterance. Speech-act theory has permitted us to see that contextual considerations can be systematic and hence rule-governed. Speech-act theory is generally considered to belong to pragmatics rather than semantics and might be said to be a version of the third thesis mentioned above. In the previous chapter, I proposed systematic ways of treating contextual considerations in the case of metaphor—some of these were pragmatic, but others, I claimed, were semantic.

The Context-dependence of Literal Language

I have challenged the view that a rule-governed conception of meaning requires context-independence. The greater challenge to standard assumptions about the bounds of semantic theory is the claim that not only is metaphor subject to contextual considerations (which may or may not be amenable to a rule-governed treatment) but that the meaning and, in fact, the truth conditions of literal language must be understood to be similarly constrained by contextual considerations above and beyond those indexed by reference to speaker, time, and place.

There are several ways of arguing that literal language is no more context-free than metaphor is, each revealing different aspects of the context-dependence of both literal and metaphorical language. The first emerges directly from the study of metaphor itself; the second concerns the implicit background assumptions against which all language is understood; the third involves the profound ambiguity inherent in most terms of a natural language. The first two are directed against the contextual independence of sentence meaning; the last at that of word meaning.

Considerations from metaphor. A challenge to the contextual independence of literal language is posed when we consider how we come to recognize that an utterance is metaphorical. The following sentences, which we have seen earlier,

   3.1 Smith is a plumber.
   3.2 The rock is becoming brittle with age,

may be interpreted literally or metaphorically. 3.1 is metaphorical if we know that Smith is not a plumber but a surgeon; 3.2 is metaphorical if we are speaking of an ageing professor emeritus. Similarly, sentences such as 3.3, 3.4, and 3.5 are standardly given a metaphorical interpretation, but they need not be:

   3.3 I can kill two birds with one stone.

3.4 He is up against the wall.

3.5 Time flies.

The possibility that 3.5 may be treated literally is perhaps the least obvious. Still we see the sentence used literally in an old children's joke:

3.6 'Time flies.' 'You can't. They fly too fast.'

These considerations suggest that we can give a metaphorical reading to sentences ordinarily construed literally and a literal reading to sentences which might ordinarily be construed metaphorically—although a literal reading may sometimes be very bizarre. If we now say that it is the context which supplies the basis for the judgement that a sentence is metaphorical, then it is also the context which determines that the sentence should be interpreted literally. In that case, literal meaning is, at least, context-bound in that we cannot supply a literal interpretation, and hence literal truth conditions, without a consideration of the context of the utterance.

But here a Davidsonian may simply reply: why do I need any contextual material to know that the truth value of 'Man is a wolf' is always false? For the T-sentence gives me the condition that this sentence is true if and only if man is a wolf and clearly men are not wolves. Yet Davidson (1981, 259) himself provides an example of a literal use of a sentence which would generally be interpreted as a metaphor:

3.7 The men are pigs.

The sentence would in most contexts be metaphorical, and literally false, regardless of how the indexicals are specified; but when uttered by Ulysses of his men in Circe's palace, we are to suppose that these are meant as literal and truthful words. In this example and others that he cites, Davidson recognizes that the context determines the metaphorical nature of the appropriate interpretation, but he does not attend to the natural corollary, that if the determining factor in the case of metaphor is context, then context plays the same determining factor if the sentence turns out to be literal.

Again, a recognition of the metaphorical nature of the sentence has an immediate impact on the truth conditions of the sentence. An example Davidson (1981, 257) elicits for another purpose will serve to demonstrate this without recourse to the fantasies of poetic fiction.

Davidson cites the headline the New York *Mirror* used when Hemingway's aeroplane crashed in Africa:

3.8 Hemingway Lost in Africa.

At first, it was presumed that Hemingway was dead. 'Lost' was used metaphorically (euphemistically?) to suggest that Hemingway had died. When it was discovered that he was alive, the headline was allowed to remain. But now it was to be understood literally. In contrast to the usual rendering of metaphorical sentences, the sentence turned out to be true if taken literally but false if understood metaphorically.

Davidson's point in making use of this example is to say that to understand the sentence metaphorically, we must only *hold* the sentence to be false. The actual truth or falsity of the sentence is not at issue. But this is wrong. To say of Hemingway that he was 'lost' in Africa, thereby suggesting that he had died, did not necessarily preclude the additional meaning that he had literally been lost before he perished. We can say that Hemingway was lost in Africa 'in both senses'. We should say that the two readings have two independent sets of truth conditions. But to say this is to concede that how we assign truth conditions to a sentence depends on whether we understand it literally or metaphorically.

One could argue that to do so is not to concede that this is an issue of semantics, and that how we assign truth conditions to a given occurrence of a sentence is a matter of pragmatics. The semantics will assign a truth condition for each possible interpretation of a sentence. It is a matter of pragmatics as to which assignment is the correct one in this particular instance. A metaphorical reading will then be on par with other literal readings of the sentence and will be treated as a case of ambiguity. But the assignment of multiple sets of truth conditions will not help where one reading is metaphorical. On Davidson's account, the meaning of the metaphorical utterance is simply the literal meaning of the words of the sentence. Therefore, except in the case of an ambiguity between literal readings, we can assign only one set of truth conditions to that sentence. Given that a metaphorical interpretation is not just another reading of the sentence, the above argument establishes, minimally, that Davidson cannot be right both in asserting that the meaning of a sentence is given by its truth conditions and in his claim that a metaphorical sentence has no meaning apart from its literal meaning.

Were it the case that only a few sentences posed the sort of difficulties noted here, we could say that *these* sentences lacked a clearly understood logical form. These were sentences whose analyses must await a deeper understanding of logical form. Hopes of consigning this problem to that messy drawer are dashed when we realize that virtually any word, phrase, sentence, or group of sentences we may employ could, in the right context and in the right circumstances, conceal a metaphorical meaning. This very essay might be a political treatise in which the argument for the context-dependence of literal language serves to remind us of our mutual interdependence in a struggle for freedom. Fantastic? Not if we lived in a sufficiently repressive society. Repression and censorship, as Freud realized, are prime motivations for the circuitous symbolic presentations characteristic of dreams and metaphor. I am claiming that we can make metaphor of whatever linguistic materials are to hand. Therefore we can make metaphors of sentences which, when read literally, have a perfectly clear canonical form. If this is right, then we cannot both claim that a metaphorical reading puts these in the class of sentences lacking a clear canonical form *and* maintain that there is no metaphorical meaning apart from the literal meaning of the words in the sentence. For if it were true that the metaphorical sentence, be it literal or metaphorical, has just one meaning, then the metaphorical sentence would have to have the same canonical form as the literal one.

One might reply that the literal meaning is always the preferred one and that only special contextual circumstances will pick out metaphorical interpretations. But this is not so. It requires a special context to give 'The men are pigs' a literal interpretation. This is equally true of 3.5 and during Richard Nixon's administration after the Watergate affair, the literal would not be the preferred meaning of the phrase:

3.9 Nixon's plumbers.

Thus without any mention of metaphorical meanings, it appears that the truth conditions appropriate to a sentence's interpretation are affected by the understanding, gained through contextual considerations, of whether the utterance is to be interpreted literally or metaphorically.

From this argument, two points emerge which ought to trouble the Davidsonian: first, that whether a sentence is to be understood literally or metaphorically may alter the truth-value of that sentence—that is, metaphor appears to have some bearing on the issue of truth conditions and meaning; and secondly, that context, in some manner—at least, when the sentence is clearly ambiguous between a literal and a metaphorical interpretation—determines the meanings and truth conditions of literal sentences.

Contextual background assumptions. That context determines whether a sentence is to be understood literally or metaphorically is only the beginning of its involvement in meaning. Once again, the quintessential and supposedly context-free literal sentence

3.10 The cat is on the mat

turns out to be highly ambiguous once we suspend some of the background assumptions against which we understand this sentence.

As Searle (1979) argues, the truth conditions of the sentence are none the less dependent on these contextual background assumptions. He asks us to consider the truth conditions of 3.10 uttered by a speaker referring to a cat and a mat as they float about outside the earth's gravitational field: do we still say the cat is on the mat when its position, relative to our gravitational field, would be described as being under the mat?

We might ask whether it is not the case that these background assumptions are to some degree simply built into the meaning of the terms. For example, in its occurrence in 3.10, the term 'on' is used to mean 'on top of'. We could say that this includes the presupposition that what is considered to be on top is so relative to the gravitational field of the earth.

But this turns out not to be the case, as is evident when we engage in another Searlean thought experiment. We are travellers on a spaceship. Each time we look out, we see a cat together with a mat in one of two positions. From our vantage point on the spaceship, the cat appears to be either on the mat or under the mat. In that case, Searle says, 'The cat is on the mat' would be a clear and literal response to the question: 'Where is it now?' If this is right, as I believe it is, then we see that 'on' cannot include as its meaning the supposition that what is on top is so in relation to our gravitational field—that circumstance does not apply to travellers on a spaceship.

To Searle's focus on the significance of our background assumptions, we can add another consideration that emerges from semantic field theory. When we encounter the sentence 'The cat is on the mat', we expect this to be a plausible answer to a question such as: 'Is the cat *on* the mat or *off* the mat?' Nor are these exclusive possibilities. The cat could be *under*,[1] *beside*, or, if it is sufficiently mischievous, *wrapped up inside* the mat. Questions based on these possibilities suppose that the world meets our usual expectations and form part of our background default assumptions. Default assumptions provide the ground from which we understand the implicit affinities and contrasts that specify the meaning of a given term in a sentence. These relations of affinity and contrast (see Chapter 2, p. 53, above) are represented by the *semantic field indicators*. The default assumptions assure us of the fact that when we speak of the cat's position relative to the mat, we mean the cat's position relative to its upper surface—for that is how a cat on a mat would be located relative to a mat, given the gravitational force as we usually experience it—the fact that we place mats on the floor, and the fact that we generally consider only the surface of the mat when it is so placed. This surface is generally coincident with the earth's surface, so that the position of the cat, relative to the mat, is the same whether we consider it in relation to the earth's surface or to the viewer's perspective. (If stating all this is very tiresome, so it is for our most basic default assumptions—and that is precisely why they generally get relegated to background assumptions.)

The two thought experiments cancel some of these default assumptions. Without the default assumptions in place, it is not clear to which set of contrasting questions the statement 'The cat is on the mat' is an answer. However, the context could specify these relevant contrasts. In the first experiment, the context does not provide sufficient information to permit the reader to give 'on' a determinate meaning. But in the second experiment, we see that we are concerned with the cat's position relative not to a given surface of the mat but to the object in its entirety. The relevant contrast is not *on* or *off*, but *on* or *under*. And the latter contrast, we infer from the context, is relative not to the earth's surface but to the viewer's perspective.

Searle's examples and the utterances 3.5–3.9 indicate that when we are faced with phrases or sentences sundered from their context, we read them in such a way as to preserve our usual presumptions and expectations concerning the world. Sometimes this is facilitated by the fact that the expression in question is comprised of terms which have a conventionalized, though non-literal meaning (for example, 3.5): here it is especially clear that the literal meaning is not always the preferred

---

[1] But, as A. Lehrer notes (personal communication), 'on' can sometimes mean 'under', as in 'The fly is walking on the ceiling'.

one. In 3.5, 3.7, and 3.9, were all the terms read literally, a world very different from our own—one in which different expectations were the norm—would be presupposed. Quite sensibly such suppositions are not readily made. We would sooner alter the meanings of the words than alter our basic conceptions and trustworthy empirical expectations. To interpret utterances such as 3.5 and 3.9 literally, we should need to ask: why should one want to clock the speed of a fly? Why report on the plumbing repairs in the White House? To understand 3.7 literally we must imagine a world in which change of species is possible. And to understand the sentence 'The cat is on the mat' without any context forces us to hold constant the world as we normally experience it.

The point to be made here is that, when a given sentence has been artificially taken out of context (or rather out of *its* context), the features of the world that we take to be normal, and our usual expectations of our world (in so far as these are relevant to the utterance), serve as an implicit context (the default frame) determining our interpretation—be it literal or metaphorical—and belie the claim to intelligibility of context-free sentences. Because we draw on these background assumptions, and because the beliefs and knowledge we bring to bear on the presumably context-free sentences are so much in the background, we tend to think that our interpretation is context-free. In a somewhat different context, Davidson himself notes:

If the vast amount of agreement on plain matters that is assumed in communication escapes notice, it's because the shared truths are too many and too dull to bear mentioning. What we want to talk about is what's new, surprising, or disputed. (1974a, 321.)

The sort of background assumptions Searle speaks of, and to which even the most evidently literal statements are relative, are just those 'plain matters' which escape our notice but which none the less are operative in our understanding of language.

Context-dependence based on systematic ambiguity. We now turn our attention to the thesis that word meaning is context-free. We may ask: why does this thesis need to be addressed? The fact that words can have several meanings which are only disambiguated in a sentence is well recognized. Since Frege, at least, most philosophers of language have held that a word has meaning only in the context of sentence. But most renderings of this view assume that we can specify the few different meanings for a word, each of which would be listed as a disjunct in the set of disjuncts that would serve as the dictionary entry for the polysemous term. Further, it is assumed that a relatively limited portion of the vocabulary is polysemous, for example, homonyms such as 'pen', 'bank', etc. The context-dependence of word meaning would appear not to threaten the contextual independence of literal language at the sentential level. Sentences containing the polysemous terms either disambiguate the term sufficiently, or we simply attribute a set of separate truth conditions for each of the several meanings (cf. Davidson 1967 and 1974*b*). Furthermore, we can say that even when the sentence does not suffice to disambiguate a term and context must be considered, there are a few principles or factors, to which we relativize the sentence, which will yield an unambiguous reading. We can then reassert the contextual independence of the relativized sentence.

The position maintained here will be that polysemy is a pervasive feature of word meaning, one which has the potential to generate an indefinitely large set of meanings for each word. While the context of the sentence may significantly disambiguate word meaning in many sentences, in many others the resulting semantic ambiguity will be such that it cannot be incorporated in a truth theory positing a set of disjunctive truth conditions for each reading. Rather than assert that context allows us to distinguish between pre-given senses of a term, we can say that the contextual environment serves to confer different meanings on a given word, a multiplicity of meaning to be distinguished from vagueness.[2] To get a flavour of the richness of polysemy, consider that we can:

'*draw* a picture', '*draw* a curtain', '*draw* a lot'; we may just have '*dressed* the chicken', 'got *dressed*' or 'got *dressed* up'; we might '*drop* a book', '*drop* a subject', or '*drop* a hem'; if we *dust* the furniture we *remove fine particles* (called *dust*) from it; but if we *dust* an infant with baby powder we *apply fine particles* (not dust but powder) to her.

Can we adequately treat polysemy by considering each different sense a disjunct in a dictionary-like entry? In reponse to criticism by Bar-Hillel that the ability of a native speaker to disambiguate

3.11 The box is in the pen

---

[2] The following discussion relies extensively on the recent work by Ross (1981) and Cohen (1985; 1986). For an argument that multiplicity of meaning may be distinguished from polysemy, see Cohen 1985, 130.

cannot be matched by a machine translation, Davidson responds that a theory might handle this type of ambiguous sentence along the following lines:

'The box was in the pen' is true for an English-speaker x at time t if and only if either the box was in the playpen before t and the circumstances surrounding x at t meet condition c, or the box was in the writing pen before t and the circumstances surrounding x at t meet condition c'. (1974b, 246.)[3]

Cohen (1985) argues that c and c' cannot be exhaustive of all the conditions under which the sentence is spoken. There may well be circumstances such that we fail to disambiguate the sentence. (If there were no such circumstances, we would not feel the force of the ambiguity so clearly.) In the case that neither c nor c' obtains, so that we are unable to disambiguate the sentence, the predicate will not be satisfied and sentence 3.11 will be false. But, Cohen remarks:

Where the ambiguity is a deliberate pun the point of the pun would be lost if the assertion had to be regarded as false. And where the ambiguity of the assertion is due to carelessness in matching sentences to circumstances appropriate for their utterance the author of the assertion is being convicted of a crime that he did not commit (viz. the crime of asserting what is not the case) and not convicted of the crime that he did commit (viz. speaking carelessly). Yet to prevent such anomalies it looks as if the semantics would have to admit the possibility of truth-value gaps. (1985, 131.)

It appears that a truth-theoretic semantics is faced with the difficulty that if it treats ambiguity as amenable to the sort of treatment exemplified by the T-sentence assigned to 3.11, it must either admit truth-value gaps or admit the sorts of anomaly suggested above. These anomalies might be acceptable if polysemy were rare and limited to the occasional homonym. But they become problematic if it can be shown that polysemy is pervasive. One may argue that, even if verbal ambiguity were not infrequent, but the number of different meanings a word had were few, then there might be a way in which to specify all the meanings by a set of exhaustive disjunctive conditions that would specify a given predicate. Note, however, that given the thesis of compositionality, were each word in a six-word sentence to have five differ-

---

[3] It is noteworthy that this passage is deleted, without comment, in the latest reprinting of the essay in Davidson (1984). Perhaps Davidson recognized that this was not an effective way to respond to the criticism.

ent meanings, the possible reading for a sentence would be about 15,000![4]

Of course, projection rules and selection restriction rules would considerably reduce the viable alternatives. Still the prospect makes a Davidsonian set of disjuncts appear formidable. But this may not yet pose a theoretical problem for this model. A more troublesome prospect is that for most words in the language the number of possible senses is indefinitely large, so that we can never say that *now* our disjunctive set is exhaustive. Only if a term's senses are relatively few and determinate can a dictionary entry be a set of disjuncts which are manageable and learnable.

Much of our language is polysemous, as even a cursory examination of a good dictionary will show. Although homonyms such as pen (writing-pen/play-pen) are relatively infrequent, most polysemy involves different related senses of a word. And this polysemy is importantly context-dependent.[5] Consider the polysemy that results from the familiar fact that many words may be understood to refer to either a given thing or its representation: 'a face' may refer to a face, or to a representation of a face, or to some representation of a representation of a face, etc. Similarly, we know that terms denoting ability may have occurrent and dispositional senses, for example, 'driver', 'leader', 'orator', etc. Many other terms can denote either acts or objects, for example, 'perception', 'utterance', 'regulation', etc. We understand

---

[4] I am indebted to Richard Grandy (in a personal communication) for this observation.

[5] The psychological literature has been very instructive in its efforts to demonstrate the context-dependence of our interpretations of utterances. In Tulving and Thomson 1973, the authors report on a number of experiments designed to show the role of context in recall tasks. In one, subjects were presented with a list of paired terms such as 'white : black'. They were then given another list that used some of the words in the previous list, but now accompanied by different words—e.g. 'black' would appear accompanied by 'train' rather than by 'white'. Subjects had to recall which words on the second list had previously appeared on the first list. A second group of subjects were presented with a similar list of words, but ones which were not paired, and then with a second list which included words from the first list. Again subjects were asked to recall those words that had appeared on the second list and had also appeared on the first. The results strongly indicated that subjects in the first study would fail to recognize those words on the second list that had appeared on the first list but accompanied by different terms—e.g. subjects would fail to recognize that 'black' had appeared on the first as well as on the second list. When words were presented unpaired, subjects had far less difficulty recalling which words appeared for a second time. Apparently, the context of 'white' as opposed to the context of 'train' so significantly influences the subjects' recall, that the term itself is not recognized as the same.

instances of these principles even though they may never have occurred before in the language.

We could say that these are identifiable lexical principles—for example, 'a word which names an object, situation, or substance may also be used to name a representation of that object, situation, or substance'—and that we can circumscribe the parts of the lexicon which are susceptible to them. We ought perhaps to confine the meaning of, let us say 'lion', to the animate object. When it is used in combination with 'stone', as in 'stone lion', we understand that the lexical principle above applies. This may suffice for certain cases. But consider the following sequence of sentences, cited by Ross (1981, 33):

3.12 She *dropped* a stitch.

3.13 She *dropped* her hem-line.

3.14 She *dropped* her book.

3.15 She *dropped* a friend.

3.16 She *dropped* her courses.

Most of these are literal uses of 'dropped', and each occurrence of the word is different in meaning. This difference is evidenced by our inability to substitute the antonymous phrase 'picked up' for 'dropped' in the various sentence frames: for example, 'She picked up her book' expresses the contrary of 'She dropped her book', but 'She picked up her hem-line' is not even a clearly acceptable sentence and is not the contrary of 'She dropped her hem-line'.

The variety of meaning, Ross claims, arises through analogy. The different senses of 'dropped' in the sentences 3.12–3.16 are analogous to one another. The range of analogous meaning may be indefinite, although, I would insist, constrained by the α, and β-components of the sense representation. The view, propounded by Ross (1981) and Cohen (1985; 1986), and endorsed here, is that words, in combining with other words, evince different possibilities of meaning and that these possibilities are indefinitely numerous.[6]

The principle of analogy that is responsible for multiplicity of word meaning is nicely illustrated in the notion of *craftbound discourses*, discourses that are particular to specified domains of human activity:

'Craftbound discourse' connotes that *skill in action* is necessary for a full grasp

---

[6] Cohen claims that word meaning is infinitely polysemous. His arguments (1985; 1986) do not seem to support the conclusion that the polysemy is infinite, but they do suggest that we can generate an indefinitely large number of possible senses.

of the discourse . . . The basic vocabulary of these kinds of discourse is similarly anchored to benchmark situations (legal cases, Scripture stories, scientific experiments, particular professional observations and responses) that structure and stabilize the central meaning relationships. (Ross 1981, 158.)

The craftbound sense of 'will' in legal discourse bears an analogous relation to that of 'will' in the equally craftbound discourse of philosophy. The very fact that such discourses abound in natural language is a deep source of ambiguity and polysemy.

One might note the similarity between craftbound discourses and Wittgensteinian language games. The discourses provide an implicit context for much literal language. Once again children's material is a rich source of the possibility of ambiguity which results from the presence of such discourses. Through stories and jokes, children are taught to appreciate the fact that there are many interpretations attributable to particular words and sentences and that the distinct interpretations are context-dependent. Amelia Bedelia, the context-insensitive heroine of a children's book's series that bears her name (by P. Parish), is introduced as a newly hired maid, faced with a list of chores. When asked to 'dust the furniture', she uses a powder-puff to spread face powder on the furniture; when required to 'draw the curtains', she produces a sketch of them; and when asked to 'dress the chicken', she puts a miniature pair of trousers and shirt on a bird intended for that night's dinner. Amelia Bedelia has failed to differentiate the craftbound uses of 'dust', 'draw', and 'dress' in housekeeping.

In a later episode, in which her charges attempt to teach her baseball, Amelia Bedelia causes havoc by continually misunderstanding the distinctive craftbound uses of those baseball terms which are also found in other parts of the lexicon: she steals bases by removing them from their positions on the field; she hits a home run and responds to the children's cheer, 'Go Home, Amelia Bedelia,' by running, with the stolen bases still in her arms, all the way back to the children's home, wondering all the while what a peculiar game baseball is! Amelia Bedelia's difficulty is her failure to recognize the multiple meanings of words and the specificity to context of the various interpretations. Her linguistic incompetence causes her to have her victories fortuitously and in spite of the rules of the games which, whether one is keeping house or playing baseball, all depend on this linguistic competence.

If one held the third thesis of context–independence one could maintain that, in the case that the sentence alone did not sufficiently disambiguate a word meaning that was ambiguous between an object and its representation, we would have a semantic principle that generated two possible disambiguating sentences; similarly, we could find semantic principles that would disambiguate sentences containing words with distinct craftbound meanings. Such a principle would relativize the sentences, in a way that would be not unlike the relativization of sentences to indexical factors. This relativization would go a long way towards disambiguating much ordinary speech. But, as we have seen, not all polysemy is due to craftbound discourses. Such relativization might not suffice.

One might respond that the various uses, particularly craftbound uses, of a term are 'derived' from one of a few primary meanings a word may have. We would then need to specify semantic principles that applied in the case of different sorts of derivations. That efforts to locate and differentiate such primary, as opposed to derived, meanings are often futile is suggested by the following examples (Nunberg, 1979, 148). In each pair, the two senses are obviously related, but it is far less clear that we can designate one sense as primary and the other as derived:

(i)   The window was broken. (= 'window glass')
(ii) The window was boarded up. (= 'window opening')

(i)   The newspaper weighs five pounds. (= 'publication')
(ii) The newspaper fired John. (= 'publisher')

(i)   The chair was broken. (= 'chair token')
(ii) The chair was common in nineteenth-century parlours. (= 'chair type')

(i)   We got the news by radio. (= 'medium')
(ii) The radio is broken. (= 'radio set')

(i)   France is a Republic. (= 'nation')
(ii) France has a varied topography. (= 'region')

(i)   The game is hard to learn (= 'rule')
(ii) The game lasted an hour. (= 'activity')

These examples can easily be multiplied. The difficulty of locating a primary meaning from which others are derived is illustrated by the numerous things to which the word *cell* may refer:

. . . to cells of the body, prison cells, battery cells, Communist cells, photo-cells, the cells of a matrix, and so on. And it is tempting to say that all of these are members of a single 'vague' extension—say, the set of things that are the uniform constitutive parts of a large structure. But . . . we can speak of single-celled organisms. And we can use *cell* to refer to the parts of a political organization only when they are clandestine . . . Similarly, prisons and monasteries can have cells, but libraries or cruise ships can't, for all that the latter may be divided into compartments. (Nunberg, 1979, 171.)

For many, if not most terms, polysemy cannot be reduced by appealing to a distinction between a primary and a derived meaning. In that case, ambiguity cannot be resolved by positing a set of truth conditions for each possible meaning without such sets becoming absurdly numerous. In the account of a relational theory of meaning in section 2 of this chapter, I adumbrate an alternative approach.

If we take seriously the proposition that a theory of meaning is a theory of understanding, that is, a theory of what we must know if we understand a word or sentence, then we should conclude that we must understand how context (sentential or extra-sentential) helps determine the meanings of words and sentences. Contextual considerations are inseparable both from word meaning and sentence meaning, and they are as inseparable from the meaning of literal sentences as they are from the meaning of metaphorical sentences. A context-free sentence is an abstraction which has, at best, methodological usefulness. Ultimately, in spite of the prevailing wisdom to the contrary, a true semantics of natural language cannot ignore the dependence on context for the interpretation of all sentences. If metaphors seem particularly context-bound, it is only because a literal interpretation yields statements which are at odds with the ordinary background assumptions and the constraints of craftbound discourse to which the meaning of literal language is relative.

Use and Meaning

But if literal language is context-dependent, several questions arise concerning metaphorical meaning. Since contextual independence has generally been taken as the point of demarcation between language use and language meaning, is there still a useful distinction to be drawn between semantic and pragmatic concerns? And if so, on what side of the line does metaphor fall? In other words, the question still remains: Is it legitimate to speak of metaphorical meaning?

Searle thinks that the context-dependence of literal language does nothing to disturb the distinction between sentence meaning and speaker meaning, a distinction he sees as coincident with the meaning/use distinction on which Davidson depends. Searle assimilates metaphor to speaker meaning, a move I have challenged, asserting instead the stronger claim that metaphorical meaning is significantly related to the nature of the utterance-type itself. But even on Searle's weaker claim, speaker meaning is meaning still and it bears on truth conditions. Once we allow context to function in the case of literal meaning, then, as Searle's move indicates, the distinction which remains between use and meaning shifts. The shift is such that metaphor influences meaning, and its truth conditions need consideration in a semantic theory.

This point can be reinforced by considering Davidson's comparison between the metaphor and the lie. The sentence 'Lattimore's a Communist', according to Davidson (1981), can be used to make an assertion, a true or false accusation, or a metaphor. Certainly, he would concede that it might be stated ironically—for example, if it were used to speak of an ostentatious capitalist handing a beggar a penny. Let us contrast an utterance of the sentence as a lie with its utterance as a piece of irony, since in both cases it is false and known by the speaker to be false. A crucial difference is that in the former case it is important that the audience does not realize that the speaker is aware of the falsehood of his sentence. From the speaker's perspective, at least, the success of his communication depends on it. In the case of the ironical utterance the reverse situation pertains. For the sentence to be correctly understood, that is, correctly interpreted, its context must reveal that the speaker knows that Lattimore is not a Communist. When teaching students to detect Socrates' irony, we must teach them how to read the text so that they recognize that the irony is evident in the text itself. The liar who can similarly be read as a liar is a poor liar indeed. My point here is that lying is indeed a use of language which necessitates no further semantic explanation. But metaphor, like irony, would be futile if it could not be 'read off the text'. Because their proper interpretations require identifiable elements of what I call the *discourse situation*, metaphor and irony demand an analysis which is, at least in part, semantic; they are not simply forms of language use.

My claim may be stated within the confines of a truth-conditional semantics. A lie is a case of use and not meaning of language because the truth-value of the sentence does not in any way depend on whether the utterance is a lie—although if it is a lie its truth-value will normally be 'false'. In contrast, I have argued that the truth-value of a sentence will depend on whether or not it is given a metaphorical interpretation. That non-literal language has an impact on truth-value in this fashion indicates that we have here cases of meaning, rather than merely use, of language. Whenever it is possible to construe the discourse in which the sentence is situated so that the proper interpretation of the sentence (and hence semantic properties such as its truth conditions) depends on the discourse situation itself, we have language meaning. And this is precisely what fails to be the case for lying. The reader may grant the above arguments, claim that my argument applies to utterance meaning, not to sentence meaning, and note that no one denies that context influences the meaning of *utterances*. What I have attempted to argue is that, within natural language, sentence meaning, if construed as independent of context, is an empty abstraction, and that, within natural language, semantic considerations ought to bear on utterance-type.

Philosophers of language and most linguists are accustomed to speak of semantics in terms of word meaning and sentence meaning and, therefore, the inclusion of features from the discourse situation appears to be contextual and pragmatic rather than semantic. By investigating metaphor, we learn that not only does a word only have meaning in the context of a sentence, but a sentence, too, lacks a definitive meaning outside its linguistic and situational context—its discourse situation.[7]

In the preceding discussion, I have proposed that the truth conditions of a sentence are altered when a sentence is interpreted literally rather than metaphorically (or ironically) and have taken this to indicate that whether an utterance is metaphorical is a semantic matter. That is to say, we have taken altered truth conditions as an index of semantic pertinence. This ought not to be understood as an implicit endorsement of a truth-theoretic semantics for natural language. Rather, the above arguments are meant to show that even within the framework of a truth-theoretic semantics, that is, within the constraints of what constitutes a semantic concern within a truth-theoretic semantics, metaphor must be given a semantic account.

---

[7] My claim is meant to be stronger than the claim which concedes that most sentences may have to be relativized to speaker, time, and place. Davidson (1967) remarks that a sentence has a meaning only in the context of a language, and at the same time maintains the contextual independence of the sentence. He is upholding the contextual independence of a *sentence relative to a given language*. While I do not dispute that a sentence has a meaning only relative to a given language, a point which seems either quite profound or quite trivial depending on how it is taken, the claim that a sentence has a meaning only relative to a given context has an importantly different focus. It is neither a holistic nor an atomistic view of language.

Let us look once again at how I assigned truth conditions to sentences such that these turned out to be different for a literal and a metaphorical understanding of the sentence. According to Davidson, what is required for us to assign 'true' to a sentence is that we *hold* it to be true. Let us take the *Mirror* headline 3.8. Understood literally, the sentence was true for a given speaker, at a given time, and in a given place. Understood metaphorically, the headline was false for a given speaker, etc. In order to assign the value false we have had to construct a T-sentence which runs something like

3.17 'Hemingway is lost in Africa' is true if and only if Hemingway has perished in Africa, for speaker x, at a given time t, in a given place y.

But on the right-hand side we have to interpret the metaphor and offer a translation into the metalanguage which amounts to a literal paraphrase of the metaphor. It appears, then, that in order to give a semantic account of metaphor within a truth-theoretic semantics, we are required to reduce metaphor to a literal paraphrase, which is then assigned the truth condition appropriate to that literal sentence.[8]

Essentially, what we have done in 3.17 is to paraphrase 'Hemingway lost in Africa' as 'Hemingway has perished in Africa' and implicitly assign a truth condition to the former sentence on the basis of the truth condition for the latter sentence. More precisely, 3.17 is really shorthand for the conjunction of 3.18 and 3,19 below:

3.18 'Hemingway is lost in Africa' is true if and only if 'Hemingway has perished in Africa' is true.

3.19 'Hemingway has perished in Africa' is true if and only if Hemingway has perished in Africa.

In the case that 'lost' is used as a euphemism for 'died', there is not much that the paraphrase fails to capture. But if metaphor is not merely a decorative use of language, then a literal paraphrase ought not to be able to capture the meaning of the metaphor, except perhaps for very worn metaphors. The strategy described above is such that we lose the metaphor. Beyond the literal paraphrase to which we assign

---

[8] This is essentially the strategy employed by Bergmann (1979), using however, a modal semantics (see Chapter 5 below). Bergmann shows how we can assign truth-values to metaphors which are not the truth-values of the sentence understood with the literal sense of its constituent words.

truth conditions, the metaphor has only an ornamental value or an emotive force. But this is precisely the trap Davidson wished to avoid by assigning to metaphorical sentences the truth conditions of the literal meaning of the sentence rather than assigning to metaphor the truth conditions of some literal paraphrase. Davidson presumed that denying to metaphor a semantics, and insisting that metaphor was an issue for pragmatics only, was a side-stepping manœuvre. But it is one that fails in virtue of the context-dependence of literal as well as metaphorical sentences.

We have cleared the ground for providing metaphors with a semantic analysis. A truth-theoretic semantics, however, does not promise to provide the needed account. The Davidsonian account (exemplified by his position in Davidson 1981), fails to account for how the collocation of terms generates new meaning, whether the new meaning is literal or metaphorical, and hence is incapable of adequately addressing the question of metaphor.

The Dreamwork of Language

Davidson begins his essay on metaphor with the following words:

Metaphor is the dreamwork of language and, like all dreamwork, its interpretation reflects as much on the interpreter as on the originator . . . So too understanding a metaphor is as much a creative endeavor as making a metaphor, and as little guided by rules . . . These remarks do not, except in matters of degree, distinguish metaphor from more routine linguistic transactions: all communication by speech assumes the interplay of inventive construction and inventive construal. (1981, 200.)

Davidson's remarks provoke two related sets of comments: one is motivated by Davidson 1986; the other by Freud's own understanding of dreamwork.

The remarks concerning the inventive construction and construal of all language receive in Davidson's later essay a far greater importance than in any of his previous work. Inspired by the fact that we manage to understand the intent of sentences which contain malapropisms, Davidson concludes that efforts to penetrate what a language might be, when we take into account Donnellan-type phenomena, malapropisms, mistakes—intentional and unintentional—and all the idiosyncratic facts about our speech, must ultimately result in the truism that we have a language when we manage to understand one another. In the lines I have quoted from his 1981 essay, Davidson merely hints at such a result. The remainder of the essay reaffirms language as based on a truth-conditional semantics, in which metaphor has no place as such; metaphor can none the less use the resources of that language, but it brings nothing semantic to the language. The later essay has little to say about a truth-conditional semantics. The method of radical interpretation becomes a method of continual reinterpretation. In all this, one must wonder whether there is not a new turn to Davidson's view which has an impact on his views on metaphor.

In a passage noteworthy enough to quote at length, Davidson, speaking now not of metaphor but of language generally, says:

> But we might try to say in what a person's ability to interpret or speak to another person consists: it is the ability that permits him to construct a correct, that is, convergent, passing theory for speech transactions with that person . . . This characterization of linguistic ability is so nearly circular that it cannot be wrong: it comes to saying that the ability to communicate by speech consists in the ability to make oneself understood, and to understand. It is only when we look at the structure of this ability that we realize how far we have drifted from standard ideas of language mastery. For we have discovered no learnable common core of consistent behaviour, no shared grammar or rules, no portable interpreting machine set to grind out the meaning of an arbitrary utterance. We may say that linguistic ability just is the ability to converge on a passing theory from time to time—this is what I have suggested, and I have no better proposal. (1986, 173.)

And this, of course, is just what he had to say about the interpretation of metaphor in the passage we quoted earlier. But in that case, metaphor is not the linguistic pariah we might earlier have thought. Instead it should be embraced as the very paradigm of linguistic interpretation.

Beyond this, Davidson goes on to say:

> But if we do say this, then we should realize that we have abandoned not only the ordinary notion of a language, but we have erased the boundary between knowing a language and knowing our way around the world generally. For there are no rules for arriving at passing theories, no rules in any strict sense, as opposed to rough maxims and methodological generalities . . . I conclude that there is no such thing as a language, not if a language is anything like what many philosophers and linguists have supposed. (1986, 173–4.)

Surely, if there is no distinction between language and knowing our way around the world generally, then there is nothing on which to hang a use/meaning distinction and thus no way to differentiate metaphor from any other means by which we understand one another. If we understand each other's use of literal sentences through a convergence of theories about how we use our terms and how we expect our audience to expect us to use our terms, then we must understand metaphorical sentences in the same way. But this requires that we should develop a different passing theory for the sentence understood metaphorically than for the same sentence understood literally. If that is correct, and if the passing theory is a theory about what sentences mean, then it must be the case that metaphorical sentences must mean something more than the literal meanings of the words, or how else could they be understood as metaphors? In short, if Davidson abides by the position he lays out in his 1986 essay, he must alter his position on metaphor.

Ultimately, however, I do not think that we can erase 'the boundary between knowing a language and knowing our way around the world generally'. Although I agree that there are many and significant continuities between knowing a language and knowing our way around the world, language is too distinctive a capacity and is too productive of general features of human life to allow us to rest with Davidson's results. The special significance of language requires that we should make a better attempt at arriving at a satisfactory theory. If our theory cannot make the distinction between knowing a language and knowing our way about the world then I think we have simply arrived at an inadequate theory. While Davidson's former views of language were too exclusionary, his new position is too inclusive. Not only is there now no difference between knowing a language and knowing our way about the world, but also within language there is no difference between how we interpret a literal statement, a malapropism, and a metaphor. Since the same sentence may be any of these, we must interpret them differently. Again, if our theory can tell us nothing about these differences, the theory is inadequate.

As we have seen, Davidson (1981) claims that metaphors are the dreamwork of language. Davidson means to remark on the extent to which the creativity required in the interpretation of metaphor precludes the elaboration of rules for understanding and interpreting both dreams and metaphors. But we know that Freud conceived of the interpretation of dreams as a scientific project which would yield invaluable understanding of the workings of the human mind. Freud wrote: 'The interpretation of dreams is the royal road to a knowledge of the unconscious activities of the mind' (1965, 617). These unconscious activities underlie our conscious thoughts, and the latter are but a taming, censoring, and making reasonable the well-springs of mental activity. Thus an understanding of dreams provided for Freud a mediation between these otherwise hidden well-springs and manifest, conscious mental activity. If we understand Davidson's dreamwork metaphor in this context, then his metaphor is especially apt for philosophers of language who want to gain insight into the well-springs of human language. For if dreams provide the royal road to understanding the unconscious, then metaphors provide the royal road to understanding what I take to be the primary role of language: its expressive capacity (about which I shall have more to say in Section 2 of this chapter).

Freud distinguished between two modes of thought—primary process and secondary process.[9] The former, Freud believed, produced dreams, neurotic symptoms, and creativity. Thought which is literal and follows logical lines of implication he identified as secondary processes. Cavell (1984) utilizes Freud to suggest that metaphor is prior to literal language, and criticizes the notion of metaphor as second-order meaning to the extent that it indicates that literal language is primary. To this, I respond that when we speak of priority we must speak of it relative to some concern. In relation to logical analysis of language, metaphor is secondary. And we might need to say that within a logical reconstruction of how we interpret language, metaphors are also secondary structures. Yet there remains a sense in which metaphor is prior, and here the analogy with Freud becomes especially valuable.

Contrary to the main contesting theories of language, language ought to be understood as serving primarily neither a referential function, nor a calculative role, nor yet a communicative end, but as having the capacity to perform all these functions through its inherent capacity as an expressive medium. Language is a mode in which most humans are capable of acting, communicating, expressing their thoughts, feelings, and desires, and making an impact on their surroundings. Literal language, with its referential and logical impetus, is a pruning of this rich expressive medium, just as conscious thought is a constraint on and a pruning of the rich resources of the unconscious—a constraint which is necessary and productive, but which is a constraint none the less.

The dual conceptual content of metaphor, captured in the notion of second-order meaning, manifests the dual structure of all linguistic

---

[9] These remarks are due to Cavell 1984.

meaning. Whenever we have meaning we take one thing to stand for another—thus, we have the dual structure of the expressive sign and its content. A prerequisite for natural language may well be our ability to take what is to hand, whatever its content, and utilize it to express something else—perhaps something which is related. In literal, first-order language, the expressive sign is emptied of all content not pertinent to a given conceptual organization which provides its content and which it serves as a vehicle. Whenever that conceptual organization fails us, we revert to a duality of structure which is not constrained by the given unities of a conceptual scheme. Language arises out of a metaphorical displacement of a meaning, desire, or purpose on to a sign. The metaphorical move collapses into literality and conventionality—necessarily so if we are to have a viable working language—but language must be able to use new metaphorical displacements and metaphorical organizations to bring new meaning and concepts into language. Thus metaphor is both first and last—both primary process and second-order meaning.

By studying metaphor, we can understand the creative process that is involved in language generally, and understand how the process of interpretation can, in fact, proceed, given the difficulties Davidson sees so clearly in his 1986 essay. To stay within the confines of Davidson's old or new theories will not lead us down the royal road we desire. Davidson has led us down some enticingly straight lanes—but they all lead to dead ends. We must resume a more tortuous path, less elegant, but more sure, in the hope not only of understanding metaphor but of appreciating the lush resources of natural language.

2 A RELATIONAL APPROACH TO MEANING

A Relational Theory

Metaphorical meaning has to do with the capabilities of language to generate meaning. When a term is used metaphorically, a 'new' sense is generated. Yet we want clearly to distinguish metaphorical sense from merely another sense such as we might locate in a dictionary. The sort of polysemy of which Cohen and Ross speak is not limited to additional dictionary entries for a given term. They are concerned with a generativity of related senses, and this generation of meaning is clearly closer to metaphor than is the multiple meaning found in the distinct senses of homonyms. We shall still need to distinguish metaphorical meaning from literal polysemy, but Cohen and Ross are directing us towards principles of language, generation, and analogy which figure prominently in metaphor.

Insulationist theories, such as, Davidson's, have not taken into account the shifts of meaning to which we continually accommodate ourselves as we encounter words in combination:

According to the insulationist account the meaning of any one word that occurs in a particular sentence is insulated against interference from the meaning of any other word in the same sentence. On this view the composition of a sentence resembles the construction of a wall from bricks of different shapes . . . We may sometimes need to look at neighboring words in order to discover the sense in which a word is functioning in the sentence in question, as we might infer the concavity of one brick from the convexity of its neighbour. But even then the meanings that we discover are not made what they are by one another, any more than the presence of a convex brick actually alters the shape of its neighbor. Rather, the words in the sentence have been given these meanings by diachronic facts of etymology. (Cohen 1986, 223.)

In contrast, I want to identify an *interdynamic* theory,[10] wherein the interdynamic between words in a grammatical string is productive of multiple meanings. This leads to a *relational* theory of meaning. The relational view grows out of an understanding that the specific sense of a given word emerges from its relation to other words in a language. There are two parameters for such relations. Once is the interdynamic between collocating terms—terms that obey the syntactic rules of well-formed sentences in coherent and cohesive discourse. The other is the systematic relations characterizing a term's affinities and oppositions to other terms in a given synchronic state in a language. The first parameter constitutes a contrast between insulationist theories of sentence meaning and theories which stress the interdynamics of words in a phrase or sentence or longer grammatical string. The second parameter forms the basis of a theory of semantic fields—a relational rather than an atomistic theory of word meaning. I shall postpone a full discussion of semantic fields until Chapter 6.

---

[10] Cohen (1986) has opposed insulationist theories with *interactionist* theories of sentence meaning. I am employing Cohen's distinction. I have substituted *interdynamic* for interactionist only because the latter term is already used somewhat differently to name a theory of metaphor. The interactionist theory of metaphor ultimately requires an interactionist theory of meaning. None the less some confusion may be avoided by the substitution of a different term in the case of sentence meaning.

The meaning of a word as I proposed to represent it in Chapter 2 is such that the α- and β-components provide indicators and constraints for the possible meanings a word may have. But within these constraints there are indefinitely many possible specifiable meanings. The γ-component, that is, the semantic field indicator, specifies the meaning by situating the word as it appears in a given context, that is, by situating it in an appropriate semantic field. To situate a term in its appropriate semantic field is just to specify the affinities and contrasts which emerge within this contextual setting. I shall later stress, in explicating semantic field theory, that it is the differences in affinities and oppositions that are at once indicative of and responsible for differences in meaning.

The semantic representations formulated in the previous chapter are to be considered encodings of certain informational content along with indications and constraints for how to make accessible that aspect of the informational content which pertains to the contextual environs in which a term is found in a given utterance on a given occasion. The timeless meanings and the applied timeless meanings are not yet full specifications of how the term is to be understood on a given occasion. The timeless meanings must allow for all the indefinitely many occasion meanings a term may have, without us requiring of the timeless meaning that it be an indefinitely large disjunct. Our schema of the triple ordered set is only an approximation of what an adequate representation of the meaning of a term would ultimately be. In order to suggest the direction for further inquiry, I propose, below, an information-theoretic framework for elucidating the relational approach.

Expressive Capacity and Semantic Theory

> Expressing oneself in one's natural language(s) is a *medium of thought*. Some of our thoughts subsist in their verbal expression the way a Wyeth painting subsists in egg tempura on board, having no existence apart from it and yet not being made *out* of it, as a chair is made out of wood, but being made *in* it, as joy can *be*, not merely be exhibited, in a dancer's movement. (Ross 1981, 12–13.)

At the heart of a relational theory is Saussure's concept that language forms a system. The elements of the system are not independent but exist, and are identified, by virtue of the interrelations they form with other elements of the system. This thesis, as applied to the question of meaning, yields the principle that the meaning of a term is a function of the system in which the term is embedded. Rather than explicating meaning by *reducing* it to some extra-linguistic entity—a behavioural response or disposition, a referent, a mental process, etc.—a relational theory aims to speak of meaning as emerging from the interconnections inherent in the structure of language itself.

These interconnections allow for an ever expanding expressivity in language. *Expressivity* is that capacity of language to make itself available to ever new articulations of experience. We sometimes think of expressivity in terms of its affective import only; but I mean to stress its *cognitive* import. The cognitive import derives from the articulations which make possible the sorting, differentiation, discrimination, and identification of experience.

What I mean by expressive capacity can perhaps be best illustrated by a scene in François Truffaut's film *L'Enfant sauvage* (1970), based on the account of Dr Itard in whose care was placed 'the wild child of Aveyron'.[11] The doctor has modest success in getting the boy to articulate the sound 'lait'. On one occasion, the boy sees a glass of milk through the window of a cupboard and eagerly gestures for it. The doctor tries to exploit the situation by getting the boy to utter 'lait' in order to obtain the desired milk. The boy, however, is simply baffled by the doctor's refusal to hand him the drink. With a sense of great failure, the doctor finally gives it to him. Having emptied the glass, his desire satisfied, the young boy at last says, 'lait'. The triumph experienced by the boy and the audience alike is not shared by the doctor. Itard is convinced that this utterance is an insignificant event, that all his efforts have been futile: the mere utterance of the word does not constitute the use of language. For the utterance to have been a linguistic act, his ward would have had to use the word in a purposive fashion, that is, as a means for obtaining the milk.

Although the doctor was correct in his belief that the mere utterance of a word did not constitute a use of language—witness the parrot's mimicry—he was mistaken in thinking that only uttering the word *to request* the beverage would have indicated that the boy had understood its linguistic import. The doctor's despair was conditioned by a concept of language which was, if not mistaken, certainly partial. The doctor took the primary functions of language to be referential and communicative. Instead the boy used the word expressively: not simply to express his satisfaction, but to *mark* an experience now *delineated*

---

[11] For a full account of this intriguing story see Itard 1932.

and *articulated* through the word 'lait'. In its expressive capacity, language provides such articulation of our experience. It marks off bits of experience, or conceptualization, or perception as distinctive—and contrariwise unites and unifies disparate experiences. Natural language is a subtle, efficient, and responsive instrument to accomplish such articulation. The capacity to achieve a finely articulated experience allows us greater facility in communication, in conceptualization, and in manipulating the world.

The articulative possibilities in language inhere in the pattern of affinities and oppositions among words of a language—specified with regard to a given synchronic language-state—and in the fact that 'words differentiate in suitably contrasting environments' (Ross 1981, 22), as we saw illustrated with the term 'drop' earlier. Metaphor is a means available within natural language to extend that expressive capacity in often radical ways. We use metaphor when the resources of literal language are inadequate to articulate significant distinctions or unities.

We use metaphor in order to communicate, to help us make certain calculations, and even to refer.[12] However, it is only the expressive role of language, its articulative capacity, that makes intelligible our use of metaphor. The linguistic and conceptual detours of metaphor seem merely extravagant unless we consider that, when, in metaphor, we take the contrasts and affinities that pertain to one part of the lexicon and apply them to a distinct domain, we make possible a set of articulations not previously available. Metaphor expands these articulative possibilities by exploiting the inherent, contrastive possibilities in natural language. Our goal is to explain how metaphor works so that we can at once integrate metaphorical meaning into a general theory of meaning and illuminate its distinctive character. To achieve this, we have to employ a complex of notions: the contextual nature of both literal and metaphorical meaning; a relational theory of meaning; and the expressive capacity of language. This complex, I claim, permits us to situate the study of metaphorical meaning.

Informational Content/Semantic Content

I want to speak of linguistic meaning as the expressive capacity of language. But if meaning has to do with expression, then it must be

---

[12] See Elgin 1983, Goodman 1968, Ricoeur 1978*b*, and Chapter 8 below.

expressive of some content. That content is conceptual; but I propose to understand concept in information-theoretic terms.[13]

There is clearly some relation between meaning and information, but the nature of this relation is not one of equivalence. The sentence

3.20 The person wearing the red-hooded cloak is a woman

is meaningful, but need not inform us that the person wearing the red-hooded cloak is a woman. There may be no such person; it may not be a woman but a man or a child; the garment may not really be a cloak, etc. But if 3.20 is true, then it does inform us that the person wearing the red-hooded cloak is a woman. And it so informs us *because of what the words mean*. In addition, if I know the meaning of 3.20 and I know that it was uttered with the intent to inform, by a competent speaker of English who is generally well informed and is generally not deceitful, I can assume that it is *probably* the case that the person wearing the red-hooded cloak is a woman. If these circumstances pertain, the assumption is warranted again, because of the meaning of the sentence. That is, there is a high probability of a correlation between the meaning of words and the information they provide, that is, if that probability is conditioned by the sorts of considerations mentioned above.

On the other hand, fictional sentences, and statements in the suppositional and modal contexts of novels are often false. None the less, they are not only meaningful but also informative. If the Brothers Grimm write:

3.21 The person wearing the red-hooded cloak is Little Red Riding Hood,

although I know that Little Red Riding Hood is a fictional character, I do have more information concerning the happenings in the story. I have information in a *differential* sense. I am now informed, for example, that neither the Grandmother, nor the Wolf, nor the Hunter, nor any other character is the one in the red-hooded cloak. But similarly, without knowing the truth of sentence 3.20, I have some con-

---

[13] I rely on the account of information theory presented by Dretske (1983). I recognize that there are some objections to his semantic theory of information, in contrast to the mathematical theory of information of Shannon and Weaver (1949). In particular, there are objections to Dretske's attempt to reconstrue information theory along non-probabilistic lines (see Grandy 1987*b* and Suppes 1983). Since some of these objections to Dretske's theory are pertinent to the use I make of Dretske's account of information theory below, I make use of a modified version of Dretske's account that allows for a probabilistic notion of information (see n. 17 below).

ditional and differential information: I am informed that if there is such a person as the one spoken of in 3.20 (and she is a woman and she is wearing a red-hooded cloak) that person is a woman rather than a man or a child. I also know that (if she exists) she is wearing a red-hooded rather than a brown-hooded or unhooded cloak, etc. If I place the stress on *Little Red Riding Hood* in 3.21, then it is the identity of the character that is at stake; if I place the stress on *red*, in either 3.20 or 3.21 then it is information about the colour of the cloak which is of interest. The nature of the differential information conveyed depends on such 'contrastive stress' (Dretske 1972) of the sentence.

We can say that a meaningful utterance will—at the very least—carry differential information. That differential information will be available both for actual states of affairs and for counterfactual situations—fiction, or future (or mere) possibilities.

While meaning is not information, it does have an information-theoretic basis. The content of linguistic expressions—at least to the extent that it is of cognitive significance—is potentially informative. It is potentially informative, first, in a probabilistic sense: given the intent to inform, etc., an utterance informs us that there is some non-zero conditioned probability that the meaningful content of the utterance applies or is the case. It is potentially informative, secondly, in a counterfactual, conditional, and differential sense: certain alternatives would be instantiated, while others would fail to be instantiated, were it the case that the state of affairs in the utterance pertained (or, in the case of an utterance which was not also a statement, that the utterance had an applicability)—for example, in 3.20—were there a person wearing a red-hooded cloak, that person would be a woman rather than a man. When I speak of the *informative content* of words or of the informative content which constitutes a concept, I mean to speak of such conditional and differential information. The information-theoretic basis of meaning will, I believe, help to provide an explanatory framework and a ground for a relational theory of meaning.

In speaking of the information-theoretic basis of meaning, however, we ought not to neglect the formative role provided by the structure of language itself. Language not only carries information but it also *in-forms* the content it carries: the contrastive and affinitive relations between words give shape to the content we express through language. By serving as a medium, language makes information that we receive informative *to us*. Language provides a way for us to focus and highlight that information which is interesting or significant for us.

Interestingly, the nature of information, in so far as it is to be useful for cognition, is such that language can and needs to serve as more than a mere conduit of information. This is due to three features underlined in a semantic theory of information: that information which serves as semantic content is *digitally* encoded; that all information is *nested*; that information is such only against a background of *possible alternatives*.

The first salient information-theoretic point is that no information arrives as an isolated piece of information. All information is related to other information—it both includes and is included in other information. If we receive information that *s* is a square we also receive information that *s* is a rectilinear plane. This is a relation of *nesting*, which is defined by Dretske as follows:

> The information that *t* is *G* is nested in *s*'s being *F* carries the information that *t* is *G*. (1983, 71.)

All information is 'nested' within other information and has nested within it still other information. The sentence

3.22 Mary is a woman,

if it informs us that Mary is a woman, also provides the information that she is human, female, and adult; that she is breathing, requires nourishment and liquid; that blood flows through her veins; that she *probably* has the potential to bear children, etc.[14] We should, however, point out that the sentence can carry such information only if it is understood relative to the hearer's knowledge and our general background default assumptions. If it turns out that we are speaking of Martians, the sentence may not give us the information that Mary is human, or that blood flows through her veins, etc., but only the information that she is adult, female (and perhaps a person).[15]

---

[14] If we take our stand on the fact that informational content need not have a conditional probability of 1, then including nested probabilistic information is not problematical. Dretske, in attempting to recognize some of the problems in his insistence that the conditional probability should be 1, offers the following suggestion: 'The best we can do in such cases [where the conditional probability that *s* is *B* is high but less than 1] is to say that the signal carries the information that *s* is probably in state *B*. This comes closest to satisfying our definition of informational content, since (we may suppose) the conditional probability of *s*'s *probably being B*, given *r*, is unity . . . When there is no sentence describing the situation that does exist at the source which satisfied our definition of informational content, and we none the less wish to give propositional expression to the quantity of information that is transmitted, we are forced to adopt the expedient of talking about the fact that *something is probably so* as the informational content of a signal' (1983, 69–70, author's italics).

[15] cf. Dretske's (1983, 225–28) discussion of Putnam's Twin Earth example.

Because information is nested, no signal can be said to carry a unique informational context. The related information is nevertheless *different* information, and in different situations we are interested in extracting some and eclipsing other information carried by a signal. The different pieces of nested information may be spoken of as different *informational shells*.

The generalization and classification required for the formation of concepts demands a selectivity with respect to information. When we encode information about *t* in one concept rather than another, we engage in a *semantic* process that requires highlighting, and focusing on some information about *t* and eclipsing other information about *t*. This selectivity is the *digital conversion* of information that we receive in *analogue form*.[16] The digital conversion selects the most specific information relevant to the purpose in hand or to the classificatory scheme invoked. The concepts, which are the semantic content of words, are the potential informative content encoded in digital form. When we speak of information that is digitally encoded, we speak of the most specific information about *t* that the encoding carries. The semantic description of the α-component in our semantic representation are concepts in this information-theoretic sense.

A difference between the meaning of an utterance-type and the information conveyed by the utterance-type has to do with the specificity of the information that is encoded in the utterance-type.[17] A signal

---

[16] I employ Dretske's adaption of the terms 'digital' and 'analogue'. These are self-consciously non-standard uses of the terms. Information that *s* is *F* is in *digital* form 'if and only if the signal carries no additional information about *s*, no information that is *not* nested [*see below*] in *s*'s being *F*. If the signal *does* carry additional information about *s*, information that is *not* nested in *s*'s being *F*, then I shall say that the signal carries this information in analog form' (1983, 137). Dretske adds, 'The most specific piece of information it carries (about *s*) is in digital form. All other information (about *s*) is coded in analog form'.

[17] Because of the constraint that information needs to be true or probable, whereas concepts may not be concepts of anything true, or even probable, we have to devise this awkward formulation. Dretske believes that all concepts ultimately have at their origin the digital encoding of some information. This, he claims, is directly true of 'primitive concepts', in that we learn primitive concepts through exposure to their informative instantiations, and indirectly true of 'complex concepts', which are built of primitive concepts. Dretske writes: 'The meaning of a [semantic structure] derives from the *informational* origins of that structure, but a structure *type* can have its origins in information about *F*-ness of things without *every* (indeed, without any) subsequent token of that type having this information as its origin' (1983, 193, author's italics). This updated Lockean view is not entirely convincing and may result from Dretske's insistence that informative content must have a conditional probability of 1. But something can be informative if it suggests that it is more likely that *x* is *Y* rather than *Z* without telling us that *x* is either. This puts the emphasis on the differential and probabilist nature of information. I suspect that with such a formulation we need not be bound to the Lockean view of concepts that Dretske presents.

which has semantic content, that is, a *semantic structure*, *S*, may convey
many pieces of information. But its semantic content is to be identified
with that information in which is nested any other information carried
by *S*. The informational shell that contains all the other information
about *t* is called the *outer informational shell*. The information which is
contained in the outermost informational shell is information that it
carries in *completely digitalized* form. The information that *t* is *F* is in
completely digitalized form if

Structure *S* has the fact that *t* is *F* as its semantic content =
  (a) *S* carries the information that *t* is *F* and
  (b) *S* carries no other piece of information, *r* is *G*, which is such that the
       information that *t* is *F* is nested . . . in *r*'s being *G*. (Dretske 1983, 185.)

We see that the outermost informational shell is of special semantic
significance. For a structure to be semantic, it must encode the outermost informational shell. The word 'woman', understood in 3.22 as
this sentence is understood against our general background default
assumptions, does not *mean* 'blood flows through the veins of the individual denoted'. That information is nested in the information
encoded in the concept 'human', although again, that is not what the
term 'human' means. The fact that an informational shell is outermost
'does not mean that there are no larger information shells *in which* this
piece of information is nested. All that follows is that there are no
longer shells representing more specific information' (Dretske 1983,
183) encoded in a signal. This encoded information, we have said, is
completely digitalized. In the case of 'woman', as it is used in 3.22, we
may say that it contains the informative content of the concepts
[human], [adult], [female]. These would function as the semantic descriptors of the α-component.

Although we are able to give dictionary definitions of words in which
we specify their sense—each specification encoding completely digitalized information—I suggest that these specifications of meaning are
useful abstractions only. Instead the meaning of a term is specified by
the context. That is until words combine and their senses are specified,
they do not yet encode completely digitalized information. When a
term has been interpreted, it has been completely digitalized. By this I
mean that the semantic content of words remains somewhat indeterminate until they combine with other words, and often the semantic
content of a sentence is indeterminate until it combines with other
sentences. The indeterminacy concerns the question of which infor-

mational shell is outermost.[18] Until words combine, they are only partially digitalized; much information is left in analogue form. When words combine, that analogue information is selectively digitalized so that some pieces of nested information are highlighted or eclipsed, thereby completing the digitalization. But the complete digitalization can take place in what may be indefinitely many different ways. For a complete digitalization is the process of selecting, to highlight or eclipse, pieces of information which, prior to the specification of meaning, existed in analogue form. That some information remains in analogue form is the source of the multiple ambiguity illustrated in Section 1 of this chapter.

Let us consider one of Nunberg's examples:

3.23 The newspaper weighs five pounds.
3.24 The newspaper fired John.

In 3.23 the newspaper signifies the physical object; in 3.24 it signifies the institution. We can also say:

3.25 The newspaper is on strike.

In this case we are speaking only of the unionized workers at the newspaper (the institution). We can also invoke the type–token distinction, as in

3.26 The newspaper is torn.
3.27 The newspaper is printed on recycled paper.

We can plausibly speak of 'the newspaper' in all these different senses, because the informational content conveyed is all part of the informational content we derive from the phenomenon of a newspaper. Which aspect of that phenomenon we choose to focus on and highlight will depend on what is of interest in a given context. That, in turn, will be reflected in the words with which the term 'newspaper' combines in a given setting. In the combination, the salient information is picked out and becomes the semantic content—the outermost informational shell—of the term 'newspaper' understood in this setting.

The representation of the indeterminacy resulting from the incomplete digitalization of the informative content will, therefore, generally not be best served by a set of disjuncts meant to capture the various

---

[18] This indeterminacy is different from, but may be related to, Quine's indeterminacy of translation.

ambiguous readings possible. The complete specification of word meaning requires a context—one which is often extra-sentential. That is why the interdynamic we have seen illustrated can take place. The interaction between words and contextual features, such as default assumptions of both the general and special sort, specify a sense, and thus completely digitalize the informative potential of the utterance. But to understand how the same term may have different, though related, informational content we must understand the relation between a word and other words with which it contrasts and the infor-mation-theoretic analogue of this semantic notion. This brings us to another salient feature of information.

It is a property of information that it exists against a set of alterna-tives: 'no information is generated by the occurrence of events for which there are no alternatives' (Dretske 1983, 12). This notion is also formulated as the proposition that the amount of information in a sig-nal is a function of the reduction of uncertainty. That is, a signal is informative to the extent that the state of affairs it informs us of pro-vides a reduction in the possible alternative states of affair. Therefore, if we are to ascertain the amount of information we are receiving, we must know the range of alternatives possible. For example, if the sen-tence 'Mary is a woman' is to be informative, there need to be things that are not-woman. More informative still are the contrasts which pertain to the *outermost information shell* in which other information is nested. The sentence 'Mary is a woman' provides information that Mary is not a man, or perhaps that Mary is not a girl. In Ursala LeGuin's science-fiction novel, *The Left Hand of Darkness* (New York, 1969) in which all persons undergo periodic sex-change, the sentence would provide the information that Mary is not *at this time* in her male cycle (and the conditional probability that she can bear children now approaches 1). What contrasts are pertinent depends in part on the language, in part on the context, and in part on the default assump-tions.

The fact that the content that is informative is linked to other con-tent in a relationship of contrast (alternate possibilities) or affinity (the nesting of information) serves both to explain why meaning is rela-tional and to require that it should be. A given word has the meaning it has, that is, it encodes a given informational content, only against a background of alternative possibilities. A semantic field theory is the semantic analogue of the information-theoretic principle that to be informative a stimulus must reduce uncertainty. Similarly, the fact that information is always nested means that nested in the informational content encoded by a word will be other information which is not encoded but which can be made available, can be highlighted (and hence 'completely digitalized', in Dretske's terms) when it is presented together with other informational content.

I do not want to deny that we can make assignments of timeless meanings to words in our language. Both such assignments are either abstractions of the many distinctive senses a word will display as it enters into combination with other words, or they are paradigms of some particular applications, or they may be no more than samples of possible applications. Here we have an important kernel of truth in Davidson's holism. We abstract or single out applications of words from their use in the language taken as a whole. But it is a mistake, I believe, to be led by the idealization to think that *these* are the (fixed) meanings of the words. To take this position is to run into the prolife-ration of ambiguous interpretations of which I spoke in Section 1 of this chapter.

Let us consider this issue in the light of the information-theoretic considerations which have now been introduced. I pointed out above that, if we take a noun such as 'lion', it need not only mean the real animal but it can also designate a representation of the animal. I sug-gested that one way to treat this was to introduce the representative use as a distinct meaning; I also suggested that we could introduce a semantic principle as follows: 'a word which names an object, situ-ation, or substance may also be used to name a representation of that object, situation, or substance'. Using information-theoretic notions, we may say that the principle applies because information concerning the configuration of an object is part of the informational content of the noun naming the object. The term 'lion', for instance, includes the information concerning the distinctive shape of a lion.

If we were to claim that 'lion' is ambiguous between the real animal and a representation, we should have to claim that it was ambiguous between the real lion, a two-dimensional representation, and a three-dimensional representation.

A sentence such as

3.28 The column was surrounded by four lions

is ambiguous between

(i) The real column was surrounded by four real lions.

(ii) The real column was surrounded by four stone (or alabaster or bronze) lions.

(iii) In the two-dimensional representation of a real scene a column was surrounded by four live lions.

(iv) In the two-dimensional representation of a real scene a column was surrounded by four stone lions.

(v) In the two-dimensional representation of an imagined scene a column was surrounded by four live lions.

(vi) In the two-dimensional representation of an imagined scene a column was surrounded by four stone lions.

(vii), (viii), (ix), (x), (xi), (xii) A representation of (i)–(vi) as in a story including a description of (i)–(vi).

And the further question arises: ought we to say that readings (i)–(xii) are also ambiguous between a baby lion (a cub) and an adult lion; and between a female lion (a lioness) and a male lion, since 'lion' is ambiguous between lioness and lion? It seems preferable to say instead that all of this information is contained in analogue form in 'lion' and leave it to context to highlight the specific information relevant to the purposes in hand. That is, we leave it to the context to completely digitalize the informative content of the term. Again, what should we say that the *meaning* of 'lion' is? We can say that, while we can give a dictionary definition of some paradigmatic sense of lion, and take this to be the conventional fixing of what we take as the outer informational shell, when we understand the word in its setting, it is the contextual (sentential and extra-sentential) considerations that specify its meaning.[19]

In the case of 'lion', the paradigmatic application of the term is to an adult animal, belonging to the cat family, and having certain species-specific characteristics which distinguish it from other felines. But if we speak of a 'stone lion', we cannot make sense of the term understood in the paradigmatic fashion. Instead we highlight the informational content which informs us of three-dimensional configurations. Similarly, a 'paper lion' highlights the information concerning two-dimensional configurations. A stimulus which presents us with an actual lion, carries with it information concerning the three-dimen-

---

[19] Sometimes this occurs according to specifiable semantic principles, but often the way in which we find it possible to construct a message out of combined informative contents is less amenable to easily specifiable semantic principles. That is not to say that the processes are not rule-governed or are random but only that they involve a lot of complex considerations.

sional and two-dimensional configurations. (Conversely, the ability to understand representations in two or three dimensions ordinarily allows us to infer what the actual thing would look like. Thus, having seen pictures of lions, we should tend to recognize the real thing if we saw it. However, this is not necessarily so. We are familiar with situations in which we have seen a photograph or sketch of a person and yet fail to recognize the person when encountered in real life.)

I believe that this approach can also help to explain why it is the case that, when terms combine, the impact they have on one another is not always equal. In most contexts, if we speak of 'stone lions' we assume that we are speaking of a stone that has been fashioned to look like a lion and not an actual lion that we can somehow speak of as having the properties of a stone—though I can imagine a metaphorical construal of the phrase that would allow such an interpretation. In the two phrases 'dropping a friend' and 'making a friend', *friend* remains fairly stable in meaning; in the phrases 'dropping a friend', 'dropping a hem', 'making a friend', and 'making a hem', the meanings of *drop* and *make* are significantly different, while the meanings of *friend* and *hem* remain fairly stable. This is the phenomenon that Ross (1981) speaks of as words 'dominating' other words or 'being captured by' other words. Let us say that we do have two terms, A and B, and that we combine these into the utterance AB. And let us say that the context supports a sense of A which encodes the outermost shell of A in what we have called a paradigmatic sense, but fails to support the outermost shell encoded by a paradigmatic sense of B (if there is one). In order to make sense of AB, that is, in order to glean information from the utterance, we need to access information in an inner shell of B. And we are guided by the sense of A to choose an inner shell of B that in combination with the outermost shell of A is informative. This is a situation in which the term A dominates B. It will then be information encoded in such an inner shell that will fix the meaning of B in its combination with A. That inner shell now becomes its outermost shell and its sense in the utterance AB. For some terms, the outermost informational shell is relatively firmly fixed by the conventional, paradigmatic sense. Some technical terms are of this sort and resist an invasion of the inner informational shells. Other terms have only a weakly established outermost informational shell and are subject to much variation of meaning, for example, 'make'. What we take 'make' to mean depends on what is being made, who or what is making it, etc. Such terms are easily dominated. Interestingly, they are not frequently used metaphorically.

For some terms there may not be a paradigmatic sense. The term 'cell' as quoted above from Nunberg illustrates this. To say of *x* that it is a 'cell' is not very informative without a context. If we say, 'The organism is a cell,' or, 'The room is a cell,' we have (at least potentially) informative statements. Yet the two senses are not entirely separate. There are structural features of both rooms and organisms to which the term 'cell' pertains. That is, the content of 'cell' is such that, at least in its non-homonymous instances, it conveys some sort of information about the structural features of that to which the term is applied. But the specification of that information must await its predication of some particular sort of entity. We ought perhaps to say that a timeless meaning or a dictionary definition of 'cell' would provide *samples* rather than a paradigm of the way the term was to be used. The semantic content of 'cell' will also contain certain restrictions governing the sorts of things that can literally be termed cells—restrictions which would be represented by the β-component. As Nunberg pointed out above, while monasteries have cells, libraries and cruise ships do not.

Taking into account information-theoretic considerations, we should look once more at β, the semantic concatenation conditions. These conditions indicate to us the possibility of forming or specifying the conceptual or informational content resulting from the combination of terms. That possibility is constrained by the conceptual organization underlying and governing linguistic usage and by the imaginative limits of stretching and altering that conceptual organization. The possibility of deriving a coherent message, one that has at least a differential informative content, is also constrained by whether our discourse applies to the actual world, to possibilities inherent in the actual world (given the nature of our conceptual organization and our system of beliefs about the empirical world), or to a fanciful, imaginative, or exploratory vision, not bound tightly to our current conceptual organization or to our beliefs about the empirical world. Here we see one way in which empirical considerations may enter as conditions on word combinations: beliefs concerning empirical matters enter into our conceptual organization in that they can constitute limits on what we take to be possible. Thus some new beliefs and some new data are easily assimilated, while others are met with scepticism; still others require a different way of talking and thinking.

Except to the extent that we are pressed to give a dictionary-type definition, where general or special default assumptions form an implicit context, words out of context have informative content that is digitalized, but not yet completely digitalized. For that content to be completely digitalized, the pertinent contrasts and affinities must be specified. I have said that the contrastive relations that a term has with other terms in the language is the analogue of the fact that a stimulus is informative only in relation to a set of alternatives; and the affinitive relations a term bears to other terms is the semantic analogue to the nesting of information. The semantic fields which are comprised of terms and their affinitive and contrastive relations are therefore neither arbitrary nor eternally fixed. They are constrained by the informative content of the terms and are reactive to the different functional demands which selectively pick out some information among all the information available—that is, which determine what information needs to be encoded as the outermost informational shell. The default assumptions and the requirements of a given discourse will help to shape particular fields for given purposes, while the contrasts and affinities available in the language will provide a fairly stable supply of semantic fields which reflect current conceptualizations of information.

But how are these contrasts and affinities made available? They are made available by the combination of terms according to syntactic rules. When we combine terms in sentences and sentences in texts we come to understand the contrasts and affinities which pertain to the use of a given term in a given context. Sometimes a sentence suffices to delimit the pertinent semantic field relations, especially when understood against a set of default assumptions. More often a sentence alone will not do. A more extensive context is necessary. Thus we can say that a term is ambiguous—that is, its informative content, while digitalized, is not yet *completely* digitalized—until its meaning is further specified by the context. When we can locate the pertinent semantic field and the pertinent contrasts and affinities within that semantic field, then we have specified the meaning. This is precisely what the γ-component is meant to represent.

The need for contextual considerations to specify meaning—for the contextual considerations are required to completely digitalize the informative content—underlie language's profound polysemy, its processes of meaning differentiation, and its expanding expressive capacities. When words combine, their informative content is selectively pruned so that the resulting message is coherent and appropriately informative, at least when there is a warranted assumption that all speakers adhere to the Co-operative Principle. The informative content of words taken singly is still sufficiently in analogue form for the generation of meaning illustrated above to be possible. That generation, then, involves the further digitalization of the information forced upon us in the process of combining terms.

On the one hand the relational nature of information—that it requires a background set of contrasting possibilities and that it is always nested—means that a structure which is to be able to carry information (that is, to be informative) must accommodate these relational features. A relational theory of meaning accomplishes just this. On the other hand, language must be able to convey new information. The interactive nature of meaning—the fact that new meaning can be generated through the appropriate combination of words—means that information which has not previously been encoded, or perhaps not previously been digitalized may, none the less, be *expressible* by the appropriate combination of words. The differentiation of meaning exemplified above increases the expressive possibilities of language. That context can provide a term with contrasts and affinities which are not already provided by the language means that the expressive capacities of language can expand to meet the demands newly posed.

In metaphor, the generative process takes a radical turn. The attempt to arrive at a coherent informative content, through the processes of the projection rules described in Chapter 2, results in an incongruity of a conversational or conceptual sort. Thus, while metaphor is an instance of the generation of meaning, it is so in a special way. And while all meaning is context-dependent, the dependence in the case of metaphor takes a particular form. The context does not simply serve to digitalize further the informational content. Instead of a shift or specification of meaning, it requires a transference of meaning: a transference of relations of contrast and affinity across semantic fields.

As was stated in Chapter 1, metaphor, from Aristotle onwards, has been thought to be a transference of meaning from one term to another. With a relational concept of meaning, the traditional definition of metaphor is transformed. A transference of meaning is not a simple displacement of an atomistic meaning but a move from one system to another, from the system embedding a term in its literal–conventional sense to another system which will give the term its new metaphorical significance. This conception of meaning accords well with the perspectival view of metaphor presented in Chapter 1. The perspectival view of metaphor which I found in Chapter 1 to be most amenable to explaining its cognitive potential calls upon an acceptance of the thesis that metaphor involves not two isolated terms or ideas but two systems, whether these be systems of terms, of labels, or of extensional realms. But my argument in this chapter has the consequence that metaphor involves systems, and not isolated ideas, because language and meaning generally require that linguistic terms be systematically related. The view that metaphor is a transference across semantic domains has been arrived at by two different routes: first, by considering the question of the cognitive import of metaphor; and secondly, by a search for an adequate semantic theory.

In the following chapter, I shall give a detailed account of the process of interpreting metaphor. We shall see just how context functions and how the incongruity serves the interpretation, and I shall discuss how contextual features determine the semantic fields involved in the metaphorical interpretation.

4

Interpreting Metaphor

IT will be the task of this chapter to explore the nature and structure of that second-order meaning which results from a particular mapping of first-order meaning and which yields metaphor. The second-order meaning of metaphor results from the double semantic content carried by metaphor. As we saw in Chapter 2, one content can be identified as an appropriate first-order meaning of the vehicle term. Selecting this meaning, the first step in interpreting a metaphor, requires us to recognize that the background assumptions presumed by the context of an utterance are in conflict with such a first-order interpretation. The second content is drawn from the context that frames the vehicle term. In this chapter we see how our second step is to extract a content from the context which serves as the second content of the metaphor. I shall say that the first content, that of the term(s) used metaphorically, the vehicle, is a semantic field which is distinct from the semantic field of the context in which the metaphorically used terms are embedded. The second content or semantic field provides the topic of the metaphor. The final step, then, is to transpose the semantic relations that a term or terms have within their own semantic field on to a new conceptual domain—the one given by the context—thereby reordering the second domain in virtue of the relations which pertain in the first. The result is the second-order meaning that the term acquires in its metaphorical use. The notion of second-order meaning will allow us to understand both what is distinctive in metaphor and how metaphor fits into a more general conception of language meaning and use.

I METAPHOR AS SECOND-ORDER MEANING

Resolving Some Perplexities about Metaphorical Meaning

In the previous chapter I set forth a relational theory of meaning. It is a theory of meaning that insists on the importance of accommodating certain contextual factors within a semantics. By including these, we make room for the notion of a second-order meaning. But it may be observed, that in positing a second-order meaning, we can answer some of the objections to metaphorical meaning that Davidson and others have put forward, even without further insistence on a relational theory of meaning.

I have said above that if we were to include metaphorical sentences among the totality of sentences for which we could form T-sentences, and if we were to say that these had metaphorical meanings in addition to their literal meanings, the intermingling of literal and metaphorical meanings would make it impossible to abstract word meanings in the manner that Davidson thinks necessary for an account of how sentence meanings are dependent on word meanings. But if we separate out first- and second-order meanings, then metaphorical meanings no longer pose such a problem, for then the forming of T-sentences would pertain only to first-order interpretations of these sentences. However, for there to be a distinction between first- and second-order meanings, we need to relativize meanings to contexts in such a way that we assure ourselves that we are formulating the truth conditions for first-order interpretations. Such relativization to context may be seen as an extension of the relativization to speaker, time, and place which Davidson already acknowledges to be necessary. The further indices may relativize meanings to salient background assumptions, the nature of the discourse (whether it is craftbound, speaks of fictional or imaginary worlds, etc.), and so on. To recognize the importance of context in our understanding of language, literal or metaphorical, is only a first step. The second and far more painstaking step is to learn how to specify the significant elements of context. Of course, the difficulty of such an endeavour, or other considerations such as those presented by Cohen (1986) in reference to truth-theoretic semantics, may urge us to jettison the very idea of a truth-theoretic semantics. But regardless of how first-order discourse is characterized, I maintain that to regard metaphor as second-order will permit a more coherent semantics of first-order discourse without at once relegating metaphor outside the bounds of meaning.

To say, then, that metaphorical meaning is a second-order meaning is to leave much in first-order discourse intact. This view asserts, with Davidson, that the first-order meaning of metaphorical utterances is indeed operative in the meaning of a metaphor. But while it may be possible to construct artificial languages which exclude the particular special structures which characterize metaphor and indirect speech, these cannot be excluded from natural language, nor can they be characterized by the logical form of first-order meaning. Thus, to posit a second-order meaning for metaphor is to disagree with proclamations such as the following:

> The work of applying a theory of truth in detail to a natural language will in practice almost certainly divide into two stages. In the first stage, truth will be characterized not for the whole language, but for a carefully gerrymandered part of the language . . . The second part will match each of the remaining sentences to one (or in the case of ambiguity) more than one of the sentences for which truth has been characterized. We may think of the sentences to which the first stage of the theory applies as giving the logical form or deep structure of all sentences. (Davidson 1973, 320.)

If a truth-theoretic semantics is appropriate to natural language, then the first stage to which the theory applies will give the logical form or deep structure only of sentences interpreted in their first-order meanings. Second-order discourse also has a deep structure which requires investigation and which will not submit to the logical form of first-order discourse. It may be possible to construct artificial languages which exclude the particular iterative structures which characterize metaphor and indirect speech, but these cannot be excluded from natural language, nor can they be characterized by the logical form of first-order meaning.

Davidson suggests that if metaphors had a special meaning then 'we might be able to specify the special meaning of a word in a metaphorical setting by waiting until the metaphor die[d]' (1981, 208). While it is true, as Davidson says, that this cannot be done, we ought not thence to conclude that metaphors have no special meaning. Rather, if instead of a second meaning, as in the case of ambiguity, they have a second-order meaning, we understand why this cannot be done. For a genuinely dead and unrevivable metaphor is one in which no second-order meaning is recognized by speakers of the language—the word acquires as a first-order meaning the sense which previously only contributed to its second-order meaning. If we are dealing with a phrase composed of several words, the entire phrase is treated like a single lexical item (and is learned as a single lexical item) with the literal senses of the constituent words forgotten in favour of its new first-order meaning. But as we saw in Chapter 1, most metaphors never die completely, and, while they may seem merely to acquire new first-order meanings, their special structure can often be evoked in the right context. This is what characterizes them as dead *metaphors* rather than as new lexical items.

Introducing the notion of second-order meaning also helps explain the relation between metaphor and similes. Davidson introduces the issue of simile because he believes that a consideration of simile shows us what is mistaken in the idea that metaphors have a special meaning and a special cognitive content. He says:

> Just because a simile wears a declaration of similitude on its sleeve, it is, I think, far less plausible than in the case of metaphor to maintain that there is a hidden second meaning. . . . We might then say the author of the simile intended us—that is, meant us—to notice that similarity. But having appreciated the difference between what the words meant and what the author accomplished by using those words, we should feel little temptation to explain what has happened by endowing the words themselves with a second, or figurative meaning. (1981, 210.)

By positing a difference between a first- and a second-order meaning, we see that to claim that metaphors have a distinctive meaning is not to endow 'the words themselves with a second, or figurative meaning' but only to attribute a meaning to the result of words functioning together in certain contexts. This is a meaning derived from certain rule-like operations on the usual meanings of those words. Thus I have virtually no disagreement with Davidson when he says that 'the unexpected or subtle parallels and analogies it is the business of metaphor to promote need not depend, for their promotion, on more than the literal meanings of words' (1981, 211). But I should add that, in addition to the literal meanings of words, we require the rules for second-order discourse specific to metaphor. These rules are just the ones that identify the utterance as metaphorical and that direct us to making 'the subtle parallels and analogies it is the business of metaphor to promote'. And it is the business of metaphor to promote parallels and analogies which are not accomplished through literal comparison and which use the resources of second-order discourse.[1]

Second-order Meaning and Second-order Interpretation

By properly identifying the metaphorical unit, I have been able to specify those rules of first-order meaning whose violation signals the

---

[1] Simile accomplishes some of the same cognitive ends, but uses different linguistic resources. A simile is not a connotative semiotic and has no second-order meaning. But the nature of the comparison is metaphorical. In particular, the 'like' in simile should be understood metaphorically, for it signals a *cross-categorial* comparison. See my discussion in Chapter 1.

potential for a second-order interpretation. By reconceiving the relation between context and meaning, I have argued for the viability of the concept of metaphorical meaning. The nature and representation of metaphorical meaning now requires specification. Essential to our understanding of metaphorical meaning is the concept of a second-order meaning. By characterizing that second-order meaning which is metaphor, we can formulate rule-governed procedures that exhibit the linguistic competence to interpret metaphor.

Second-order meaning, I have claimed, is a function of first-order meaning. The first-order meaning of an utterance is derived from an appropriate combination of the first-order meaning of its constituents as they are set within a given context or, in the absence of a sufficiently explicit differentiating context, as they are understood within a *default frame* of *background default assumptions.* (Differences in specific default assumptions will manifest themselves in those meanings that are viewed as most entrenched given those default assumptions.)

Second-order meaning is obtained when features of the utterance and its context indicate to the hearer or reader that the first-order meaning of the expression is either unavailable or is not appropriate— but when the first-order meanings of the words of the utterance are none the less relevant to its appropriate interpretation. As examples of second-order meaning other than metaphor I cited tropes such as irony, non-figurative utterances which Searle has called indirect speech acts, and other non-figurative utterances which have *two illocutionary forces.*

Once we have determined that a second-order interpretation is required, we need to determine some appropriate function to be applied to a selected first-order interpretation to obtain an appropriate second-order interpretation. I shall now characterize a function, $\dagger$, whose application to a first-order interpretation will result in a second-order interpretation. Later, I shall define a metaphorical operator, μ, which will be a particular instantiation of the more general function. Let us recall that $I(u)$ is the first-order interpretation of the utterance $u \in U^k$. By $I^*(u)$ I shall denote a second-order interpretation of u. That second-order interpretation is a function of first-order interpretation may be formally expressed: there exists a function $\dagger$ such that $I^*(u) = \dagger(I(u))$. But this statement needs further refinement. In the case that $k > 0$, a first-order interpretation may not be available. Thus we shall have to give the conditions for arriving at a second-order interpretation when there is no first-order interpretation of $u \in U^{k > 0}$.

Since u will have constituents, we shall operate on the highest-level constituents which are subject to first-order interpretation. Those highest-level constituents which belong to the same semantic field specified by the context of the utterance will require one mapping. Those which belong to a distinct semantic field will require another mapping. The nature of these mappings will be determined by the nature of the second-order interpretation. A precise statement of the procedure is given below.

Schema for obtaining a second-order interpretation. Given an utterance $u \in U^k$, 'a', a first-order interpretation $I(u)$ where $u = a$ or where $u \in U^{k-1}$ is a constituent of a, the function †, we obtain a second-order interpretation $I^*(a)$ as follows:

  (i) where $k \geq 0$, and where there is a $I(a)$, † maps $I(a)$ on to $I^*(a)$;

  (ii) where $k > 0$, but there is no $I(a)$, that is, a first-order interpretation of a is blocked, we

    (1) determine an utterance $u \in U^{k+1}$, call it 'c', such that a is a constituent of c,

    (2) determine the highest-level constituents of a which belong to the same semantic field as c; let us say that these are $(u_{t1}, u_{t2} \ldots u_{tm}) \in U^{k+1}$,

    (3) determine the highest-level constituents of $u \in U^k$ which belong to distinctly different semantic fields from that of $u \in U^{k-1}$; let us say that these are $(u_{v1}, u_{v2} \ldots u_{vn}) \in U^{k-1}$,

    (4) our function, †, will map $(u_{t1}, u_{t2} \ldots u_{tm}) \in U^{k-1}$ on to itself and will assign a mapping to $(u_{v1}, u_{v2} \ldots u_{vn}) \in U^{k-1}$ which will give the interpretation appropriate to the nature of the second-order meaning.

We are primarily interested in second-order meaning in so far as it gives us a way to account for the interpretation of metaphorical utterances. But, to give scope to the notion of a second-order meaning, consider once again a sentence such as 'You are stepping on my toe', when we desire not merely to inform but to request the person addressed to get off our toe. Many such indirect speech acts have a conventional second-order meaning. The conventionality, however, is not due to their lexicalization but to a rule most competent speakers have mastered—a rule that maps assertions or questions of a certain sort, questions to which a literal, first-order response is inappropriate or insufficient, on to polite forms of requests, commands, and 'whimperatives'. For the indirect speech act expressed by S we can define a request operator: 'Please stop doing what it is asserted that you are doing in S'. (In the case of indirect speech acts, we generally encounter condition (*b*) of the definition above.)

Indispensable to all forms of second-order meaning is an understanding of the operative first-order meaning. This is indeed what makes second-order meaning *second-order* and not simply another, alternative meaning. In the case of some second-order signification, the ties between a first-order meaning and a second-order meaning are such that there is no independence of their applicability conditions. This is the case with indirect speech acts. If I were to say to Jones, 'Pardon me, you are stepping on my toe,' and Jones was not stepping on my toe, the sentence would fail as an indirect speech act, that is, as a request, and become merely a false and mistaken remark.

Codes, of the sort that cryptographers concern themselves with, are generally not second-order, but some coded language might well be. Let us say that a secret organization has agreed to the following code: a non-basic colour term[2] signals the presence of an enemy in the immediate vicinity. Were a member of the organization to hear the word 'chartreuse' in a communication addressed to her by another member, she would have to know, minimally, that it named a colour and that it was not one of the eleven basic colour terms of English. Otherwise she would fail to recognize the term as a communication of an enemy's presence. In so far as the successful communication depends on understanding a relevant aspect of the term's first-order meaning, even if what is to be communicated by the term is not what is indicated by the term's meaning$_{\text{LC}}$, we have a second-order meaning.

A Connotative Semiotic

Interestingly, the very fact that someone uses a special code, or a technical language, or jargon, or dialect may have a special significance, forcing the conclusion that more is meant than what is said. That is, the mode of expression may itself carry important information, for example, in humour, when a joke is not funny unless presented in the proper dialect. It is also apparent in literature in which dialect is

---

[2] The basic colour terms in English are black, white, red, yellow, green, blue, brown, pink, purple, grey, and orange (Berlin and Kay 1969). A discussion of *basic terms* is included in Chapter 6 below.

prominent. Information concerning the characters' ethnic, or class, or geographic origins may be revealed through dialect: often more is conveyed by Professor Higgins and Eliza through their respective dialects than through their respective dialogue.

In Chapter 1, I introduced the notion of a connotative semiotic in order to illuminate the iterative structure of metaphor whereby a term used metaphorically carries two contents simultaneously. But Hjelmslev (1961) introduced the notion to account for just such uses of dialect, tone, regional language, jargon, etc. These he called *connotators*, and they carry information which is additional to the content of the denotative sign.[3] According to Hjelmslev, all connotators involve features of the label (orthographic or phonetic sequence) which carry information additional to their usual content (or sense). Hjelmslev saw connotation enacted only by such secondary means of communication, and did not consider what might happen if we were to allow a complete conventional denotative sign to occupy the plane of expression. When a conventional denotative sign is placed on the plane of expression of a connative semiotic, we get the second-order signification pertinent to metaphor.[4] Let us look (Figure 4.1) at a modified representation of the

(u_v)	bees	/biːz/
$s(u_v)$		apian beings
$s(u_l)$		workers

FIG. 4.1

connotative structure of the term 'Bees' as used in Shelley's 'Song to the Men of England (example 1.7 above).

The connotative structure is illuminating in another regard. Even if an utterance was not intended to have this connotative structure, such a structure could be imposed on many utterances by sufficiently imaginative readers. For a metaphorical interpretation to be appropriate, the term(s) on the level of content must come from the semantic field of

---

[3] Denotative signs are simply terms with a level of expression and a level of content, in our terms, $<E(u), s(u)>$.

[4] Hjelmslev (1961) points out that metalanguage may be represented as signification in which the conventional denotative sign, i.e. a term, occupies the level of content. In metalanguage there are two expression levels, one for which the sign is itself the content, the other for which only its sense is.

the frame. The less explicitly the frame is specified, the more options there are in determining the second semantic field. Many writers on metaphor put forward sentences which, isolated and out of context, appear to demarcate the boundary between metaphor and nonsense. But that contextless 'piece of nonsense' will permit an imaginative reader to take her or his pick of semantic fields from which to select some salient features and relations to serve as a basis for metaphor.

In Chapter 2, I stated that the necessary conditions we had arrived at did not jointly constitute a sufficient condition for an utterance to be a metaphor. I suggested that this was because metaphor was a second-order phenomenon and that sufficient identifying criteria would involve rules of second-order discourse. We are now in a position to see that what is required is not a single sufficient condition as such but rather a set of alternative conditions any one of which is sufficient just in case the necessary conditions are fulfilled.[5]

Given that the necessary conditions are fulfilled, it is sufficient for an utterance to be a metaphorical utterance either if the utterance was intended to be understood metaphorically or if it is possible to attribute a metaphorical interpretation—appropriate to the context—to the utterance. These alternative sufficient conditions are dependent on a systematic equivocation that we find in metaphor and other tropes, as well as in other forms of discourse—that is, that for an utterance to be understood as taking the particular form in question it must fulfil certain necessary conditions and must either be intended as such or must be taken as such. The requirement that the utterance should fulfil the necessary conditions is indispensable since I might intend a metaphor but not understand how to produce it or be insufficiently familiar with the language to be successful, *or* I might try to take an utterance to be a metaphor which neither was intended as such nor will yield to a metaphorical interpretation. Notice that the same sort of equivocation is not true of a speech act such as promising. Regardless of how many felicity conditions are satisfied, no one can correctly take an utterance to be a promise unless the purported utterer intended the utterance to be a promise.[6] The connotative semiotic permits us to recognize a structural feature characteristic of metaphor which makes the identification of an utterance as metaphorical independent of the particular inten-

---

[5] I owe this formulation to Bernard Baumrin (personal communication).

[6] For other relevant distinctions between speech acts and metaphor see Cohen 1979 and the discussion in Chapter 3 above.

tions of a speaker.[7] The connotative semiotic functions graphically to represent the double semantic import of metaphor. The connotative structure of metaphor as I have represented it in Figure 4.1 illustrates the conception of metaphor by which we can say that a single label, that is, an orthographic or phonetic sequence, simultaneously carries two conceptual contents. A distinctive feature of the connotative semiotic that is metaphor is that the two conceptual contents come from two distinct semantic fields. A more precise statement is that the relations of contrast and affinity from one semantic field are mapped on to a distinct *content domain*. If we look at Figure 4.1 we notice that the second content level does not require its own expression in the form of a label. And indeed, often we will use metaphor when there is no distinct term or even a distinctly articulated semantic field for the topic. When the term 'current' was first used for the phenomenon of electricity, the conceptual domain of electricity was only beginning to be articulated. To date there is no separate, non-metaphorical, term for the phenomenon which today is more or less literally spoken of as 'electrical current'.

Can we incorporate this structure within a suitably modified representation of meaning as it was developed for first-order signification? This is what I shall attempt in section 2 of this chapter.

Second-order Interpretation within a Relational Theory of Meaning

On my view, then, a literal, conventional sense (sense$_{LC}$), $s(u)$ is an ordered triple $<\alpha,\beta,\gamma>$. The first-order meaning, $M(u)$, is represented as:

$$M(u) =_{df} \{s_1(u) \ldots s_m(u)\} =_{df} \{(\alpha_1,\beta_1,\gamma_1)(u)\} \ldots \{(\alpha_m,\beta_m,\gamma_m)(u)\}.$$

We represented a term in the language as a meaningful$_{LC}$ utterance-type, that is, as an ordered pair $<E(u), C(u)>$, where $E(u)$ is an expression of u (a label) and $C(u)$ is its content. We can also represent a term as an ordered pair $<E(u), M(u)>$, where $M(u)$ is the meaning$_{LC}$ of the expression u, or alternatively as $<E(u), s(u)>$, where a given sense$_{LC}$ of u has been specified. $M(u)$ represents a set of meanings$_{LC}$ or, more precisely, Grice's timeless meaning, while $s(u)$ represents a

---

[7] If this were not the case, since, in fact, we are constantly utilizing metaphors we are quite unaware of, we should have to invoke a notion of an unconscious or (given the Freudian appropriation of that term) a non-conscious intention.

particular sense$_{LC}$ or, more precisely, Grice's applied timeless meaning. A term interpreted with a second-order signification carries with it a meaning, the occasion meaning of the utterance-type, which diverges from the applied timeless meaning but which is none the less dependent on the applied timeless meaning. The divergence of meaning might result from some operation either on the label itself or on the sense. Where dialect plays an important role in understanding the utterance, we take the phonemic sequence to carry a double significance: it conveys words *per se* and it conveys a dialect which is informative, which adds content to what is said—for example, the ethnic identity of the speaker. In the case of metaphor, irony, and indirect speech acts, the added content results from an understanding of the appropriate transformation of the sense$_{LC}$.

The reader may sense a certain tension here between the criticism against insulationist theories of meaning endorsed in Chapter 3 and an account of first-order meaning that depends on Grice's timeless meanings and applied timeless meanings. The picture of sentence meaning to which I gave more than an approving nod was interactive and seemed to suggest the plausibility of indefinitely large or infinite word polysemy. Should we attempt to reconcile these apparently conflicting views, or should we simply renounce the idea of timeless meanings and applied timeless meanings? How can we espouse a relational theory of meaning and maintain a distinction between first- and second-order meaning?

I believe that, with suitable modification, all these notions can coexist. Language may well require a complex of notions of varied origin properly to represent the different ways in which we encounter them. I shall attempt to weld the theory presented here at its joints. However, I shall make no claims to have presented a water-tight vessel.

The specified meaning of an utterance is that utterance's occasion meaning, which in the case of first-order meaning is the same as some applied timeless meaning. The utterance's occasion meaning is a specification of an incompletely digitalized timeless meaning. Timeless meanings are word meanings and sentence meanings which are given outside an explicit context. Some words, and perhaps some sentences, may have meanings which are highly specified and remain relatively invariant in differing contexts. Technical terms which have not borrowed a label from some other domain, certain mathematical terms, (for example, 'rectangle'), borrowed foreign terms, and suchlike are relatively univocal in varying contexts. But most terms require a setting in which their meaning may be specified, in the sense in which I spoke in the discussion of polysemy in Chapter 3. Entries in dictionaries, it was posited in Chapter 2, are abstractions. Certainly they are often very useful ones. But, again, what we must recognize is that the meaning of the utterance-type is completely digitalized against an implicit frame of background (or sometimes discourse-specific) default assumptions and various paradigmatic contextual situations. We can use these notions with the understanding that they are abstractions.

The analogical shifts of meaning which Ross demonstrates are essentially first-order. Consider again some uses of 'dropped' in the following sentences:

4.1   (i) She *dropped* her paint can.
        (ii) She *dropped* her hem.
        (iii) She *dropped* her stitch.

Although they involve analogous meanings of the term 'dropped,' they are all literal sentences and literal uses. Now consider a text such as:

> 4.2 She had been held in high esteem when she was young and beautiful. But age and decline in beauty are difficult for an actress. She was rarely given important roles and felt her value had plummeted. She had been *dropped* and the crash splintered the fragile structure of her ego.

Here 'dropped' is used metaphorically. The terms 'crash' and 'splinter' give to the interpretation$_{LC}$ of 'drop' the sense of a physical, quick, and palpable descent. Notice that 'drop' used literally need not be a precipitous action wherein an object hits the ground, for example, when a hem or stitch is dropped. But the terms used in 4.2 specify such a sense. The context provided by 4.2 also makes it clear that this is *only* the first-order sense. There is a figurative appropriation of the sense which is metaphorical. The appropriation in 4.2 is no less analogical than in 4.1. We say of 4.1(i)–(iii) that the relation between what *she* did to her *paint can* was analogous to what *she* did to her *hem* and that these, in turn, were analogous to what *she* did to her *stitch*. And similarly we can say these are all analogous to what the *acting industry* did to the *actress*. The difference is that in the sentences of 4.1 we do not need to consider the originating source of the analogy in order to understand the full import of the utterance. In the case of 4.2 the originating source of the analogy and the appropriate disanalogy need to be jointly considered. That is to say, in interpreting the last sentence of 4.2 we are required to understand 'dropped' as having a connotative structure.

Granted that principles of analogy are operative in first-order discourse, we still ought not to say that metaphorical meanings are simply another, perhaps more far-fetched, analogical extension. Instead they are a special application in which the semantic field serving as the source of the analogy is retained as a second content in second-order discourse.

First-order discourse and literal language generally may use analogy to expand and generate meaning, but the semantic field from which an analogy is generated is dropped when the new semantic field is introduced. Analogy in first-order discourse may originate in one field and be carried to another, or it need not originate in any one particular field. It may simply be that our experience of the phenomena is similarly structured and that our language reflects this. We speak of physical fights and verbal fights. There is no reason, I believe, to take either as primary, as the model by which we understand the other. They are both experienced as fights, and one sort of abuse can lead to the other form of abuse. Domains that are so similarly structured will often give rise to potent metaphorical extensions among those parts of the domain where the structure is not given, a priori, as analogous. While an argument of a vituperous sort is literally a fight, it is probably not literally a battle. And we may speak of two people in a discussion 'sparring' with each other; thereby using a term from a particular domain of physical combat, boxing (which may, in turn, be borrowed from cockfighting), to convey something particular about the nature of the verbal dispute. The more *strategic* argument which is reasoned and deductive in nature may not be a 'fight' at all, although we may say metaphorically that 'we defended our position well'. Domains in which portions are analogically structured will have a number of *bridge terms* that will anchor metaphorical redescriptions of the remaining portions of the domains.

But in metaphor one domain will take on the role of an originating field—the field of the vehicle of the metaphor. Metaphorical analogies are asymmetrical for just this reason—that one side of the analogy has a privileged status in regard to the other. A simile based on a metaphorical analogy is not—or at best paradoxically—reversible. A simile based on a non-metaphorical analogy may well be. Compare 'My love is like a rose' with 'The tornadoes of the interior plains are like the hurricanes of coastal regions'. While we can reverse the latter comparison without significant alteration of sense, we cannot do so in the former case. In the former case the perfection and beauty of the rose are the model, the originating source of the analogy; in the latter, either can be modelled on the other. But asymmetry alone does not differentiate the metaphorical comparison. The comparative statement 'The son is like the father' is asymmetrical, but not metaphorical. (See p.187 below.) In metaphor, the originating source remains active and productive in generating the relevant contrasts and affinities:

In non-metaphorical analogy, the originating source has given way to a somewhat different set of oppositions and affinities which become distinctive for that sense of the term. Thus the fact that metaphors are a *special* application of the analogical principles operative in the general case of polysemy is nicely seen in the test for polysemy which Ross suggests. Ross (1981) claims that, if the affinities and oppositions for two uses of a term are different, then we have two different or analogous meanings. But when we try this with metaphorical uses, it often fails as a test. Consider the sense of 'light' in the following sentences:

4.3 The bag is *light*.
4.4 It is a *light* shade of red.
4.5 She feels *light*-hearted.

Its antonym in 4.3 is 'heavy'; in 4.4 it is 'dark'; but in 4.5, which is metaphorical, it is 'heavy' again (as in 'heavy-hearted'). In the metaphorical sentence

4.6 Her mood is *light* and gay

the antonymous term would again be 'dark'. In both 4.5 and 4.6 the distinct antonyms direct us to the different, though related, sources of analogy which correspond to the different, but similar, metaphorical uses of 'light'. Ross's test of analogy allows us to find the uses of 'light' analogous in regard to 4.3 and 4.4 and in regard to 4.5 and 4.6. But it fails to distinguish analogy between 4.3 and 4.5 on the one hand and 4.4 and 4.6 on the other, for here the antonyms are common to both literal and metaphorical uses. The same point could be made with 'drop'. An antonym of 'dropped' in 4.1(i) could be 'picked up'. But we do not 'pick up' a hem, we 'take up' a hem. And while a student may choose to 'drop philosophy' rather than to 'add philosophy', an American student 'picks up a subject' not if she has simply 'dropped a subject' but if she is 'short' of a requisite course. There are also interesting variations within a language. For American English speakers there is no clear antonym of 'drop a stitch', yet the British speak of 'picking up a stitch'.

This is not to say that we could not find some oppositional term which would distinguish the literal from the metaphorical uses, but in an effective metaphor many of the affinities and oppositions are carried along in the transfer of meaning. That is, in part, what I mean when I say that, in the analogous extensions which are metaphorical, the semantic field which is the originating source of the analogy is retained.

The distinction between the metaphorical and the literal is, of course, not always clear. If we say:

4.7 She *dropped* her eyes

or

4.8 She *dropped* her friend

there might well be a difference of opinion as to the literality or meta-phoricity of these sentences. The term 'drop' in 4.7 and 4.8 applies to a domain of objects which only under extraordinary circumstances might be dropped in the same sense as we can be said to drop a paint can. Of the two sentences, I should venture to say that 'dropped' in 4.7 is simply an analogous extension of the term as used in 4.1(ii) while 4.8 is a metaphorical use which has become conventionalized. 'Dropped' in 4.7 and in 4.1(ii) share some relations: in both cases the term is syn-onymous with 'lowered', and in both cases we can say that a contradic-tory sentence would result if we were to substitute 'raised' for 'dropped'. But while we 'take up' a hem, we do not 'take up' our eyes. Furthermore in the case of the two uses of 'dropped' in 4.1(ii) and 4.7 there are differences in syntagmatic relations. For example, we can easily say:

4.9 She *dropped* her eyes slowly.

But

4.10 She *dropped* her hem slowly

is somewhat odd, unless it refers to her gradually lowering her hem-line over an extended period of time. In that case, it transforms the sense of the term 'dropped' from something that happens all at once to an action which is accomplished over an extended period of time. The fact that some relations remain the same and others are altered is more characteristic of literal analogy than figurative analogy. But because so many of the paradigmatic relations remain more or less the same, this case is less clear than others.

In 4.8 'dropped' is not synonymous with 'lowered'. In 4.8, as in 4.1(i), it is partially synonymous with 'let go of' (cf. 'dropped her paint can'/'let go of her paint can' and 'dropped her friend'/'let go of her friend'). In terms of a syntagmatic relation such as CONSEQUENCE, we can say that as a consequence of 4.1(ii) the paint can was 'crushed' and as a consequence of 4.8 the friend was 'crushed'. Yet the paint can and the friend were crushed literally and metaphorically, respectively. We can transfer many implicated predicates and paradigmatic relations which will retain the metaphorical use in the case of friend. Yet the use of 'dropped' in 4.8 is so conventionalized that it hardly strikes us as metaphorical. This is because there no longer seem to be two contents understood here simultaneously. Instead the original source of the analogy is conflated with the new application. But, as we see when we draw out some of the metaphorical implications which the relations of affinity and contrast permit, we can reinstate a lively sense of the originating field. For example:

4.11 The *dropped* friend felt the full impact of the betrayal.

While 'drop' and 'impact' share a semantic field (though not in the sense of a dropped hem or a dropped stitch), 'betrayal' is not in the semantic field of 'dropped' in any sense but a metaphorical one.

Some people have claimed that all language is at its source metaphorical. Perhaps what is really meant is that all language begins with an analogical displacement in which the originating source of the analogy remains active. In literal language it is dropped, and thereafter the relations a term has with other terms (its affinities and oppositions to other terms) are no longer guided by the relations the term possessed in its originating field. Second-order meaning and a connotative semiotic express the idea that two contents are present in metaphor; that is, that the originating field continues to guide the relations a term bears to other terms in its new field of application. Furthermore, it is in this way that metaphors (re)order and (re)structure a conceptual realm or an unarticulated set of experiences. Second-order meaning, therefore, expresses the fact that metaphor is a special and perhaps a primal application of such analogical principles. Rather than there being a tension between the positing of a distinction between first- and second-order meaning and a relational theory of meaning, the distinction permits us to incorporate literal and metaphorical language within a single theory of meaning which at once reveals their commonality and their differentia.

2 THE METAPHORICAL FUNCTION

Distinguishing a Metaphorical Operator

Metaphorical interpretation (henceforth interpretation$_M$ or I_M), then, is conceived as a particular function of the literal, conventional interpretation, interpretation$_{LC}$ or I_{LC}. The purpose of the remainder of the present chapter is to specify the function peculiar to metaphor. Such a function must fulfil the following conditions:

(1) That it assigns a meaning to the focal utterance—the vehicle— that is analogous to a first-order sense.

(2) That it supplies an interpretation which results from mapping some (not all) relations of contrast and affinity that the focal term bears to other terms in its own semantic field on to a portion of the concept domain of a distinct semantic field, namely, the semantic field of the metaphorical frame—the topic of the metaphor.

(3) That it induces a structure in a portion of the domain of the topic such that this portion of the topic domain will be homomorphic to the structure of a portion of the field of the topic.

(4) That the field which serves as the source of the analogy is retained in the metaphorical interpretation, giving the I_M a connotative structure.

'The seal dragged himself out of the office' as fairy-tale. In order to specify the metaphorical operator which is the second-order function I shall contrast the interpretations that we might give to a sentence as it appears in a fairy-tale and as it appears in a passage in which it is used metaphorically. The sentence (2.10 above) 'The seal dragged himself out of the office' might well be a candidate for a metaphorical interpretation. It presents us with an empirical, if not a conceptual, oddity. Consider the sentence in a children's story in which story-book animals go to work in offices and lead lives very similar to those of humans in contemporary industrial societies. Text 4.12 is meant as an excerpt from such a story:

4.12 (i) It had been a bad day.

   (ii) Sammy had just had an unpleasant telephone conversation
         with his uncle, the giant walrus.

   (iii) The seal dragged himself out of the office.

   (iv) His one consoling thought was the refreshing swim that
         would carry him back home.

If we take 4.12 as an utterance, we can see that it meets some, but
not all the necessary conditions A–D, stated at the end of Chapter 2.
We can construct a conversion sentence that would yield a conceptual
incongruity characteristic of metaphor. 'Sammy' in 4.12(ii) is the anaphoric antecedent of 'the seal' in 4.12(iii). Thus by the appropriate
cohesive projection rules we get the conversion sentence:

4.12(ii′) The seal had just had an unpleasant telephone conversation
         with his uncle, the giant walrus.

But telephone conversations are restricted in their collocatability to
terms with a marker [human]. Thus the empirical oddity of a seal
appearing in an office is rendered a conceptual oddity. There is also a
conceptual oddity in the attribution of an avuncular walrus to a seal,
since walruses and seals do not interbreed. Depending on how one
chooses to draw the synthetic/analytic distinction, this could be an
empirical or a conceptual oddity. It would be conversationally odd in
most discourses. None the less, this latter oddity is particularly characteristic of the conventions of children's stories. The existence of such
literary conventions suggests that the world described in 4.12 is not
one we normally experience but is one conjured up in a fairy-tale.
Therefore sentence 2.10 (4.12(iii)) in the context of 4.12 would most
likely not be interpreted metaphorically because here it fails to satisfy
condition B:

That there is nothing in the context to persuade us that the world to
which the utterance applies is substantially different from our own,
or that our usual expectations are not met.

To see how we might interpret 4.12(iii), let us represent it as
follows:

4.13 { [(The seal)] [(dragged himself)(out of)(the office)] }.

Terms not bracketed are elements of U^0; terms enclosed in ( ) are
elements of U^1; terms enclosed in [ ] are elements of U^2; and terms

enclosed in { } elements of U^3. The sentence, an element of U^3, is itself a constituent of the text 4.12. That text can be said to be an element of U^4.

The projection rules first operate on the elements of U^0 and bracket them as elements of U^1. These are then bracketed as elements of U^2, etc., until the entire sentence is interpreted. The partially interpreted lowest-level constituents each have a number of senses, and these combine to give a set of potential interpretations on the next level of complexity where all combinations not proscribed by sc-rules are represented.[8]

We can say further that the range of analogically related meanings is controlled by reference to a given set of default assumptions and to the larger context. If a permissible reading is obtained, then that will normally constitute the interpretation that the hearer will accept. If more than one acceptable reading is obtained, then we need to consider the alternative interpretations in relation to the utterance that is at the next level of complexity, in this case U^5, if such an utterance is available. If it is not available, then the utterance remains ambiguous.

Interpretation proceeds not only from the bottom up but also from the top down. In the downward interpretation, the default assumptions and the larger context play a major role in the selection of semantic fields such that terms cohere and that the appropriately specific informative content is selected. That is, through the downward interpretation, we choose the contrasts and affinities which are relevant to what is being talked about. In information-theoretic terms, we decide what the relevant alternative possibilities are as well as the pertinent informative outer shell which is to be considered the semantic content of the utterance.

The fact that an interpretation takes place both from the bottom up and from the top down means that an interpretation is always revisable in the light of a larger context. The fact that an utterance may always be so revisable also helps to account for the fact that an utterance

---

[8] The linguistic forces of 'resistance' and 'dominance' of which Ross (1981) speaks, should, I believe, ultimately be incorporated in an adequate formulation of the projection rules. In the sentences of 4.1 and 3.12 the sentence frame 'She dropped her . . . ' remains the same, while the different terms that complete the sentence alter the sense we attribute to 'dropped'. The completion expressions in this case *dominate* the term 'dropped'. Ross states: (1981, 9) 'No word dominates all other words and all words are dominated some of the time. Some words are dominated in a great variety of ways, especially common words like "make", completed with "time/trouble/way/appointment/bed/money/merry/haste/cake/dinner/love/war" ' (1981, 9).

which results in an empirically or conceptually odd interpretation can be revised to yield an utterance which is true on a first-order interpretation when its context is expanded, and that an utterance which appears to have a perfectly acceptable first-order interpretation may require a second-order interpretation when its context is expanded. The expanded context may well tell us that the default assumptions operative have altered, thus requiring us to reinterpret the utterance in the light of newly *indexed* projection rules.

If, within the confines of the only available context, there results some empirical or conceptual incongruity, given the general background default assumptions, the literal interpretation(s) are questioned. Were we to encounter the sentence bracketed in 4.13 above and apply the projection rules as referenced to the general default assumptions, we would find that it yielded an empirical oddity. As we have seen, a context such as 4.12 would, in fact, result in a violation of sc-rules, indeed one which would be a selection-restriction violation, through the conversion sentence 4.12(ii'). This would force us to revise a straightforward literal and conventional interpretation of the sentence.

In so far as we have an acquaintance with children's stories and have inferred some of the conventions of this literary form we interpret an empirically odd sentence such as 4.12(iii) so that it has applicability to a world substantially different from our own. This involves to some extent replacing the general background default assumptions with the discourse-specific default assumptions, namely, assumptions specific to the world described in children's stories and fairy-tales. We adopt default assumptions which do not preclude seals going to work in offices, uncles and nephews or nieces belonging to different species, and seals (as well as other animate beings) having telephone (and other sorts of) conversations.

It also involves to some extent revising the meaning of terms so that the participants in 'telephone conversations' need not be restricted to humans or so that 'seal' takes on the language-speaking features of human beings. I believe that the question of whether we could discover talking seals, that is, creatures very much like those we now call seals who had language in the sense that human beings have language, is rather like the question of whether the fluid substance on Twin Earth which looks, tastes, smells like our water, but has the chemical composition XYZ, is water. Perhaps the correct analysis here is that both the 'talking seal' and the Twin Earth 'water' are seals and water only in some extended analogical sense—an analogical sense which becomes possible only with revised default assumptions. Revising the meaning of the terms in the case of the children's story, then, involves extending the range of entities which can be said to engage in 'conversation'.[9] To introduce information-theoretic notions here, the term 'conversation', as understood against our general background default assumptions, includes in its sc-rules, the descriptor [human] as a restriction on both the subject and the object of its prepositional phrase ['with noun phrase']. But the concept of *conversation* has nested within it the informative content of an *interchange*—perhaps an interchange that can be behaviourally manifested. It also has nested within it a notion of *co-operative behaviour* as well as a number of other related concepts. When we talk about a conversation between a seal and a walrus—as in a fairy-tale—the default assumptions are altered, and with the suspension of default assumptions—which is a suspension of disbelief—what is identified under the usual default assumptions as the outer informational shell is no longer the outermost informational shell. We utilize some inner shell to specify the meaning of the term in this context.

Analogical shifts may be reflected in revised selection-restriction rules. Furthermore, it may be the case that certain selection restrictions on a term can more easily be revised than others without significantly changing the meaning of a term, especially in the light of the revision or suspension of the empirical beliefs which may be importantly tied to selection restrictions.[10] When we read the sentences 4.12(i)–(iv) as a text, we interpret them so that they cohere. And yet this text results in conversion sentences which violate selection restric-

---

[9] Notice that, given the general background default assumptions common to those of us who live in an age of telephonic communication, the appropriate restriction on telephone conversations is not to humans *per se* but to operators utilizing human speech. We now regularly speak to tape-recording machines on the telephone, and we are not unlikely to receive unsolicited calls from computers with simulated human voices. We might still question whether such telephone experiences are 'conversations', since that term generally implies spontaneous communicative interactions and tape recorders are not interactive, while computer-simulated voices are not spontaneously generated. These considerations demonstrate the need for language to be sufficiently fluid to respond to empirically changing conditions in the real world, let alone fairy-tale worlds. It is language's very adaptability to apply to fictive instances such as the one pictured in (4.12) that is exploited in its accommodation to changing circumstances of the reality to which it must apply.

[10] It is not within the scope of this book to explore the ways in which selection restrictions may be related to empirical beliefs, but as this discussion and n. 9 indicate, a change in the latter does necessitate a change in the former, if our language is to remain intelligible.

tions, for example, 4.12(ii′). We need to describe some procedure by which we ascribe an interpretation to such conversion sentences. We must understand that the 'he' referred to in 4.12(ii) is the 'seal' of 4.12(iii), and therefore we must be able to interpret the two sentences together so that we can make sense of a seal participating in a telephone conversation. If we were interpreting 'seal' as it occurs in 4.12(ii′) we should need to modify its α-component. In particular, we should conjoin the marker which serves as a selection restriction on the subject of the predicate 'to have a telephone conversation', namely, [human] (or perhaps [humanoid], with the α-component of 'seal'. Or we would displace the feature [human] to seal. Interpreting the 'seal' in text 4.12 involves the addition or deletion of semantic descriptors. Several accounts of the interpretation of metaphor maintain that metaphorical interpretation consists primarily of the addition or deletion of semantic features (or descriptors). This view, which I shall call the *feature addition/deletion thesis*, will be discussed in detail in Chapter 5. But now we have seen that, contrary to this thesis, strategies for the construal of sentences in which there are apparent semantic selection restrictions by the addition or deletion of features need not result in metaphor. Although seals do not, in fact, have telephone conversations, and although we need to alter the concept of a telephone conversation somewhat in order that sentences such as 4.12(iii) become intelligible, the manoeuvres of feature addition or deletion do not necessarily result in metaphorical interpretations.

I am unsure whether we should say that the interpretation I have given in the case of 4.12 is second-order or first-order. On the first view, we should claim that a second-order interpretation was required, because the feature addition/deletion strategy, while not metaphorical, still requires that some terms—for example, 'seal', 'phone conversation'—should be given an interpretation that is a function of their literal and conventional senses. The function is one which conjoins the features of the α- or β-component of one term with (or disjoins them from) the α- or β-component of another. On the second view, we should claim that here, as in many other literary conventions, we were moving into a domain of discourse with a relatively standardized set of assumptions—discourse-specific default assumptions. Were we talking about actual seals, we should have to say that it was impossible or nonsensical for them to carry on telephone conversations, but the very concept of *fairy-tale seals* was such that it did not preclude *them* from executing such feats. Thus, on the second view, we should not have to alter meanings or apply functions to understand and utter 4.12(iii). The change in default assumptions automatically makes this sentence interpretable$_{LC}$, as long as we understand the subscript C to stand for fairy-tale language conventions rather than general background conventions. Nevertheless, the first view would hold, the altered default assumptions still require that we pay heed to the ordinary first-order meanings of terms such as 'seal', and that we perform some standard function on a sentence such as 4.12(iii) to transform the ordinary meaning of 'seal' into the meaning it has in fairy-tale discourse. It would therefore qualify as second-order.

At present, it appears to me that in the case of discourse-specific language in which the default assumptions are fundamentally altered from ordinary background defaults either position can plausibly be maintained. But this is not to say that we can always maintain such an indifference regarding the question of whether a first- or second-order interpretation is appropriate. The alternative to a second-order interpretation described for fairy-tales does not exist for non-discourse-specific language. In the case of indirect speech acts, no change of default assumptions will accomplish what second-order interpretation accomplishes. Beyond this, we can say that once we decide such an issue for discourse-specific domains, the fact remains that the interpretation of a sentence such as 4.12(iii) is significantly different in the case of the fairy-tale and in the case of a story in which it is used metaphorically. In brief, its interpretation remains within a denotative semiotic—it is not connotative in the sense I defined above.

'The seal dragged himself out of the office' as metaphor. Let us now contrast the fairy-tale interpretation with a metaphorical one. Consider sentence 2.10 as it appears in the text below:

4.14 (i)   The corporate existence was becoming too much for Mr S, whom many thought was the ultimate corporation man.

  (ii)   He was constantly on display, trotted out before prospective clients, a performing seal who knew all the requisite clever tricks needed for success in the corporation.

  (iii)   The endless meetings and the tedious details of his job left Mr S bored and weary at the end of the day.

  (iv)   At last, it was five o'clock.

  (v)   The seal dragged himself out of the office.

In 4.14(i), 'Mr S' is in apposition to 'the ultimate corporation man', and these two terms cohere with 'he' and 'seal' in 4.14(ii) and 4.14(iii). We can form the conversion sentence:

4.14 (i′) The corporate existence was becoming too much for the seal, whom many thought was the ultimate corporation man.

Clearly we have an incongruity of a conceptual sort in the apposition of 'seal' and 'man'. What it is to be a man necessarily excludes what it is to be a seal. Through the projective cohesion rules we know that seal and man are co-referential so that the referent of the subject of 4.14(v) must be man, although the subject is 'seal'. In interpreting a text metaphorically, we want to preserve the incongruity marked here by the co-referentiality of two terms whose usual domains of applicability are clearly disjoint—terms which are situated in two distinct semantic fields. Anaphoric reference, the manifest identification of Mr S as a man (through use of the apposition in 4.14(i)), and the co-referentiality of man, seal, and Mr S, close the option that we might be talking of some fanciful Disney-like character, an executive seal.[11] There are no discourse-specific default assumptions which would neutralize this sort of incongruity. Thus, unlike text 4.12, text 4.14 does appear to meet condition B, as well as conditions A, C, and D. If conditions A–D are satisfied then we can suppose that some terms in the text are not to be given a first-order interpretation.[12]

The locus of the incongruity is the term 'seal', the *vehicle* of the metaphor. Its semantic field is substantially different from that of

---

[11] Note that an alternative text does not entirely eliminate such a possibility:

  (i) The corporate existence was becoming too much for Mr S.
  (ii) Again today he was constantly on display, trotted out before prospective clients.
  (iii) As he prepared to leave for the day he thought, 'I am just a performing seal and all I know are some clever tricks that please and amuse my superiors.'
  (iv) The thought disheartened him.
  (v) The seal dragged himself out of the office.

Only a still larger context could disambiguate this text for us. Yet without any evidence to the contrary, our default assumption would be that 'Mr S' named a man.

[12] No doubt, we could embed 4.14 in a larger text such that condition (B) was not met. We could have a science-fiction account of men who were transformed into seals at five o'clock. Embedding a text in a still larger text is always possible and can almost always alter the interpretation of the text in crucial regards. And just as a sentence can be infinitely long, so a text can be infinitely long. In this sense, determining what constitutes a text is somewhat problematic. Yet it is an issue we often resolve through conventional or pragmatic means. There exist conventional and pragmatic ways in which we mark a given text as an *entire* text. However we resolve this issue, the point made above holds for 4.14, as it stands.

which the text speaks: human beings, in general; employees of a corporation, in particular. The field of which the text speaks provides the *topic*. How can we represent the interpretation of 4.14 which will capture the metaphorical use of the term 'seal' and of related terms such as 'clever tricks'? Can we fashion a representation which permits the semantic concatenation of the terms and yet retains the incongruity we claimed as a necessary feature of metaphor?

Conditions Ciii and D are especially important in directing us towards a metaphorical interpretation, for the incongruity specified in Ciii and D will help define the metaphorical operator μ. Given the validity of the strong thesis (condition D), the selection-restriction violations direct us to the divergent semantic fields.[13]

Context Selects out Relevant Semantic Fields

In the case of example 4.1 we have a field which includes seals and a field which includes human office workers. In this case, the captive seal exploited by humans in contrast with the free animal provides the contextually relevant field of features and relations. The relation of the performing seal to his audience, of an exploited animal to his exploiter, of natural capacities used for the benefit of the species to the distortion of these capacities for the idle amusement and benefit of others, provide the contrasts and relations that are transposed on to the corporate human animal and those he serves. The metaphorical mapping of the sentence 2.10 in the context 4.14 induces a structure in the field of human relations in the corporate world which is transposed from the field of seals as performing animals. But both the range and the domain of the function is selected by context.

Were we to place sentence 2.10 in a context such as 4.15 below, the metaphorical function would induce a differently structured set of relations and features.

4.15(i) Mr Harris was a man in his late forties.

---

[13] But that a sentence contains a violation of selection restrictions is not sufficient to guarantee that its constituent terms come from distinct semantic fields. Even within a semantic field, one can form a sentence that violates selection-restriction rules:

Fry the onions in a pan with water.

When 'fry' takes a prepositional phrase beginning with 'with', the noun phrase which follows must be [[fat] v. [oil]]. This constitutes a selection restriction on the object of the prepositional phrase. Yet water is within the semantic field of cooking terms. See Lehrer 1974.

   (ii) His habitual black suit had by now developed a fine sheen, not unlike a seal's coat.

   (iii) His black hair was worn slicked down, and he waddled as he walked.

   (iv) He seemed to have descended not from tree-climbing apes but from primeval sea mammals.

   (v) Tonight he worked late, completing a long and tedious assignment.

   (vi) At last his work was done.

   (vii) The seal dragged himself out of the office.

Again in 4.15 the topic is the office worker and the vehicle is the seal, but in the case of 4.15 it is the appearance and manner of seals which are salient: the black shiny suit, the dark slicked-down hair, the waddling walk. Again, we can talk about the metaphorical transposition not as a transfer of one-place predicates but as a transfer of relations from the semantic field of the vehicle to the conceptual domain of the topic. The seal's physical features and aspects of his manner are the elements and their relations are those they bear to one another and to a seal's environments. Thus the relation of a seal's fur to his body is analogous to that of a man's hair and clothing to his body; the placement of fins on the ground to a pattern of the man's walk, etc.

While the elements of each field remain undisturbed, the relational features between these elements are mapped on to the analogous features of the semantic field of the metaphor's topic. This point will be further illustrated and elaborated in Chapter 7.

As I have tried to illustrate through the juxtaposition of 4.14 and 4.15, most terms belong to a large number of semantic fields. Which semantic fields come into play in the interpretation of the metaphor depends on what interpretation$_{LC}$ we have chosen for the term, and this, we should remember, depends on which, if any, of its senses$_{LC}$ we have chosen for the term to cohere maximally with other senses$_{LC}$ of the other terms in the unit of discourse of which it is a constituent. The focal term or terms of a metaphor will generally not properly concatenate with the terms of the frame, so that it may appear puzzling to say that the sense$_{LC}$ that we choose depends on how the term will maximally cohere with other terms in the discourse. But there will generally be other terms from the topic's semantic field which will provide the necessary context for choosing the relevant sense and field. For example, in the case of both 4.14 and 4.15, we tend to eliminate the sense of 'seal' which is an 'inanimate stamp' because the cohesive projection rules bracket it with 'dragged himself'. There may also be terms which may apply both to the field of the vehicle and to the field of the domain, terms I call *bridge terms*, that may guide the interpretation$_{LC}$ of the focal term. In the case of 4.15 'performance' may be predicated of workers within a corporation as well as seals in captivity.

In the interpretation of an utterance, I shall say that the semantic field indicator is only determined, that is, fully specified, when we obtain the most complete interpretation$_{LC}$ of the utterance in which the term's sense$_{LC}$ is a constituent. The *contrast sets* of the vehicle's semantic field are determined by the senses$_{LC}$ which enter into the interpretation$_{LC}$ of the utterance, if one is available, or the interpretation$_{LC}$ of the constituent terms in so far as they are specifiable as we move from the partially determined lowest-level constituents to the highest-level constituents.[14]

What I have broached here is the difficult question of how a context selects out relevant semantic fields, for both first- and second-order interpretation. Work has yet to be done in this area. The considerations of which I have spoken thus far are primarily semantic. Additional semantic, as well as pragmatic, considerations can also be brought to bear on the problem. A logic of questions sensitive to the issue of semantic fields may help provide answers. We can speculate that the context (linguistic and situational) will give rise to those questions which delineate the appropriate semantic fields, questions which query relevant relations of contrast and affinity. Also pertinent may be

---

[14] Here Ross's (1981) notion of *dominance* is again helpful. Terms that dominate determine the relevant field and relevant relations within a given field of the terms that are dominated. We can speculate that terms that dominate are ones whose meanings are highly specified, which carry very little of their informative content in analogue form. The dominant terms help specify the γ-component of the term(s) they dominate. I suggested above (see note 8) that such dominance relations would participate in the operation of the projection rules. For example, the term 'hook' would be dominated by terms such as 'fish' or 'coat'. If it collocated with fish then we would choose a sense of hook which belonged to the semantic field of fishing terms. Within the field of fishing terms, 'hook' would bear important relations of contrast and affinity to words like 'fish' (noun) and 'to fish' (verb), as well as to 'line', 'rod', 'trout', 'angle'. Its relation to other terms in the field, for example, 'whale' or 'net', would be comparatively insignificant—except if these terms appeared in the context that highlighted these relations. (Note that terms that are easily dominated, terms such as 'make', 'good', and 'very', are unlikely to function metaphorically. To serve as a metaphorical vehicle, a term must be sufficiently resistant to the domination of the topic terms so that we have a metaphor and not merely a literal sense.)

the work in philosophy of science which relativizes explanation to relevant alternatives. (See Van Fraassen 1980, for example.)

A useful pragmatic consideration, *differential* or *selective relevance*, combines the two Gricean maxims 'Be informative' and 'Be relevant':

An explanation or reason is selectively relevant to the question, just in case what it asserts appropriately about one of the possible alternative answers it does not say about all. Information is provided about the topic at hand that is not part of the common knowledge of the audience. (Adler 1984, 167)

A particularly useful passage in which Adler illustrates a 'failure of selectivity' follows:

If you ask me how Tom is doing, as he jogs on by, and I respond, 'Tom's breathing', you will probably construe my remark as implicating something like: 'Tom's exhausted'. Part of the reconstruction of your reasoning would involve the assumption that I am acting under the CP, and would not violate the maxim of informativeness by telling you something that is common knowledge. In this context we would expect the set of relevant alternatives to be (Tom's moving well, Tom's slowing a little, Tom's barely running . . .) (1984, 167)

Adler suggests that we construe 'Tom's breathing' as 'Tom's exhausted' because construing the statement to mean only that Tom's lungs are functioning would be uninformative in a differential sense. That his lungs are functioning would be equally true of all the relevant alternatives.[15] In other words, the contrast {breathing, not breathing} is not the contrast operative here, and we must understand 'breathe' in a special sense that will give it a place among the relevant contrasts. I think that we can construe this passage to suggest that the context provides an implicit set of questions with pertinent alternatives to which any given statement can be viewed as providing an answer. What counts as the implicit set of questions depends on the sort of information that is required within a given context. What counts as the alternative responses has to do with what sorts of things will provide relevant answers. In terms of field theory we could say that the context supplies the conceptual domain within which a query arises and that the alternative responses are given, in part, by the articulations (available in the language) of the pertinent conceptual domain.

But this still leaves certain questions unresolved. How do we

[15] Cf. Chapter 3, Section 2, above, with regard to the information-theoretic importance of relevant alternatives. Cf. also the discussion of the *diagnostic principle* in Tversky 1977 and the discussion of Tversky in Kittay 1982.

transform the context into such a set of questions and how do we
establish the upper and lower bounds of relevance? Adler suggests
some factors which provide the lower bounds of selective relevance.
Many of these are factors that have already proved significant in the
identification of an utterance as metaphorical. They include 'sufficient
mutual knowledge of the topic to provide a shared set of irrelevancies'
(Adler 1984, 168). This notion may be seen to be congruent (or perhaps
identical) to my notion of default assumptions. Where it is pertinent,
knowledge of the craftbound nature of the discourse is important.
That is to say, we need to know not only the formal definitions of the
terms used in a context but also the practices which pertain to that
which is being discussed. Similarly we need social knowledge, for
example, of customs, social behaviour, etc. The context will also sometimes provide explicit reference to what ought *not* to count as relevant.

Another way of putting this is to use Adler's notion of *rather-about*,
which is meant as a restrictive form of selective relevance: 'A sentence
S is *rather-about* an object *a* only if what S asserts about *a*, it does not
say about all relevant alternatives to *a* in the appropriate context'
(1984, 168). A semantic field may be said to include as its elements all
the relevant alternatives to *a*. And the context has the job of providing
for us the information necessary to ascertain what it is that a given
statement is rather-about. This job is accomplished through semantic
means such as selection restrictions, and sentential and cohesive projection rules, and through more pragmatic considerations such as
default assumptions, craftbound knowledge, knowledge of social practices, etc., references to data bases and stereotypes, and explicit affir-
mations and denials. Furthermore, through semantic fields, relevant
sets of alternatives become encoded in the language.

We may note here that the use of models and extended metaphors
set up certain semantic fields as selectively relevant and thereby help to
establish both upper as well as lower bounds for selective relevance.
This is one reason why the use of metaphors and models proves both
fruitful and potentially limiting for a given research programme. This
is a point I shall explore further in the following chapters.

Properties of the Metaphorical Function

The way in which first-order interpretations guide us to a second-
order metaphorical interpretation is through the specification of the
semantic fields and the relevant relations of contrast and affinity
involved in the metaphorical transfer. To account for such metaphori-

cal transfers, I shall posit a function f_M. When we interpret a metaphor whose topic domain is already structured, we make that function homomorphic, that is, we make the function *a relation-preserving mapping from some subset of the semantic field of the vehicle to a subset of the content domain of the topic*. If the metaphor's topic domain (or the relevant portion thereof) is largely unstructured, the function *induces* the structure of relations from the relevant portion of the field of the vehicle. The mapping imposes a structure which exists among the elements of the range upon the elements of the domain. The range of the function contains the appropriate contrast set(s) from the semantic field of the vehicle. The domain contains the appropriate elements from the content domain of the topic. The semantic field of the vehicle is determined by the γ-component of the focal terms; the semantic field of the topic is dependent on the γ-component of the terms of the frame.

I have said that the metaphorical function f_M assumes the property of being *homomorphic*. Discussions concerning metaphor have spoken of an *isomorphism* between the vehicle and the topic (where the topic is already structured). But the function need not be one-to-one; it may be one-to-many or many-to-one. What is important is that it is a relation-preserving property. For example, we may say:

4.16 Jones [a tennis player] was hot early in the day, but cooled down to a mere lukewarm during the last set.

We are then transferring the graded antonymy between 'hot' and 'cold', with the intermediate terms 'warm', 'lukewarm', 'cool', etc., from the field of temperature terms to the domain of tennis—in particular, to the evaluative contrasts of the performance in the game. The relations of affinity and contrast determine the *position* of a term within a field. In 4.16, the mapping must preserve the relation of the graded antonymy; it matters little if one field contains a greater or fewer number of terms than the other. What matters is that the relative *positions* of the terms within their fields are preserved in the transfer and that these positions are interestingly exploited or modified through the metaphorical transfer.

In determining the f_M which will map pertinent contrast sets of the vehicle's semantic field on to the content domain of the topic, we examine the γ-components of the interpretation$_{LC}$ of the metaphorical utterance.

The operation of the metaphorical function. The metaphorical function f_M is a homomorphic function. A contrast set $\{C_a\}(V)$ is defined as an

ordered n-tuple, $<v_1,v_2 \ldots v_n, \varrho^v a>$ belonging to the semantic field
V. If ϱa^v is a relation which orders elements $v_1,v_2 \ldots v_n$ in the contrast
set $\{C_a\}$ in the semantic field V of the vehicle, this relation induces a
structure in a portion of the content domain, $t_1,t_2 \ldots t_n \in T$ of the
topic.

Thus f_M maps $v_1 \rightarrow t_1, v_2 \rightarrow t_2 \ldots v_n \rightarrow t_n$.

This induces the relation ϱ^{t*} between $t_1,t_2 \ldots t_n$. We define ϱ^{t*} such
that, whatever was in ϱ^v, its image will be in ϱ^{t*}.

The asterisk * indicates that ϱ^{t*} is not a relation that is normally in
T. The resulting contrast set will similarly be marked, $\{C_a^*\}$ (U).

Note that:

(a) If the topic belongs to an articulated semantic field, then the
    elements of the semantic field belonging to the pertinent con-
    trast sets are read as having not their usual position within their
    own semantic field but a new set of relations—namely, those
    belonging to the vehicle's field—and thus a new position in
    their own field.

(b) If the topic belongs only to an as yet unarticulated content
    domain, then the structure of the relevant sub-portion of the
    semantic field of the vehicle induces a structure on the content
    domain, and the content domain of the topic becomes articu-
    lated by the terms and relevant relations from the field of the
    vehicle.

I represented the content domain of the topic by $t_1,t_2 \ldots t_n$. Where
(a) pertains, we can identify $t_1,t_2 \ldots t_n$ as concepts. But what of (b)?
How can we pick out anything as $t_1,t_2 \ldots t_n$ in case (b)? Where the
domain is not articulated, it is more pertinent to say that $t_1,t_2 \ldots t_n$
represent relatively discrete *experiential* phenomena rather than unarticulated concepts. They are, then, discrete experiential phenomena
which have been conceptualized only to the extent that they have been
assigned some content domain. The role of metaphor is often to bring
the process of conceptualization to the point of articulation. In this
case, we have in the metaphor the apposition of two contents—one is
in analogue form, the other is completely digitalized. The apposition
leads us to engage in the appropriate mapping which induces structure
and permits the digitalization of the information previously in analogue
form. In this way, the articulative (or expressive) possibilities of the
language as manifest in one semantic field in*form* another content.

Thus, language not only carries content but forms the content it carries. Where no labels exist within the topic domain, the labels $v_1, v_2 \ldots v_n$ will often be adopted, along with the relation ϱ. Again, the use of terms such as 'current' and 'flow' for electrical phenomena illustrates this point. Beyond this, once we have ϱ^{t^*} which orders $t_1, t_2 \ldots t_k$, we may find that the relation posits a t_j not originally part of the experiential phenomenon on to which the contrast set was mapped. This is part of the interest and generative capacity of metaphor. This will be illustrated in Chapter 7.

Some metaphors, particularly poetic ones, leave the domain of the topic somewhat indeterminate. In Chapter 1, I pointed out such an instance in the lines from T.S. Eliot that include the phrase 'the butt ends of my days and ways'. The field of the vehicle is clear enough, but 'my days and ways' are most likely to be understood metonymically. We have a figure operating upon a figure. In interpreting this metaphor, we have to consider possible mappings on to different, although related, conceptual (and experiential) domains. My 'days' may be the successive days of my life or the accumulation of all the days of my life. My 'ways' may be the direction of my occupation, my habits, etc. By considering all the possible distinct domains on to which we map 'butt ends', we also consider the experiential merging of these different domains such that they constitute the single topic of this metaphor.

But even when the metaphor is such that the topic is articulated as a distinct semantic field, we may well want to suspend the usual articulation. We may be looking for a conceptualization which articulates a different experience of the phenomena. Then we find, once again, that we lack appropriate labels to apply to the domain of the topic. The poetic metaphor used by Artistotle, 'sowing around a god-created flame', quoted in the Introduction above, is a good illustration. We do not lack terms for speaking of the rays of the sun. None the less the ϱ relating 'seed' to 'sow' induces a new structure in the domain of the topic such that we now have, as Aristotle says, 'a nameless act'. Again, this is often why we want to use metaphor, to allow us to reconceptualize a familiar domain.

We have viewed semantic fields as consisting of contrast sets, where each contrast set defines a relation between certain elements of a semantic field. From the context which selects the relevant semantic field, we cannot necessarily delineate only one such contrast set. Often the term bears a number of relations to other terms in its field. The metaphorical mapping can potentially carry any of these contrast sets into the topic's content domain. Much of the fluidity and fecundity of different interpretations of a metaphor, all suitable, is due to the different contrast sets that can be employed in the metaphorical transfer. Different interpretations need not be mutually exclusive, if they reflect the different relations a term bears to other terms in its field and hence the different contrast sets of which it is an element. Even if the utterer of the metaphor intended only one such contrast, the reader is free to construe as many as will in fact result in interesting induced relations. Such a reader will not properly be accused of misreading the metaphor. What we commonly say here is that the metaphor reveals more than what was intended by its creator. Our representation provides a nice mechanism by which to account for the multifarious and non-exclusive possibilities inherent in metaphorical interpretation.

The construals which result from the newly induced structure in the topic will be either interpretations of the metaphor or *implications* which result from a particular interpretation. The cognitive and rhetorical rewards of making metaphors lie primarily in the spinning out of metaphorical implications made possible by the conceptual connections effected within semantic fields.

In order to give a semantic representation of the metaphorical utterance, we suppose that the domain of the topic is newly articulated by the relations from the vehicle. In the discussion that follows, v is a term from the semantic field of the vehicle V and t is a term from the semantic field of the topic T.

Semantic Representations of Metaphor

The metaphorical function f_M is a mapping between the content domains. In order to obtain a representation of the interpretation of a linguistic utterance, we also need to posit a metaphorical operator μ, which maps the linguistic constituents of an utterance on to a second-order meaning.

We now want to represent the altered semantic representation of the resulting utterance. We introduce an operator μ, which transforms the interpretation$_{LC}$ of $u \in U^k$, $I(u)$, or, in the case that we can not obtain $I(u)$, which transforms $<I(v), I(t)>$, where v and t are the highest-level interpretable utterances bracketed by the projection rules, into a metaphorical interpretation of u, $I_M(u)$. This operator is meant to reflect the mapping of the f_M in the semantic representation of a metaphorical interpretation of an utterance.

In defining μ, I am assuming that we are working within specified default assumptions that do not alter as our interpretation of u proceeds from the interpretation of its constituents. In the case of a metaphorical interpretation, we have identified an utterance which contains an incongruity (or obeys the IAC) so that we can identify terms coming from two distinct semantic fields; and we assume that we have chosen u as being a *complete metaphorical utterance* containing both the focus and the frame. The focus and frame will serve as the highest-level interpretable constituents of u, in the case u that is not first-order interpretable. We designate v the focal term(s) (or vehicle), and t, the frame term(s) (that is terms from the topic domain).

We express $I_M(u)$ as $\mu(I(u))$, if $I(u)$ is obtainable, otherwise as $I_M(u) = \mu{<}I(v),I(t){>}$. We define the operator μ in terms of two other operators μ' and μ'', whose domains are limited to the selected first-order interpretations of the focal terms and the frame terms, respectively. Then we can say that:

$$\mu({<}I(v),\ I(t){>}) = {<}\mu'I(v),\mu''I(t){>}$$

The operators μ' and μ'' will be defined below.

Procedure for obtaining a metaphorical interpretation of u. We begin by selecting a first-order interpretation of the highest-level interpretable constituents of u, v and t, which we identify as the vehicle or focal term(s) and the frame terms, respectively.

We then define two operations μ' and μ'' that will operate on v and t, respectively. Recalling that $I(v) = s(v)$ (definition of first-order interpretation) and that the term $v={<}E(v),\ s(v){>}$, we define μ as the mapping:

$${<}E(v),\ s(v)\ {>}\ \rightarrow\ {<}E(v),\ s(v),\ s(t'){>},$$

where $s(t')$ is the concept from the domain of the topic on to which v was mapped by f_M.

We now have the result that:

$$\mu'I(v) = {<}s(v),\ s(t'){>}.$$

That is to say, μ' transforms the focal terms into a connotative structure. Again, recall that, by the definition of s_{LC},

$$s(t') = (\alpha_{t'},\ \beta_{t'},\ \gamma_{t'}),$$

where γ_t consists of a semantic field indicator, which directs the speaker and hearer to the semantic field, and pertinent contrast sets which are selected out by the context. But since f_M has resulted in altered relations in T, we see that μ' maps:

$$(\alpha_{t'}, \beta_{t'}, \gamma_{t'}>) \rightarrow (\alpha_{t'}, \beta_{t'}, \gamma_{t'*}),$$

where * indicates an altered ϱ in $\gamma_{t'}$.

To the extent that the α-components of v are excluded by the β-components of t' they fall out of the interpretation of the utterance, for it is primarily the α-components of t' that will cohere with the β-components of t. The function of the β-component of v will similarly be taken over by the β-component of t. Within a frame of terms from T, the concatenation rules of t will dominate. Thus, all that remains of v is the semantic field indicator. And essentially, that is the function of a term used metaphorically, that is, to indicate semantic relations which come from its field that can be made pertinent to the domain of the topic. Finally, then:

$$\mu'I(v) = <\gamma_v, (\alpha_{t'}, \beta_{t'}, \gamma_{t'*})>.$$

We now define μ''. With regard to the interpretation of t, we proceed as above. By the definition of I_{LC} and s_{LC},

$$I(t) = s(t) = (\alpha_t, \beta_t, \gamma_t).$$

Again, the metaphorical function has altered ϱ's of the domain of the topic. Therefore, μ'' maps:

$$(\alpha_t, \beta_t, \gamma_t) \rightarrow (\alpha_t, \beta_t, \gamma_{t*}).$$

At last we have the metaphorical interpretation:

$$I_M(u^k) = <\gamma_v, (\alpha_{t'}, \beta_{t'}, \gamma_{t'*})> + (\alpha_t, \beta_t, \gamma_{t*}).$$

Although the second-order interpretation has dispensed with the selection-restriction violation, it has not yet dispensed with the incongruity needed not only to identify metaphor but also to give metaphor the conceptual edge with which it serves its creative function in language and thought. Below I shall address the question of why this incongruity serves a cognitive end. For now, let us note that the metaphorical interpretation results in a structure distinct in form from a first-order interpretation. Within the metaphorical interpretation we find the presence of what is literally designated by the vehicle, but only through the γ-component of its pertinent sense$_{LC}$ and by the peculiarly altered γ-component of the term(s) belonging to the topic. In this analysis the second-order meaning is not a new meaning attached to a word, whether it is a focal term or one of the frame terms.

To return to text 4.14, in which the metaphorical seal is a corporate man dragging himself home from the office, we can say that we commonly understand 'seal' in a very different sense from its ordinary sense. On our account, this is true in so far as the interpretation of the utterance involves the suppression of the actual concepts and selection restriction rules which comprise part of the meaning$_{LC}$ of 'seal'. But the semantic field indicator, the aspect of the meaning of the term which directs us to the contrasts and affinities 'seal' has with other terms in its pertinent semantic field, remains active in the utterance. We might say that a more radical reinterpretation is given to the world of corporate workers, for these are now understood in the aspect of a performing seal's relations to its master and to the free, unfettered animal. But each reinterpretation can only occur through the complete metaphorical utterance. Notice also that only certain aspects of the topic's field get reinterpreted—offices *per se* remain the same under the metaphorical transformations. They do not enter into the relevant contrasts that are mapped.[16]

Individuation of Semantic Fields

I have spoken of the need to introduce two distinct semantic fields, or at least a semantic field and a distinct content domain. The question of the individuation of semantic fields necessarily arises here. Theoretically this appears to be a vexed question. Yet, pragmatically it is hardly a problem at all. It is generally fairly clear to us when we are speaking of two different matters. Even when the same word is used in two senses such that it would be placed in two distinct semantic domains, we can find the appropriate questions to ask about the two uses to determine if these belong to one or two semantic fields. Semantic fields are, however, not so clearly distinct that there are not overlaps, bridges, and more or less distant fields. It seems likely that empirical

---

[16] Were we to use a conversion sentence possible given this text, 'Mr Harris was a performing seal', we would have to raise the question of whether names belong to semantic fields. If names do not have sense, then perhaps they cannot belong to *semantic* fields. Yet we conceive of people in terms or relations of affinity and contrast, and we do refer to people in terms of their different aspects. In a loose sense we may say that we can establish *ad hoc* contrast sets in which the elements can include proper names belonging to identifiable persons and conceived of in specifiable terms. What is evident is that we use proper names in metaphors, both as topic as in 'Juliet is the sun' (see Introduction) and as vehicle: 'She was his Juliet'.

research in linguistics, psychology, and psycholinguistics could begin
to delineate conceptual areas and semantic domains, and even establish measures of distance (see Sternberg and Nigro 1978). In the
meantime we should be wise to take the counsel Quine gave in regard
to other matters, namely, that we should individuate to the degree that
is relevant to us. We may wish to individuate forests, trees within a for-
est, branches on a tree, leaves on a branch, or the cells which comprise
the leaves of a tree. At what point we individuate these nested entities
depends on our purposes. Similarly we can view semantic fields as
nested and decide to individuate as we see fit for the purposes in hand,
purposes which can generally be discerned from the context.

The Prodigal and Prodigious Child

If the account I have given of the interpretation of metaphor accords
well with a perspectival conception of metaphor, it is because it is
intended as such. However, it is also intended to be more precise than
previous accounts and to capture, through the notion of semantic
fields, the relational nature of metaphorical transfer of meaning. It is
also meant to show how a perspectival view of metaphor can be given
an expression in linguistic terms without the incongruous elements of
the metaphor being conflated. In giving metaphorical interpretation an
expression in terms that build from literal and conventional interpretations, I hope to have shown how metaphors can violate certain
linguistic rules without forfeiting the linguistic goal of mutual understanding. The violation is seen as relative only to the rules governing
first-order discourse. These rules give way to a second set of rules—
ones which are far less constraining but which none the less establish
procedures for and define bounds of interpretation. This is true of
metaphor and of the many phenomena which Grice has subsumed
under the umbrella concept of conversational implicature.

We can say that metaphor is a *meta-* phenomenon. But unlike metalanguage, which takes as its object linguistic terms, metaphor is *meta-
nomological*—its object is a set of linguistic rules or principles. If we
move from a discussion of *violation* to a discussion of *creativity*, we get a
clearer view of what I mean to say. As Dell Hymes points out, the
linguistic creativity to which Chomsky has alerted us, the ability to produce and understand novel sentences, is concerned with the systemic
potentiality of the language. In contrast, the use of metaphor exhibits
' . . . that kind of creativity which consists of the discovery of possibilities implicit in a [linguistic] system, but not yet discovered, not yet

known' (cited in Basso 1976, 116). To this, Basso adds: 'Creativity in Chomsky's sense consists in the unfolding of existing structures. Creativity in metaphor consists in the use of existing structures to forge new ones . . . What distinguishes the two even more sharply, I think, is that the former is achieved through adherence to grammatical rules while the latter is achieved by breaking them' (1976, 117). But merely breaking rules is not sufficient for metaphor; it is only *certain* rules that are broken, and this too is accomplished in a systematic and even rule-governed manner. It is to this systematic procedure that we have turned our attention in the previous chapters.

Like the Prodigal Son, who violates the rules of the community by straying off but, on returning home, is still more prized than the ever-obedient child, metaphorical use of language is often more valued than literal use. Its contribution is not only linguistic but conceptual, for the violation of conceptual constraints inherent in the meaning of the terms brings about a new conceptualization, a new way of conceiving some content domain.

5

Alternative Approaches: A Critique

NOW that a theory of metaphor has been set forth, we are in a good position to evaluate other attempts to formulate a theory of metaphorical meaning. In this chapter I shall critically examine some of those alternative approaches. I shall limit the scope of my critical comment to those theories incompatible with my own. Theories which are important predecessors have been discussed in Chapter 1, and theories, such as Lakoff and Johnson's (1980), which are compatible in many regards with my own are treated in passing throughout the text. The one significant exception is the view of Davidson which it proved important to examine earlier (Chapter 3, Section 1) in so far as it posed a serious challenge to the very enterprise of constructing a theory of metaphorical meaning.

The investigation will consist of two parts. In Sections 1 and 2, I shall look at alternative theories of interpretation. In Section 3, I shall show how theories of metaphor which are based on the major non-relational theories of word meaning are inadequate. Sections 1 and 2 look at two theses which recur in countless contemporary works on metaphor: the predicate transfer thesis and the feature addition/ deletion thesis. Section 3 completes the task, begun in Chapter 3, of justifying the need for a relational theory of meaning. While, in Chapter 3, I argued against Davidson's non-relational theory of sentence meaning as an adequate base for a theory of metaphor, in Section 3 of the present chapter, I shall similarly argue against non-relational theories of word-meaning.

The countless theories—of philosophers, linguists, psychologists, and literary theorists—proposing detailed accounts of how we interpret metaphorical expressions may be comprehended under Scheffler's (1979) six-fold classification: intuitionist, emotive, formulaic, intensional, interactional, and contextual.

According to the *intuitionist*, metaphors, unlike literal statements, cannot be construed from the meaning of their parts. Hence their interpretation requires an act of intuition and defies analysis. For the *emotivist*, metaphorical meaning is derived from the word's (or words') emotive force rather than from its (or their) cognitive meanings. Metaphorical interpretation, therefore, requires that we suppress the cognitive meanings of the words used in a metaphorical utterance in favour of their emotive sense. In the account given in Chapter 4 we have seen how metaphorical meaning is derived from the constituents of the metaphorical utterance, in a manner analogous to the way in which literal meaning is so derived. We need no more intuition to interpret metaphors than we need to interpret literal language. Similarly, we have seen that we need posit no additional emotive sense, and that the metaphorical meaning of an utterance is derived from (though not identical to) the literal meanings of the constituent terms. These two groups of theories will not be examined further.

The *formulaic* approach contrasts particularly with the intuitionist one, and maintains that we can analyse metaphorical interpretation by regarding metaphors as implicit comparisons for which we need to supply the formula that gives us the full statement of the comparison. Formulaic approaches are characterized by their emphasis on the possibility of finding appropriate formulas through which to explicate metaphor, and by their insistence that the relation between the components of metaphor is a comparison.

The *intensionalist*, like the emotivist, takes the view that metaphorical interpretation involves attending to a sense distinct from that which is taken as the denotative or designative sense of the metaphorically used words, and that this connotative sense, which is latent, becomes prominent when the denotative sense is blocked. But the intensionalist believes that the meaning we attend to is still cognitive. For the intensionalist, metaphorical interpretation involves an incongruity which causes the suppression of the designative sense of the vehicle in favour of the connotative meaning; connotations generate predicates which are then available to be attributed to the topic of the metaphor.[1]

Scheffler distinguishes the intensional from the *interactional* approach in that the latter is not constrained by non-designating predicates which are indeed true of the vehicle. According to the interactionist, in interpreting a metaphor we may consider properties which are known to be false but which are generally believed to be true of the metaphorically used terms. More correctly, I believe, we should say that the intensionalist holds that the *intension* of the vehicle term is to

[1] Scheffler largely attributes intensionalism to Monroe Beardsley.

be considered, while the interactionist prefers to speak of the associations or implications of the term. For the interactionist, the associated or implicated predicates are, whenever possible, made to 'fit the principal subject . . . either in normal or in abnormal senses' (Black 1962, 41).

When we examine most versions of the formulaic, the intensionalist, and the interactionist approaches, we find that they embody one of two theses, both of which I believe to be faulty. I shall call these the *predicate-transfer thesis* and the *feature addition/deletion thesis*. In the predicate transfer thesis, the interpretation of metaphor is seen as involving the displacement or projection of predicates of (or attributes of, or implicated assertions about) the vehicle term on to the topic of the metaphor (or, in the case of the interactionist, displacement or projection from the topic to the vehicle term as well).

An emphasis on interpretation has led a number of theorists to integrate metaphorical interpretation into the most prominent linguistic theory of interpretation, componential semantics. These writers do not speak of predicates, but regard metaphorical interpretation as the addition or deletion of semantic features, linguistic or empirical, of the terms involved in the metaphorical utterance. This I shall call the feature addition/deletion thesis.

Both theses falter in the crucial respect that they cannot give an account of the double semantic relation to which Henle (1965) has called our attention, and they cannot describe, in linguistically specific ways, the double semantic content which I have argued is critical for an understanding of the cognitive import of metaphor. Without an account of the double semantic content of metaphor, we cannot give a clear answer to the question Davidson raises when he writes: 'Why does Black think a literal paraphrase "inevitably says too much—and with the wrong emphasis"? Why inevitably? Can't we, if we are clever enough, come as close as we please?' (1981, 215.)

Scheffler attributes *contextualism*, in its initial form, to Goodman. Goodman's (1968) relatively early account is, I believe, still among the most interesting, and it does not succumb to the criticism I level at the above theses. The contextualism Scheffler advocates and elaborates depends on the context for the 'set of cues relevant to [the utterance's] interpretation' (Scheffler 1979, 118). Scheffler also argues that context alone is not sufficient, but that a knowledge of the term's literal application is necessary to guide the interpretation of metaphor. While Scheffler's emendation is somewhat helpful, I shall argue that it is the

nominalism of both Goodman's and Scheffler's accounts that is difficult to reconcile with the double semantic import Goodman himself
wishes to attribute to metaphor. In the account that I have given, I have
attempted to specify how context functions in the interpretation of
metaphor without conflating the two distinct semantic contents in
metaphor. The writers I criticize have often recognized the significance of the double semantic movement in metaphor. But they have
not been able to incorporate it in their analyses of how we interpret
metaphor.

I THE PREDICATE TRANSFER THESIS

Intensional and Interactional Approaches

According to the Aristotelian tradition, metaphor was regarded as the
application of a name to something which was not its proper one, the
basis for the transfer being similarity between the thing usually named
by the term and its new denotatum. It has now become fairly standard
practice to regard metaphor as a matter of predication rather than
naming (see, for example, Ricœur 1978b). Those who wish to take a
less linguistic and more conceptual approach speak of the transfer of
'attributes' or 'implicated assertions'.

Both the positions taken by Black, in his early and in his revised versions of interactionism, are representative of the predicate transfer
thesis. The most systematic statement concerning the inner workings
of a metaphor in Black's original position may be found in the following passage:

The effect, then, of (metaphorically) calling a man 'wolf' is to evoke the wolf-
system of related commonplaces. If the man is a wolf, he preys upon other animals, is fierce . . . Each of these implied assertions has now to be made to fit
the principal subject (the man) either in normal or in abnormal senses . . . A
suitable hearer will be led by the wolf-system of implication about the principal
subject. But these implications will *not* be those comprised in the commonplaces *normally* implied by literal uses of 'man.' The new implications must be
determined by the pattern of implication associated with literal uses of the
word 'wolf.' Any human traits that can without undue strain be talked about in
'wolf-language' will be rendered prominent, and any that cannot will be
pushed into the background. The wolf-metaphor suppresses some details,
emphasizes others—in short, *organizes* our view of man. (1962, 41.)

This sounds helpful, but it cannot be quite right. To begin, the implications of 'the wolf-system of related commonplaces' must be indefinite and perhaps infinite. Therefore it is absurd to think that *each* of these implied assertions (and why must they be assertions?) gets applied to the principal subject. Following Scheffler (1979), we can note that, even if we confine ourselves to commonplace beliefs concerning the subsidiary subject (the vehicle), there are many predicates which can be formed, such as 'are not ironing-boards', believed to be true of wolves, which have no import whatsoever in the interpretation of the metaphor.

Indeed, as Black himself realizes in his 1979 essay, just what characteristics get chosen depends in large measure on the topic, or principal subject—this, one may assume, is part of what is 'interactive' in interactionism. Hence, the system associated with 'wolf' used as a metaphorical vehicle for man will differ significantly from that associated with the term used as a vehicle for, let us say, the wind, as in the line:

5.1   In the deserted land, the wind, a lone wolf, howled in the night.

Commonplaces cited by Black—the wolf as scavenger, fierce, hungry, predatory, etc.—figure little or not at all in the wolf-system when it serves as a vehicle for the wind. It is not that they cannot be made *to fit* the principal subject; it is rather that most of these attributions would not even be chosen in this figuration. As we have seen, Black suggests that we construct a set of implications, *an implication complex*, guided by the primary (formerly principal) subject and projected on to the secondary (formerly subsidiary) subject: 'the presence of the primary subject incites the hearer to select some of the secondary subject's properties' (1979, 29). Thus, Black believes that he has resolved the issue of which predicates are to be chosen, ruling out the sort of objections Scheffler and I have mentioned.

However there are still problems, not addressed in the revised interactionism, with the view that metaphorical interpretation is a 'projection' of implicated predicates from the secondary subject (or vehicle) on to the primary subject (or topic). We recall that in speaking of the man as wolf metaphor, Black suggested that those human traits which became prominent could 'without undue strain be talked of in wolf-language'; the rest would be 'pushed into the background'.

Two sorts of difficulty remain. First, there are predicates applicable to wolves which offer no strain whatsoever when applied to man. These are the predicates or implications which apply to (or concern) *both* the topic and the vehicle of the metaphor. For example, in the *man as wolf* metaphor, W1–W3 are believed true of wolves and are easily and literally applied to man:

W1 Wolves are living, animate beings.
W2 Wolves are mammals.
W3 Wolves are carnivorous.

We could construct a parallel implication-complex which was literally true of man, but this would be of no interest or help in interpreting 'man is a wolf', although we would still be guided by the principal subject in forming the implication-complex W1–W3. We would need criteria for determining which implications and predicates of the vehicle, literally applicable to the secondary subject, were significant in the interpretation of the metaphor.

Secondly, it may be true of banal metaphors such as 'man is a wolf' that what is made prominent are those predicates of the vehicle that can be projected on to the topic without undue strain. But most interesting metaphors involve a great deal of strain on language and thought. Witness some of the metaphors I have already discussed: gardens as 'slums of bloom', and life as cigarette 'butt ends'. The strain experienced in these metaphors has to do with the *tension* between vehicle and topic. It is a tension which Black himself acknowledges to be an important aspect of metaphor.[2]

Curiously, Beardsley, who is responsible for the *controversion theory* of metaphor—'A metaphor is a significant attribution that is either indirectly self-contradictory or obviously false in its context' (1958, 142)—adopts a position in which the tension, while crucial for identifying metaphors, is again resolved in their interpretation. He writes:

The problem of construing the metaphor is that of deciding which of the modifier's connotations can *fit* the subject, and the metaphor means *all* the connotations that can fit—except those that are further eliminated by, because they do not fit, the larger context. (1958, 143.)

Beardsley, who serves as Scheffler's paradigmatic intensionalist, would be immune to the objection I raised to an analogous position of Black's when I pointed to sentences W1–W3. Beardsley could say that such properties were part of the definition rather than the connotation of 'wolf'. Connotations such as aggressiveness, fierceness, etc. would be

---

[2] Wheelright (1962; 1968) is important in emphasizing the tensive theory of metaphor.

made to fit the topic of the metaphor and these would enter into our interpretation of the metaphor.

But if we want to preserve the tension, we cannot give an account of interaction which neutralizes all tension between vehicle and topic. Unfortunately, this is what appears to happen in Black's and Beardsley's accounts. Unless this tension is preserved, the 'suppress[ion of] some details' and emphasis of others does not really *organize* our view of man, for unless the categories of man and wolf remain distinct we cannot use one distinct entity—with its systematic interconnections—to reconceive the other. Instead the metaphor would serve as a neologism naming a hybrid creature, part-man, part-wolf. Rather than one subject serving as a perspective on a second, the two subjects are merely conflated.

In the revised interactionism, the more precise analysis using the implicative complexes gives rise to the question of how we are to understand statements that result from the projection of predicates from the secondary subject on to the primary subject. Let us consider Black's example; 'Marriage is a zero-sum game'. He outlines the implication-complex of 'game' as follows:

G1 A 'game' is a *contest*;
G2 between two opponents;
G3 'in which one player can win only at the expense of the other.' (1979, 29)

Accordingly, on at least one possible interpretation, marriage would have projected on to it the following claims:

M1 A marriage is a struggle;
M2 between two contestants;
M3 in which the rewards (power? money? satisfaction?) of one contestant are gained only at the other's expense.' (1979, 30)

Are we to understand M1–M3 as literal or as metaphorical assertions? Black means them to be literal: 'Here, the "projected" propositions can be taken literally—or almost so, no matter what one thinks of their plausibility' (1979, 30). But I do not believe that they can be so understood. First a 'struggle' describes an activity. While marriage, understood as an institution or contractual agreement, is not the sort of thing that can be properly described as a 'struggle', living the married life may perhaps be literally so described. Still, literally to predicate of marriage that it is a struggle need imply nothing about contestants. We mean to say only that it is difficult to achieve the happiness, harmony, etc. desired of the married life. Both partners can struggle together, rather than against each other. Secondly, the persons who are married are literally spouses or (given current parlance) literally husband and wife, or perhaps (given a conception of marriage as a contractual agreement between spouses) marriage partners. But they are 'contestants' only if marriage is already metaphorically conceived of as a game or struggle involving contestants—they are not literally 'contestants' at all. To call them 'contestants' involves what Lakoff and Johnson (1980) have called a metaphorical (rather than a literal) implication.[3]

Lastly, in so far as any human enterprise can involve 'rewards', in the sense of some desired end or goal, that notion can indeed be literally applied to marriage. But rewards 'gained only at the other's expense' are a case of winning only when the participants are conceived of as contestants—when there is some measure of equality to be challenged such that there can be a contest in which one may emerge as superior. If we expunged the metaphorical 'contestant', we would have something more akin to exploiting than to winning. And, at least within certain feminist construals of male–female relations, the concept of exploitation would be literally, not metaphorically applied to marriage. But it is not a literal explication consonant with the leading metaphor of *marriage as a zero-sum game*. Thus what appears in M3 to be a literal explication appears so only relative to what is already a metaphorical reconception of the topic. That is, M3, like M2, appears literal only if we have already accepted the framework (which is metaphorical) of marriage as a zero-sum game. Within *that* framework it is not incongruous and not metaphorical to call the spouses 'contestants'. To call them 'contestants' is only metaphorical if we maintain, simultaneously, our conception of marriage as, let us say, a societal practice of a certain sort that precludes its conceptualization as a contest.

Must the projected predicates be literally applied? If the predicates (or implications) transferred are to be applied metaphorically, then the problem of interpreting metaphors has merely been pushed back one step. We would now have to ask how we interpret the metaphorical

---

[3] Lakoff and Johnson, whom I would not characterize as predicate transfer theorists but who do speak of the complex of implications involved in the interpretation of a metaphor, are willing to grant that these implications are only sometimes literal, and more often metaphorical. Yet they do seem to suggest that there is an ultimate reduction of these metaphorical implications to literal implications.

interpretation of a metaphor. An account would have to eventuate in
a set of literal projections—unless, that is, we make the claim that all
language is metaphorical. The account of Lakoff and Johnson (1980)
comes close to this latter view. Metaphoric interpretation is characterized as a spinning out of metaphoric implications, implications
which themselves might not be grounded by literal projections. Yet
even Lakoff and Johnson, whom I do not consider as predicate
transfer theorists, appear to insist that the metaphorical conceptual
systems are grounded on certain concepts which are directly experienced and may be taken as literal. These are the 'emergent concepts'
(1980, 59). None the less, Lakoff and Johnson's account is not really
a theory of metaphorical interpretation. They are more concerned
with demonstrating the prevalence of metaphor in our language and
conceptual schemes than with questions of how we interpret a metaphorical utterance when we encounter one. The relevant point here
is that, while Lakoff and Johnson do take much of our language to
be metaphorical, they still see the metaphorical schemes, whether
linguistic or conceptual, as grounded on the literal. They provide no
argument that could give succour to the predicate transfer theor-
ist who might want to maintain if we had a set of metaphorical projections we would have no need to reduce these further to a set of
literal projections.

But the interactionist who insists on literal projections faces a
dilemma. If interpretation must ultimately be rendered in terms of
literally applied predicates or implications, assuming that such a
reduction is possible, then in what sense can the interactionist consistently maintain that metaphors are irreducible to literal
paraphrase? It would appear that the set of predicated or implicated
claims literally true (or believed to be true) of the vehicle, which
are to be literally applied to the subject of the metaphor, are
equivalent to a literal paraphrase of the metaphor. Therefore it
seems that one cannot consistently hold the interactionist position
and maintain that interpretation is a process of predicate transfers,
literally applied.

The Formulaic Approach

Ortony (1979*b*; 1979*c*) seems to escape both the antagonism between
interactionism and the predicate transfer thesis and the difficulty
concerning the choice of predicates to be applied to the topic of the
metaphor. Ortony's views may be regarded as a sophisticated version

of the formulaic approach.[4] That is to say, rather than claiming that metaphor is an implicit comparison, the explicit form of which is simile, Ortony believes that while 'it is probably not possible to map all metaphors into similes', for simile and metaphor alike, 'the process of making comparisons is of fundamental importance' (1979c, 188–9). Ortony's views are of special interest because, unlike Henle and others who emphasize the role of similarity in metaphor, he works with a distinctive theory of similarity, that expounded by Tversky (1977).

Tversky proposes a feature-matching model to oppose to the standard geometric model of similarity. The received view takes similarity as the relation of distance between objects regarded as points in geometric space. On the geometric model, if *a* is similar to *b*, then *b* is similar to *a*. When similarity is thought of as a measure of distance between objects conceived as points in a geometric space, then, as Black (1962) has pointed out in criticizing the comparison view, we can always find some regard in which two objects are similar. But in the feature-matching model, we conceive of objects as clusters of features, and judgements of similarity as feature-matching procedures. On this view, the similarity between two objects is a 'linear combination of the measures of their common and distinctive features'. (Tversky, 1977, 327). Moreover, within a given matching, not all the features of an object are salient and *diagnostic*, that is, determinant in characterizing the similarity between the two (or more) objects. Which features will be salient and diagnostic will depend on the grouping in question.[5]

On the geometric model, similarity is symmetrical since the distance between point *a* and point *b* is equal to the distance between *b* and *a*. But on a feature-matching model, judgements of similarity need not be symmetrical. Tversky points out that we are more likely to claim that the son is like the father than that the father is like the son. If we were to make the latter claim, its significance would be quite distinct from the former claim. While not all judgements of similarity exhibit this asymmetry, metaphors and similes always do. This, Ortony claims, is a 'radical asymmetry', in which lies the key to the interpretation of

---

[4] This holds true of the views represented in Ortony 1979c and in the section of Ortony 1979b, in which he speaks of 'salience imbalance'. However, those portions of the work in which he speaks of 'domain incongruence' do not easily accommodate themselves to the formulaic approach.

[5] It would be interesting to ask if some form of the diagnosticity principle is not at work in the interactive process through which the meaning of a word is specified by its context. In another work, Kittay 1982, I have used the diagnosticity principle to show how similarity is 'created' in the case of metaphor.

metaphor. We should make the latter statement if we wanted to remark on the childishness of the father or the fact that the father shared some prominent characteristic of the son. However, he believes that Tversky's view of similarity as feature-matching needs to be supplemented. Ortony points out that not only do features, taken by themselves or within a given context, have different degrees of salience, but that, independent of context, the same feature may have one degree of salience as a feature of object *a*, and a different degree of salience as a feature of object *b*:

Being made of iron is a more important attribute of magnets than it is of railroad tracks; and even though not necessary for either, being red is a more important attribute of a fire truck than it is of a brick. (1979*b*, 163.)

One of Ortony's central theses is that metaphors and similes arise when a comparison between *a* and *b* involves an imbalance of the salience of certain features in *a* and *b*.

To understand Ortony's point, consider the comparative statement '*a* is like *b*' in the case that there are features f_1, f_2, and f_3 which *a* and *b* share and which are:

(i) salient in both *a* and *b*;
(ii) salient in *a* but not in *b*;
(iii) salient in *b* but not in *a*;
(iv) not salient in either *a* or *b*.

Ortony claims that (i) would result in a literal comparative statement, (ii) and (iv) in nonsensical or trivial claims, and (iii) in metaphor or simile. Stated another way, simile and metaphor depend on a *salience imbalance* weighted towards *b*. Indeed it may even be the case that it is not known beforehand that features f_1, f_2, and f_3 are in *a*, but that these features get projected on *a* (in the form of predicates applied to *a*, because they are salient in *b* and are predicable of *a*).[6]

Thus Ortony provides the criteria, missing in Black's account, by which to pick out the features or attributes of the vehicle made relevant by the subject of the metaphor. The criteria select features which are *both* literally true of the subject and pertinent to a metaphorical interpretation of the utterance. These need to be highly salient for the vehicle but not highly salient for the topic of the metaphor. These will

---

[6] Later in 1979*b*, Ortony discusses 'domain incongruence' as a source of metaphor. This is not subject to the criticisms I make of salience imbalance.

be those highly salient attributes of *b* which may be applied literally to *a* (or, if they are metaphorical implications applicable to *a*, then we presume a recursive procedure whereby there is ultimately some attribute which is literally applicable), while other highly salient attributes of *b* cannot be applied to *a* at all. Ortony (1979*b*, 164) states: 'If two things share some characteristics that are important to both, then those things will be perceived as literally similar.'

But is this latter claim true? Consider, Shelley's metaphor of workers as bees in example 1.7 above. Certainly, a *high level of activity* is a highly salient attribute of bees which is pertinent to the metaphor and literally applicable to workers forging 'many a weapon'; yet it is also a highly salient attribute of workers. Hence it appears that we have a counterexample to Ortony's rule that the attributes metaphorically projected should not be salient in both topic and vehicle.

Ortony appears to be prepared for such a counterexample since he also claims that salience imbalance is not the only source of metaphor. He claims that when an attribute is highly salient in both subject and vehicle, but there is what he calls a 'domain incongruence', the attribute in question is indeed not likely to be the *same* attribute but rather a *similar* attribute; that is, the attribute of the vehicle needs some suitable modification in order to become an attribute within the domain of the vehicle. His example is the predicate 'is a channel for carrying liquids' (1979*b*, 166). This highly salient attribute of both blood vessels and aqueducts may be thought of as the basis for the simile:

5.2 Blood vessels are like aqueducts.

But, Ortony claims, because there are so many kinds of channels and so many sorts of liquids that might flow through these channels, it is rather misleading to say that the predicate 'is a channel for carrying liquids' is the same when attributed to blood vessels and to aqueducts. We ought instead to say that there are two similar attributes, expressed by the predicates 'is a channel for carrying blood' and 'is a channel for carrying water', which are similar, and that it is the *structural* similarity of these across distinct domains, the domain of blood vessels and the domain of aqueducts, that is the source of metaphor. This is reminiscent of the valuable remarks made in Black 1962 and stressed in Black 1979 concerning the isomorphism between the implicative systems of the topic and vehicle. It also resonates with our discussions concerning analogy and polysemy.

One might well adopt such an analysis for the *bees as workers* metaphor and the attribute of having a high level of activity. I believe Ortony's strategy to be correct here.[7] But it is worth noting that to deal with what Ortony speaks of as a 'higher order' of similarity, that is, the similarity of attributes as opposed to the similarity of objects having those attributes, or to speak of an isomorphism between two systems of implications, it will not do to enumerate the relevant predicates of the vehicle and merely project them on to the subject. The predicates would need to be altered, and altered in a systematic fashion, to accommodate the incongruity of the two domains. For this purpose, Ortony himself employs a diagrammatic representation of schemata for 'aqueduct':

Aqueduct Schema—isa $(x,$ Aqueduct)
A1: isa $(x,$ channel)
A2: flows through (water, x)
A3: purpose of (A1,A2)
(etc.)

and for 'blood vessel':

Blood-Vessel Schema—isa $(x,$ Blood vessel)
A1: $(x,$ channel)
A2: flows through (blood, x)
A3: purpose of (A1,A2)
A4: isa (artery, x)
(etc.) (1979b, 167)

The diagrammatic representation is far more suitable for representing both the systematic nature of the differences in the predicates appropriate to the two domains and the openness of the interpretive process generated by such a conception of metaphoricity. This openness is not evident when one conceives of metaphorical interpretation as an enumeration of transferred predicates. Both the systematicity and the openness within the constraints of the systematicity are what make literal paraphrase of metaphor ultimately so elusive. The schematic representation of the source of metaphoricity as 'attribute inequality in incongruent domains' is much closer to the mark than

---

[7] Though later in the same essay (Ortony 1979b) he writes that he believes salience imbalance to be a *necessary condition* for metaphoricity, even in the presence of 'attribute inequality'. Yet there appears to be no important salience imbalance either in the bees as workers metaphor or in the blood vessel as aqueduct metaphor. Ortony, I believe, errs in considering the 'attribute inequality' to be of greater moment than the fact that the comparison takes place across incongruent domains.

salience imbalance. Salience imbalance presumes what I have called the predicate transfer thesis, although it modifies that position by offering constraints on the predicates that can be transferred. Without denying that salience imbalance can often be found in metaphor, I believe that it is not a distinct source of metaphoricity, but is itself derivative of domain incongruence. I have argued that a necessary condition for an utterance to be a metaphor is that the subject and vehicle must come from two distinct semantic fields. If non-literal comparison involves a comparison across distinct and incongruent domains or semantic fields, then the fact that highly salient features of the vehicle fail to be highly salient features of the subject is not at all surprising, for the domain to which an object belongs is generally determined by those of its features which are highly salient. And when a feature appears to be highly salient for objects in distinct domains, it is generally, as Ortony so perspicuously notes, because it is not the *same* feature, but a feature that bears an analogous structure or, we might add, an analogous position in the two domains. Thus if domain incongruence is indeed a necessary condition for metaphor, then the two separate sources Ortony identifies, salience imbalance and attribute inequality, both, in fact, derive from a comparison across incongruent domains.

In the end, predicate transfer as metaphorical interpretation will not do, even if only the appropriate and relevant predicates can be selected. The predicate transfer thesis will not distinguish metaphorical discourse from other non-standard, though literal and non-anomalous, discourse such as fairy-tale language or certain technical language in which ordinary words are used in a special fashion.

This sort of concern is less problematical in the case of simile than in the case of metaphor and most problematical in the case of metaphors in which the subject is not explicitly mentioned. Compare the following:

5.3 Coming into the office, the wolf created quite a stir.
5.4 The man who came into the office was a wolf.
5.5 The man who came into the office was like a wolf.

In the case of 5.5, we are explicitly comparing a man to a wolf, although the basis of the comparison may well be a non-literal one. But if 5.4 occurred in a science-fiction story or other fanciful tale in which persons were mysteriously transformed into beasts—as Gregor Samsa, in Kafka's tale awakens to find himself transformed into a 'monstrous kind of vermin'[8]—it would be meant as a literal statement. The interpretation of 5.3 is still more problematical. From 5.3 alone, we do know if the sentence concerns an actual wolf who has found his way into an office, an implausible but not impossible state of affairs; if it speaks metaphorically of a human being as a wolf; or if we are in the midst of a literary fantasy in which wolves perform actions not unlike those of persons within our own culture, and may even work in offices.

Black (1962) claims that, in the metaphor 'man is a wolf', the human traits that can be spoken of as wolf traits become prominent; and those that cannot, recede in importance. Let us say that using the concept of salience imbalance we have resolved which wolf traits we wish to employ in our interpretation. But the strategy of applying wolf traits to the subjects of 5.3 and 5.4 fails to distinguish the distinct interpretative processes involved in each of the aforementioned interpretative possibilities. Often there is only a thin line between a metaphor and the creation of a fictive entity. In the predicate transfer view of interpretation, we have no clue when we cross over the line from the literal, though fanciful, use of language that makes possible a fictive creation or an implausible but not impossible situation of some creature in a possible world very much like our own actual world to the metaphorical use of language by which we remain, at all times, concerned with man as we know and can imagine him within the constraints of our actual world, but speak of him in non-literal terms. Even if we were to grant that the predicate transfer thesis, when adequately accompanied by suitable criteria, specifies which predicates are to be transferred, it fails to capture the special problem of interpretation posed by metaphorical language. In contrast, in my account of metaphorical interpretation in the previous chapter, I have shown how the nature of the semantic representations will distinguish the literal, though fanciful, interpretation from the metaphorical.

Contextualism

Goodman's position, which I have referred to above, and which Scheffler has called contextualism, does much to amplify our understanding of the double semantic move. The vehicle provides a scheme of labels. But rather than applying the labels to their familiar realm, we

---

[8] In Kafka's (*Metamorphosis*, trans. by A. L. Lloyd, (New York: The Vanguard Press), 1976) story, the transformation is literal, although the story as a whole may be meant to be understood metaphorically.

apply them to a novel realm. Although the new application is in some way guided by the habitual realm, we need posit no pre-given similarity or iconic relation between the two realms. While Goodman's willingness to do without the notion of resemblance is a kind of intellectual heroism in the field of metaphor studies, Scheffler detects a lack in Goodman's theory which is probably attributable to this radical stance. Scheffler complains that Goodman provides inadequate criteria for choosing to which new realm the label is meant to apply. That is, Goodman does not explain how the habitual use of the vehicle is to guide the new use.[9] Scheffler tries to supplement Goodman by suggesting that it is context which provides the needed guidance. My own account above has proved Scheffler right, and it has, moreover, made explicit the contribution of context in this regard. However, while context plays a critical role in the interpretation of metaphor, I have argued that context also plays a crucial role in the interpretation of non-metaphorical utterances. The important question for metaphorical interpretation, is not, as Scheffler seems to suggest, *whether* but *how* context plays its part. As we have gained some understanding of how context works in specifying the meaning of a word, phrase, or sentence, we have been able to supplement Goodman's views accordingly.

A more particular difficulty with the Goodman–Scheffler[10] theory concerns their insistence on a nominalism which robs the double semantic move of a double semantic content.

Goodman writes:

In all this, the aptness of an emphasis upon labels, of a nominalistic, but not necessarily verbalistic orientation, becomes acutely apparent once more.

---

[9] One wonders what Goodman might have to say to Tversky's conception of similarity. It appears to me that Goodman might well be amenable to Tversky's views; for these strike me as not entirely incompatible with Goodman's conventionalism.

[10] To this group we may add Elgin (1983). Elgin pulls together the pieces of Goodman's views on metaphor and adds a number of valuable additional insights. She addresses certain prominent difficulties of a nominalist theory of metaphor. An extensionalist semantics such as Goodman's, Scheffler's, and Elgin's would appear to have difficulty explaining how we can use terms with a null extension metaphorically. Goodman's answer, which Elgin elaborates, is that these are cases of metaphorical *exemplification*, rather than metaphorical denotation: 'Whatever I am getting at when I say that Smith is a Don Juan, I am not (even metaphorically) consigning him to the null set. The metaphorical application of a fictive term reflects rather the way the term itself is sorted [Goodman, 1978*b* . . . There may be no single literal predicate that serves as the basis for metaphorical transfer. Applying "Don Juan" metaphorically to Smith may bring about a likening of Don Juan-descriptions and Smith-descriptions that no literal predicate captures' (Elgin 1983, 60). However, she does not address the problems I present below.

Whatever reverence may be felt for classes or attributes, surely classes are not moved from realm to realm, nor are attributes somehow extracted from some objects and injected into others. Rather a set of terms, of alternate labels, is transported; and the organization they effect in the alien realm is guided by their habitual use in their home realm. (1968, 74.)

'Label' sounds comfortably neutral in regard to any epistemological or ontological position. But when we ask exactly what Goodman means by 'label', we find that either some non-nominalistic claims are smuggled in or the whole problem is reduced to incoherence.

Goodman's labels carry no conceptual baggage—they have no content, only application. They even have habitual applications. This distinguishes them from the pair 'ping' and 'pong', which Saussure might have called pure signifiers. The habitual applications, Goodman appears to assume, constrain the labels, when used literally, to a given realm. Applications to new realms are metaphorical. But Goodman's assumption here is not warranted. Some schemes have only minimal constraints on the realms to which they may apply. The labels in such schemes tend to be commonly used adjectives or adverbs. Lehrer, for example, points out that 'the lexical set (*hot, warm, cool, cold*) have meaning in the general domains including temperature, personality type, colors and sensation' (1970, 349).

Evaluative adjectives and adverbs are still more loosely tied to a field of application. Within Goodman's sparse ontology, nothing marks these realms as realms appropriate to the application of these terms beyond given past usage. The more domains in which a set of labels, a schema, or a lexical set has application, the less the term can be used metaphorically. It is for this reason that it is difficult to find metaphorical uses of terms such as 'good' or 'bad'. They are purely evaluative terms, attached to no particular content domain, and, except in so far as one considers evaluation itself as a content domain, they float over virtually every other domain whose referents may be subject to evaluation.[11]

---

[11] Numbers are difficult to assess in this regard. Whether we say that numbers have or have not an inherent field depends on our philosophy of mathematics—whether we are realists or nominalists in regard to mathematical entities. If we are nominalists we can say that when numbers are applied to a given domain they organize that domain non-metaphorically, in accordance with the relations which organize the numbers themselves. If we are realists, we can say that numbers organize the field by transferring the relations which organize the domain of mathematical entities to a new domain. As long as the field of mathematical entities is kept in mind together with the recipient field, the organization is metaphorical, not literal, and it has the dual semantic content character-

The point is that this set of labels is not likely to find a metaphorical use, because it has no content-bearing domain of its own. Goodman claims that it is prior habitual use which guides the way in which the transferred set of labels are used in their new realm of application. But prior use alone will not do. 'Good' and 'bad' have a long—even revered—history of past usage, but they have no home territory, hence no informative content (beyond relative evaluation) to bring with them to a new territory. The same point may be made of lexical sets consisting of demonstratives.[12] It is that informative content which serves as a mediation between a set of labels and a new application, a mediation which makes metaphorical statements, in the phrase of Myers (1968), 'mediatively informative'. Without such content, a metaphor is not 'a happy and revitalizing, even if bigamous, second marriage', as Goodman (1968, 73) says; it is merely an ordinary divorce and subsequent second marriage. It is for this reason that the nominalistic orientation of the contextualism Scheffler assigns to his own and Goodman's views will not, I believe, work in explaining metaphor. Goodman unwittingly slipped content into his nominalistic labels to produce the '*bigamous* second marriage'.[13]

istic of other metaphors. We could say that this dual semantic content was lost either in so far as we disregarded the domain of real mathematical entities or in so far as we believed that the 'topic' domain had, in fact, a structure isomorphic to that of the mathematical field. It appears to me that this speculation may have some interesting consequences for understanding the connection between metaphor and the use of mathematical models in science.

[12] Indexicals have some specifiable content in that they are indices of a certain sort—person, time, or place—and as such can be used metaphorically. Proper names, which presumably have no conceptual content even within most intensionalist semantics, are interesting in this regard. In a certain sense, we never use proper names metaphorically. However, we do occasionally say of someone: 'She's a veritable Einstein', or 'Honest Abe, there, will repay every cent.' In these cases, I suggest, we are not using the names as true proper names for which the reference is given, as in Kripke's causal theory of proper names. If, for example, it turned out that the man generally credited with Einstein's accomplishments was not the man we have called Einstein, but some other person let us say, Kramer, the sentence given above would retain its intelligibility. And if Kramer signed all his papers 'Einstein', it might even retain its truth value. Although capitalized and treated as proper names, these names are more like names of natural kind terms. And it is not entirely clear that the causal theory of reference provides an account of the meaning, let alone the reference, of natural kind terms. Natural kind terms, on my account, do have a conceptual content that can be exploited in the making of metaphor.

[13] For a related criticism that insists on 'properties' rather than conceptual content, see Beardsley 1978.

2 THE LINGUISTIC APPROACH: FEATURE ADDITION AND DELETION

The Feature Addition/Deletion Thesis

A number of writers have taken the position that the question of meta-phorical interpretation presents characteristically linguistic problems whose resolution requires the application of specifically linguistic devices. If, as I have argued, metaphor *can* be treated linguistically, in part at least, it is reasonable to utilize our best theoretical linguistic resources to explain how we interpret metaphor. The position has been favoured by linguists and linguistically minded philosophers, par-ticularly those who have been impressed by the power of a componen-tial approach to semantics.[14] Its major thrust is to utilize, and if necessary to extend, the formal apparatus of (some version of) trans-formational grammar in order to provide an interpretation of meta-phorical expressions. As a result, we have various accounts of what I term the *feature addition/deletion thesis*. According to the thesis we can say that, given a sentence which is semantically deviant, a metaphorical interpretation involves the addition/deletion or transfer of certain semantic features from one component of the metaphor (that is, the topic or the vehicle) to another component of the metaphor.[15]

It is important to note that the notion of semantic deviance plays an important part in most versions of the feature addition/deletion thesis. I have already pointed out many of the limitations of an insistence on the semantic deviance of metaphor. None the less, the temptation to regard metaphor as semantically deviant is very strong, particularly

[14] For a summary account of what I mean when I speak of a componential semantics, see Chapter 2, note 10 above.

[15] The theorists differ on whether to consider metaphorical interpretation a matter of semantics (e.g. Cohen 1979, Levin 1977, Weinreich 1966, Mack 1975) or pragmatics (e.g. Matthews 1971, Sadock 1979); and on whether the semantics of the grammar ought to be interpretive (e.g. Matthews 1971), or generative (Sanders 1973), or struc-tural, i.e consisting of binary oppositions (e.g. Bickerton 1969). Generally, those who believe that metaphor is properly a matter of pragmatics do not see any point in provid-ing an account in terms of a componential semantics. Matthews is an exception, only because he wants to show that the mere deviation of metaphor from the representation of literal sentences suffices as an account of metaphorical meaning. According to Matthews, this deviance is a necessary and sufficient condition. We shall see later that this position is untenable.

There is still disagreement also on whether the features, or components of the mean-ings of the lexical items in the language, are purely linguistic and conceptual or whether they are to include empirical knowledge as well. The position given in Chapter 2, note 10, above, is the one on which the theorists mentioned here may be said to agree.

when one has available the technical notion of a selection restriction. According to standard interpretive semantics, a term may have a number of selection restrictions, each governing the different grammatical categories and subcategories with which the term may combine. A verb such as 'chase' will have <human> v <animate> as a selection restriction on the subject variable and <object> as a restriction on the direct object variable. Sentence 5.6 would then be marked *semantically anomalous*:

5.6 The blackboard chased away the yellow.

Many metaphors appear to be precisely statements which result when one violates a selection restriction rule. Using the term 'chase', consider the following sentence:

5.7 The champagne chased away the blues.

Here, as in 5.6, the selection restrictions on 'chased' are violated by the terms 'champagne' and 'the blues'. Though 5.7 strikes us as being clearly a metaphorical utterance and 5.6 seems simply anomalous, we can attribute the difference to nothing other than the fact that we are familiar with the metaphorical use of 'blues' for unhappiness and of 'chase' to describe what alcohol and other mood-altering substances do to unhappiness. In contrast, it requires some resourcefulness and originality to give 5.6 a metaphorical interpretation. But all that is required to turn a semantically deviant sentence like 5.6 into a metaphor is to set it in a context where a metaphorical interpretation is available for it.

According to Matthews (1971), the violation of selection restrictions is a both necessary and sufficient condition for an utterance to be a metaphor, providing only that the utterance is not intended to be meaningless. The competence to understand metaphor, which is equivalent to the competence to interpret that class of deviant sentences that violate selection restrictions, is completely analogous to the way in which we understand non-deviant sentences. In metaphorical sentences we are guided by the selection restriction violation to de-emphasize those features[16] of the appropriate lexical item that violate

---

[16] Matthews construes lexical features more broadly than Katz (1972). For Matthews, lexical features, including selection restrictions, are simply the '*common uses* of the lexical entry and thus lexical features might be viewed as *elucidations* of literal usage rather than as an analysis or definition of the lexical entry' (1971, 419 my itals).

the selection restriction rules so that we may then proceed as we should in understanding a non-metaphorical sentence. Matthews regards this procedure as a performance rather than a competence, and therefore does not build into his grammar the addition or deletion of features necessary for a metaphorical construal of a deviant sentence.

Weinreich (1966), one of the earliest proponents of the need to build such procedures into a grammar, realized that, in virtue of the fact that their task is to block the interpretation of semantically deviant sentences, selection restrictions are not the appropriate vehicles to assign readings to metaphorical sentences. Convinced that the technical apparatus of a language must be sufficiently flexible to account for the interpretability of poetic language which violated the conventions of non-poetic language—in particular, language which violated selection restriction rules—he rejected selection restrictions in favour of *transfer features*. Weinreich's transfer features contain approximately the same information as selection restriction rules. But rather than serving as a rule proscribing the interpretation of certain collocations, a transfer feature simply moves from one term to that with which it is collocated. Consider the phrase:

5.8 Rosy-fingered dawn.

We can say that the feature [+ human] belongs as a transfer feature to the term 'rosy-fingered'. In 5.8 [+ human] would be transferred to 'dawn'. But 'dawn' presumably has a feature [− human], thereby creating the incongruity so characteristic of metaphor. We now have a phrase which contains a contradiction of sorts. To interpret the phrase, Weinreich introduces the *semantic evaluator*, which assigns the degree of deviance in accordance with the interpretability of the metaphor. What remains unclear is how such an evaluator is to distinguish between one contradiction and another, for the transfer of features marked '+' or '−' has reduced all deviance to logical contradiction and logical contradiction is not a matter of degree. (P & −P) is not more or less contradictory; it is always simply a contradiction.

Although both Matthews and Weinreich assume that the features to be de-emphasized or transferred are connected with the violated selection restrictions, neither considers that modifying the features in the offending word and modifying the selection restriction itself would result in different interpretations of the metaphor. For instance, if we employ an example used by Matthews (1971)

5.9 The volcano burped

do we de-emphasize the features of 'volcano' which are in violation of selection restrictions on 'burped' or do we de-emphasize the features of 'burped' which are in violation of the selection restrictions on 'volcano'? That is, do we interpret 5.9 to mean that we are speaking of the eruption of a volcano as a gigantic 'digestive' release of air, or that we are speaking of a baby who has burped 'explosively'? Both the fact of such ambiguity and the strategies we employ for resolving the ambiguity are left unanswered in the versions of the feature addition/deletion thesis I have discussed.[17]

Six Construals of 'The Stone Died.'

Levin (1977) points out that for 'semantically deviant' sentences such as 5.9 as many as six construals are possible, and he provides rules by which to get all six readings. The rules specify the adjoining or displacing of semantic features of the key terms. Because Levin's is the most developed version of the feature addition/deletion thesis, its careful consideration will be most useful.

Levin illustrates the six construals of semantically deviant sentences, four of which involve adjoining features and two of which involve displacing features, with the sentence:

5.10 The stone died.

The construals may be described as follows:

(1) If we *adjoin* features of the *verb to the noun* and *disjoin* these in the semantic representation of 5.10, we get the construal which will attempt to find something which is both [human] (or [animal] or [plant]) and [mineral], such as a natural physical object. The construal would be: 'The natural physical object died' or 'Something died'.

(2) If we *adjoin* features of the *verb to the noun* and *conjoin* these in the semantic representation of 5.10, we get a construal in which the transferred feature is fused with the host term. Thus we get a humanized, animalized, or 'plantified' stone, depending on whether from the term 'died' we choose to transfer the feature

---

[17] Indeed, few theorists have paid attention to the systematic ambiguity in the interpretation of metaphor, first pointed out by Sanders (1973). See Chapter 1, Section 2, above.

[human], [animal], or [plant]. Choosing the feature [human], we get: 'The "humanized stone" died'.

(3) We *adjoin* features of the *noun to the verb* and *disjoin* these in the selection restriction of the verb. In the semantic representation of 5.10, the transferred feature, let us say [mineral], is disjunctively adjoined to such other disjuncts as [human] in the selection restriction on the subject of the verb die. We then generalize over the disjuncts and construe 5.10 as: 'The stone ceased to be/exist.'

(4) We *adjoin* features of the *noun to the verb* and *conjoin* these in the selection restriction of the verb. In the case of 5.10, we find it difficult to get a construal in which the transferred feature is fused with the host term. Levin suggests that the construal could better be exemplified by a sentence such as:

5.11 His ego died.

To illustrate this fourth mode of construal, Levin writes of 5.11, 'the meaning of *die* would be construed so as to mean what *die* means but of an object that was both human and abstract' (1977, 46).

(5) We *displace* features of the *verb to the noun*. If we take the reading of 'stone' as follows:

stone: [[[object] [physical]] [natural] [mineral] [concreted]]

we can displace [mineral] with one of the disjunctive selection restrictions on died, <human>, to get

stone: [[[object] [physical]] [natural] [[human] [concreted]]]

yielding a set of possible interpretations of the variety: 'An unfeeling (or indurated, or stupid, or doltish) person died.'

(6) We *displace* features of the *noun to the verb*. If we take the reading of 'die' to be

die: [[[process] [[result] [[cease to be] [living]]]X] <[human] v. [animal] v. [plant]>]

then, replacing the selection restriction disjuncts with [mineral], we get

die: [[[process] [[result] [[cease to be] [living]]]X]
<Mineral>]

with the resulting interpretation: 'The stone disintegrated.'

Each of the above modes of construal is formalized by Levin in a series of six construal rules which utilize the technical apparatus of generative grammar and substitute for selection restrictions the transfer features recommended by Weinreich (1966). The six construal rules comprise what Levin calls the Theory (T).

Let us compare the readings given under the different construals:

(1) 'The natural physical object died' or 'Something died'.
(2) 'The "humanized stone" died.'
(3) 'The stone ceased to be/exist.'
(4) Empty in the case of 5.10.
(5) 'An unfeeling (or indurated, or stupid, or doltish) person died.'
(6) 'The stone disintegrated.'

Construals (5) and (6) seem the most natural and likely metaphorical interpretations of 5.10. Construal (1) seems hardly metaphorical at all, and (3) seems to be a most general way of expressing (6). The second construal is not intelligible as it stands and seems to me to need some subsequent construal, while (4), on Levin's own admission, has no apparent interpretation in the case of 5.10. However, Levin's point is less that semantically deviant sentences are all construable in each of the six ways he suggests than that semantically deviant sentences which receive a metaphorical interpretation will receive that interpretation through one of the six construal rules. The question now arises whether Levin's Theory (T) characterizes the metaphorical interpretation of utterances.

Although theory (T) is perhaps the most sophisticated version of the many feature addition/deletion theses, it shares deficiencies with more naïve versions. In demonstrating the inadequacies of (T), I hope to show the general failure of the feature addition/deletion thesis.

Critique of Levin's Theory (T). The inadequacies of (T) involve the following three points: its failure to encompass semantically non-deviant sentences which are none the less used metaphorically; its inability to distinguish metaphorical from non-metaphorical modifications of a word's meaning; its failure to capture metaphor's double semantic import. Let us take these considerations one at a time.

First, construal rules do not encompass cases in which the metaphorical utterance is not a semantically deviant sentence. While Levin recognizes that not all metaphors are semantically deviant sentences and speaks of 'pragmatic deviance' as characterizing a whole class of sentences of this sort, he does not go beyond stressing Grice's (1975) conversational maxims to deal with these cases. While the maxims are particularly helpful for arriving at the identification of an utterance as metaphorical, the pragmatic considerations do not help to establish its *metaphorical interpretation*. The argument may be that since these are not deviant sentences they would be interpreted just as other non-deviant sentences are. Our familiar, if slightly altered, example, 5.12 below, would be such a case if it were used metaphorically to speak of, let us say, a person of a certain demeanour.

5.12 The stone has become brittle with age.

But a literal construal of 5.12, in which we are concerned with the state of concreted pieces of mineral substance, and a metaphorical one, in which we are concerned with a person, are two readings sufficiently distinct to warrant different truth conditions and different semantic representations. In that case, we would need a different theory to account for cases of 'pragmatic deviance'. Yet it is not clear why one theoretical framework should not account both for sentence 5.10 and for 5.12 when both are used metaphorically to speak of a person.

Second, theory (T), like the predicate transfer thesis, does not enable one to distinguish between the representations of a metaphorical utterance and of one which adheres to a set of conventions not completely congruent with the conventions of quotidian language, for example, the conventions of technical language or descriptions in science fiction or fairy-tales. In these latter situations, we do not take a word in its usual sense but according to certain modifications prescribed by the context. These modifications could very well be described according to some of Levin's construal rules, and yet would not be metaphorical interpretations of the utterances.

One might claim that (T), unlike most versions of the feature addition/deletion thesis, has the virtue of positing several different modes of construal. Thus, although one construal of a semantically deviant sentence will clearly be non-metaphorical, it is still conceivable that another construal will represent the metaphorical interpretation. When the fairy-tale tells us that

5.13 The wolf said, 'I'll huff and I'll puff and I'll blow your house down,'

it is not in some metaphorical sense that the wolf so threatened the little pigs. Using (T) to represent a construal of 5.13, we should say that the feature [animal] in 'wolf' was adjoined as a disjunct to the selection restrictions on the subject of 'said', in other words, it would follow the model of the first mode of construal. If 5.13 were used to describe (in jest, one would hope) what a rakish man said to a resisting woman, then the appropriate construal would be the displacement of certain lupine features incompatible with the transfer feature [human] from the selection restriction on the subject of 'said', namely, the fifth mode of construal. Consider:

5.4 'And the dog said to the little boy . . .'

The sentence might appear in a children's story or in a dialogue of some dog-lover who endows dogs with human capacities. But if (T) is correct, then how is one to distinguish 5.14 as it occurs in a fairy-tale and in the speech of our dog-lover, where 'said' is not used literally. But in both cases, the feature [animal] in 'dog' is adjoined as a disjunct to the selection restrictions on the subject of 'said'; in other words, the interpretation of both would follow the model of the first mode of construal. In the fairy-tale, the construal suggested by (T) appears to be a perfect rendering of the process of interpretation. (T) does not do justice to the shifts in meaning in the process of metaphorical interpretation. This failure is a direct consequence of the inability of this theory to represent the dual content of metaphorically used terms, as we shall shortly see.

Terms in technical language will often involve only a few of the lexical features which could be said to define them in ordinary language. Consider 'power', 'rank', 'chain', and 'nest' in mathematical set theory, 'spin' in physics, 'person' in law, etc. In terms of (T), we could say that their interpretation in a sentence of the technical discourse involved one of the displacement construals. Yet these terms are not metaphors when they are used in their technical sense. According to the feature addition/deletion thesis we should interpret both metaphorical and technical discourse in precisely the same way. This is an intuitively unacceptable conclusion, and it is certainly unacceptable if the conclusions of the previous chapter are justified. For these provide us with the possibility of giving distinct semantic representations to the different interpretations.

Third, theory (T) does not capture the notion of a double semantic relation in the sense in which we are forced by a metaphor to attend at once to both the sense of the vehicle and the content of the topic. Although it seems plausible to say that in understanding a sentence metaphorically we do something to the lexical features of the words of the sentence so that we may resolve the selection-restriction violation, the transfer or deletion of features does not tell the whole story. Consider Yeats's metaphor 'child-bearing moon' in the opening lines of the poem 'The Crazed Moon'.

5.15   Crazed through much child-bearing
         The moon is staggering in the sky.

Let us assume that to construe this metaphor we displace the features in 'moon' which violate selection restrictions on what may be 'child-bearing', for example, [inanimate], and replace them with just the features appropriate to entities which are child-bearing [animate], [human], [female]. Thus to make sense of the phrase we must presumably disregard the inanimate, non-human, sexually neuter attributes of 'moon'. Such a conception of the moon strikes us more properly as mistaken than as metaphorical. It is through the metaphor that the meaning of the moon, as an inanimate object, is transformed into something animate and life-giving: the moon, in its literal sense, becomes the bearer and possessor of those female cycles with which it is associated. This phrase is a metaphor not because some features of 'moon' are de-emphasized, but because it is capable of making the reader grasp *both* the actual barrenness of the moon and its seeming procreative cycle as it grows from a thin sliver to the rounded shape of a pregnant woman. It is the apprehension of these two, not easily reconciled, concepts, held together in the metaphor and consequently held together in the mind, that I want to evoke when I speak of the double semantic relation or the double semantic content of metaphors. Only an account which avoids conflating vehicle and topic will represent this double semantic content. And it is this characteristic of metaphor which is, at least in part, responsible for its special cognitive interest and its unparaphrasability.

The account I have presented in Chapters 2–4 has incorporated some aspects of a componential semantics without falling into the errors of the feature addition/deletion thesis. Some aspects of a componential analysis have been importantly modified by the relational approach to meaning. Many of the defects of the feature addition/deletion thesis result from considering the metaphorical unit to be a sentence. By speaking of utterance meaning instead of sentence meaning, I have been able to represent the semantic interpretation of metaphors so that it is not necessary to construct one theory for metaphors which appear 'semantically deviant' and another for those which are not. Furthermore, the account I have given allows us to differentiate between metaphorical and non-metaphorical (even non-figurative) divergences from a term's ordinary meaning. This is because I have sought to capture the incongruence which marks metaphor, that is, the tensive relation between the two components of the metaphor, within the semantic representation itself.

To accomplish this, I required a notion of second-order meaning and the linguistic frame provided by a relational theory of first-order meaning. My relational theory makes the meaning of expressions (consisting of words combined according to syntactic rules) interactional and requires a semantic field theory of word meaning. In Chapter 3, I criticized an insulationist theory of sentence meaning and substituted an interdynamic theory. But I postponed a full account of semantic field theory. Prior to giving this detailed account, I want to indicate how alternative theories of word meaning give us unsatisfactory results in regard to metaphorical meaning.

3 A CRITIQUE OF ATOMISTIC THEORIES AS BASES FOR A THEORY OF METAPHOR

Theories of word-meaning may be atomistic or relational.[18] What I have chosen to call 'atomistic' theories of word-meaning generally posit an *atomistic entity* of sorts as the meaning of a linguistic expression. This is the position Wittgenstein, with ironic wit, caricatured: 'Here is the word, there is the meaning. The money and the cow you can buy with it' (1953), 49). Atomistic theories may be extensional (or referential), intensional, or behaviouristic. An extensional atomistic theory identifies the referent or extension of a term with its meaning.

[18] Cohen (1981) explores much the same sense of a relational conception of meaning and contrasts it with what he also calls an 'atomistic conception'. My use of the term developed quite independently of his, but we use the notion in very much the same way. I believe the coincidental set of concerns results from the fact that we have both been struck by Saussure's insight into the significance of systematic linguistic interrelations for meaning.

Within atomistic intensional theories the meaning of a linguistic term may be taken to be something objective—a Fregean concept or a Platonic idea—or it may be understood to be subjective. It has been variously proposed that meaning is an idea (in someone's mind), a brain state, an intention (to mean something by uttering that word), or a functional role (one that the term's concept plays in a person's psychology). Theories which are atomistic and behaviouristic identify the meaning of a term with a high degree of statistical probability that the given term will be uttered in the presence of a certain set of circumstances or, alternatively, with a measure of the frequency of a response or the disposition to respond elicited by a term. A more sophisticated version of behaviourism, favoured by thinkers such as Morris and Skinner, takes the 'disposition to respond' as constitutive of the meaning of a linguistic expression.

Extensional Atomistic Theories

How might an atomistic extensional (referential) theory explain the metaphorical use of the word 'bees' in the phrase 'Bees of England' (example 1.7 above) in Shelley's 'Song to the Men of England'? According to a referential theory we would say that the literal meaning of 'Bees of England' is its reference, namely those apian beings which are found in England. Or we could say that the extension of 'bees', that is, all the things which satisfy the predicate 'is a bee', constitutes its literal meaning. Clearly, the usual extension of this expression does not provide the meaning Shelley intended, nor does it provide the meaning that the reader understands in Shelley's poem. How then may 'Bees of England' come to be used to speak of the men of England? One claim may be that for most terms there are literal extensions which correspond to literal meaning and metaphorical extensions which correspond to metaphorical meaning. In Shelley's poem, 'bees' has a metaphorical extension, namely, workers. But what if 'bees' were used metaphorically, in another context, to speak of, let us say, a group of industrialists? Would we then say that 'bees' had these two (opposing) metaphorical extensions, workers and industrialists? But normally what will satisfy the predicate 'is a worker' will not satisfy the predicate 'is an industrialist'. In that case, then, nothing would satisfy the metaphorical predication 'is a bee' and these metaphors would be unable to refer to anything at all. Thus they would no longer have a meaning, but would be nonsensical.

In reply we may say that the metaphorical extension should not be workers *and* industrialists, but workers *or* industrialists. We add a new disjunct for each innovative metaphor employing 'bees'. But there is no apparent limit to the possible innovative metaphorical uses. Throughout, I have argued that the only constraint on the metaphorical application of a term is that the term should be used as a vehicle for a topic from a distinct content domain (though this is not to deny that some topic domains will yield more interesting metaphors than others). And it is possible to argue that there is no limit to the number of content domains. Therefore, there can be no limit to the possible metaphorical meanings. The metaphorical meaning of a term then consists of an infinite string of such disjuncts. Such infinite strings, however, are not learnable. Even if these strings were not infinite, but only indeterminately large, we should need to explain how we could understand each addition to such a disjunctive string, and no explanation is forthcoming. Thus, it appears that the alternative to multiple and sometimes contradictory metaphorical uses which empty the term of any metaphorical meaning is, at worst, to make such metaphorical meanings unlearnable. At best, our understanding of as yet uncodified metaphorical senses would be mysterious.

To attempt to treat these multiple metaphorical meanings as we treat homonyms and simply create new dictionary entries for each new use would present us with similar problems. At best, each new metaphorical use would swell the dictionary entries to an unwieldy size. At worst, if the uses were indeed infinite, and if we treated a term with a metaphorical meaning as a primitive in our language (just as we treat a term with a literal meaning), then this would seemingly make the language itself unlearnable.

Davidson (1979) puts forward, only to attack, yet another extensional approach. Rather than say that a term used metaphorically now has a second, though metaphorical, extension, we say that the sense is extended by including additional entities under the term's *extension*. In the example Davidson provides, 'the Spirit of God moved upon the face of the waters', 'face' acquires a metaphorical sense in that it now refers not only to all faces, but also to waters. Davidson, rightly I believe, points out that such an account cannot be correct, since if 'face' is to apply correctly to waters then water must really have faces. The metaphor is lost, and there is little difference now between a metaphor and a new term introduced into our vocabulary.

Intensional Atomistic Theories

The intensional theory suffers from similar difficulties. As with an extensional theory we may take one of two routes. We may regard each metaphorical application of a term as representing an intensional entity which is additional to the literal intension of the term (regardless of what intensional entity we posit for our semantics). The difficulties here are analogous to those we saw in the case of extensional theories. In the case of intensional theories we have the additional problem of unconscionably multiplying intensional entities with each distinct metaphorical application. Again, the problem becomes: how can we understand each new application? The intensionalist may also take the tack suggested by Davidson and say that a metaphorical use extends the sense of a term, but that it is the intension which is extended. This is precisely the thesis which lies at the heart of the feature addition/deletion thesis examined in Section 2.[19] In short, according to the claim that metaphorical meaning extends a word's literal meaning (conceived intensionally or extensionally), we must construe metaphorical meaning either as generating paradox or as collapsing into some new, fanciful, technical, or mistaken literal meaning. Finally, to the extent that a theory of meaning does not explain the existence or production of distinct but kindred senses, it will be unable to relate the literal and metaphorical senses.

Theories of Reference

Above I have located metaphor within the scope of various theories of meaning. But semantic theory has two branches: a theory of meaning and a theory of reference. Rather than identifying reference with meaning, many take a theory of meaning to be, at best a separate project, at worst a futile, misguided, or otherwise mistaken one. Are there theories of reference which would be able to give a better semantic account of metaphor than the theories of meaning we have thus far encountered?

Referential theories exhibit many of the same defects as extensional

---

[19] Interpretive semantics may be viewed as a relational theory of sentence meaning, and feature addition/deletion approaches are based on some componential semantics. But a componential semantics is relational only to the extent that it regards semantic features as somehow mapping the given term within a network of other terms. Once the semantic representations of words become hypostatized entities which 'belong' to the word, they lose their relational capacities and the theory becomes another atomistic intensional theory. See the discussion in Chapter 6, Section 3.

atomic theories—that extension is not here identified with the meaning of the term seems to matter little. Within such theories, the same problems that arise for identifying the meaning of a metaphor arise for identifying the reference of a metaphor. More thoughtful are those advocates of referential theories who would consign the study of metaphor to pragmatics. But as I have argued in the previous chapters, pragmatic considerations alone do not suffice to account for metaphor.

Consider, for example, an attempt to account for metaphor in a causal theory of reference. There are two possible ways we might do this. First, we could say that when Shelley called workers of England, 'Bees of England' he effectually 'baptized' the workers of England 'Bees of England'. In spite of the tendency to insist that only sentences can be metaphorical, there is an intuitive sense in the idea that a metaphor is (a sort of) name. 'Bees of England' would serve as a rigid designator whose reference would now be the workers of England to whom Shelley referred in his poem. If we now wanted to make any counterfactual statements concerning these workers, we could use the term 'Bees of England' and still refer to *those* workers in a counterfactual state of affairs. Of course, the complication is that 'Bees of England' already refers to the apian creatures that are found in England. With our new baptism have we enlarged the extension of the term to include new entities, or has the new baptism replaced the old? In either case, it would seem from our previous arguments that the metaphor is lost.

Beyond this, it seems that if the term is a rigid designator then those individuals who are the workers of England could not in any state of affairs be bees. Therefore, we can no more speak of a possible world in which *apian beings* are *human workers*, than we can speak of a possible world in which a circle is a square. This attempt to provide a possible worlds account has again led us to assimilate metaphors to nonsensical utterances.

The second way of accounting for metaphor in a causal theory of reference differs from the one just given by conceding that perhaps 'Bees of England' is not a rigid designator. Perhaps instead 'Bees of England' is part of a descriptive cluster used in a baptism. So it is the case that in our actual world the workers of early nineteenth-century England could satisfy the assigned predicate 'is a bee', but in other counterfactual situations they might not. For example, in a state of affairs, that is, a possible world, in which workers of England revolted, they would not be 'bees of England'. We might say that this was a definite description meant to capture the relation of the workers to the aristocracy—a relation which would have been vitiated had there been such a revolt. Thus we could find one model in which, given the specific metaphorical interpretation we gave to Shelley's metaphor, 'is a bee' would be satisfied and another model in which it would not be satisfied.

Bergmann (1979) has proposed a formal semantics of metaphor along these lines. She uses the distinction between the content, intension, and extension of a term. The content provides the set of properties determining the things to which the term applies. The intension is the class of all possible things to which the term might apply, while the extension is the set of actual things to which the term does apply. In metaphor the content is at once expanded to include properties not usually within the content of the term and narrowed to exclude other properties normally included in the content. There is generally a corresponding expansion and narrowing of intension and extension. Context will importantly determine the content for a given metaphorical interpretation. While Bergmann agrees with Davidson (and others) that metaphor is context-bound and literal language is independent of context, she does not take this to be a serious hindrance for a semantics of metaphor as long as that semantics is given for a specific interpretation.

An attractive feature of this analysis is that it provides a formal representation of an intuitive sense that metaphors (and models, in both the non-mathematical and the mathematical sense) have a modal character. In particular, metaphors and models encapsulate counterfactual states of affairs. Thus rather than being able, in the actual world, to apply 'bees of England' to the workers of England, we should say that the metaphorical phrase as applied to the workers of England was a sort of counterfactual statement, which we could rewrite as the antecedent clause of a counterfactual conditional: 'If the workers of England were bees, then . . . ', or perhaps 'If bees were workers of England then . . . '. The consequent clause would then speak of whatever Shelley had to say about the 'bees of England'. Thus, the model for metaphorical interpretation posits some possible world in which we can say that workers are bees, where 'bees' is given a specific metaphorical interpretation. The intuitive appeal of this approach is that it captures the 'as if' sense of a metaphor: we think of workers as if they were bees.

In its modal aspect, we can say that a metaphor presents us with *possibilities* that are often not evident without the model or metaphor.

This modal aspect is often important in the use of metaphor for didactic purposes and for the purpose of suggesting explanation with predictive consequences. When Socrates called himself a 'midwife' he implicitly suggested the possibility that the relation a teacher bore to a student was such that the teacher could not simply impart knowledge that the student never before had within him. The metaphor presents the possibility that we look at knowledge as something inherent in the student that the teacher must facilitate in bringing out—just as the role of the midwife is to facilitate the birth of a being already existent within the mother. Bergmann's model states that, given an appropriate context for a sentence like 'Socrates is a midwife', there is a world such that we can give a specific metaphorical interpretation of 'is a midwife'. The interpretation would appropriately expand and narrow the content of the term 'midwife'. Given the domain of individuals in that world, the context, and a metaphorical interpretation function (as well as a literal interpretation function and the class of all interpretation functions), we can assign a value to the predicate which is to be interpreted metaphorically: 'is a midwife'. Given the interpretation suggested above, we may say that while Socrates satisfies the predicate, Protagoras does not. Furthermore, in that model, Socrates' mother (who was, in fact, a midwife) does not satisfy the predicate as metaphorically interpreted.

Bergmann's model depends on the specificity of an interpretation. She is correct to point out that a semantics which demands the specification of truth conditions demands that a given interpretation should be specified in order to assign values to predicates and sentences. A metaphor for which a specific interpretation has been chosen can perhaps be given a form of a counterfactual conditional, for example, 'If the skill of midwives were applied to extracting knowledge from students (rather than delivering women of babies), teaching would be conducted by a method of question and answer', or 'If bees were manufacturing goods (as workers do), the products would go to the drones who do not labour'. But her formal model does not provide an understanding of how we derive an interpretation which is or is not a satisfactory one. Nor does it elucidate why a statement that would provide the interpretation could not simply be considered a literal paraphrase of the metaphor. In that case, it would really be the literal paraphrase to which we assign values and not the metaphor itself. This involves us in questions very similar to the ones raised by Davidson's truth semantics.

An account such as Bergmann's may indeed be helpful in formaliz-
ing certain aspects of a semantic theory of metaphor, but it alone is not
sufficient to provide a semantic theory of how we interpret metaphor.
A causal theory of reference and a possible world semantics do not
provide a complete account of metaphor. At most, they raise the problem at a different point in the inquiry.

Behaviouristic Accounts

It seems that to try to give a behaviouristic account of metaphorical
meaning only underscores the inadequacies of behaviourism as a
theory of word meaning. Bloomfield speaks of the meaning of a
linguistic form as just the response that it calls forth, in the situation in
which it is uttered. He claims that each word has both a central and a
peripheral meaning, and that a metaphor makes use of the peripheral
meaning (1933, 146). We can infer that the central and peripheral
meanings are determined by the higher or lower frequency, respectively, of one set of situations in which the speaker utters a term and by
the response which is called forth. The flaws in this view are many.

First, is it really the case that metaphors simply utilize a peripheral
meaning? This claim is reminiscent of Ortony's view that the less
salient properties of the vehicle are utilized in metaphor. Again, we
respond that when we call workers 'bees' we are employing a rather
central part of the meaning of 'bees', that is, as busy, productive, and
social beings. Furthermore, if, as Alston remarks, 'a moment's reflection should suffice to bring out the great variety of situations in which
almost any given word is uttered' and 'there is nothing in common to
all these situations which is distinctive of the word' (1967, 236), then
the situation is even more acute in the case of metaphors. The presumed responses elicited by such metaphorical uses range from baffle-
ment to wildly elaborate verbal interpretations. Similarly, the stimuli
we might identify which purport to produce any metaphorical utterance are so diverse and so rarely predictable (except for dead or conventional metaphors) that an attempt thus to specify a peripheral
meaning seems quixotic.

The more sophisticated version of behaviourism, espoused by figures
such as Morris and Skinner, posits the disposition to respond as constitutive of the meaning of a linguistic expression. But all such attempts
fail in dealing with metaphor because all dispositional accounts of
meaning depend on a certain predictability, measured perhaps as a
statistically predominant distributional frequency of an expression.

Metaphors (again except perhaps for dead and conventional metaphors), by virtue of novelty and creativity, confound such predictability and escape the measure of statistical probability.

Fixed and atomistic conceptions of word meaning have made metaphor an anomaly, and its comprehension a mystery. And because metaphors never come as isolated words, metaphors are inherently problematic for atomistic theories of word meaning. A theory of metaphor requires a theory of the meaning of terms as they are combined according to syntactic rules.

But a theory of word meaning is none the less important for the full account of metaphor. There is a systematic connectedness between metaphors in a given language, both those which are novel and those which are more entrenched.[20] That systematicity derives from the relatedness between words within the lexicon, a relatedness which constitutes an important aspect of word meaning. Since it is the theory of semantic fields that attempts to give the grounds of the relations a word bears to other terms in a language, it is now time to turn our attention to the particulars of this theory.

---

[20] In exploring the systematic interconnections of extended metaphors, Kittay (1978) and Kittay and Lehrer (1981) discussed the importance of such connectedness among metaphors. Our work was done independently, prior to the appearance of Lakoff and Johnson, and is consonant with the findings of the latter. The virtue of the latter study is that it exhibits the systematic character of conventional metaphors found throughout our language that are not *intentionally* constructed as extended metaphors.

6

Semantic Field Theory

WE have criticized atomistic theories on the grounds that such conceptions of the meaning of a word cannot yield an adequate account of metaphor. And just as we required a relational theory of sentence-meaning, so we require a relational theory of word-meaning. In the previous chapters I have employed the concept of a semantic field with only a cursory explanation of the theory justifying such a notion. In this chapter, I want to offer a fuller description of semantic field theory and to argue for its inclusion within a complete semantics of natural language.

I THE HISTORICAL AND CONCEPTUAL BASIS OF THE THEORY

The Primacy of Value

Semantic field theory develops, historically and conceptually,[1] from the work of Ferdinand de Saussure.[2] Saussure (1966) put forward the view of language as an interconnected system of signs such that an alteration of any of the elements involved a change in the entire system:

Just as the game of chess is entirely in the combination of different chess

---

[1] For the historical antecedents of contemporary semantic field theory see Bally 1940; Trier 1931; Porzig 1950. See also Ohmann 1953 and Ullman 1957, for a discussion of the history of field theory. For the conceptual link with contemporary theory see Lyons, 1963, 59–90; 1968, 473–570; 1977, pp. 230–336; Lehrer 1974.

[2] The structural semantics of which I speak must be distinguished from Bloomfieldian structuralism. Lyons (1977) makes clear the distinct and even contradictory aspects of the two schools of linguistics which have both been called structuralist: the Saussurean and the Bloomfieldian. The latter structuralism is applied to a methodology and theoretic framework in which the very notion of semantics is properly excluded from linguistic study. Bloomfieldians generally consider meaning to be too subjective a matter for the presumably scientific methodology of their school. Furthermore, while Bloomfieldian structuralism is in direct conflict with many of the principles of generative grammar, there is far less conflict between Saussurean structuralism and generative grammar.

pieces, language is characterized as a system based entirely on the opposition of its concrete units. (1966, 107)

The holism here, for those more familiar with Quine than with Saussure, will seem rather reminiscent of the Quinean interanimation of sentences. But while Quine speaks of the sentence as the unit of language, Saussure speaks of the sign as the unit. (For natural language we can take the sign to be the meaningful word.) For Quine, language is anchored to the world to which it refers at a few central points in the network. Saussure's emphasis is on an apposition of two *systems of differences*, a differential system of *signifiers*—the expressive medium of language, a system of acoustic or inscriptional difference—and a differential system of *signifieds*—the conceptual content of language. The coming together of these two differential systems creates positive signs, that is, signs with a positive content which can then be used to refer. For Saussure, meaning is made possible through such apposition alone, and serves as a precondition of the referential use of language. We may note that Grice stresses the primacy of the intentions of speakers. For an utterance x to mean y requires, ultimately, that a speaker has (or that some speaker had) the intention of acting upon another speaker in the manner describable by a set of 'looped' intentions (see Chapter 2 above).[3]

In this section I want to argue that the Saussurean position, that meaning emerges from the apposition of two differential systems, calls attention to features of the language too easily obscured by a Quinean account or by a Gricean emphasis on the intentionality of the speaker. I do not wish to insist that the conceptual validity of semantic field theory or the theory of metaphor I have presented hinge on a Saussurean conception of meaning, or to argue that a Quinean or Gricean alternative is necessarily incompatible with a theory of semantic fields. Some of the Saussurean arguments may be seen as supplemental to Quinean and Gricean considerations. However, if we recognize the validity of the Saussurean view, the claims of semantic field theory to be an integral part of any semantic account become more natural than they would be on either Quinean or Gricean grounds. Thus I offer the following as considerations favouring the Saussurean position and as offering a preliminary justification of semantic field theory.

My argument (which follows Saussure's) is that even an act as

---

[3] Grice himself produced several versions of the formulation of these intentions.

elementary as ostension requires first, that the language speakers share an understanding of what constitute the salient acoustic (or inscriptional) differences among the acoustic (or inscriptional) phenomena; and secondly, that the language speakers share an understanding of what counts as a salient differentiation within the conceptual frame of the language.

To substantiate the first point, let us consider that to specify the meaning (or reference or semantic role) of a term in a language we must be able to say when two (or more) acoustic (or inscriptional) tokens belong to the same type. Since each acoustic (or inscriptional) token will vary somewhat, not only from speaker to speaker but from occasion to occasion, and since acoustic (or inscriptional) tokens may vary very slightly before they are distinct acoustic (or inscriptional) types, deciding when we have different acoustic (or inscriptional) types, given two or more acoustic (or inscriptional) tokens, is not a trivial problem.

None the less, one might claim that to fix the reference of a term such as 'rabbit', we need merely to identify a rabbit (or rabbit stimuli), utter the sound 'rabbit', and thus confer upon that sound the meaning that will fit the desired referent. Quine has already shown us how fraught with difficulties such an apparently simple procedure really is—particularly in the case of *radical translation*. But by pointing to difficulties Quine did not stress, we can see some justification for the Saussurean position. First, we note that if we wish to repeat that bit of sound, applying it once again to the 'same' entity, we need to establish what will constitute the 'same' sound. Saussure's insight was to recognize that two sounds are the 'same sound' not because they possess the 'same' phonetic attributes, but because they are differentially similar, given the range of phonetic possibilities.

Quine, in elaborating the difficulties that face us in the course of radical translation, makes short shrift of phonetic matters. But these are not trivial and have a substantial impact on our understanding of language and word meaning. For the ethnographer may well get rather bizarre results if she has not correctly differentiated small phonetic (or other acoustic, for example, tonal) distinctions. Quine hypothesizes, 'A rabbit scurries by, the native says "Gavagai" ' (1960, 29). The ethnographer, testing the hypothesis that 'Gavagai' means 'rabbit', may find that she receives an affirmative response on one occasion, a negative response on another.

The reason may simply be a small distinction in the way in which these two tokens differed, a distinction which is insignificant in our own language, yet very significant in the language of the native. Or the ethnographer, intending to test whether 'gavagai' means 'rabbit' or 'animal', tries out the term, given the stimulus of a lion. The native assents to the utterance in the presence of the lion stimulus. What our ethnographer does not as yet realize is that this language contains tonal variants, that, quite coincidentally, she has uttered the term in the high tonal pitch, and that the sound in a high tonal pitch applies to a lion. We can further imagine that our interrogator consistently uses this high pitch to prompt an affirmative or negative response and thus consistently gets an affirmative with the lion stimulus and a negative with the rabbit stimulus, even though the native consistently volunteers 'gavagai', uttered in a medium-range pitch in the presence of a rabbit but never in the presence of a lion.

Of course, differences such as these would ultimately yield to radical translation, since a clever ethnographer would eventually learn which acoustic discriminations were significant and which were indifferent. The point, however, is that grasping the significant acoustic differences is not a trivial problem and that these constitute a system of difference which makes possible the system of language.

Moreover, these discriminations are discovered in conjunction with the differentiations which mark the native's conceptual scheme— differentiations about which the ethnographer, of necessity, hypothesizes using the differentiations which exist in her own conceptual scheme. Where the differentiations do not coexist in two languages, we can predict a difference in meaning of some words in the language which can and eventually will be discovered by a competent translator.

On the one hand, organizing sounds as differentially similar provides a 'system of differences'. On the other hand, the identification of such differential similarity is made possible in virtue of the fact that this system of differences is placed in apposition to a set of conceptual differences which are to be marked phonetically. A difference in each system is fixed by reference to the other system, and thus they mutually mark out the positive, reiterable sign which can be used referentially. Certainly, without such reiterability, it is not clear whether we can speak of linguistic meaning—natural language depends on signs which are types and not tokens. A precondition of an account of linguistic meaning is an account of how we identify the same term on different occasions.

This can be illustrated further by another difficulty which emerges in Quine's project of radical translation. Quine invites us to 'Suppose the native language includes sentences S_1, S_2, and S_3, really translatable respectively as "Animal", "White", and "Rabbit" ' (1960, 29) and asks how we should come to differentiate these. Clearly, it would be through an empirical procedure of inquiry and observation.

But suppose that S_1 is not translatable as 'Animal'. As it turns out, it is translatable as 'ancestral spirit'. And suppose that some, but not all, of those beings we call 'animals', the natives call by a term we should translate as 'ancestral spirits'. And just as we have a theory which allows us to call rabbit stimuli both 'rabbits' and 'animals', the natives have a theory which allows them to call rabbit stimuli both 'S_3 ' and 'S_1'. It would require a certain change in the perspective of the ethnographer for her to begin to understand this, for here the set of differences which is in apposition to the acoustic types is significantly different from our own. To understand S_1, S_2, and S_3 would require paying attention to the native's system of salient conceptual differentia. The difference in conceptual scheme here need not ultimately land us in the sort of indeterminacy of translation Quine has in mind, although we should either have to understand a significant portion of the language of the native or have to have formed some very good hypotheses concerning the beliefs of the native from non-verbal behaviour to be able to form the appropriate analytic hypotheses for these sentences.

To say that S_1 means something like 'ancestral spirit' rather than 'animal', suggests, with Saussure, that the second system of differences is the system of differences between concepts. If the natives had an ontology of 'stages' such that they spoke only of rabbit stages, lion stages, person stages, then their system of differences between concepts would not really differ from our own. The indeterminacy of translation would indeed be there and it would be, as Quine maintains, inscrutable. But if it is the *differences* between concepts which are the salient differences of meaning, then such indeterminacy is ultimately insignificant—it *signifies* nothing and therefore it fails to appear as a feature of a translation manual. But the difference between calling the same stimulus both a rabbit and an animal, in the case of the language of the ethnographer, and calling it a 'gavagai' and 'S_1', in the case of the native's language, where we would translate 'S_1,' as 'an ancestral spirit', is a difference with a significance that will eventually be discovered by the ethnographer. Such a difference must appear in any adequate translation manual—for it is one which, when paired with the appropriate set of acoustic differences, results in a difference of meaning.

To recapitulate, and to illustrate the interdependence of the two appositional differential systems in the formation of meaningful terms, let us go on to suppose that our natives consider some rabbits ordinary animals but consider other rabbits to be the repositories of ancestral spirits. Now let us say that the natives call ordinary rabbits either 'gavagai' or 'gafragai'. What appears as a phonetic difference in our language does not appear as a difference in their language. In contrast, the fact that a native stresses the first syllable, rather than the second, indicates that this is not an ordinary animal but a visiting ancestral spirit: 'ga*va*gai' and the 'ga*fra*gai' are both translatable as our familiar rabbit; but not '*ga*vagai'. The native's semantic distinction between 'ga*va*gai' and '*ga*vagai' is not a feature of our language (probably because it is not a feature of how we regard rabbits or ancestral spirits). We must translate using a sentence or so to describe the native's beliefs about rabbits and ancestral spirits. Without an awareness of the relevant acoustic and conceptual differentiae, the naïve ethnographer would take '*ga*vagai' and 'ga*va*gai' to be two tokens of the same type. She might suspect that 'ga*va*gai' and 'ga*fra*gai' were two distinct utterance-types and search for differences in reference (or stimuli)—perhaps the sex of the rabbit—to account for the acoustic differences.

Now I wish to stress a related point. Were the ethnographer to hold (if only temporarily) these mistaken views, then, on the one hand, what the native would take to be *one* sort of thing, an ordinary rabbit indifferently called 'gavagai' or 'gafragai', the ethnographer would take to be *two* sorts of things, perhaps a male rabbit ('gavagai') and a female rabbit ('gafragai'). And, on the other hand, what the native considers to be *two* sorts of things, namely, an ordinary rabbit and a rabbit possessing an ancestral spirit, the ethnographer would mistakenly consider to be *one* sort of thing, namely, that to which the natives apply the term 'gavagai'. Thus, in addition to encountering the need for systems in order to establish the referential use of 'rabbit' to name a given sort of stimulus, we find that it is not possible even to maintain the numerical identity of the referent without a set of concepts or labels to designate that object's differentia, that is, to designate what the object is not.

It is considerations such as these which lead me to say, with Saussure, that the net of language is fixed through the apposition of two systems of difference, one acoustic and the other conceptual. This apposition is logically prior and conditions the sign so that we can use it to fix reference.[4] Quine seems to imply that the making of the linguistic net and the tying of certain nodes of the net goes on simultaneously. And that may be right, once we already have the beginnings of a net. Saussure stresses that we must begin with at least a rudimentary net before any nodes are referentially fixed.[5]

Saussure called the relation between salient differentia *value*. When elements of the acoustic (or inscriptional) system (*signifiers*) are fixed in apposition to elements from the conceptual system (*signifieds*), we have *signification* and the emergence of a system of positive signs. For Saussure, *signification* results from the arbitrary, but conventionally established, assignment of a given signifier to a given signified. But to speak of a 'given signifier' and a 'given signified' seems to presume the existence of pre-established bits of sound which can be correlated with distinct ideas. Saussure's claim is rather that sounds and ideas have no articulation, that is, they do not exist as distinct delimited entities prior to their combination signs. They exist, and each on their own plane, in an undifferentiated state.[6]

---

[4] Proper names, if Kripke's causal theory of reference for proper names is correct, would seem to be immune from this sort of systematic embeddedness. But notice that at least the phonemes in an acoustic representation of the name would be part of a system of acoustic differentials. And we implicitly work within a conceptual frame in which persons are so individuated that, given the system of acoustic differences, we can individuate words which name by virtue of their repeated use to apply to the 'same person' (a notion which, while philosophically problematical, only occasionally presents genuine difficulties for us in the daily interactions in which we use names).

[5] I have made this point as a claim for the possibility of language and meaning. If it were made as an empirical claim—positing practical rather than logical priority—then I would have to maintain some form of an innateness hypothesis.

[6] Two somewhat controversial consequences appear to result from such a claim. The first is that we appear to make ontological claims concerning the nature of reality that have Whorfian consequences. The second is that people who do not possess the capacity to engage in natural language seem to be deprived of the capacity to think.

But Saussure's claim need not involve an ontological view such as that often adopted by Saussureans influenced by Whorf (1956): that reality is a continuum, broken up into distinct and differentiated entities by the action of language. Saussure's claim is instead psychological or, perhaps more appropriately, linguistic, involving no ontological commitment. He insists that both the signifiers and the signifieds exist only in the mind of the speakers and hearers familiar with the language. Saussure's view is consonant with a conception of meaning utilizing information-theoretic ideas. The information that is 'out there' is not yet 'digitalized', in Dretske's sense. The digitalization comes about through the intentional structure of language.

The view that the concepts which are the signifieds have no articulation prior to their combination with signifiers is even compatible with a Platonic ontology, since Platonic ideas have an objective status while signifieds, as psychological entities, are at best intersubjective. For Whorf there can be no Platonic heaven of universal and eternal ideas. A Saussurean can maintain the relativeness of a given signified to a given language without

The system of positive signs is no longer purely differential. The positive sign, with its signification, can then be used referentially. If Saussure's contention that the signifier and the signified each receive articulation through their coming together in a sign is correct, then one cannot bring together an isolated signifier and signified; value becomes indispensable for signification. The sign, or in the case of natural language, the meaningful word, the term, has not only signification but value in relation to other terms in the language. It is the value of the terms in the language which underlies the idea of a semantic field.

To rephrase these insights in terms of notions we have considered in the previous chapters, terms more familiar to the analytic tradition in philosophy, we can say that, while an understanding of the meaning requires an understanding of the content or function of a term (where that content or function is conceived as something which stands outside the system of linguistic entities—that is, what a term denotes or what role it may play epistemically or communicatively), it also requires an understanding of the relation the term bears to other specifically linguistic entities. And, further, without its relation to other specifically linguistic entities, the term cannot function as a relatum of the non-linguistic entity in a signifying fashion. If these linguistic relations are meant to be captured in the notion of semantic fields, then they provide the justification for insisting on an account of semantic fields to complete any semantic theory.

One consideration against a Saussurean position might come from an extreme Gricean position in which all meaning was reduced to utterer's intention meaning. The radical reductionist would claim that meaning required only that A uttered x intending to mean y, along with other appropriate Gricean intentions. We would not need to depend on any system(s) of differentials—we would not need the notion of value. Let us assume a case of radical translation—better still a case of *radical* radical translation. In the case of radical translation *simpliciter*, A

denying the possible existence of universal and eternal ideas. These eternal and universal ideas, in order to enter into our language system, must be mediated through the system of concepts which are the signifieds of that language—they are not directly accessible, that is, they are not immediately nameable by a portion of sound. Once brought into the language by the mediating system of signifieds, the ideas would then be relative to that language.

To remedy the consequence that the Saussurean thesis results in the claim that deaf mutes and very small children do not possess differentiated concepts, we can modify Saussure's thesis thus: concepts become differentiated within some system of differentiated labels (signifiers). Natural languages, while particularly well suited to such articulations, are not the exclusive means of such differentiation.

and *B* do not know each other's language. In the case of *radical* radical translation, *B* neither knows if *A* speaks a language or if *x* (the presumed utterance) is a part of a language, and, similarly, *A* has no way of knowing, prior to receiving an appropriate response from *B*, if *B* has a language or can understand that *x* is to *mean something*, much less *mean y*.

It is true that *A* can utter *x* *intending* to induce a response in *B* by uttering *x*, and that *A* can have all the other requisite Gricean intentions without either *x* or what it signifies, *y*, belonging to a system of differences. But for *x* to *mean y*, or for *B* to understand that this is what *A* intends, it is less obvious that we do not need to rely on some system of differences. How is *B* to understand that *A* intends what *A* intends in regard to *x* and *y*? First *B* must form some hypothesis concerning *A*'s behaviour. Let us assume that *B* has correctly hypothesized that *A* is attempting to communicate something to *B*. *B* now forms an hypothesis that *x* means *y*. The fact that this act of communication turns out to be successful does not as yet confirm the hypothesis. It is possible, from *B*'s vantage point, that had he taken *x* to mean *z*, or *h*, *i*, *j*, *k*, the communication would have been equally successful. To confirm that *x* *means y*, *B* would have to explore competing hypotheses. In the discussion of information-theoretic basis of meaning in Chapter 3 above, we saw why this must be the case. If *x* means *y*, then it is at least potentially informative. This is to say that when *A* utters *x* and means *y* by uttering *x*, it is only against a background of alternative possibilities that *x* means *y*. But these competing hypotheses would be formed on just what I have defined as the system of conceptual differences. And the considerations we explored with regard to the acoustic differentia would again apply to the reiterated tokens of *x*.

When language is regarded from the perspective of the intentionality of the utterer, it may appear that the appositional systems of which we have spoken are unnecessary for signification to take place.[7] But

---

[7] I believe that the fixing of reference itself requires *either* the apposition of two differential systems *or* the Gricean 'looped' intentions. We can speculate that within a limited communicative situation, in which there are few speakers and only a few utterance-types, the reduction of meaning to the looped intentions of speakers is not implausible. And we can speculate further that, once we have more speakers than we can communicate with personally and once the number of utterances becomes sizeable, it becomes essential, both for the purpose of our semantic memory and for the purpose of communicating with persons to whom we can never communicate our intentions directly, to posit systematic interconnections between the various utterance-types. At that point in the development of a language or communicative system the meaning of an utterance-type will have less to do with the intentions of a speaker and more to do with

language is essentially social, as Wittgenstein's private language argument demonstrates and as the other Gricean intentions attest. And it is the social fact of language which is at once responsible for value. In a passage reminiscent of Wittgenstein's argument against a private language, Saussure writes:

> The social fact alone can create a linguistic system. The community is necessary if values which owe their existence solely to usage and general acceptance are to be set up; by himself the individual is incapable of fixing a single value. (1966, 113.)

The reduction of all meaning to speaker's intentions can bypass value only to fall into the trap of ignoring the inherent social character of language. And it is ironic for a Gricean reductionist programme to fall into such a trap. As a theory of communication, Grice's view importantly acknowledges the social aspect of language, but as an intentionalist reductionist programme it fails to do so.

Early Semantic Field Theory

The Saussurean notion that the meaning of a term is, in part, determined by its position in a system of differences or contrasts was taken up by a number of linguists—Charles Bally (Saussure's student), Jost Trier, and W. Porzig, to mention only the most significant. Especially influential was the investigation of Trier into the lexical fields of intellectual terms occurring in both thirteenth- and fourteenth-century German. He claimed that the shift from a set containing 'wisheit', 'kunst', and 'list' to one in which 'wizzen' replaced 'list' marked a shift in the meanings of all the terms, one which reflected altered political, sociological, and cultural conditions. Briefly, in the thirteenth century, 'list' referred to all skills and knowledge pertaining to courtly and chivalric achievements, while 'kunst' referred to non-courtly modes of knowledge. 'Wîsheit' could be used for either 'kunst' or 'list', or could serve as a global term for all human wisdom. Around 1300, the distinction between courtly and non-courtly attainments dissolved, and none of the terms now covered the whole realm of human knowledge. 'Wîsheit', was reserved for religion and mysticism, while 'kunst' and

---

the systematic interconnections of utterance-types. Furthermore, these systematic interconnections can generate possibilities of meaning never intended by any speaker of the language. It is with such thoughts in mind that I argue, with Saussure, for 'the primacy of value' (see above).

'wizzen' marked the beginnings of a division between art and knowledge. 'List' degenerated into 'cunning'.

Lyons (1963) specified a set of what he later called 'sense-relations'
in his attempt to work out the semantic field, or more specifically the
lexical field, of knowledge words in Plato's corpus. These sense-
relations include varying types of contrast between conceptually
related words. Lyons regarded these sense-relations as a specification
of Saussure's insights. He writes:

At least some vocabulary items fall into lexical systems and the semantic structure of these systems is to be described in terms of the sense-relations holding
between the lexical items. This statement is intended as a more precise formulation of the principle that 'the meaning of a term is a function of the place it
occupies in its own system.' (1963, 129.)

It is the investigation of the semantic systems which constitute a term's
value and which function in providing the meaning of a term which will
occupy us now. We shall attempt to discover how these systems are
constituted, and how their elements and relations can be characterized.

Semantic Fields, Lexical Fields, and Content Domains

The Saussurean insight that the system of signs results from the apposition of two differential systems has its root in the understanding that
semantic fields are constituted by the application of a set of labels to an
area of thought, perception, or experience. In the appropriation of
Saussure by semantic field theory, the system of signs becomes an
interrelated set of terms which serve as elements in a semantic field.
Terms, let us recall, were represented (in Chapter 2) as ordered pairs
$<E(u), C(u)>$. The system of signifiers becomes a set of labels or *lexical field* which provides the expression level $E(u)$, of term; while the system of signifieds becomes the *content domain* providing the informative
content, $C(u)$, of the term. We need to explore these notions.

A **lexical field** consists of a set of *labels*. A label is an uninterpreted
lexical item. As such it can serve as the expression level of a term. A
simple label is monolexemic; that is, its meaning cannot be determined
from the meaning of its parts. Simple labels are generally 'word-forms'
of single words. Sometimes compounds, idiomatic expressions, and
conventionalized phrases acquire a meaning not (readily, at least)
determinable from their parts. When appropriate, these too may be
considered *simple labels*. The uninterpreted labels are related in a field

when we can identify a scheme of contrasts and affinities for a set of labels. For the uninterpreted set of labels {ping, pong} we can specify a contrastive relation of *complementarity*, such that *A* is ping only if *A* is not pong. The set {hot, warm, cool, cold}, independent of its application to any particular domain, marks out a lexical field characterized by the relation of *graded antonymy*. I define these relations in Section 2 below.

A content domain denotes a domain from which we determine the interpretation of an element of a lexical field. Content domains may be variously identified. They may be perceptual and as general as the domain of colour or shape, or as specific as that of ice-cream flavours. An identifiable activity, such as woodworking or fishing, may constitute a content domain, as may something as generally experiential as the life cycle. A domain could have its source in cultural institutions—for example, marriage and the socially significant kinship relations. A domain may be conceived of as conceptual, having its unity derived not from an activity or a perceptual mode but from an interrelation of concepts. Scientific theories would be paradigmatic conceptual content domains. As these examples suggest, a content domain is an area of thought, of inquiry, of activity about which we require or desire *information*.[8] It will provide the *informative content* of a term. In short, a content domain is whatever a set of labels that have contrastive and affinitive relations may be *about*.

A content domain is identifiable but not exhausted by a lexical field. When a lexical field and a content domain are in apposition the contrasts and affinities of the lexical field segment and organize, that is, they *articulate*, the content domain. By *articulation* I mean a sorting or ordering of the content of the given domain, in which salient contrasts and affinities are specified. Notice that such articulation is required if we are to acquire information about a domain. If a signal is informative only against a background of alternate possibilities, it is precisely through an articulation of a domain by a set of salient contrasts that what we experience can be informative. The affinitive relations come to our attention when we recognize that all information is nested. Again, for something to be informative to us, we must sort out and highlight some, rather than other, nested shells of information that are all carried by a 'signal'.

---

[8] I speak of 'information' as including the merely conditional, differential information of which I spoke in Chapter 3, Section 2.

The question will arise: are these articulations given by an objective reality (do they 'cut nature at its joints'?) or are they imposed by our conceptual structure? That is, does the notion of articulation commit us to realism or idealism? I believe that some phenomena are fairly well articulated through the coincidence of our perceptual apparatus and the world exterior to our sensory mechanisms, for example, the force of gravitational pull and hence our experience of *up* and *down*; other phenomena are articulated in the absence of all but cultural constraints for example, some cultural mores and institutions; and most involve a gradation of constraints imposed by the external world and our internal make-up, for example, colour terms, kinship relations, etc. But the notion of articulation itself is relatively neutral to ultimate ontological questions. Regardless of how well defined 'nature's joints' may be, we require the sensory and conceptual means by which to gain such information. That is, the structures by which we become informed about our world must themselves be attuned to identify the articulations, hence to be able to establish contrastive relations between experienced phenomena. Put simply, whether we consider a content domain to have an objective structure, which we need to capture with a set of contrasts and affinities, or whether we conceive of the content domain as a continuum upon which we impose a scheme of contrasts and affinities, it is the requirements of information that dictate the articulation of the domain by contrasts and affinities.

We generally recognize a content domain in virtue of the fact that we can locate a number of terms which appear to be semantically related. That is, these terms bear semantic relationships to one another, such as synonymy, antonymy, complementarity, etc. But the fact that there are terms which are semantically related is an epistemic criterion for a domain. Content domains should be so conceived that it is intelligible to think of there being some that have yet to be articulated by a set of terms. Otherwise we ignore the possibility that new domains emerge. The poet who attempts to express and communicate a unique perceptual experience, an imaginative vision, charts out a new content domain. When the new sciences of electricity, magneticism, genetics, and molecular biology emerged, they were exploring previously unarticulated content domains. Such an understanding of the content domain is especially important for the project of understanding the cognitive role of metaphor. It is precisely to provide such an articulation that we often require metaphor—in the case of metaphor, the structure of another, articulated or *formed* content domain is used to provide the articulation of the as yet unarticulated or *unformed* content domain.

A content domain may be identified and not yet articulated. We identify a phenomenon as distinct prior to gaining any understanding of it. In the history of science, electricity and magnetism provide a good example. While the ancient world knew of the attractive effects of magnetite and amber, the domains of magnetism and electricity did not receive studied attention until the sixteenth century; and the unification of the two domains as one did not occur until the early nineteenth century. The discovery of radiation gives us another example from the history of science in which a new content domain was opened to be explored and charted by future empirical and theoretical work. Using Dretske's adaptation of the terms *analogue* and *digital*, we can say that a domain not yet articulated can, at best, provide us with analogue information. (Or using epistemic concepts, we may say that we have *knowledge of* without yet having *knowledge that*—that is, we have knowledge *of* x without knowing *that* y may be predicated of x.) To acquire digitalized information (or propositional knowledge), we require that the domain be articulated. To avail ourselves of a set of articulations, that is, contrasts and affinities from another (possibly related or homologous) domain, allows us 'epistemic access' (Boyd 1979) to the domain under inquiry. We acquire a way in which to digitalize information about the domain, supplying hypotheses that, by abduction, lead to empirical testing. In the case of electromagnetic phenomena, the articulations were heavily borrowed from the domain of fluids (and indeed at various periods, electricity, or electromagnetism, was believed to be a special sort of fluid): we speak of 'electric currents', 'electromagnetic waves', and in slang of 'electric juice'.

To draw the distinction between a content domain articulated by a lexical field and one identified but not articulated, we may say that the former is constituted by *formed content*, the latter by *unformed content*.[9] The articulation which segments a content domain by contrastive and affinitive relations results in *formed content*. Formed content can provide us with information which is digitalized. Clearly, when the temperature continuum is segmented by a lexical set such as {cold, cool, warm, hot}, we can express and convey information that we could not convey without some form of differentiation of temperature states.

---

[9] See Hjelmslev 1961, esp. 36.

(Equally clearly, we do not require lexemes—a numerated scale or a differentiated set of behaviours would also serve this limited function, with differing degrees of informativeness.)

If we wish to speak in terms of concepts, we can say that formed content may be identified as a concept, but only in so far as it is a concept expressible in some sign system or language.[10] A concept, on this account, is not a 'disembodied' thought. Content domains provide the conceptual substratum underlying language, independent of any particular language; but in so far as such conceptual substrata are independent of any language, or more generally of any expressible set of articulations, they are also unformed. As we shall see below, we can none the less speak of concepts that transcend the linguistic bounds of a given language, but a concept, as formed content, must be expressible in some language. Conceptual substrata are unformed content, whereas a specified concept (and to be specified it must be articulated in some sign system) is formed content. Notice that the contrast is not between form and content but between what has been differentiated (formed content) and what has not been differentiated (unformed content).

Formed content can be defined using the notion of isomorphism, as follows. If we had two languages Q_1 and Q_2 (or finite subsystems of two infinite sign systems) that were isomorphic and articulated the same content domain, then the word meanings would be given the same representation in both Q_1 and Q_2. For any given term t_1 in Q_1 we could find a term t_2 in Q_2 so that both would have as their content the same concept or concatenation of concepts. This content would be formed content, and it would be the same formed content although it had two different forms of expression. It would remain the same formed content because the two articulations which the content domain received were isomorphic. Given a third language Q_3 which was not isomorphic to Q_1 and Q_2, but which articulated the same content domain, then, to the extent that Q_3 was anisomorphic to Q_1 and Q_2, we should not be able to find an expression t_3 to which we could assign the same formed content as t_1 and t_2.

The anisomorphism between different natural languages, that is, the fact that for every term of a natural language it is often not possible to find a corresponding term in a second natural language, can be seen in

---

[10] If the reader is more comfortable with beliefs than with concepts, then the notion of a content domain can be reformulated as a related set of beliefs, both actual and possible, attributable to a given language community.

cases in which there is a term t in Q_1 which is a superordinate term such that all the subordinate terms find a translation in Q_2 but there is no superordinate term in Q_2 which translates t. Lyons (1977) points out that the Greek term *demiourgós* has as subordinate terms (hyponyms, see below) *tékton*, *iatrós*, *auletés*, *skutotómos*, *kubernétes*. These may be translated by the English words 'carpenter', 'doctor', 'flute-player', 'shoemaker', 'helmsman'; yet English has no superordinate term for all of these. (We may note that the issue of conceptual relativism is closely related to such anisomorphism between different languages. Conceptual relativism receives a pertinent, if brief, discussion in the concluding chapter of this book.)

Formed content, as we have defined it, is not identical to the term of which it is the content, nor is it independent of the articulation which is given to the conceptual or experiential continuum. As *formed content*, there is no difficulty in individuating concepts, for they are the formed content of some lexical item.

Semantic fields are constituted by content domains that have been articulated by lexical fields. If there exists an isomorphism between two lexical fields which apply to the same content domain, then they also define the same semantic field. However, if there is an anisomorphism, then we must say that, while these two fields cover the same content domains, they define different semantic fields.

The question arises whether the terms of a semantic field completely cover a content domain without gaps or overlaps. Such were the earliest conceptions of semantic fields, especially that of Trier. Lehrer suggests that rather than regarding fields as mosaics, we should view them as comprised of terms whose application to a content domain centres on certain foci.[11] This conception accords very well with the claims of *prototype theory* that the members of a category share prominent features of the prototypes and are related to one another in the manner characterized by Wittgenstein as 'family resemblance'.[12] The

---

[11] Berlin and Kay (1969), in their study of colour terms, elicited responses from an individual speaker at different times, from different speakers of a given language, and from speakers of a number of different and unrelated languages. They found that for each basic colour (see below, n. 16), a focal point could be identified which remained remarkably stable even across unrelated languages, while the boundaries of each colour term, even in a given language, are very unclear (indeed, they may vary for the same speaker questioned at different times).

[12] See Rosch (1973, 1975*a*, *b*), Rosch and Mervis (1975), Rosch *et al.* (1976). Semantic fields may, in turn, provide prototype theory with a more convincing theoretical base than is possible if we ignore semantic fields. (See Grandy 1987*a*.)

terms for the prototypes would provide the foci of the field. On this model, gaps and overlaps are to be expected, and while each concept or term has a clear focus it may have indeterminable boundaries.

Considerations of polysemy, information-theoretic concerns, and arguments borrowed from structural semantics lead us to the view that words have their meaning in part because they contrast with other terms in the language.[13] Furthermore, the view that our semantic memory is in fact structured through contrasts between related terms has received appreciable empirical confirmation (Gleitman 1981). We ought to see that the potential for the subtle articulations which give natural language its rich expressive capacity arises not only because we can posit a difference between any two terms but because we can group related terms and posit differences between them. Within a language, we recognize certain relations holding between words: synonymy, antonymy, part–whole, etc. Saussure's system of differences may be characterized as sets of terms bound by relations of affinity and contrast.[14]

2 THE STRUCTURE OF SEMANTIC FIELDS

Contrast Sets

We begin with the notion of a *simple contrast set*. A simple contrast set contains a covering term and two or more terms which contrast with one another. For example, the terms 'sibling', 'sister', 'brother', form the simple contrast set {sibling: sister, brother}, in which the covering term is 'sibling'. Another example of a simple contrast set includes the terms naming the seasons {season: summer, winter, spring, autumn}, in which 'season' is the covering term. Following Grandy (1987*a*) we can characterize a simple contrast set as follows:

---

[13] The conception of semantic fields that I shall attempt to portray here will be an amalgam of the views of Lehrer (1974) and Lyons (1968; 1977), new work being done by Grandy (1987*a*), and my own additional insights. Finally, the work of Ross (1981) and Cohen (1985, 1986) will provide this brew with its salt and pepper. I attempt to construct a notion of semantic fields which, in spite of the varied origins of the elements of the theory, will form a coherent assemblage.

[14] Ross speaks of affinities and oppositions, Lehrer and Lyons of sense-relations, and Grandy of contrasts. I choose to speak of affinities and contrasts, rather than contrasts alone, because affinities as well as oppositions characterize the related but differentiated sets of terms that we shall call semantic fields; and I chose the term contrast rather than opposition, for the latter suggests a polarity of meanings, while the former suggests a variety of available differences. See Chapter 2, n. 12, above, for a justification for abandoning the use of the term 'sense-relation'.

Definition of a simple contrast set. $<L: E_1 \ldots E_m>$ is a simple contrast set if it satisfies the following conditions:

   (a) If, in a given language, $E_1 \ldots E_m$ are all monolexemic terms, then they all belong to the same grammatical category, i.e they are all nouns, or all verbs, or all adjectives, etc.

     (i) if $E_1 \ldots E_m$ are all nouns, then L will be a noun;

     (ii) if $E_1 \ldots E_m$ are all verbs, then L will take a form such as 'verbs of . . . ', e.g. $<$ (verbs of) cooking: boiling, baking, simmering, frying, steaming, etc.$>$;

     (iii) forms analogous to (ii) will hold true of other non-nominal forms.

   (b) All speakers competent with regard to L, E_1, . . ., E_m would believe that all speakers competent with regard to these expressions would believe that, for each i between 1 and m inclusive, all E_is are Ls and that, for each distinct i and j, the domain of application of E_i is (generally) not coincident with the domain of application of E_j.[15]

According to condition (a), L, E_1, . . . , E_m should be *paradigmatically related* terms. Terms or expressions are paradigmatically related if, in substituting one for another in a syntactically well-formed string, we preserve syntactic well-formedness.

Some simple contrast sets will be widely accepted and recognized as such, for example $<$colour: red, green, blue, white, black, yellow, etc.$>$. These cohere with our most general background default assumptions, assumptions shared by virtually all competent speakers of the language. Among simple contrast sets we can differentiate *basic contrast sets*. In a basic contrast set, all Es are *basic terms*. The criteria for basic terms can be demonstrated by considering colour terms. Basic

---

[15] See Grandy (1987*a*) for a justification of this formulation, especially condition (*b*). Grandy and I disagree, however, with regard to the necessity of maintaining the disjointness of E_i and E_j. Many contrast sets will form an opposition between terms which generally apply to disjoint (extensional) classes but which need not, as a matter of the meaning of the terms, apply to disjoint classes. Kinship terms, such as 'mother', 'father', 'sister', 'brother', are elements of a contrast set whose covering term is 'blood relative', but some of the elements need not have disjoint domains of application—as the Oedipal myth reminds us.

terms are monolexemes that are not restricted to a narrow application (excluding 'blond', which can refer only to human hair, complexion, and—in the USA—wood furniture) and that meet certain established criteria of psychological saliency, for example, a tendency to occur at the beginning of elicited lists of colour terms, stability of reference across informants and across occasions of use, and occurrence in ideolects of all informants. Terms are suspect if they are morphologically complex, for example, 'blue-green'; if they are recent loan words; or if they fail to have the same distributional potential as established basic terms, for example, in English we can add '-ish' as a suffix to basic colour terms, as in 'reddish', 'greenish', but we cannot say 'aquaish' or 'chartreusish'.

Basic terms establish the important contrasts within a larger field of related terms.[16] We can say further that the basic contrast sets of a language provide the most widely accepted contrasts available in the language. We may note that while a basic contrast set is a simple contrast set, not all simple contrast sets are basic. To the basic contrast set we may add *peripheral terms*. In the case of colour, these would include 'crimson', 'scarlet', 'chartreuse', 'aquamarine', etc. These peripheral terms may have different degrees of importance. If a basic term is added or eliminated over time, there are important shifts throughout the contrast set and the larger semantic field to which the contrast set belongs. If a term on the periphery is added, there is relatively little effect on the other terms. In the realm of colour terms, Berlin and Kay (1969) determined that if a language did not have a term for, let us say, green, then the different shades of what we call 'green' would, according to their hue and tone, be included within the denotation of one or more of the other colour terms: a light shade of yellowish green might be called by the term we translate as 'yellow', while a deep, dark green would be called by the term we translate as 'black'. Adding a term for

---

[16] See Lehrer 1974, 10. Lehrer modifies the criteria for establishing a field's basic words used by Berlin and Kay (1969) in their important study of colour terms. In that study, eleven terms are taken as basic: 'white', 'black', 'red', 'green', 'yellow', 'blue', 'brown', 'purple', 'pink', 'orange', and 'grey'. Terms such as 'crimson', 'scarlet', 'blond', 'blue-green', 'bluish', 'lemon-coloured', 'salmon-coloured', 'the colour of the rust on my aunt's old Chevrolet', are excluded on the basis of the criteria I have mentioned above. These criteria are held commonly by Berlin and Kay, and Lehrer. Berlin and Kay include the following criterion, which Lehrer holds to be relevant but too restrictive for generalization: the signification of basic terms is not included in that of other terms of the field, thus 'crimson' and 'scarlet', for example, are eliminated as these are both kinds of red for most speakers of English.

'green' to the other colour terms of the language would significantly alter the denotation of other colour terms.

Sometimes we want to speak of a set of related terms, not all of which are monolexemic. *Mixed contrast sets* are defined in the same way as simple contrast sets above, but allowing polylexemic expressions— for example, in a set of terms contrasting different fishing methods, we would include 'angling', 'trolling', 'harpooning', but also 'fishing with a net'; the set of terms for silverware, in addition to the basic 'spoon', 'fork', and 'knife', would include 'dessert spoon', 'soup spoon', 'sauce spoon' (found on the tables of restaurants influenced by *nouvelle cuisine*), 'salad fork', 'fish knife', etc.

So far I have defined simple, basic, and mixed contrast sets. A contrast set *simpliciter* is a simple, a basic, or a mixed contrast set. From the notion of a contrast set, we can develop the notion of a semantic field. In our contrast set, we want L to be a term which delineates the domain to which the lexical items $E_1 \ldots E_m$ apply. Grandy (forthcoming *a*) points out that one possible objection to his formulation of a contrast set is that <kidney or oak: kidney, oak> seems to fit the criteria of a contrast set. Grandy's problem applies to simple and mixed contrast sets, not to basic contrast sets. For the latter we have fairly strict membership criteria. But, as we have seen, we do not want these criteria to apply to all contrast sets. Grandy suggests that we add the condition that 'specific frames such as "that's not an E_1, it's an E_j" are non-anomalous' and that 'no matter exactly how anomalous one thinks "That's not an oak, it's a kidney" is, it is at least somewhat anomalous unlike "That's not an oak, it's a pecan." ' The difficulty, I believe, pertains to how we decide what constitutes a domain to which a set of terms might apply. If we speak of a conceptual domain, we appear to make a commitment to some sort of conceptual substratum. Grandy simply does not want to make any commitments to any notions beyond the empirically ascertained judgements of the language speakers. I am not sure that we can proceed in this uncommitted fashion. But if we are to appeal to some notion of anomaly which is not wedded to a synthetic–analytic dichotomy, then we need to amend Grandy's discussion with the concept of a default assumption introduced in Chapter 2. Default assumptions will help us with the question of when to exclude certain disjunctive groupings from being considered contrast sets.

In the discussion of default assumptions (and in particular of discourse-specific default assumptions) in Chapter 2, the examples given alluded only to general or widely recognized discourses. But even within a particular text, or within a particular conversation, we can alter or temporarily suspend the operative default assumptions in certain ways. This makes what might otherwise appear to be anomalous sentences not anomalous at all. For example Katz and Fodor take 'The wall is covered with silent paint' (Fodor and Katz, 1964, 493) to be anomalous. Sanders points out that this sentence 'might refer to a specially developed paint that is noiseless when applied with a roller' (1973, 60–1) as opposed to producing the squishy noise that generally ensues. Our usual default assumptions are such that we do not attribute noise or silence to paint. Given certain developments, within a given discourse—say, about these particular properties of paint—we alter some of our ordinary default assumptions, so that we can accommodate the contrast: silent paint, noisy paint.

Rather than posit degrees of anomaly and say that contrast sets must be clearly non-anomalous, I believe we need to say that, given our general background default assumptions, we have a non-anomalous set. But default assumptions can be temporarily altered when we explicitly posit the conditions which differ from the default assumptions. This might well be the case were the contrast between a kidney and an oak somehow made salient—one could, for example, speak of the difference between a kidney bean and an acorn, or want to differentiate between two shapes, one of a kidney, the other of an oak. I suspect that regardless of how far-fetched the examples may be, it will always be possible to conjure up some context in which we suspend our usual default assumptions (for example, that kidneys and oaks have nothing of interest in common—thus, they would not form a suitable contrast set) to allow what otherwise would seem incongruous, anomalous contrasts.

The key notion here is context. It is context which determines whether we adopt a given set of default assumptions: the context will guide our choice of default assumptions, if they are not to be simply the general background default assumptions, or will offer grounds for suspending default assumptions and provide the material for forming alternative (temporary) assumptions. Context, in ways suggested in Chapters 3 and 4 above, then mediates between default assumptions and the contrastive sets operative in a particular bit of language. But we have yet to understand precisely how context accomplishes such mediation. It is to be hoped that current interest in pragmatics will eventually make this process less opaque.

Ordered Contrast Sets

The contrast sets so far discussed do not specify the nature of the contrasts and affinities that we find in semantic fields. To indicate the specificity of contrasts, Grandy (1987*a*) has suggested introducing an *ordering* among the elements of a field, but notes that 'ordering here cannot have its usual set-theoretic meaning of a transitive, irreflexive relation'. As a preliminary step in setting forth a proper sense of ordering, he introduces a *successor function*.

A successor function will be a one-to-one function on the elements of the contrast set such that there is at least one element which generates the entire set. . . . Successive applications of the function produce all members of the set other than the originating one. If these applications also eventually produce the originating element the set is cyclically ordered.

These will generate *ordered contrast sets*: 'an ordered pair of contrast set and successor function'. As an illustration he provides the following: <<days of the week: Sunday, Monday, Tuesday . . . Saturday>, d.a.> where 'd.a.' is the 'day after' function that maps 'Sunday' on to 'Monday', 'Monday' on to 'Tuesday' . . . and 'Saturday' on to 'Sunday'. Such a successor function is too specific to be of general use, but we can think of a function with greater generality that would serve the purpose, namely the 'unit following', where the unit is given by the covering term, with an additional provision that the set is cyclically ordered. This function would then also be operative in the ordered contrast sets of months of the year, seasons of the year, hours of the day, etc.

Most semantic fields have terms in differing relations to one another—some affinities, for example, synonymy, partial synonymy, hyponymy, part–whole relations (see below), and some contrasts, for example, incompatibility, antonymy, converse terms, complementarity (see below). A field will generally include several such ordered contrast sets. While Grandy aims here at a needed generality, it is not yet clear whether the successor function will be able to characterize the different sorts of relation that we find within semantic fields. Furthermore, the orderings which will be most useful to us in exploring metaphorical transfers of relations require a specification of, rather than a generalization about, the different relations of affinity and contrast. I leave it to future theorizing to bring the general formalization attempted by Grandy into line with the empirically derived relations provided by

Lyons and Lehrer. Where it is enlightening, I shall employ Grandy's more formal notions.

From an ontogenic perspective we could say that we take a set of words which appear to constitute a lexical set—our test might be something empirical, such as eliciting associative lists and seeing what items appeared most frequently—and then ask how we can characterize the relations or ordering within these sets. Having established a regularity in such relations, we can then establish the presence of such relations as a criterion for the existence of a semantic field. While such a procedure would appear to be circular, it is not viciously circular, and is not very different from the way in which many scientific concepts become established. We could call this the 'bootstraps theory of semantic fields'. Thus we can say that it is our ability to posit relations between terms which in large measure determines that we have a semantic field.

These relations are, at least for the purposes of constructing a theory of metaphorical meaning, the core of contemporary semantic field theory. So let us now consider them, beginning with the paradigmatic relations.[17]

Paradigmatic Relations of Affinity

Among affinitive relations, *synonymy* has probably exercised philosophers most. Contemporary linguistic philosophy has given us cause enough to be wary of synonymy[18] construed as interchangeability in all contexts, *salva veritate*. For linguistic philosophers who take the central questions in semantics to be the questions of truth conditions, synonymy plays a central role in the theory of meaning. Quine writes:

Once the theory of meaning is sharply separated from the theory of reference, it is a short step to recognizing as the primary business of the theory of

---

[17] These are given by Lyons (1963; 1968; 1977). Neither Lyons nor Grandy treat syntagmatic relations. I shall suggest a number of syntagmatic relations later in the chapter. An alternative set of relations is put forward by Ross (1981), although Ross himself does not conceive of these as defining a semantic field, but as defining 'predicate schemes'. The relations Ross (1981, 40–7) uses are derived from Aristotle's remarks in the *Topics* (i, 15, 106^a–107^b), in which Aristotle offers different tests for whether a given term has the same meaning in different occurrences. Lyons's sense-relations seem to me to be preferable here, since they more closely adhere to the sorts of semantic relations philosophers and linguists discuss today.

[18] I refer here to cognitive synonymy. For a justification of the priority of cognitive synonymy, see Lyons 1968, 449.

meaning the synonymy of linguistic forms and the analyticity of statements; meanings themselves as obscure intermediate entities, may well be abandoned. (1963, 22)

But if the sense of a term is a function of the way in which that term relates to other conceptually related terms, then questions of sense are not reducible to questions of truth conditions, and meaning is not simply that which fixes reference. There is a sense in which we reverse the interdependence of meaning and truth. Rather than it being the case that the meaning of a sentence is dependent on its truth conditions, the truth conditions are dependent on how the meanings of the terms are established. And the meaning of terms are established through contrastive relations with other terms, as these terms apply to a given domain. Of the various relations, synonymy contributes least to establishing these contrastive relations; hence it figures less prominently in a relational semantics than in a truth semantics.[19] As a result, we can still adopt the notion of synonymy but be less subject to the consequences of affirming the existence of such a relation between terms. We can also loosen the requirement of preserving truth in *all contexts*, since meaning does not hinge on synonymy. Instead, the criterion of interchangeability which preserves truth in all contexts is altered to interchangeability that preserves *meaning* in a *context-relative* fashion.

For meaning to be preserved would mean that the other oppositions and affinities displayed by the putatively synonymous terms would be maintained in the given context of the term. That is to say, if 'unmarried man' is synonymous with 'bachelor' in the context

6.1 Amanda vowed that, after her experience with Edward, she would never again be involved with a man who was not a bachelor,

where Amanda is unmarried and Edward is married, then we can substitute 'unmarried man' for 'bachelor' and the antonymous term in both cases would be 'married man'. Similarly, the covering term would remain the same (though there is no monolexemic covering term). All other salient affinities and relations of the one term would be retained by the other.

In contrast to the definition of synonymy as interchangeability which

---

[19] Contrast this with Quine's (1963, 11) remark that when we give the meaning of a term we are simply giving a synonym.

is truth-preserving in all contexts, our notion makes synonymy relative to a given context.[20] Following Lyons, we adopt a broad and encompassing notion of context. Context includes the spatio-temporal situation of the utterance; what has been said earlier, in so far as this is known by speaker and hearer and is pertinent; other 'mutual knowledge'; (for an oral utterance) concurrent, and salient, non-verbal behaviour on the part of speaker and hearer; and 'the tacit acceptance by the speaker and hearer of all the relevant conventions, beliefs and presuppositions "taken for granted" by the members of the speech community to which speaker and hearer belong' (Lyons 1968, 413).— The latter condition accords, roughly, with our default assumptions.

By making synonymy context-dependent, we de-emphasize the importance of any notion of absolute synonymy and replace it with a notion of *partial synonymy*. Partial synonymy is synonymy to a certain degree. We bypass the difficulty of establishing an absolute synonymy, which we could say is synonymy in all possible and significant contexts, by positing differing degrees of synonymy. The greater the number of possible contexts in which two terms, *x* and *y*, may be substituted, preserving relations of contrast and affinity, the greater is their degree of synonymy. Partial synonymy may be illustrated in the following context:

6.2 My — has just had puppies.

In 6.2 the terms 'dog' and 'bitch' are completely interchangeable. The context has neutralized the difference between these two terms, and within this limited context they are synonymous.[21] This is because there is a semantic field which includes the terms 'dog', 'bitch', and 'puppies', with specified relations between them such that if the context can absorb some of the information regarding their relation, a limited type of synonymy can be posited between some of the terms. But in the context

6.3 I should like to mate my pure-bred golden retriever bitch with another pure-bred golden retriever,

[20] Lyons (1968) takes a similar tack, one which is adopted in Kittay (1978) and Kittay and Lehrer (1981). The introduction of contrast sets makes some of Lyons's apparatus redundant.

[21] Contextually determined synonymy also illustrates the general principle that the same information may be conveyed in language either syntagmatically or paradigmatically.

'dog' and 'bitch' do not preserve the same contrasts.[22]

We can see that the strategy employed suggests, as does Lyons, that not only synonymy but also other affinities and oppositions are context-dependent. An extremely important relation of affinity is *hyponymy*, a taxonomic relation which is the reverse of *superordination*. The covering term, L, in both the simple and the basic contrast set is generally in a relation of superordination to $E_1 \ldots E_m$; and $E_1 \ldots E_m$ are generally all hyponyms of L. We may say that if x is a *kind of y* then x is a hyponym of y (and conversely, y is a superordinate term with regard to x). 'Scarlet', for example, is a hyponym of 'red'; 'scarlet' and 'red' are both hyponyms of 'colour', and are therefore *co-hyponyms* of 'colour'. Lyons defines hyponymy as unilateral or asymmetrical implication: '*x is scarlet* will be taken to imply *x is red*; but the converse implication does not generally hold' (1968, 455).

Hyponymy is related to the formalized concept of *inclusion* in the logic of classes. But inclusion is appropriate only for extensions. We reject inclusion in a class as a definition of hyponymy for the same reason that Grandy (1987*a*) rejects a definition of contrast sets in terms of the extension of terms: 'we want the containment of elements in the covering term and the disjointness of the elements to be linguistic matters not possibly accidental extensional matters'. 'Unicorn' is a hyponym of 'mythical beast' although both terms have a null extension. On an extensional account, 'mythical beast' and 'dragon', would also be hyponyms of 'unicorn'.

It is important to note that hyponymy operates neither as comprehensively nor as systematically in natural language as it does in scientific taxonomies. There are *gaps*, *asymmetries*, and *indeterminacies* in lexical areas. Without discussing hyponymy explicitly, Grandy (1987*a*) makes use of the relation between prototypicality and hyponomy in his 'contrast set with prototype theory'. He writes:

For many contrast sets, speakers competent with regard to the contrast set have internal representation of a particular kind of similarity (associated with

---

[22] We should notice that, if questions of truth conditions are regarded as the only appropriate ones in semantics, then it will not do to consider synonymy as context-dependent. One can choose contexts so as to make words which are clearly different in meaning interchangeable, *salva veritate*. For example, in speaking of a 6 ft. tall, dark-haired, blue-eyed man named Harry, we can say that the three adjectival phrases and any combination of them are all interchangeable, without change in truth value, in the following context: 'Harry can be described as being — '. And we should certainly not want to claim that we had even a limited synonymy in this case, as we do in the case of 'dog' and 'bitch'.

the covering term) and prototypes of the members. An object is categorized as E_i just in case it is more similar (in respect L) to the E_i prototype than to any E_j prototype.

The term L, expressing the particular kind of similarity, is the super-ordinate term of which the different prototypes of the members are hyponyms. Similarity to a prototype, an inherently problematical notion, is rendered far less problematical when replaced by the notion of 'more similar to a given E than to any other E, with respect to L'. Using the apparatus of 'more similar-with-respect-to-L', Grandy characterizes three kinds of contrast set:

A contrast set is *strongly cohesive*, just in case for each i any two members of E_i are more similar-with-respect-to-L to each other than to any member of any E_j.

A contrast set is *prototypical* just in case it is not strongly cohesive and for each i one can find a member (the prototype) of E_i such that any member of E_i is more similar-with-respect-to-L to that prototype of E_i than it is to the proto-type of any E_j.

A contrast set is *weakly cohesive* just in case it is not prototypical and for each i for any member of E_i it is more similar-with-respect-to-L to *some* other member of E_i more than it is to any member of any E_j.

Scientific and technical taxonomies are generally strongly cohes-ive—for example, the contrast set of chemical elements. Here there will be no overlaps and no gaps, although the list of elements may not yet be exhausted. Biological taxonomies are mostly strongly cohesive, though they may be partially prototypical. But contrast sets involving biological terms in natural language would more close resemble proto-typical characterization. Colour terms would be a very good example of a prototypical contrast set. Here there will be some boundary disputes, some overlaps, and perhaps some gaps, as well. A contrast set of differ-ent sorts of furniture for sitting on, for example <chairs, sofas, arm-chairs, settees, etc.> would exemplify a *weakly cohesive* set. Here there are many overlaps, gaps, and indeterminacies.

When, in metaphor, relations of affinity and contrast are transferred across semantic fields, the cohesiveness and prototypicality of the con-trast set most likely guides the selection of the contrast set. Alterna-tively these may be carried over in the transfer, as are the contrasts and affinities. I shall speak later of 'the furniture of our minds'. If the meta-phor has any plausibility, it resides, in part, in our ability to think of the contents of mind as being organized into the same sort of weakly cohesive sets to which furniture terms belong. Contrast this metaphor with the aviary metaphor in Plato's *Theaetetus* (197c–200a). There the contents of mind are pictured as having a prototypical organization characteristic of a natural kind.

To the above relations we may add two suggested by Lehrer (1974). *Part of* is an affinitive relation like *hyponymy*, but unlike the latter it is not always transitive.[23] *Part of* probably covers a variety of different forms of connection between terms. The sense in which a fingernail is a part of a finger is different from the sense in which a cell of epidermal tissue is part of a finger. *Overlapping segments* is one special type of the *part of* relation, but one which is contrastive at the same time as it is affinitive. *Overlapping segments* is a relation which holds between terms of the set <time interval: second, minute, hour, day, week, month, year, decade, etc.>. We can either say, 'That lasted an hour, not a minute', or we can say, 'That lasted not merely a minute, but a full hour.' In the first sentence, 'minute' and 'hour' are simply contrastive; in the second, they are affinitive as well. (Contrast the anomalous: 'He punched her in the eye, not in the face'.)

Paradigmatic Contrastive Relations

Incompatibility is the most basic contrast to be found. The relation posited between the *E*s of our simple contrast set is a relation of incompatibility—for example, 'blue', 'green', 'yellow', 'red', etc. are all incompatible terms. Two otherwise identical sentences containing incompatible terms are contradictory. (In the case of colour terms, we arrive at such contradictory sentences when we assume that the sentence attributes two incompatible colours to the same coloured portion of the object.) Incompatibility is importantly different from mere difference of meaning. Indeed one could say that two terms which are incompatible are more closely related in meaning than two terms which are not incompatible.

Antonymous relations involve different kinds of opposition of meaning. In *antonymy* properly so called, the assertion of one antonymous term implies the denial of the other but not vice versa. Take the

---

[23] In certain technical uses *part of* is always transitive; for example, in geometry, if a line segment AB is part of a line segment AC, and AC is part of a line segment AD, then AB is part of AD. However, in many other uses *part of* is not transitive. For example, the retina is part of the eye and the eye is part of the face, but the retina is not part of the face. (See Lyons's discussion of part–whole relations in 1977, 311–17.)

example, 'good' and 'bad'. The sentence 'John is good' implies 'John is not bad', but 'John is not bad' does not always imply 'John is good'.

Complementarity is a special case of incompatibility holding in lexical sets containing only two items. Any two terms x and y are *complementary* if and only if the denial of x involves the assertion of y and the assertion of x implies the denial of y. If 'John is single', then 'John is not married', and if "John is married', then 'John is not single'. While antonymies are gradable, complementarities are ordinarily neither gradable nor qualifiable. One can be partially good and partially bad, and something can be somewhat high, but one cannot be partly married and partly single, or slightly pregnant. At best, these latter expressions would need special interpretation to be intelligible.

Converse terms include pairs such as 'buy' and 'sell', 'husband' and 'wife', 'parent' and 'child'. These are not complementary, for it is not the case that if 'x does not buy y from z' then 'x sells y to z'. Rather, as is the case with antonymy, if 'x sells y to z' then 'x does not buy y from z'. But converses, unlike antonymies, are not gradable. Grandy points out that converse are really several different relations:

In the relevant sense husband/wife is a two-place relation such that

x is the husband of y iff y is the wife of x

whereas the relationship for buy/sell involves a permutation of the first and third elements rather than the first and second:

x buys y from z iff z sells y to x

Grandy suggests that converses require a permutation relation, that is, an ordered triple specifying the permutation and the two linguistic items so related.

Oppositions may be *privative* or *equipollent*. In the former case two terms are distinguished in so far as a positive property attributed to one is denied of the other, for example 'animate' versus 'inanimate'. In linguistic terms, this is a distinction between a 'marked' and an 'unmarked' term. Equipollence is an opposition between two terms, both with distinctive but opposing positive features, for example, 'viral' versus 'bacterial'.[24] The pair, 'male'/'female', are often used meta-

---

[24] Lyons (1977) gives 'animate', 'inanimate' as an example of a privative opposition, and 'male', 'female' as an example of equipollence, and they are themselves revealing of the extra-linguistic forces which sometimes invade considerations that are presumed to be purely semantic. Morphologically 'animate' versus inanimate' would seem to indicate privative opposition. But certainly some ecologically minded persons might object that the properties of being animate and of being inanimate are distinctive beyond the

phorically and even mythologically to label many oppositions we would call equipollent, for example the Yin–Yang dichotomy. But the opposition between male and female is often ambiguous with regard to equipollence or privation—an ambivalence preserved in many metaphorical transfers.

Directional contrasts may broadly be understood to include change of state as well as change of place. Lyons writes:

> Looked at from this point of view, arriving in Paris stands in the same relation to being in Paris, as getting married is to being married . . . and departing from or leaving Paris is in the same relation to being in Paris as dying is to living or forgetting is to knowing. (1977, 281)

Regarded in this sense, directional opposition is at the basis of much lexical structure. It also provides an elementary example of the relational character of such standard metaphors as a 'journey' to speak of death and of those (dead) metaphors which use a change of place as a metaphor for an epistemological change, for example, 'I *arrived at* the idea'.

Orthogonal and *antipodal* contrasts are illustrated within the contrast set <compass points: north, south, east, west>. The antipodal contrasts are between 'north' and 'south', 'east' and 'west'. The orthogonal contrasts are between 'north' and 'east', 'south' and 'east', 'north' and 'west', 'south' and 'west'. Antipodal contrasts are diametrically opposed to one another, while orthogonal contrasts need not be exclusive oppositions. Using our example, we can posit a point which is north-east but never a point which is north-south. Orthogonal and antipodal oppositions need not be spatial. The contrast in English between black and white is an antipodal contrast. The striking character of this antipodal contrast is preserved in the widespread metaphorical use of these opposed terms. Lyons (1977, 284–6) suggests that contrasts in semantic fields of kinship words are often best seen in terms of orthogonal and antipodal oppositions. The lexical set <spring, summer, autumn, winter> also illustrates that the question 'What is the

presence or absence of life. More striking is the opposition between male and female. Throughout the written record of the thought of men there have been theses put forward which characterize the opposition between male and female as a privative one—a woman is a man *manqué*. The view that the opposition is an equipollent one has had an equally long history and has constituted a competing view. Given the public ideology of today, few would attempt to pronounce the male v. female opposition a privative one, but this should not blind us to the fact that, for many using the opposition, past and even present, it is the privative and not the equipollent opposition which they have in mind.

opposite of *x*?' has several answers depending upon the type of opposition one has in mind. Spring is the antipodal opposition, while summer and winter are orthogonal oppositions, to autumn.

Some sets will be *cyclical*. Employing Grandy's successor function, we can say that if successive applications of the function 'eventually produce the originating element then the set is cyclically ordered',—for example, <seasons: spring, summer, autumn, winter>. If successive applications produce all but the originating element, then the set is *serially* ordered. Sets may be *determinate* or *indeterminate*. The field of season words is *determinate*. The field of evaluation is *indeterminate* because, to the set of serially ordered grading terms <evaluation: excellent, good, fair, poor>, we could add terms at either end of and in between the terms cited above, for example, 'superb', 'awful', 'very good', etc. This last contrast set also exhibits the relation of *ranking*.

Rank, added by Lehrer (1974), describes the relation between such serially ordered, incompatible terms, which are *scalar*—for example, <general, colonel, major, captain, lieutenant, sergeant, etc>. Graded antonymies are also scalar, for example temperature terms <hot, warm, cool, cold>. Rank is a commonly transferred relation in metaphorical use: to call someone a 'general' is clearly to place him at the highest rank of whatever his endeavour is. With rank, as with other scalar terms, the use of one term very often results in the productive device of similarly using the related scalar terms metaphorically. Thus if we call a head chef a 'general of the kitchen', then we might call one of his *sous-chefs* a 'lieutenant'. This type of productive use of a semantic relation is not limited to scalar relations, but it is most easily identified among such relations.

Among the serially ordered sets, there is a distinction to be drawn between those in which the terms are a series of stage-like progressions and those in which the terms denote continual accretions marked by a set of regular intervals. This distinction, overlooked by Lyons, will be discussed in Chapter 7 Section 1, where it plays an important role in the metaphors analysed there.

Syntagmatic Relations

Of the early field theorists, only Porzig (1950) discussed semantic relations between terms that collocate. Contemporary field theory has focused largely on paradigmatic sense-relations. Lyons (1977), cites McCawley's (1968) view that 'kick' has as part of its meaning 'with a foot', for it is worse than odd to say, 'I kicked him with my elbow'.

Lyons suggests that 'kick' *encapsulates* 'with a foot', as 'bite' encapsulates 'with teeth'.

I shall take the *syntagmatic relations* of a field to indicate the basic underlying structure of sentences that can be formed in a given semantic field or to indicate rules and relations specifying what collocations are possible given certain semantic considerations, that is, the considerations which govern the constituents of a given field. For example, semantic contrasts and affinities govern what elements are to be constituents of the semantic field of fishing. 'Fishing' would be a covering term for a set contrasting the various instruments we fish with or methods of fishing: <fishing: angling, trolling, harpooning, fishing with a net>. (Compare a contrast set which includes 'kicking with . . .'; it allows no paradigmatic alternative to 'foot'.) What we fish for also yields a contrast set: <fish: trout, salmon, pike, etc.>. And one who fishes may be a 'fisherman', or an 'angler' or a 'harpooner', etc. The various terms of these contrast sets, for example, 'fisherman', 'angler', 'to fish', 'fishing', 'fish', 'trout', 'rod', 'net', etc., are clearly related. These elements may relate to each other as alternatives in a grammatical string, for example, 'fisherman' or 'angler', or as elements in a collocation, for example 'the fisherman fishes for trout'. While paradigmatic relations specify which elements serve as alternatives for one another, and the nature of the alternative (synonymy, antonymy, etc.), the syntagmatic relations indicate how members of sets of alternatives (paradigmatic sets) collocate in a manner specific to the semantic character of the field.

We can use the notion of role-relations to help us indicate the ways in which semantic, as opposed to syntactic, relations are specific to a given field.[25] The *syntagma*, or grammatically well-formed string of words, characterizing the role-relations particular to a given field will serve as a model, even a paradigm, for other related syntagmatic formations of the field. Such a paradigm is a *model syntagma*. In the case of

[25] I owe this suggestion to Adrienne Lehrer. The role-relations, as they pertain to sentences rather than to the skeletal syntagma of a semantic field, are considered by some to be more basic than the noun phrase/verb phrase structure of sentences. The question then arises whether the role-relations which noun phrases bear to the verb of the sentence should be considered to be at the base in a transformational grammar. Fillmore (1968) clearly takes this view. Langendoen (1970) took this view, but has subsequently repudiated it. For Jackendoff (1972), however, thematic relations are assigned by the semantic component to the output of a Chomskian deep structure. This controversy need not concern us here. My point requires only that there are syntagmatic considerations, that is, questions of collocatability, which are intimately related to the semantic properties of sets of words.

fishing terms, 'the fisherman fishes for fish' is a model syntagma. This model is an abstraction, sometimes got by examining common usage, sometimes derived from more special and specific contexts. It is a skeletal structure consisting only of the syntagmatic relations around which the paradigmatic relations form the fleshed-out body and to which the syntactic rules of both deep structure and surface structure give life and motion.

Fillmore (1968), using case grammar, and Langendoen (1970), using grammatical roles, each identify a number of relations between a verb and its noun phrases. Consider the following four sentences (Langendoen 1970):

6.4 *John* sent *the news to the Congressman by telegram.*
6.5 *The Congressman* received *the news from John by telegram.*
6.6 *The news* reached *the Congressman by telegram.*
6.7 *A telegram* conveyed *the news to the Congressman.*

In each of the sentences the same nominal expressions (with the possible exception of 'John', see below) stand in the same semantic relation to the verb of the sentence, although they each occupy different syntactic positions in the various sentences. In each, 'the news' is the object of the action, a role which, in grammars with a well-developed case structure, is usually designated as the accusative case. One can drop the case terminology altogether, as does Langendoen, and refer to the role played by 'the news' in the above sentences as that of the PATIENT; it 'suffers' the action of verb.[26] 'The Congressman' is the GOAL, that is, that towards which the action of the verb is directed, in all four sentences. The INSTRUMENT, or means by which the action is carried out in each of the sentences, is 'a telegram'. 'John' is the AGENT, the one by whose agency the action of the verb is performed, in 6.4. A role related to AGENT (which is more likely to occupy syntactic positions other than subject) is SOURCE. In 6.5 'John' is the SOURCE. Notice that AGENT involves some intentionality, or potential for intentionality, not required by the SOURCE. A sheet of paper with confidential material on it left lying carelessly about might be the SOURCE of a news leak, but it could not be the AGENT of such a leak. Other grammatical roles which nominal expressions might play

---

[26] An alternative terminology, accompanied by a somewhat different theory, is provided by Gruber's *thematic relations*, cited and used by Jackendoff (1972). Using Gruber's theory we should say that 'the news' as the object of the action is the *theme* of the sentence.

would be the RESULT of the action, the LOCATION, and the DIRECTION. While the number of roles must be rather small if they are to assume any theoretical importance in the structure of language, the ones cited here most likely constitute an incomplete inventory.

The syntagmatic relations specify the semantic roles occupied by nominal expressions that are required, permitted, or prohibited by the verb which 'dominates' the field. The field of colour words does not exhibit these syntagmatic relations—although it can be a paradigmatic set within a larger field of vision which would in turn exhibit syntagmatic relations.

Fillmore and Langendoen use case grammar to analyse the deep structure of specific sentences.[27] I am using it as a means of specifying syntagmatic relations of a semantic field. In my adaptation of role-relations, these skeletal structures of fields are not sentences. Sentences are generated by specifying elements among the paradigmatic contrasts; by specifying which, if any, optional case relations are used; and by syntactic transformation, involving such considerations as tense, modality, determinates, etc.

A semantic field which is ordered by syntagmatic relations can be thought of an ordered sequence (a syntagma) of paradigmatic contrast sets, such that each set occupies a given place (a grammatical role) in the syntagma. Because the terms that are syntagmatically related belong to different grammatical categories they cannot be represented together in a contrast set. Allowing for semantically related words in a syntagma to be represented in a semantic field permits us to include the various paradigmatic categories within a single field. This ensures that when we move from one part of speech to another (for example, from a noun to a verb, as in from 'resonance', to 'resonate'), we have not thereby moved from one semantic field to another.

The various relations we have discussed, whether paradigmatic or syntagmatic, cannot be regarded as definitive. The work in semantic field theory is still preliminary. As the theory evolves and becomes

---

[27] Jackendoff (1972), in fact, proposes that role-relations, which he calls 'thematic relations' after Gruber, should not be taken as the underlying deep structure of a sentence (see below), but should be incorporated in the semantic representation of verbs. I am not sure how to handle such collocations as 'blond hair' which seem to involve syntagmatic relations and which do not involve a verb. Other modifying adverbs and adjectives are so related to nominal expressions, but apart from specifying selection restrictions or using the notion of *encapsulation* I do not know how to characterize what seems to be a syntagmatic relation which involves only non-verbal expressions.

more widely known, the notions used here will be refined and altered. None the less, a theory that takes seriously the affinities and contrasts between words as a factor in word meaning will need to account for the described phenomena, and will, at the very least, resemble the theory sketched above.

Semantic Fields and Contrast Sets

We can now say that a semantic field consists of a set of contrast sets, some or all of which may be ordered contrast sets, related so that:

(1) they share a covering term, generally but not necessarily mono-lexemic—disjunctive covering terms are suspect;

(2) 'any expression [*excluding the covering term*] which occurs in a contrast set with an element of the semantic field is also in the field' (Grandy 1987a).

Condition (2) assures us a 'kind of downward completeness—the contrast set <animal: dog, cat . . . > qualifies as a semantic field on its own, but if we are to include "German shepherd", then we must also include all the contrasting terms ("poodle", "corgi", etc.)' (Grandy forthcoming *a*).

In addition:

(3) terms which are morphological derivatives of the elements of one contrast set will belong to another contrast set in a syntag-matically ordered semantic field; and

(4) the elements of the contrast sets may be arranged syntagmatically to form a *model syntagma*.

3 SEMANTIC FIELDS AND WORD MEANING

Value and Word Meaning

If we consider the semantic field of sound terms,[28] the fact that English contains the term 'silent', or some synonym thereof, affects both the intension and the extension of terms such as 'loud' and 'soft'. 'Quiet', for example, can be synonymous with either 'silent' or 'soft' depending on the contrasts relevant for a given context. But if we had no term for silence, then 'soft' would probably include the ground now covered by 'silent', altering the *content* of the term. Similarly, consider

[28] See Lehrer 1974, 36 ff., for an illustration of this type of information for a subset of sound words.

the field of cooking terms. If the term 'broil' were deleted from English, while the culinary practice continued, the content of the adjacent terms, such as 'fry', 'grill', 'roast', would be altered. They might each cover the ground now covered by 'broil', in addition to that which they already denoted, or only one term might serve this purpose. If we no longer broiled food, the term might remain in the language but shift its content. It would thereby cause the other terms to shift in meaning also.

Saussure drew a distinction between value and signification. I have been stressing the notion of value—a notion much neglected in Anglo-American linguistics and philosophy of language. What Saussure called signification has generally been treated in theories of meaning, especially intensional theories of word meaning. As suggested earlier, most theories of meaning attempt to define meaning in terms that are themselves non-linguistic. Value is that aspect of meaning which derives not from some non-linguistic entity, but from a term's relation to other terms. And yet language hooks on to the world and to our conception of the world—words signify, they have content. We cannot do without signification.

Semantic fields, as now formulated, do not provide us with a term's signification, with its content. For example, if we were learning English, and all we knew about the terms 'loud' and 'soft' was that they were a graded antonymy and that the pair contrasted with silence, we would not know the meaning of the terms. Similarly, knowing that 'broil', 'fry', 'grill', and 'roast' all contrast in a particular way, for example, are incompatible co-hyponyms, does not help us to know what to do if we are ordered to roast a chicken. Knowing the appropriate covering terms helps, but it is not sufficient.

A good illustration of the interrelationship between value and signification and their relation to field analysis is afforded by colour terms. In the culinary field, if a language fails to have a term for 'to sauté', it is possible that the culture simply has no such culinary procedure; whereas, if a language has no term for green, it is fair to assume that speakers of that language still have that perceptual stimulus. While we can assume the same perceptual apparatus in humans who speak different languages, not all languages name colours in the same way. The field of colour is a continuum which can be variously apportioned by a language. The study of colour terms by Berlin and Kay (1969) indicates that there are a number of focal points which remain fairly constant as the reference of the basic colour words in any given language.

That is, speakers of different languages (even vastly different languages), which each possess a name of one of the eleven basic incompatible colour categories (see n. 16 above) will each identify the same coloured chip as the paradigm for the reference of that term.

However the value of a given colour is different in a language which has, let us say, only two colour terms and in one that has, let us say, eleven colour terms. To illustrate, we shall say that in language *A*, Arbish, there are only two contrasting colour terms, 'arbash' and 'garbash', respectively.[29] Language *B* is English. It contains all eleven basic colour category terms, including the terms 'black' and 'white'. Both the speaker of *A* and the speaker of *B* will agree on the foci of black and white, given a colour chart of graduated hues and brightness. Arbish has no term for that category of hues termed 'green' in *B* and might classify some shades of green as 'garbash' and others as 'arbash'. Thus 'arbash' and 'garbash' have different significations from 'white' and 'black'—differences due to the difference in value, since, in Arbish there is no separate term for green and hence no contrast for such a term. We see that value and signification are importantly linked.

The Relationship between Field Theory and Semantic Components

The various versions of componential analysis may be interpreted as theories of signification. A semantic component is used to represent

---

[29] Berlin and Kay (1969) testify to the fact that such languages exist. In their study, of which the data included colour terms in ninety-eight languages distributed over a wide variety of linguistic families, eleven basic colour categories emerged. The presence of terms for these colours in a language was restricted by the following rules:

    (1) No language has only one colour term.
    (2) If a language has only two terms, those two terms refer to black and white.
    (3) Additional terms appear in the following order:

$$\begin{bmatrix} \text{white} \\ \text{black} \end{bmatrix} < [\text{ red }] < \begin{bmatrix} \text{yellow} \\ \text{green} \end{bmatrix} < [\text{ blue }] < [\text{ brown }] < \begin{bmatrix} \text{purple} \\ \text{pink} \\ \text{orange} \\ \text{grey} \end{bmatrix}$$

'For distinct colour categories (*a,b*) the expression *a<b* signifies that *a* is present in every language in which *b* is not present' (Berlin and Kay 1969, 6). And where colours are enclosed in square brackets we have an equivalence class such that a language which has all the preceding colours might have either colour of the equivalence class. For example, if a language has four basic colour terms, then the rules predict that those colours will include, white, black, red, and *either* green *or* yellow; if the language has five terms, then it will have both green and yellow as well as white, black, and red; if a language has six colour terms then it will have those of a five-colour-term language and blue.

the concepts which, in some complex arrangement, constitute the sense of a lexical item. Other components, selection restrictions or transfer features, concern the combinatory or syntagmatic aspects of the semantics of the word (see Chapter 2, n. 10).

How might we characterize the relationship between semantic field analysis and componential analysis? One might be able to specify the members of a given semantic field in terms of the semantic features held in common, or alternatively in terms of the selection restrictions held in common. An early, cursory attempt to integrate semantic components and semantic fields in this way was made by Bierwisch. He writes:

By redefining this conception [*that of Trier*, 1931] in terms of semantic components, we might indicate precisely the organization of particular fields and the relations among their members. (1970*b*, 170.)

He suggests that a field may be constituted by lexical entries (in a dictionary) which have a common configuration of components. For example, the semantic field of kinship terms is marked by the shared features [animate], [human], [relative]. There are then subfields, for example, those of male relatives, or lineal (v. collateral) kinship, as well as more inclusive fields, for example, that of social roles, of which the kinship terms form a subset. Bierwisch also proposes that fields may be formed by groups of words which all have a feature relating them to some other feature, as in part–whole or hyponymic relations. For example, 'arm', 'hand', 'finger', all denote parts of the human body and must contain some component which will relate them appropriately to other terms which contain the feature [human]. Finally verbs such as 'talk', 'think', 'dream', form a field in so far as they are activities carried out by humans, that is, they are verbs which have as a selection restriction on the subject of the verb, the feature [human].

This presentation makes it appear as if lexical fields presuppose semantic components; it is, however, equally true that components presuppose a lexicon structured as fields (see Lehrer 1974, 53–4). That is, the organization of words in a field can be the basis for a componential analysis of these terms.[30]

Furthermore, if as we have argued, contrasts and affinities are important features of a term's meaning, then it should be the case that componential analysis will fail to capture certain important features of

---

[30] This procedure is often followed in ethnosemantics. See Bendix 1966.

a term's meaning. If semantic fields can be reduced to componential analysis, then it should be possible, first, to pick out the members of a field by examining the components of lexical entries; and secondly, to derive the semantic relations governing terms as they organize a field from a componential analysis of the constituents of a field.

The first condition may be satisfiable, but only given a simple account of how semantic features are organized within a dictionary entry. We could perhaps try to specify the elements of a field by collecting terms with common semantic markers. Here we must assume that the semantic representation of a word can be given as a conjunction of simplex semantic features.[31] A field would then have a degree n, where n is the number of common simplex features. But as simplex features must be the most general sorts of concepts (perhaps [entity] might be sufficiently unanalysable to be a simplex marker), fields of a low degree would be extremely large, unwieldy, and generally uninteresting. One might decide that only fields above a certain degree had potential for exhibiting interesting features, and for actually characterizing the way in which speakers organized content domains. For this reason, one might even refuse to call fields of a degree lower than some specified n fields at all, coining another term, let us say 'superfield', to designate these fields of low degree, while calling fields of a high degree 'proper fields'. This could be viewed as an elaboration of Bierwisch's suggestion above.

The problem with this suggestion is three-fold. First, our assignment of degrees to fields such that they could be classed as either superfields or as proper fields was based on the assumptions that all features could be reduced to simplexes and that features were merely conjoined. Both these premises are problematical. Certainly it is in practice untenable to reduce all complexes to simplex concepts. No one is even clear about what a single simplex might be. Nor is it inconceivable that a dictionary assigning semantic components to lexical items would, like an ordinary dictionary, be circular, that is, without simplexes.[32]

Moreover, it is generally agreed that features are not merely con-

[31] Componential theories require redundancy rules in order to prevent dictionary entries from growing too large. The feature [animate] is itself a complex composed of [physical], [alive], etc. [Physical] can be decomposed as [object], [solid], etc. The simplex markers are the primitives from which the complex markers are built.

[32] Within an ordinary dictionary each term is defined by means of another. But it is the immense semantic territory encompassed by the resulting circle and the occasional grounding in the referential that makes this circularity non-vicious.

joined[33] and that all features do not have the same status. Bierwisch (1971) suggests that some are predicative and others delimiting. Others (Fillmore 1971; Langendoen 1970) have proposed a division between features used assertively and presuppositionally. Word association studies indicate that markers may be hierarchically ordered (Clark 1970). Lehrer (1974) introduces the distinction between obligatory and optional components. Optional features are those which are often, but not always, thought to belong to the meaning of a word, while the obligatory features do not provide enough information to differentiate between many members of a field. Finally, the work of Ross (1981) suggests that the salience of any given marker may be significantly altered in different linguistic environments. Thus commonality of a sufficient number of markers would serve as a very poor criterion for deriving the elements of a proper semantic field.[34]

The second objection is directly related to the fact that semantic fields consist of elements ordered according to certain relations. Unless a componential analysis can provide this ordering, we cannot consider a field reducible to it. The mere commonality of markers does not provide any information concerning the ordering.

It is precisely in regard to ordered contrasts and affinities that componential analysis is weakest. Some relations, such as synonymy, can easily be defined componentially. Two words are synonymous if they contain all the same components. However, the componential analysis of words which are part of scalar contrasts, for example, gradable antonyms, is problematical.[35] For example, if we are to understand the meaning of the term 'hot', semantic markers will supply the information that the term applies to a certain thermal state of an object. We also need to know that 'x is hot' does not entail that 'x is cold'. It may be warm or cool. Componential analysis has thus far failed to provide an adequate account. Furthermore, the ordering of fields such as <compass points: east, west, north, south> would be difficult to represent componentially for any given term without also including all the other elements of the field. (See Grandy 1987*a*.)

Thirdly, it is sometimes the case that we want to use a term in a

---

[33] Weinreich (1966, 1972) suggests linking, nesting, and ranking. Katz (e.g. 1972) uses logical constants and bracketing.

[34] It may none the less be possible to distinguish 'proper fields'. The basic level objects posited by prototype theory (Rosch 1978, 30 ff.) may provide a minimal level of generality for the constitution of a proper semantic field.

[35] See Lehrer's (1974, 67–8) critique of such attempts.

sense that expresses its relation to some terms and not to others. For example, I may sometimes wish to distinguish 'dog' from 'wolf'; at other times I want to contrast 'dog' and 'cat'; at still other times I want to oppose 'dog' to all other domesticated animals. We can talk about the different semantic fields which are pertinent given certain contextual constraints and specifications. But if these different contrasts were all to be represented in semantic markers, the semantic representation would become unwieldy or it would continually have to change. Neither option is attractive. Semantic field analysis is not reducible to componential analysis. A theory of signification is required to supplement, not supplant, semantic field theory. We still need to adopt an account of signification in order to be able to speak of a term's meaning. We want to eschew theories of word meaning which are atomistic. Since signification is intimately bound up with value, an atomistic theory of signification could not merge with a theory of value. We need an account of signification that can be made to cohere with semantic field theory.

Semantic Descriptors

Componential analysis, considered as a theory about semantic simples, the universal atoms of meaning from which all word meaning can be construed—a 'Democritean theory of word-meaning'—cannot readily be incorporated into semantic field theory. Such a theory is non-relational. There is none the less a way in which we can think of the conceptual, informative content of a term as represented by semantic features which *function* in signification in much the same way as semantic components, yet have their grounding in a relational theory of meaning. I have called these *semantic descriptors* in Chapter 2. The α-component in the semantic representation of a term is composed largely of such descriptors, and they are also a factor in the semantic concatenation rules of the β-component. There is no presumption that some descriptors are simplexes, from which all other descriptors are composed. The descriptors give us the information that identifies the content domain and the differentia that constitute the contrast between terms. Thus the semantic descriptors for 'woman' in a contextual setting where it contrasts with 'man' would include [human] (a partial identification of the content domain), [adult] (again a partial identification of the content domain), [female] (the sexual contrast between 'woman' and 'man'). Again the descriptors themselves, as lexical items, will be analysable into a number of semantic descriptors: 'human' will include [animate], [animal], [mammal], [primate], [homo sapiens], each in part identifying a content domain and differentiating 'human' from other possible contrasts.

If we made room for semantic descriptors in our relational theory of meaning, then we should know, not merely that 'boil' and 'fry' are related as incompatible hyponyms of 'cook', but also that the incompatibility is in virtue of the descriptors [water-based liquid] and [oil] (or [fatty liquid]) and in terms of [liquid]$_s$ and [liquid]$_l$, where s = small quantity and l = large quantity. The opposition between 'fry' and 'boil' is one of [fatty liquid]$_s$ versus [water-based liquid]$_l$ $\vee$ [fatty liquid]$_l$. Similarly, we should be able to tell that 'simmer' and 'boil', which are incompatible hyponyms of 'boil' are so with regard to the antonymous set of features [cooking action]$_f$ and [cooking action]$_g$ where f = fast and g = gentle (or slow).

Before we admit semantic descriptors into our relational theory of word meaning, we need to raise a question concerning their status. If they are concepts, then we face the problem of individuating *bare* concepts, concepts not embodied in a word. If descriptors are lexical items, such as the words of which they are representations, then a dictionary composed of such entries would be circular. Some descriptors may not easily be formulated as monolexemic terms and in some cases it may be warranted to speak of descriptors which are not bound by a given language. For reasons largely motivated by the conception of a semantic field as composed of a lexical field covering a content domain, it seems preferable to regard descriptors as concepts.[36] But I do not regard these concepts as independent of some articulation in a language. Instead, I view these concepts as *formed content*. Descriptors, then, are concepts articulated by, though not necessarily bound to, a particular linguistic expression. Whether or not some descriptors are universal becomes an empirical question: are there some content domains that receive isomorphic articulations in all natural languages?

By virtue of the systematic nature of language and the interconnected nature of what we choose to talk about—of what will constitute information—some of these descriptors will recur through various

---

[36] Lewis (1972) objects to componential analysis, claiming that it is merely a translation into 'Markerese'. A translation requires two independent expression-forms E_1 and E_2 such that if E_1 expresses content C and E_2 expresses C then we can translate E_1 as E_2. If we understand descriptors to be formed content, as I claim here, then they cannot be a translation since they do not have an independent level of expression. This response is also pertinent to componential analysis.

contrasts in the language. Grandy (1987*a*) speaks of making '*the specification of the contrast part of the contrast set*', thereby expanding the definition of semantic fields to include such specification—for example, the contrast set <horse: stallion, mare> would include a specification of the contrast by sex, while <$horse_1$: $horse_2$, colt> is a contrast by maturity. We could also include such descriptors within the semantic representation of a term, in the manner suggested in Chapter 2 above, a manner that follows a model established by componential analysis. The two strategies need not be incompatible. In either case, we can see the recurrence of certain descriptors, or concepts, across the language. Semantic descriptors are the co-ordinates of a map. A given term is conceived of not as having its own distinct meaning, separable from other words (and thus separable from the way in which a word is used), but as representable by semantic descriptors which are meant to exhibit systematic interconnections between different elements of the lexicon. That 'mother' has the same markers as 'father', except for the one relating to sex, indicates the connection between these two words—that they are close in some posited semantic space which provides the concepts, the co-ordinates resulting in the meanings of words.

Thought of in these terms, the descriptions are not the building blocks of meaning, but the points of interconnection through semantic fields. Ultimately we will need a three- (or multi-)dimensional model to capture the interconnections within language rather than the two-dimensional model given by the notion of a field. Because the descriptors capture such interconnections, for example that the concepts of female/male recur as the contrasting element in the pairs 'woman'/'man', 'girl'/'boy', 'mare'/'stallion', 'goose'/'gander', etc., they also are important in governing permissible combinations of words in first-order meaning. Thus, for example, verbs that are also differentiated by a female/male factor, for example, to be pregnant, will combine to produce a first-order meaning only with a noun which has the appropriate descriptor in its semantic representation. The semantic anomaly resulting from selection-restriction violations results from a failure to respect certain semantic interconnections between contrast sets—whether the contrast sets belong to different semantic fields or to the same semantic field. If the semantic anomaly results from the violation of selection restriction rules, and therefore involves conceptual incongruity, this is because the semantic interconnections revealed through recurrent descriptors are importantly tied to the conceptual understanding we have of ourselves and our world. I have said that anomaly is relative to our default assumptions. We can also say that they are relative to our organization of our information. The differentiations that govern the construction of contrast sets and semantic fields are part and parcel of our understanding of the world and our sorting of information. First-order meaning is then capable of accommodating new information only in so far as that new information is already possible through the current organization of information. As soon as there is a need to accommodate information not easily accommodated in the current organization of information, we encounter the incongruity of metaphor. Through metaphor different organizations exist concurrently. This is a point to which I shall revert in the concluding pages of this work.

7

Semantic Fields and the Structure of Metaphor

IN the first section of this chapter I shall examine three poems and one prose piece to show that the transference of meaning, which Aristotle took to be the critical feature of metaphor, can be seen as a process in which the structure of one semantic field induces a structure on another content domain. Behind this effort lies the claim that the conceptual interest of metaphor is to be found in such reordering.[1]

To facilitate the analysis, I shall look at extended metaphors. In the case of an isolated metaphor, the pertinent semantic field may be underdetermined by the context. The more extended the discourse, the more evident are the semantic fields relevant to an understanding of the metaphor. In fact, the extended metaphors will supply most of the terms of the relevant fields. The extended metaphor also provides us a structure sufficiently rich to allow us to explore the shifts of meaning and thought that characterize metaphor. The semantic field of the vehicle will be referred to as the *vehicle field* and the content domain of the topic as the *topic domain*.

In the second section of the chapter I shall explore some differences between metaphor, as it has been characterized in this study, and other tropes such as irony and metonomy. We shall see that the use of semantic field theory permits us a convenient, if only tentative, characterization of figurative language other than metaphor.

I DISPLAYING THE STRUCTURE OF METAPHOR

'Once did She hold the gorgeous East in fee'

Wordsworth's poem 'On the Extinction of the Venetian Republic', reproduced in full below, provides a good point of departure.

---

[1] Section 1 of this chapter is based on Kittay and Lehrer 1981.

On the Extinction of the Venetian Republic

Once did She hold the gorgeous East in fee,
And was the safeguard of the West; the worth
Of Venice did not fall below her birth,
Venice, the eldest child of liberty.

She was a maiden city, bright and free;
No guile seduced, no force could violate;
And when she took unto herself a mate,
She must espouse the everlasting Sea.

And what if she had seen those glories fade,
Those titles vanish, and that strength decay,—
Yet shall some tribute of regret be paid

When her long life hath reach'd its final day:
Men are we, and must grieve when even the shade
Of that which once was great is pass'd away.

The first incongruity in the poem develops in lines 2–4: 'the worth/ Of Venice did not fall below her birth,/ Venice, the eldest child of liberty'. We speak of the 'birth' of a nation in a virtually literal fashion, in which 'birth' is partially synonymous with 'origin'. But in the fourth line the metaphorical quality becomes apparent, as the idea of 'birth' is exploited for its relation to the ideas of parentage, sibling order, and social standing (high birth/low birth). We understand this as a metaphor rather than as another use or misuse of language in virtue of the poem's title and established literary conventions. This understanding, together with the evident incongruity of speaking literally of parentage etc. of a nation, initiates the move towards a second-order meaning, the assignment of a connotative structure to the terms used incongruously, and the subsequent transfers of meaning relations. The topic of the metaphor is the Venetian Republic. As we read on, we see that the life of a noblewoman constitutes the vehicle field.

As construed in the poem, the vehicle field, the life-cycle of a woman, consists of a paradigmatically contrasting set of lexemes that are serially and non-cyclically ordered. Each stage (given in the first line of Figure 7.1) which is a paradigmatic element in the semantic field of the life history of a noblewoman may be represented as itself involving other terms and relations, both paradigmatic and syntagmatic. A birth may be 'high' or 'low' and involves a set of syntagmatic relations between the child and the parent. Additional relations are given in the remaining lines of Figure 7.1.

To turn to the topic domain, a history consists of a set of narrative events, or a narrative description of events, arranged as a chronological ordering. A chronology is an arrangement of data in the order of occurrence in time, in which time is computed by regular divisions, and events or transactions are assigned their proper dates. Thus, a simplified short history of Venice exemplifying a chronology would be something like this:

In the late 5th century refugees fleeing the Lombard invaders of Northern Italy sought safety on the largely uninhabited islands. The communities organized themselves (697) under a doge . . . [T]he communities grew, and by the 9th century they had formed the city of Venice. The city secured (10th century) most of the coast of Dalmatia, thus gaining control of the Adriatic, and began to build up its eastern empire . . . In 1204 the doge, Enrico Dandolo . . . led the host of the Fourth Crusade in storming Constantinople . . . After defeating (1380) its rival Genoa in the War of Chioggia, Venice was indisputedly the leading European sea power . . . The decline of Venice can be dated from the fall (1453) of Constantinople to the Turks, etc. (from *The New Columbia Encyclopedia*, Columbia University Press, 1975, p. 2875.)

Wordsworth imposes the stages of the life-cycle on the chronology of events in the history of Venice, making the history of Venice conform to a certain model; the events must then occur in their appropriate position in that model.[2] This model provides an interpretive or reinterpretive frame from which the events themselves can be inferred. The reordered field of Venetian history is represented by Figure 7.2.

When Wordsworth speaks of Venice as having not fallen 'below her birth' we engage the antonyms of 'high birth' and 'low birth' as an interpretive device for regarding the establishment of Venice and the syntagmatic relation of *being born of some parent(s)*. (Venetians claim their origin from the Romans who fled the mainland during the barbarian invasions.) Similarly, maidenhood is a stage defined negatively in terms of the domination of a woman by some male agent:

$$
\text{A maiden is} \begin{bmatrix} \text{not married} \\ \text{not violated} \\ \text{not seduced} \end{bmatrix} \text{by some agent.}
$$

---

[2] While the historian assumes a stance of objectivity, the poet can openly acknowledge a guiding model for his perception of historical events by use of explicit metaphor. The poet allows the reader to judge his interpretation on the strength of his metaphor.

BIRTH	CHILDHOOD	MAIDENHOOD	MARRIAGE	CHILDBEARING	OLD AGE	DEATH	AFTER DEATH (MOURNING)
high or low	youngest oldest middle	bright free (not) seduced (not) violated	spouse	optional, not mentioned in the poem	glories fade strength decays titles vanish	final decay died passed	neglect or tribute or regret paid grieve
x is born of y & z	x is child of y & z	x is not $\{$seduced / violated$\}$	$x \{$marries / espouses$\}\ y$				$y \{$mourns / grieves / neglects$\}$ death of x
Verb | Result | Source/Cause(s)	Verb | Patient | Source	Verb | Patient | Agent	Verb | Agent | Patient		Verb | Patient | Source/Cause		Verb | Agent | Cause
x | | y & z	x | | y & z	x (implied)	x | | y		fade decay vanish | old woman's glories title strength | old age		y | | death of x

FIG. 7.1.

BIRTH	CHILDHOOD	MAIDENHOOD	MARRIAGE	OLD AGE	DEATH	AFTER DEATH
Romans' high social standing Venice is born of Romans and liberty Venice is created by the Romans who fled barbarian invasions, i.e. Romans seeking freedom from invaders	Created by those seeking freedom, Venice was in turn one of the earliest republics which vigilantly guarded against despotism	Venice remained invaded by no one	Venice, by virtue of her position on the sea and her seafaring power, was able to control trade and build an Empire	Venice suffers deterioration of political and economic stability at home and influence abroad	Napoleon conquers the Republic	We must pay tribute to a great fallen Republic

Fig. 7.2

The metaphorical identification of early Venice and the maiden is given through anaphoric reference in lines 4 and 5. The agent to whom Venice, as maiden, would not yield is any power, in particular the Ottoman empire, which attempted to conquer the never-before-conquered Venice.

The marriage of Venice to the sea is a standard metaphor one ritually enacted every year. The poem presumes that the female Venice weds the sea and that the power she wielded,

> Once did She hold the gorgeous East in fee
> And was the safeguard of the West:

came from the appropriate union. Like other noblewomen, her power is at its zenith when her high birth is coupled with a sufficiently potent male. (The metaphor of potency, sexual and political, serves well in this context.) The transfer of relations illustrated in the Wordsworth poem is relatively straightforward. The reader can continue the analysis using Figures 7.1 and 7.2 as guides.

Two further points are noteworthy. First, the life-cycle metaphor suggests the naturalness and inevitability of an end to the empire. Just as all people, no matter how great, eventually die, so all empires must end. In this regard the metaphor is predictive. It also suggests the appropriateness of a tribute; we mourn and pay tribute to a great personage at her death, and so we must do with Venice. In this regard the metaphor is prescriptive. Secondly, Wordsworth neglects a standard stage of a woman's life history, namely, childbearing. While the poet may have had his reasons for the omission, it is an element which could be inserted, allowing us to form or predict the formation of other metaphors which draw on the relation of mother and child. We could speak of the artistic and cultural achievements of Venice as her children, the 'products of her labour', or alternatively of the imperial expansion of Venice as the city 'giving birth to an Empire'.

'The Bait'

John Donne's poem 'The Bait' has a more complex metaphorical structure than Wordsworth's. In this poem courtship is mockingly spoken of in terms of the extended metaphor of fishing, and the metaphor develops by playing out the relations between the elements in the vehicle field. The term 'play' seems especially apt for this parody of

Marlowe's 'The Passionate Shepherd to his Love'. The poem is reproduced in full:[3]

The Bait

Come live with me and be my love
And we will some new pleasure prove
Of **golden** sands and **crystal** *brooks*,
With **silken** lines, and **silver** *hooks*.

There will the *river* whispering *run*
Warm'd by thy eyes more than the sun
And there the **enamour'd** *fish* will stay
Begging themselves they may betray.

When thou wilt *swim* in that live *bath*
each *fish*, which every *channel* hath,
Will **amorously** to thee *swim*,
Gladder to *catch* thee, than thou him.

If thou, to be so seen, beest loath,
By Sun, or Moon, thou dark'nest both;
And if myself have leave to see
I need not their light, having thee.

Let others freeze with *angling reeds*,
And cut their legs, with *shells* and *weeds*,
Or *treacherously* poor *fish beset*,
With *strangling snare*, or *windowy net*:

Let *coarse bold hands*, from *slimy nest*
The **bedded** *fish* in *banks out-wrest*,
Or **curious traitors**, *sleave-silk flies*
Bewitch poor *fishes* **wand'ring** *eyes*

For thee, thou need'st no such deceit,
For thou thyself are thine own *bait*;
That *fish*, that is not catched thereby,
Alas, is **wiser** far than I.

---

[3] The italics and bold are my own and are to be understood as follows. A word in italics, e.g. *fish*, indicates that the word belongs to the semantic field of fishing. Bold, e.g. **enamoured**, indicates that a word is used metaphorically to describe the word from the topic field of courtship. Thus, although 'fish' is used metaphorically in this poem, i.e. to talk about lovers, the fish itself is described metaphorically as 'enamoured'.

The semantic field of fishing, as it is construed in this poem, is one in which the relations are primarily syntagmatic. As indicated in Chapter 6 above, a syntagmatic field of fishing would have to include the *verb* 'to fish'; an AGENT, such as 'fisherman'; the PATIENT, or that to which the action of fishing applies, the 'fish'; and the INSTRUMENT, or means by which the fishing is accomplished, the 'hook', 'line', 'bait', etc. The first three elements, the verb, the AGENT, and the PATIENT, are essential to structuring the semantic field of fishing.[4] The role of INSTRUMENT in this field is perhaps somewhat more uncertain. While we very often do not specify with what instrument we are fishing, fishing involves an instrument of some sort. Even if we fish with our bare hands, 'bare hands' occupies the position of INSTRUMENT in the syntagma. Although to fish does not require a LOCATIVE, I have included it since the poet uses this relation. 'To fish' is like most verbs of physical activity in that the action must take place at some specifiable locale—a body of water—but the location is a peripheral part of the meaning. My representation of this field is given in Figures 7.3 and 7.4.

In Figure 7.3, the syntagmatic relations of this field are arranged in tabular form, together with the paradigmatic sets which would serve to fill the positions indicated by the syntagmatic relations. The paradigmatic relations occupying the different syntagmatic slots are varied. The verbs are co-hyponyms of 'to fish' in a contrast set: <to fish: to angle, to net, to snare, etc.> 'To fish' is also partially synonymous with the verb 'to catch'.[5] The hyponyms of 'to fish' can be arranged in order of degree of violence, or degree of skill, or ranked according to some other criterion. Thus, in addition to the relation of hyponymy, we can introduce into the field a ranking relation between the hyponyms. In terms of the development of the poem, we shall want to order the hyponyms in regard to the degree of violence or cunning involved in the method of fishing (see Figure 7.4), for this ranking will be used to help reorder the field of courtship. Here we see, incidentally, how the text provides discourse-specific default assumptions which specify the nature of the fishing field according to its contribution to the distinctive discourse. In the AGENT position we have only one hyponym of

---

[4] Even where one of the three constituents does not appear in the sentence, the element is nevertheless tacitly understood. In the sentence 'I went fishing', it is presupposed that I went fishing *for something*, i.e. fish. Similarly in, 'The fish was caught', it is understood that *someone* or *something* caught the fish.

[5] The partial synonymy is relative to the semantic field of fishing—in a less specialized context, 'to fish' is a hyponym of 'to catch'.

VERB	MANNER	AGENT	PATIENT	INSTRUMENT	LOCATIVE
catch(es)	treacherously deceitfully cunningly traitorously	fisher-man	fish	no superordinate term	brooks bath (archaic use) channel river sea, ocean, stream, etc.
fishes (for)	w/out excessive guile · · · · · ◄ *antonymous* with guile			to capture with / to pursue &/to attract	
angles	bewitchingly	angler	kinds of fish	rod with hook / bait, line & hook / lure, flies	
fly-fishes					
besets		trapper		(windowy) net — optional: bait	banks (river) with shells and weeds
nets					
traps				trap — optional: bait	
snares	strangling			snare	
out-wrests				bold course hands	slimy nests in river beds

FIG. 7.3

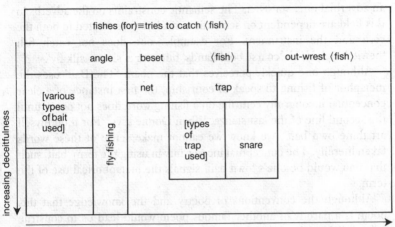

FIG. 7.4

'fisherman', that is, 'angler'. However, the other hyponyms of 'fishing' are also productive of nouns which would be co-hyponymous with 'angler', such as 'netter', 'snarer', etc. The PATIENT position can be filled either by the superordinate term, the noun 'fish', or any of its hyponyms, that is any term specifying a kind of fish.[6]

The INSTRUMENTAL relation includes instruments for two different aspects of fishing: the pursuit (or attraction) and the capture of the fish. The instrumental terms, as well as terms from other roles, such as 'angler' in the relation of AGENT, have to be lined up in the representation of the field (Figure 7.4) to collocate with the appropriate verb. One does not 'net' fish with a 'line and hook'—a fact which is reflected in the semantic concatenation rules for 'net' and 'angle'. The LOCA-TIVE role has as its paradigmatic set a number of co-hyponomous terms, designating bodies of water and the areas of land on which they border—one fishes *in* a body of water or *from* the land area bordering

---

[6] A knowing fisherman may prefer to use one method of fishing to catch some kinds of fish and not others, but this knowledge is not linguistically specified in English. However, there may be limitations of size on the kinds of fish that are caught by some of these methods. One would not ordinarily angle for a large shark or whale.

that body of water. In addition to these nominal roles, I have included an adverbial one, MANNER. The semantic constraints on the adverbs in this field are dependent on semantic considerations related to both the verb and the instrument. For example, one does not catch fish 'bewitchingly' with 'coarse bold hands' but with a 'sleave-silk fly'.

Although one quickly perceives that the poem 'The Bait' uses the metaphor of fishing to speak of courtship, the first instance of a clear conceptual incongruity centring on a fishing word does not occur until the second line of the last stanza. When Donne says, 'For thou thyself art thine own bait', we know we cannot make sense of these words taken literally. The conceptual incongruity in using the term 'bait' such that one would be one's 'own bait' signals the metaphorical use of the term.

Although the conventions of poetry and the knowledge that this poem is a parody of another famous poem would lead us to construe talk of fishing in the poem as metaphorical, the figurative phrases found up to this point are only metaphorical descriptions of fish or fishing. For example, when Donne says

> And there the enamour'd fish will stay
> Begging themselves they may betray

'fish' is being used literally, and 'enamour'd' and 'begging themselves they may betray' are being used figuratively to speak of fish. We do not literally speak of fish as 'in love' or 'enamour'd'. However, rereading these lines in the light of the poem's end (and in the light of the conventions governing the love poetry mocked in 'The Bait') we can take 'fish' as the vehicle for 'lovers', and the terms 'enamoured' and 'begging themselves they may betray' as *literal talk* about these lovers. This shift is possible because of an inherent ambiguity in *all* metaphorical utterances. In any such utterance, some terms are used literally and some are used figuratively. But which are literal and which are figurative is context-relative. A skilful use of the context can employ this inherent ambiguity for the desired (poetic and rhetorical) effect.

The textual basis upon which we can construe all the fishing terms as metaphorical depends on the incongruous use of the word 'bait'—an importance reflected in Donne's choice of the term as the title of the poem. Indeed, the line 'For thou thyself art thine own bait' has at least two interpretations, both involving an oddity or incongruity—'*bait*' occupies the position of INSTRUMENT and therefore cannot occupy the position of AGENT since each element of a syntagma stands in only *one* relation to the verb at a time. The second involves a logical incongruity so that we cannot possibly assign a referent to 'bait' if it is understood literally. For 'bait' can only be the instrument by which to attract some object other than oneself: x is bait for y and $x \neq y$ is part of the *logical structure* of 'bait'.[7]

By virtue of its metaphorical use, 'bait' transforms the setting of a lovers' meeting—the river banks where the lovers go fishing—into a metaphorical setting for the more significant activity, the courtship. One can say that in the poem, two fields—those of fishing and court-ship—are made to meet at a juncture marked out by this term. We construct our semantic field of fishing to include what is in fact an optional element (the INSTRUMENT), and we construe the field of courtship to include something analogous (homologous) to a bait.

At this point we would ideally introduce a lexical set covering the conceptual field of courtship, so that we might see in what way Donne's poem effected a reordering. But without the guidance of some context it is not clear how to construct this or any other field. In speaking of courtship, however, certain things seem fairly apparent and constant, namely, the relation of love between lover and beloved, and the attempt on the part of the lover to win over the beloved. These constant elements can be rendered simply by the schema in Figure 7.5.

VERB	AGENT	PATIENT
courts	lover	beloved

FIG. 7.5

'To fish' and 'to court' may both be said to contain the semantic descriptor [to attract]—a concept common to both. We claim that metaphor is a movement across semantic fields. Sometimes the move-ment across is facilitated by pre-established *bridges* in the form of recognized similarities between terms in both fields. At other times,

---

[7] One can imagine a literal description of a situation in which a human *body* is used as bait, i.e. by some malevolent person who is hunting sharks or other carnivorous fish with human bait. Even in these circumstances it is the human *body*, not the person, which serves as bait. But this situation is clearly foreclosed by the circumstances appropriate to the poem.

the move is a *jump* across, to be facilitated only later by the recognition of a common semantic descriptor or by a common element in a syntagmatic field—the bridge is built after the gulf has been traversed. That is to say, in some cases of metaphor there are no recognized similarities between two words and the semantic fields to which they belong; although once the metaphor has been made, we rethink our understanding of the words and their fields so as to find similarities which make the mental move from one field to another less baffling, less abrupt. These similarities, found *post factum*,[8] bridge two semantic fields and take the form of an explication. In the case of the metaphor with which we are concerned, there are at least two such bridges we can construct once fishing has been used as a metaphor for courting: (1) the common semantic descriptor for both fishing and courting, for example, [attract]; and (2) a common element in the syntagmatic field of both fishing and courting, for example, the LOCATIVE role. The presence of the LOCATIVE serves, at least in part, to provide such a transverse since the aquatic setting (brooks, river-beds, baths, springs) is not only appropriate to fishing, it is also a traditional setting for lovers. The move from the field of fishing to courtship is made via the direct route of significant descriptors (that is, not merely general semantic descriptors generated by redundancy rules) and coincident semantic descriptors in the verbs of fishing and courting, and via the more circuitous route of the common aquatic LOCATIVE.

Let us compare the fields of fishing and courtship. The syntagmatic elements include VERB, MANNER, AGENT, PATIENT, INSTRUMENT, and LOCATIVE (optional). Both fields may have humans in the position of AGENT, but only courtship can have humans in the position of PATIENT. The LOCATIVE is perhaps much less important in courtship than in fishing, as courting can be done almost anywhere while fishing must be done in or by a body of water. INSTRUMENT, as I pointed out above, is virtually obligatory for fishing. For example, the question 'With what is he catching fish?' is a perfectly normal one. (In fact, there is a certain oddity in the description of the fishing scene in the second stanza of the poem, taken as a literal rendering, in which the person addressed is presumably catching fish using no instruments whatsoever.) In courtship, however, INSTRUMENT is highly optional, perhaps even normally inappropriate. If someone says, 'He is courting her', it is somewhat strange to ask, 'With what?' Thus in the metaphorical line 'For thou

---

[8] See Chapter 8 for a discussion of such *post factum* similarities.

thyself art thine own bait', the relation of instrument is introduced into the field of courtship.

The stanza in which 'bait' appears may mean that the same referent which occupies the position of AGENT also occupies the position of INSTRUMENT,[9] that is, the woman addressed in the poem. We can indicate the syntagmatic relations and the elements which figure as the relata by means of Figure 7.6. Because the referents denoted by 'lover' and 'beloved' change in the poem, subscripts are used to indicate to whom reference is being made.

VERB	AGENT	PATIENT	INSTRUMENT	LOCATIVE
courts	lover$_W$	beloved$_P$	lover$_W$	riverbed

W = woman addressed in the poem
P = male poet

FIG. 7.6

However, the stanza is ambiguous and the situation is far more complicated than is indicated here, for this is, by convention, a love poem in which the lover is the poet and the beloved is the woman addressed in the poem. This is clearly indicated in the opening lines and in the fourth stanza, which is a sample of conventional love poetry. Thus the diagrammatic representation should have referential subscripts as in Figure 7.7

VERB	AGENT	PATIENT	INSTRUMENT
courts	lover$_P$	beloved$_W$	? (beloved$_W$)

FIG. 7.7

Thus, somewhere in the poem the occupants of the positions mapped out by the field are reversed. In the representation given in Figure 7.7, it cannot be the beloved who serves as bait because the fish swallows the bait and by analogy that would mean that the beloved

---

[9] This is in spite of the fact that the role of the INSTRUMENT is not normally filled by persons.

would simply catch? attract? herself. There is no way to make sense of such a construction. We can, however, interpret INSTRUMENT differently in Figure 7.7. In the last two lines of the first stanza of the poem we encounter four adjectives forming a set of terms describing precious and fine materials {gold, crystal, silk, silver}—terms often associated with weddings and courtship. Indeed, they are materials with which a lover woos his beloved. Moreover, the lover here is a (male) poet and a poet woos with words, words such as those composing the fourth stanza (which is otherwise the only stanza unrelated to the fishing scene and metaphor). Thus we can sketch another representation of courtship, Figure 7.8.

VERB	AGENT	PATIENT	INSTRUMENT
courts	lover$_P$	beloved$_W$	precious materials silk silver gold crystal fine words poetry flattery

FIG. 7.8

This looks rather like an ordinary representation of the field of courtship, even though the introduction of the relation of INSTRUMENT was guided by the field of fishing. But as we have seen there is also a turn-about courtship in this poem in which the woman is the AGENT and the man, here the poet, is the PATIENT. When we speak of the woman as the agent in a courtship—when the woman allures and wittingly or unwittingly attracts the man—we often do speak of *the means* by which she attracts the man: by artifice for example, make-up, clothes, *coiffure*—by natural charm, by intellect, by beauty, etc. Thus we have the representation of a turn-about courtship in Figure 7.9.

Once we have introduced the relation of INSTRUMENT, we can introduce the set of modifiers on the verb, because these modifiers, in the case of the structures with which we are concerned above, relate to the instrument at least as much as to the verb. For example, if the means of attraction is one of natural charm then the manner cannot be deceitful, whereas if the means of attraction involves artifice then the manner is

VERB	AGENT	PATIENT	INSTRUMENT
court attract	lover$_W$ (attracting person)[a]	beloved$_P$ (potential lover)	artifice charm intellect beauty etc.

Fig. 7.9

[a] Where the verb is 'attract', the AGENT need not be the lover, because the attracting person may unwittingly attract some person whom she may not love—similarly, then, the PATIENT may not be the beloved, although he may become the lover once he himself has become attracted.

not innocent or guileless. Thus we further structure the courtship relation by introducing into the field a place for MANNER.

However, the most striking way in which the metaphor of bait orders and reorders the field of courtship is seen in the following set of relations:

(1)(a)   Fisherman (tries to) catch(es) fish by means of bait.

(b)   Bait attracts fish.

(2)(a)   Lover$_P$ (tries to) catch(es) beloved$_W$ by means of . . .

(b)   Beloved$_W$ attracts lover$_P$.

(3)(a)   Lover$_W$ (tries to) catch(es) beloved$_P$ by means of . . .

(b)   Beloved$_W$ attracts lover$_P$.

(c)   Lover$_W$ attracts beloved$_P$.

In an analogue to 1 in the field of courtship, let us say 2, the appropriate completion of 2(a) would involve the insertion of 'beloved$_W$' in the blank space, a space occupied by 'bait' in sentence 1(a). But that does not work. The 'beloved' cannot at once be the prey and herself the means of catching the prey. In an analogue formulated as 3, we can insert 'beloved$_W$' in the blank space. Now we are saying that the 'lover', the woman, is attempting to attract the 'beloved', the poet, by using herself (presumably her own charms, etc.) to attract him. This is conceptually sound. However, the referential subscripts in 3(a) and 3(b) are not consistent. In 3(a) they indicate that the woman is the lover and the poet the beloved, while in 3(b), it is the woman who is the beloved and the poet who is the lover. One cannot change referential subscripts in mid-sentence without ambiguity and confusion. By substituting the formulation in 3(c) for the one in 3(b), we get the needed consistency in our referential subscripts and we have the desired conceptual coherence: the woman tries to attract the poet by means of herself.

But on this account the woman plays the role of the AGENT, the lover, and we have now lost sight of the original courting situation first established by the poem in its opening lines—that is, the (male) poet courting his lady. Various other permutations are possible, but what Donne has done is created a metaphor which on the surface seems plausible but which in fact is impossible to explicate in terms of the relations which are set up and transferred. If 'The Bait' were a serious love poem, this might be a problem.[10] But, in fact, this is not a serious love poem, it is a parody and it mocks the view of courtship presented by such traditional love poetry. This a view in which a poetic offer of the idyllic life in an idyllic setting, or rather the poem itself, is the *bait* presented by the lover-poet to his beloved, only because he himself is attracted to the bait that she is.

Another element of the parody which takes place by means of the metaphor is reflected in the paradigmatic relations of the semantic field of fishing: the movement in the poem from an idyllic fishing scene in the first three stanzas to the nasty struggle of the two penultimate stanzas. As has been mentioned above, the degree to which violence and deception are used on the part of the fisherman is one organizing principle in the field of fishing terms. In Figure 7.3 the terms which denote the activity of fishing are arranged on such a graded scale. The superordinate terms 'catch' and 'fish' are relatively neutral in this regard. In the second and third stanzas Donne portrays a fishing scene in which the fisherwoman needs no instrument to attract the fish. In fact, the fishing scene is really structured like a love scene—that is, here the field of courtship is the vehicle field for the topic domain of fishing. After the conventional verses of love poetry in the middle of the poem, we arrive at a very straightforward, literal description of fishing: first using the 'angling reeds', then the 'snare' and 'net', followed by the use of brute force ('coarse bold hands'), and finally, the ultimate villainy of cunning, beauty used in the service of betrayal ('curious traitors', 'sleave-silk flies'). With the introduction of instruments with which to catch the fish, the setting moves from the idyllic to the unpleasant ('cut their legs, with shells and weeds', 'slimy nests').

---

[10] There are, of course, many metaphors which can only be explicated in very limited ways. Of an extended metaphor such as the one in this poem, a poem written by as intellectual a poet as Donne, we can expect that the metaphor is explicable in terms of the new relations it sets up in the topic field.

All this suggests that in courtship too we move from the pleasant activity of flirtation through to the struggle of real sexual encounters and conflicts, and sometimes to the extremes of brute force, rape, and the more subtle violence, the cunning and villainy of seduction. The metaphor can imply all this, by virtue of the transfer of a set of relations: a set of relations governing co-hyponyms graded with respect to degree of violence and cunning in one field is transposed on to another field, where the reader or listener can sort out the concepts of that second field in the light of the transferred relations. Through his use of the fishing metaphor in what appears to be conventional love poetry, Donne has completely reoriented our idyllic preconceptions of courtship, introducing into it an element of unpleasantness, conflict, and struggle.

In the above discussion of 'The Bait', the goal has been to offer an example of how the topic domain of courting is reoriented in terms of the perspective offered by the vehicle field belonging to the term 'bait'. This perspectival reordering takes place not only by means of drawing similarities as given in common semantic descriptions, but by setting up relations in the topic field which mimic those in the field of the vehicle. In the Donne poem, we have the interesting additional feature of parody, which involves the reversals of relations and the absurdities into which we are led by means of the metaphorical relations established by the poem—absurdities and reversals which reflect back to the matter which forms the subject of the poem, that is, courtship, and even more pertinently, courtly poetry, as it is this poetry which is the instrument (the bait) of the poet who woos his lady.

The Use of Bridge Concepts in some Platonic Metaphors

I have said above that the aquatic setting of the love scene (seduction scene) provides a bridge between the field of fishing and the courtship domain in Donne's poem, since this location is customary for courtship as well as fishing. We can note that the exploitation of a *common boundary* between two fields is a favourite rhetorical device among certain authors for getting an audience to accept a metaphorical transposition of relations. For example, it is prevalent in many of Plato's significant metaphors. In particular, one can cite the metaphor of the sun as the good—just as the sun shines forth light by which to discern mere images and shadows in the cave from the objects themselves, so the good provides the intellectual light by which we can discern the images and shadows which are the objects of the sensuous world from the Forms of intelligible reality. The common boundary here is perception itself. Within the vehicle field (of sensuous perception) that perception which takes place in full sunlight has the greatest value; in the topic domain (of intellectual apprehension) mere sensuous perception, even in full sunlight, has very low value. As we ascend the graded scale of perceptual reality, we border on the new scale of intellectual reality. What is the top of one scale may well be the bottom of another—as we ascend one set of stairs, we find that there awaits us another flight to climb. Within the realm of knowledge, Plato induces a structure analogous to the one he so successfully elucidated in the realm of sensuous perception. The clear perception of objects in full sunlight is the top rung of Plato's ladder of sensuous perception and the bottom rung of his ladder of knowledge. The putative fact that the top rung of the ladder of perception is coincident with the bottom rung of the ladder of intellection of knowledge eases the reader's acceptance of the very existence of a domain of intellectual reality (corresponding to the domain of perceptual reality). The reader is transposing a familiar valuation on to a new domain whose existence must be presumed in order to make sense of the metaphor.

A similar use of a common boundary between fields is displayed in Plato's right hand/left hand metaphor prescribing the equal education of boys and girls in the *Laws*. The passage begins:

Athenian: Now they must begin to learn—the boys going to teachers of horsemanship and the use of the bow, the javelin, and the sling, and the girls too, if they do not object, at any rate until they know how to manage these weapons, and especially how to handle heavy arms; for I may note that the practice which now prevails is almost universally misunderstood.
Cleinias: In what respect?
Athenian: In that the right and left hand are supposed to be by nature differently suited for our various uses of them. (Plato, *The Laws*, 794 C-E, trans. B. Jowett.)

The Athenian goes on with a fairly lengthy discourse on the foolishness of training only the right hand and the virtues of not ignoring the left hand. He introduces another analogy to make his case: just as the right and left foot are equally strong because they must equally carry the burden of the rest of the body, and hence are equally exercised, so the right hand and left hand could be equally matched were they equally trained. The passage ends with the following:

Athenian: Now magistrates, male and female, should see to all these things, the women superintending the nursing and amusements of the children, and the man superintending their education, that all of them, boys and girls alike, may be sound of hand and foot, and may not, if they can help, spoil the gifts of nature by bad habits. (Ibid. 795 D.)

Clearly Plato intends us to understand that just as the hierarchical ordering of abilities between right and left hands is a consequence of poor educational policy, so the analogous hierarchy between boys and girls is also the product of misguided policies. But boys and girls not only are *like* the right hand and left hand in this regard, boys and girls *have* right and left hands which need proper training. There is therefore a cleverly engineered slippage between the two domains which makes the analogy appear very natural. Within the misogynist culture of ancient Greece, Plato's appeal must have appeared most *unnatural*, and one can well imagine that Plato's early suggestions in *The Republic* were not received with any enthusiasm. In the close to the passage cited, Plato lends added ambiguity to the metaphor by suggesting that boys and girls should be trained to utilize all their limbs fully. He thus downplays the metaphorical use of the discussion of right- and left-hand training and makes it a literal suggestion—for boys and girls alike. I suggest that this is in order that the idea of an equal education for both sexes is insinuated so that it does not meet resistance head-on as did his sexually egalitarian views in Book V of *The Republic*.

Buckminster Fuller has pointed out an interesting feature of design. If you construct three contiguous triangles, a, b, and c, in the appropriate fashion (see Figure 7.10), you create a fourth triangle, d—and a fifth, the totality of the four triangles. The appropriate use of common boundaries of semantic fields similarly yields a concept that need never be explicitly stated, and whose existence need not be explicitly asserted, for it to be operative in our understanding of the metaphor. In the case of the Cave metaphor, the very existence of the realm of Forms becomes a presupposition for the epistemic metaphor of the light given by the sun; in the case of the right hand/left hand metaphor, the suggestion of equality results from the metaphorical identification of the bilateral physiology and the two sexes. The ontological assumptions in the Cave metaphor and the prescriptive tenets of the symmetry of male and female in the right hand/left hand metaphor emerge as the fourth triangle in Fuller's image—no, indeed, as the fifth triangle. That is, as the true subject matter of the discussion carried on in terms of the vehicle.

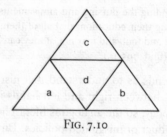

FIG. 7.10

'The Midwife'

I shall now discuss another Platonic metaphor—this time in some detail. Here too Plato exploits a common boundary between two fields, that of the creative factor in procreation and intellection. But here he does not need to convince anyone of anything as unpalatable as the equal education for men and women or the existence of a realm of pure Forms. Thus, while this metaphor also has great rhetorical force, it has less of a sleight-of-hand quality.

In the *Theaetetus*[11] Socrates speaks of himself as a midwife. The metaphor plays on the relation between creation and procreation and the fields to which these notions belong. The semantic field of midwifery has a complex syntagmatic representation; for it has an embedded sentential structure. See Figure 7.11.

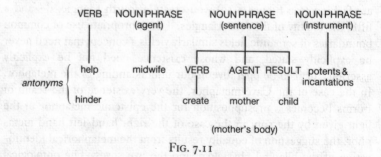

FIG. 7.11

When this field is used metaphorically to speak of a different domain, we can predict that the domain will be structured similarly

---

[11] Extracts from this work are reproduced in the Appendix to Chapter 7, pp. 299–300 below.

after the metaphor has been formed, if not before. In the case of the midwife metaphor in the *Theaetetus*, the topic domain is the relation of Socrates to his students in general and to Theaetetus in particular. That relation may be expressed as in Figure 7.12, using Figure 7.11 as a model.

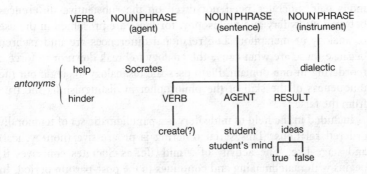

FIG. 7.12

In Figure 7.12 we have one paradigmatic relation not found in Figure 7.11, that is the opposition within the RESULT. We find the opposition between a true (or real) child and a false child. In elaborating the metaphor, Socrates remarks on the point at which the metaphor of midwife fails:

Such are the midwives, whose task is a very important one, but not so important as mine; for women do not bring into the world at one time real children and at another time counterfeits which are with difficulty distinguished from them; if they did, then the discernment of the true and false birth would be the crowning achievement of the art of midwifery. (*Theaetetus 150* A 9–B 5.)

This disanalogy differs from other differences which can be remarked on, such as the fact that Socrates acts upon men while the midwife acts upon women, that Socrates tends to souls while the midwife tends to bodies, and that Socrates aids in the generation of ideas while the midwife aids in the generation of infants.[12] These are all

---

[12] Notice that the fields generated by these syntagmas result in the identification of female creation as corporal and of male creation as mental or spiritual—an identification which makes woman an excellent metaphor for creativity of an intellectual sort, but excludes her as a participant of that intellectual creativity. Kittay (1988) contains a further elaboration of this point.

substantive differences—differences in domains, not in the ordering within domains. The disanalogy to which Socrates so carefully draws our attention is relational. While all the entries of RESULT in the midwife field are relative synonyms—that is, relative to this field, terms such as 'baby' and 'infant' would be synonymous with 'child'—the paradigm of RESULT in the student-philosopher field involves an antonymous pair. Socrates need not dwell on the substantive differences between midwifery and philosophy, for these are presumed in the use of analogy or metaphor. The relational differences are underscored because these are what cause the analogy to break down or to force a reordering in one domain. Plato uses the disanalogy to single out the uniqueness of the skill of the philosopher in distinguishing the true from the false.[13]

Included in the field of midwifery is a paradigmatic set of temporally ordered relations. This serial ordering is progressive (non-cyclical) and stage-like. The activity of a midwife, as Socrates conceives it, begins with matchmaking and continues to the post-partum period. In the temporal sequence, each element can be framed within a set of syntagmatic relations that can be represented as a verb with three noun phrases: 'midwife', 'mother', 'child'. These three noun phrases occupy various role relations in the different stages. The elements of the field are terms which are, in a sense, amplifications of the terms 'to help', 'to hinder', and 'to create' as they figure in discourse about procreation and midwifery. This field is given in Figure 7.13.

Through the metaphor Socrates presents to us a view of learning which we can structure using the heuristic model of human procreation. One might think of learning as an accumulation of knowledge. In that case, the temporal sequence is not stage-like but is ordered along a chronological continuum. Someone who is in the process of learning, and has at time t, x amount of knowledge, will at time $(t + 1)$ have $(x + 1)$ amount of knowledge. On this model, learning does not involve ruptures, radical changes of state, as it does on the model of procreation. The stages of childbirth, while progressive—with each step the mother-to-be gets closer to her goal—also involve stages in which there are radical changes and critical moments, moments at which all may be lost without the proper care and intervention of the midwife. In

---

[13] Plato might have availed himself of the notion of a false or hysterical pregnancy to provide a parallel to the birth of a false idea. Perhaps the Greeks were not aware of the phenomenon. For a modern philosopher-teacher the metaphor is available and may be a useful productive device for deriving new metaphors for different intentions.

MATCHMAKING	CONCEPTION	PREGNANCY	LABOUR	DELIVERY	POST-PARTUM	CHILD REARING
x matches y to w	z is conceived by y and w	y is pregnant with z	x uses potions & incantations to help y give birth to z	x cuts umbilical cord	x takes care of y (y recuperates (y suffers post-partum depression)	y nurtures z ---- y neglects z
x initiates conception & pregnancy			y is in labour with z	x helps y to deliver z ---- x aborts z	y nurtures z ---- y exposes z	

x=midwife; y=mother or mother-to-be; z=child; w=father or father-to-be (the father plays only a peripheral role in this field; it is essentially a field of female actors). Dotted lines indicate antonymy.

Fig. 7.13

choosing this metaphor, Socrates presents us with a view of a philosophical education which is similarly stage-like and problematical.

The stages are defined by the mother's relation to the midwife, or to the baby, or to both. Similarly, the stages of the student's progress are defined by his relation to Socrates, or to the ideas, or to both. By means of Figure 7.13 we see that if the appropriate verbs were supplied, we could replace the variable x with the term 'Socrates', y with 'student' and z with 'idea', and the field would be the reordered field of teaching as conceived by Socrates. In this sense the transfer from the field of midwifery to that of the student-philosopher is clearly a relational transfer, and this transfer is easily perceivable, if, as I have said, the appropriate verbs are supplied. To make this point clearer, I have given a schematic representation of the syntagmatic subfields of the temporal field of conception and childbirth. See Figure 7.14.

Let us take stages 3(b) and 4 and consider how the schema might be transformed to represent a syntagma concerning the relation between a teacher, his/her student, and the result of the educative process. For the variables x, y, and z we supply the interpretation x = teacher, y = student, and z = idea (or 'result of learning'). The antonymous pair 'help'/'hinder', occupying the position of the main verb, are appropriate to the domains of both childbirth and learning. The embedded verbs, the co-hyponyms 'give birth to'/'deliver' (or 'be delivered of') and their antonym 'abort' cannot be used literally in the new domain.

One could represent these terms with selection restrictions which indicate the anomalous use. We might substitute for the verbs 'give birth to' and 'deliver' terms such as 'produce' or 'create' and replace 'abort' with 'fail to produce' or 'fail to create'. Lastly, we substitute 'dialectics' for 'incantations' and 'potions'. Then we read the new syntagma as follows: 'Teacher helps/hinders student; student produces/fails to produce ideas by means of dialectics'.

In Figure 7.15 I have given another interpretation of some of the predicates, also very approximate interpretations guided mainly by the particular conception of learning put forth by Socrates. I have also formalized in Figure 7.15 the various stages given in Figure 7.14, using some notation from predicate calculus but using as connectives the phrases 'to CAUSE' and 'by MEANS of'. After the formal translation of 1–4, I give two sets of interpretations for the individual and predicate variables: one set using terms from the field of childbirth, and the other using terms from the field of learning. The purpose of this exer-

1 MATCHMAKING AND CONCEPTION
x matches *y* to *w* in order to cause *y* to conceive *z*

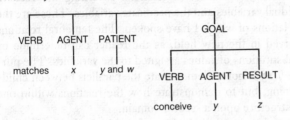

2 PREGNANCY
y is pregnant with *z*

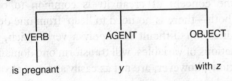

3(*a*) LABOUR
y is in labour with *z*

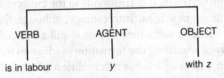

3(*b*) and 4 Labour and Delivery

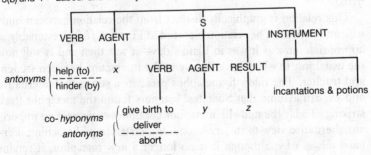

FIG. 7.14

cise is to indicate that what is preserved in the movement from the former field to the latter is a set of relations governing the relation between individual variables and the predicate variables. These are the syntagmatic relations of which I have spoken. The temporal relations are also preserved in the new field, as the reader can determine by appropriate substitutions of values assigned to the variables. The purpose of Figure 7.15 is not to demonstrate the parallels between childbirth and learning, but to demonstrate how the relations within one field induce a structure upon a second domain.

Here there may be a point in speaking of certain similarities between childbirth and the creation of ideas. The concept, or feature, of creativity is the locus of that similarity—it serves to bridge the two domains. Because the concept of creativity is common to both— indeed, is central to both—there is no need to 'leap' from one domain to the other. Thus it is not difficult to supply a verb which, given appropriate interpretations of variables, will transform one domain into another. Such transitions, however, are not as easily attained at various other stages of the field, represented in Figures 7.13 and 7.14. For example, in the second stage pictured in Figure 7.14, it is difficult to imagine what verb we might find as an appropriate substitute for 'is pregnant'. There is no verb which corresponds to the concept of being in the midst of forming a new idea. Interestingly, although the metaphor 'pregnant with ideas' is not a new one, it is still an effective one. Indeed, the usual way of regarding the formation of ideas on the part of a student is based on a field which has a very different structure from the one which we have portrayed for childbirth. The relation between student and teacher specified by the usual view may be seen in Figure 7.16.

This relation is graphically distinct from the relation between midwife and mother. The relation pictured in Figure 7.16 is presumably as appropriate now as it was in Plato's day—it was then and is still now the usual way in which we conceive of the interaction between student and teacher. The midwife metaphor presents a substantial alternative and we can assume that Socrates' listeners found the metaphor itself striking. Today the midwife metaphor continues to present an important alternative view to the traditional understanding of teaching. Perhaps this is why, although it is no longer a new metaphor, it retains much of the vigour and illumination of a novel one. One may guess that if our understanding of the act of teaching ever approached that envisaged by Socrates, the metaphor would begin to lose that vitality. It

1	$x\,M\,y\,a$ to CAUSE $y\,C\,z$	where $x \neq y \neq a \neq z$ and where M and C are non-reflexive, intransitive, and asymmetrical
2	$y\,P\,z$	where $y \neq z$ and P is non-reflexive, intransitive, and asymmetrical
3(a)	$y\,L\,z$	where $y \neq z$ and L is non-reflexive, intransitive, and asymmetrical
3(b) and 4	$x\,H\,y$ to CAUSE $y\,B\,z$ by MEANS of $I\,x$	where $x \neq y \neq z$ and H is intransitive and asymmetrical and B is non-reflexive, intransitive and asymmetrical.

FIELD OF CHILDBIRTH	FIELD OF LEARNING
$x\,M\,ya = x$ matches y to a	$x\,M\,ya = x$ introduces y to a
$y\,C\,z = y$ conceives z	$y\,C\,z = y$ formulates the idea z
$y\,P\,z = y$ is pregnant with z	$y\,P\,z = y$ thinks about z
$y\,L\,z = y$ is in labour with z	$y\,L\,z = y$ tests the truth of z
$x\,H\,y = x$ helps y	$x\,H\,y = x$ helps y
('helps' is not generally intransitive, but in this context it is)	(we shall consider 'help' intransitive in this context as well)
$y\,B\,z = y$ gives birth to z	$y\,B\,z = y$ knows the truth or falsity of z
$I\,x = x$ uses potions	$I\,x = x$ uses dialects
and	and
x = midwife	x = Socrates (or teacher)
y = mother	y = student
z = child	z = idea
a = father	a = suitable intellectual partner

FIG. 7.15

VERB	AGENT	PATIENT	INSTRUMENT	RESULT
teach	teacher	student	books (dialectics) teacher's knowledge	knowledge ideas

FIG. 7.16

would have no field to restructure because the topic domain of teaching would, in this regard, importantly resemble the vehicle field, the field of midwifery. In other words, a metaphor remains a live (and lively) metaphor as long as the two fields employed in the metaphor are structured differently in some significant manner (or in some manner that can be made to seem significant, as in the Donne poem). The liveliness of the metaphor is more likely to be a function of the degree of the sustained difference between two fields (a difference which is exploited in the process of reordering one field by means of another) than a function of the time of its initial utterance.

Plato's metaphor is also effective because the relations with which it deals are complex and varied. Moreover, it employs a paradigm of a set of developmental stages which can be extended into contiguous fields such as child-rearing (moving forward in time) and mating (moving back in time). And new knowledge about the activity of childbirth provides new, productive extensions of the metaphor. If someone feels inexplicably sad at the completion of some intellectual project, we may speak of his or her state as being a 'post-partum depression', thus offering the metaphor as an explanation of his or her state of mind. Just as a woman feels depressed at the termination of a pregnancy, when the child is no longer a part of her, so a student (writer, etc.) may feel a sense of loss at the completion of a work which is now separate from him or her. Socrates himself extends the metaphor beyond the limits of midwifery. He complains of young men with whom he has spoken but who have left him before the appropriate time (the post-partum recovery period?) and then lost their offspring through poor parenting. The ability of a metaphor to be utilized for the expression of new but related ideas we call the *productivity* of a metaphor. The productivity of a metaphor is what gives it the character of a playing out, a spinning out, of matter that is the act of creativity we associate with good metaphors. In this regard the midwife metaphor is the examplar of a good metaphor.

We have seen how a metaphor articulates the topic domain by exploiting relations among the elements of the vehicle field. The reader follows along and sees how it is possible to construct the homomorphisms between the two fields. At the end of the process, one can even draw neat diagrams reflecting the parallels. But such a diagram does not do justice to the stretching and pulling required in order to match elements in the two fields. If the match is too easy, the metaphor is banal, and its effect is decorative rather than cognitive: since the use of the vehicle field does little to restructure the topic field, the use of a mediating semantic field is relatively gratuitous.

Bees of England

Finally, I shall consider what I take to be a less successful metaphor, the metaphor of workers as 'bees of England' in Shelley's poem 'Song to the Men of England'.

The first three stanzas of Shelley's poem are given below.

> Men of England, wherefore plough
> For the lords who lay ye low?
> Wherefore weave with toil and care
> The rich robes your tyrants wear?
>
> Wherefore feed, and clothe, and save,
> From the cradle to the grave,
> Those ungrateful drones who would
> Drain your sweat—nay, drink your blood?
>
> Wherefore, Bees, of England, forge
> Many a weapon, chain, and scourge,
> That these stingless drones may spoil
> The forced produce of your toil?

Shelley presents us with a two-class society: workers (bees) and lords (drones). The bees are spoken of as if they were exploited by the drones. But the notion of exploitation is borrowed from socialist economic theory—that is, a theory about *human* behaviour. This notion is then applied metaphorically to the relation between bees and drones. Bees are pictured as producing weapons for the drones. But again, although bees do possess the weapon of the sting, the idea of them forging weapons for the stingless drones is dictated by the topic domain, human socio-economic relations, not the vehicle field.

It is significant that Shelley chooses to ignore the queen bee, certainly an important element in bee society. However, her inclusion in the metaphor could not be accommodated in the two-class system. In the socialist theory Shelley employs, the aristocracy is classed with the bourgeoisie, that is, the non-productive and exploiting class. But in bee society, the queen works unceasingly—laying eggs for new generations of bees.[14]

Shelley's metaphor is no doubt effective rhetorically, as are many other metaphors in which the topic field surreptitiously structures the vehicle domain. The vehicle field, so (re)structured, is now (presumably) used to structure the topic. It is, on analogy with a circular argument, a 'circular' metaphor. As a result, it lacks cognitive interest because the expressions from the vehicle field of bees are simply added on to the content of the topic field; they do not structure the content. On the contrary, the topic field lends structure to the vehicle field— the field whose structure is presumably being used to enlighten us about the topic field. While there may be some rhetorical effectiveness, the danger is that the metaphor soon becomes banal and begins to seem contrived. Although all metaphors have the dual structure of vehicle and topic fields, not all metaphors have much cognitive interest. The degree to which a metaphor is enlightening depends rather on the degree to which the vehicle field is going to be productive of new meaning and new insights in the topic domain.

Conclusion

If we understand the content domain of a semantic field to be the conceptual domain articulated by the terms and relations of the semantic field, then semantic fields are reflections of our conceptual schemes specified in a linguistically determinate fashion. If this understanding is correct, then the reordering of the topic field is a reflection of changes which take place in our conceptual schematization of experiential reality by means of metaphorical transfers of meaning. To view metaphorical transfers of meaning as relational shifts, which can be specified as changes in the semantic relations governing semantic fields, allows us to see, in a fairly precise manner, the way in which metaphors have such conceptual import. These changes may be very

---

[14] The bee metaphor would be more appropriate for a writer who held a political view like that of Ferdinand Lassalle: who believed that there could be a coalition between the King, the aristocracy, the army, and the workers opposing the bourgeouis. The coalition would be headed by the King who would rule in the interests of the productive, i.e. the labouring class. Using the bee metaphor would at least bring in the monarch (queen bee) with the workers in opposition to the lords (drones).

transient, lasting only for the period of the utterance itself. They may, however, result in or reflect a significant reordering which can offer a better 'fit' to our experience than the former conceptual field, and thus be descriptive, even predictive. If, for example, we adopt Donne's view of idyllic courtship, we can attribute such descriptive efficacy to the poem's central metaphor, courtship as fishing—with its predictive features in its implied description of the progression of a courtship. Similarly, Wordsworth's poem may be said to have descriptive efficacy, in addition to its prescriptive injunction to honour 'even the shade/ Of that which once was great'. Plato's right hand/left hand metaphor is also prescriptive: just as we should train both hands to perform equally, so we should train boys and girls equally. The analysis of the midwife metaphor further indicates ways in which metaphor has heuristic power, suggesting new explanations and novel courses of action. The apposition of two semantic fields, in even the most transient metaphor, makes us realize new connections and allows us to create new unities which will form the basis for future thought.

Using the medium of larger texts, of extended metaphors, we have had access to a relatively well-developed content domain in which to explore these shifts of meaning and thought, although what I have elaborated here should be applicable to metaphorical phrases and single-sentence metaphors as well. Moreover, the apparatus of semantic fields provides us with means by which to articulate the metaphorical process.

2 METAPHORICAL *v.* NON-METAPHORICAL TRANSFERS OF MEANING

In the foregoing examples, I have tried to show how metaphor involves a transfer of relations across semantic fields. But must metaphor always involve at least *two* content domains? Three considerations may be brought to bear on the question.

First, metaphors may involve *more* than two semantic fields. The connotative structure of metaphor may be further complicated as in Fig. 7.17.

The possibilities for further complicating the structure are limited only by human tolerance for grasping such intricacies. Shakespeare provides us with some excellent examples of the triplex illustrated above. Let us recall the metaphor (sentence 1.1 above) 'bare ruin'd choirs, where late the sweet birds sang'. The metaphorical use of

	expression	expression
expression		content
content	content	

FIG. 7.17

choirs to speak of autumnal boughs is, in fact, the expression plane for another principal content. The sonnet, as we learn from the opening lines and the remainder of the poem, is a love poem in which autumn (and by metonymy, the autumnal boughs) is itself a metaphor for the state of the speaker in the poem.[15] This can be represented roughly as in Fig. 7.18.

	bare ruin'd choirs	bare ruin'd choirs
bare ruin'd choirs		empty church choirs
state of the poet	autumnal boughs	

FIG. 7.18

Secondly, there appear to be transfers of relations which do not involve two distinct fields. Goodman writes: 'Among metaphors some

[15] Another way in which metaphors may involve more than two semantic fields is found in so-called mixed metaphors. A second Shakespearean example, lines 1–4 of Sonnet 33, provide us with dazzling complexity:

> Full many a glorious morning have I seen
> Flatter the mountain-tops with sovereign eye,
> Kissing with golden face the meadows green,
> Gilding pale streams with heavenly alchemy;

Consider the phrase 'gilding streams'. ('Pale' which is not clearly metaphorical, is most likely suggested by the verb 'to gild', not by what it modifies, namely, 'streams'.) If we are speaking of actual streams, clearly they can be gilded only metaphorically. In the poem it is the *morning* which is gilding the stream. But 'morning' can only be the metaphorical subject of gild. Thus the stream is acted upon by a metaphorical action performed by metaphorical agent. The action is further modified by the prepositional phrase 'with heavenly alchemy', which again can only be a metaphorical modification. Four metaphorical attributions are involved here, the vehicle of each coming from a different semantic field. Such complexity can only be handled graciously through the exercise of extraordinary skill—those with only ordinary capacities need to guard against mixed metaphors.

involve transfer of a schema between disjoint realms . . . But not for all metaphors are the realms disjoint; sometimes one realm intersects or is an expansion or a contraction of the other' (1968, 81). While the realms need not be such that they have *no* terms in common, that is, disjoint, I believe they cannot be mere expansions or contractions one of the other. There are other transfers of meaning which are not meta-phorical—they do not involve two distinct domains—but which involve transfers of relations *within* a semantic field. Hyperbole, litotes, irony, and metonymy are examples of intra-field transfers.

Thirdly, there is the difficulty, already mentioned above, of indivi-duating semantic fields. But again, although the theoretical determi-nation of when we have one semantic field and when we have more than one may be problematical, for any given instance we determine the matter by attention to the linguistic and pragmatic situation.

I maintain the position that metaphor involves at least one semantic field and another distinct content domain, and often two distinct semantic fields. The claim that metaphor involves two semantic fields theoretically puts certain restraints on what terms may be used meta-phorically for other concepts or terms. For example, we should not use 'fork' metaphorically for knife, 'chair' metaphorically for table, 'pen' for pencil, or 'swing' for slide. Each of the above pairs are pairs of co-hyponyms within their respective fields. Nor, to use an example of a part–whole relation, do we use 'branch' as a metaphor for tree, although we could use 'branch' as a *metonymic* figure for tree, that is, as a synecdoche.

There is, however, an important qualification for this constraint. Semantic fields overlap, intersect, and are embedded in one another— they are rarely completely disjoint. Thus, although we can say that two terms in the same semantic field may not be used metaphorically for one another, rarely do we find two words which exist in only one semantic field or which always appear together in a semantic field. Thus, if x and y are two terms in a semantic field A, then x will *not* serve as a vehicle in a metaphor for the content of y (and vice versa), if in whatever semantic field we find x we also find y. However, if x and y are two terms in A and x but not y belongs to some other semantic field B and y but not x also belongs to some other field C, then using the sub-script of the field to which the term belongs to indicate in what sense a particular term is being used, we can say that x_B may be the vehicle for the content of y_C and similarly y_C may be the vehicle for the content of x_B. In the metaphorical and ironical sentence 'The blind man is a seer', we have, as we shall see below, this sort of metaphor, accompanied by subsequent shifts in relations in the shared field.

The pairs of terms I have lined up above as examples of terms which would not be used as metaphors for one another serve as an open invitation to the imaginative reader to construct metaphors using one of the pair as a metaphor for the other. But if success seems at hand, I suggest that the reader carefully consider whether the terms are used in senses such that they both apply within a single content domain.

The constraint that metaphor cannot be made using elements in one semantic field is diametrically opposed to many traditional constraints on what will constitute metaphor. The latter require that metaphors should be made among things (terms or concepts) which are importantly similar—that some previous similarity must underlie a metaphor. My arguments result in the requirement that if x is to be used as a metaphor for y, x and y must be importantly dissimilar. This is crucial if metaphor is to serve its cognitive role. It is by virtue of the apposition of the dissimilar fields that certain features of the topic—ones that are often obscured—come to attain prominence. Because the two fields share so few features, it is those shared features that acquire a saliency in the grouping effected by the apposition of topic and vehicle. (See Kittay 1982).

Some of these points may be made clearer if we recall a distinction made above, Chapter 6, Section 3, between *superfields* and *proper fields*. It may be that all semantic fields overlap in some fashion, or extend into neighbouring semantic fields, so that one may speak of the entire semantic structure of a language as constituting a single, extremely large, semantic superfield. Proper fields may be spoken of as subsets of a superfield. And the superfield which would be large enough to include all proper fields as subsets would be the superfield representing the entire semantic structure of a given language. A superfield need not be so inclusive. Any field which has a proper field as a (proper) subset is a superfield. Thus, my claim can be restated as follows. Metaphorical transfers are effected across proper fields. Thus two proper semantic fields may intersect at a given point, but this point of intersection may be insignificant in the context relevant to the metaphor. In this regard my own view differs substantially from that of Goodman, for I want to claim that when two fields intersect substantially, or when one field can be viewed merely as an expansion or contraction of another, then we no longer have two proper fields, and any resultant transfers of meaning are not metaphorical.

Many transfers which Goodman (1968) discusses in this connection are ones that take place within a proper field, rather than across such fields:

In hyperbole . . . an ordered schema is in effect displaced downward. The large olive becomes supercolossal and the small one large; labels at the lower end of the schema (e.g. 'small') are unused, and things at the upper end of the realm (the exceptionally large olive) are unlabelled in this application of the schema . . . In litotes, or understatement, exactly the opposite occurs. (1968, 82–3.)

But to call a superb performance 'pretty fair', and a good one 'passable', seems to me to be not at all metaphorical: the relative measure which establishes the norm is simply displaced.

Within a given proper field the relations governing that field may be reordered by lexical and conceptual processes. These result in the figures Goodman cites as metaphorical transfers: hyperbole, litotes (understatement), overemphasis, underemphasis, and irony. I do not understand these to be *metaphorical* transfers. Let us take irony as an illustration. Irony (often considered not a figure of speech but rather a figure of thought) is a transfer of meaning within a single semantic field such that the relations between terms of that field are reversed. Let us represent the syntagmatic relations in fishing as in Figure 7.19.

PATIENT	AGENT	VERB
fisherman	fish	catch(es)

FIG. 7.19

If we say, instead, that the 'fish caught the fisherman' we have an ironical statement in which the positions of AGENT and PATIENT are reversed. Another example, a paradigmatic one, would involve Socrates' eloquent claim in the opening of the *Apology* to be using only plain speech in his defence. In the paradigmatic field of words referring to eloquence of speech, we should find a graded antonymy between plain speaking, at the low end of the scale, and eloquence at the upper end. Socrates' irony is to reverse the relation so that plain speaking occupies the higher position and eloquence the devalued, lower, position.

Often, ironical reversals have the effect of breaking down established oppositions and setting new ones in their place. If a fisherman has so devoted himself to catching fish that he has neglected his other affairs, and if, in addition, he fails to catch fish, one might utter, ironically, that this fisherman has not caught fish but that the fish have caught the fisherman. The opposition of AGENT and PATIENT is no longer that of fisherman to fish, or even fish to fisherman, but fisherman to himself, that is, what the fisherman has done to himself by means of his obsession with fishing.

When Socrates says his speech is plain, not eloquent, he adds 'unless the truth itself is eloquence' (Plato, *Apology*, 17 B 4–5, trans. B. Jowett); he thereby breaks down the opposition between eloquence and plain speaking, making them identical in regard to truth and opposing them instead to falsity. When such realignments of oppositions take place, it is often by means of an extra content domain that the new oppositions are established.

Some ironies explicitly involve metaphorical crossing of fields. To call the blind man a 'seer' is an irony and a metaphor, for in the domain of visual capacities, blind man and seer exhibit the antonymous relation of complementarity—he who is not blind sees, and he who does not see is blind. To say of a blind man that he sees is thus ironical (if not simply false). But 'seer' is in the field of terms of prophecy and knowledge and involves the metaphorical use of 'see' to describe 'having knowledge or understanding', and in this metaphorical transfer, the blind man would be he who lacked knowledge or understanding. But by means of the ironical reversal, the blind man is the one who has knowledge and is thus the seer. There is a play on the expression level (the signifier) as well, in which the productive device is used of adding '-(e)r' to a verb to transform it into a noun, so that, on the one hand, the resultant noun, 'seer', is normally the agent of the activity of that verb, and on the other, it has a distinct meaning as synonymous with 'prophet'. See Figure 7.18.

We use the relation of privative opposition to illustrate the set of transfers in Figure 7.20. The original field, that of vision, has a privative opposition between blind (man) and see(r). This relation is preserved in the metaphorical transfer, but not in the ironic reversal. In the latter, the positive and negative values of the two terms are displaced. In the *metaphorical* ironical reversal there are two opposing privative relations. The one who sees (vision field) is blind (knowledge field): the one who has the positive attribution in the vision field has the negative attribution in the knowledge field; the one with a negative attribution in the vision field has the positive attribution in the knowl-

vision	blind (man)	antonyms	see(r)	
knowledge (prophecy)	fool dullard simpleton	} *near synonyms*	prophet seer wise man	} *synonyms*
metaphorical transfer- vision to knowledge	blind man			
ironical reversal	see(r) (*from vision field*)		Blind man seer (*from prophecy field*)	} *synonyms*

FIG. 7.20

edge field. Thus, the descriptor [+ blind] in the knowledge field = the descriptor [+ see] in the vision field; the descriptor [− blind] in the vision field = the descriptor [− see] in the knowledge field. 'Blind' acquires and 'see' is divested of a positive valuation.

By pursuing such an analysis of irony, we may conclude that all non-trivial ironical reversals do in fact involve some other field besides the one within which the reversals of relations occur. At the very least this may be true of the case in which the reversal is only a first step towards a new alignment of oppositions. By means of the combined irony and metaphor, the opposed elements are not simply reversed, the very opposition is rendered inadequate and replaced with a new one.

Another group of transfers within fields (ones not included in Goodman's account) are the various types of *metonymy*. Metonymic shifts of meaning can occur among words which have either paradigmatic or syntagmatic relations between them. *Synecdoche*, a type of metonymic transfer, involves the paradigmatic relation of part–whole, for example, 'sail' for ship. Metonymic transfers may involve various other paradigmatic relations, such as overlapping segments in the metonymies 'a day' for a year, or 'a year' for a day. Metonymic associations can move from one co-hyponym to another, for example, 'cake' for bread; from a superordinate to a hyponym (or vice versa), for example, 'my word' for my promise; and from one term in an opposition to another, where the transfer is *not* ironical, antipodally or orthogonally, 'north' for south, or 'south' for east. Metonymic transfers involving syntagmatic relations may be seen in such expressions as 'a blond' to speak of a person with blond hair. We have a synecdoche of part for whole, blond hair for the person, as well as the metonymic syntagmatic transfer of blond for blond hair. The vulgar phrase 'I gave him a fistful' illustrates a metonymic use of the syntagmatic relation between punch and fist. Speaking of 'the White House' instead of the President is a metonymy based on the syntagm 'The President lives in the White House'—the LOCATION replaces the AGENT. Metonymies can also involve moving from one semantic field to another, but this generally happens by means of some polysemy or homonymy (or virtual homonymy) on the part of the word which serves as a bridge, as with puns. In extended metaphors, these metonymies will often serve to bridge the two fields involved in the metaphorical transfer.

All these transfers of meaning can become instances of *catachresis*, as are some of the examples I have used, for example, 'colossal' as the size of an olive or 'a blond' for a person with blond hair. Catachresis is, literally, a misuse of language. It is sometimes taken to refer to those cases of metaphor which arise out of a need to name some unnamed entity—standard examples include 'the leg of a chair' or the 'foot of a mountain'—or it is sometimes said to be an *abuse* of language. Quintilian, who speaks of catachresis, is inconsistent in his use of the term and in regard to its opposition to, or inclusion within, metaphor. His examples, however, are more helpful:

Flasks are called *acetabula* (vinegar flasks) whatever they contain and caskets *pyxides* (made of boxwood) regardless of their material. (*De Institutione Oratoria*, 8. 6. 35, trans. H. E. Butler.)

These are cases in which a definite and particular object or set of objects are in need of a label, and the label chosen belongs to a related object or set of objects. We can give contemporary English equivalents. We still speak of 'dialling' when we operate a push-button telephone; and we call graphite pencils 'lead pencils'. Such extensions of a term's use would be instances of catachresis. From these examples we can see that catachresis can have, at its source, many different sorts of meaning transfer.

Quintilian's *acetabula* example, in which 'vinegar flasks' becomes used as the term for flasks regardless of what they contain, is a metonymic transfer from a hyponym to a superordinate concept. In the case of 'lead pencil', the metonymic transfer is from one co-hyponym in the set of marking substances to another. 'Gaps' in lexical fields are often filled by such metonyms which become catachrestic once they are established in the language.

One can say that the distinction between metaphor and catachresis is dependent, in part, on whether we can identify two distinct content planes (in metaphor) or whether two content planes have been conflated (in catachresis). The difference between a catachresis which results from metonymic transfers and a genuine metonymy depends on whether or not the original relation between the two terms involved is operative in a term's current use. If it is, we have metonymy; if it is not, we have catachresis.

Extensions of meaning, which are the catachrestic product of transfers of meaning, may then be metaphorical (without being metaphors) or metonymic (without being genuine metonymies),[16] that is, they may take place across fields (which are then conflated) or they may take place within a field. Extensions of meaning which have lost their figurative aspect may be spoken of in terms of the notion of *obligatory* and *optional* descriptors, following a distinction introduced by Lehrer (1974). Then we can say that catachresis, whether resulting from metonymic changes or metaphorical ones, is a shift in meaning from the obligatory to the optional semantic descriptors. Thus in the catachrestic 'foot of a mountain', 'foot' simply means 'base' or 'bottom', whereas in another use of the word 'foot', for example, as a part of the body of a human or other primate [base] or [bottom] would serve as optional descriptors.[17] When metaphor turns into catachresis, the

---

[16] I owe the observation that metonymies as well as metaphors are subject to becoming catachrestic to Umberto Eco (personal communication).

[17] Even such catachrestic uses as 'the foot of the mountain' can, in the appropriate context, be revived. In Baudelaire's poem 'La Géante', the poet says he would love to have lived near a young giantess, 'as a voluptuous cat at the feet of a queen'. He speaks of her in terms appropriate to a mountain—for example, 'climb on the slope of her huge knees'. At the end of the poem he says that 'when the unhealthy suns . . . make her stretch out across the country', he would like to 'sleep without a worry in the shade of her breast, like a peaceful hamlet at the foot of a mountain'. In the poem, we begin at the 'feet of a queen' (*aux pieds d'une reine*), climb up her immense body as we would climb a mountain, and return to 'the foot', this time 'the foot of the mountain' (*au pied d'une montagne*), a catachresis which here facilitates and even seals the metaphorical juxtaposing and eventual identification of giantess and mountain. Moreover, the catachresis is returned to its metaphorical origin so that we see the mountain as a being with corporal parts like our own. That is, we see the field of parts of the human body as the vehicle field for the topic content of the topography of the mountain, and we see what might motivate the use of this vehicle field for this topic, namely the voluptuous, yet peaceful sense of lying at the foot of a 'giantess'.

term moves permanently to the field of the topic: 'foot of a mountain' is a standard part of the semantic field of mountain terms. To revert again to Goodman's immigration metaphor of metaphor, a standard metaphor results when a term that is a visitor to a new land chooses to remain as a resident alien (a standard metaphor), even after the rest of her clan returns home. Occasionally, such a term becomes a naturalized citizen and then we have a fully-fledged catachresis of metaphorical origins.[18]

In the above pages, I introduced the distinction between novel metaphors, standard ones, and catachresis, or dead metaphors. It has been suggested[19] that the metaphors which remain in the language but eventually become dead metaphors, are ones for which the metaphorically transferred term remains the only term in the language which expresses that concept, or set of concepts. This happens when we have a conceptual domain which is newly discovered and explored, and which was not previously articulated by a lexical field, as is the case with electrical terms such as 'circuit', 'current', and 'attraction'. It may also happen when there is a gap within an already articulated conceptual field. This is particularly true if the gap is made prominent by the metaphorical juxtaposition of its field with some other semantic field. For example, in the sentence, 'I *arrived at* the idea', the conceptual domain of 'idea' lacks a term indicating the concept expressed by the metaphorical use of the words 'arrived at'. Other terms used similarly, as in the sentences 'I *came to* the idea', and 'The idea has *occurred* to me', are also metaphorical and are all near synonyms in the lexical field of motion. I have called all these sentences metaphorical, but they are hardly metaphors any longer. Only by a very conscious effort do we detect two conceptual fields as operative. 'Arrived at', 'came', 'occurred', are all dead metaphors. Lakoff and Johnson (1980) have a well-elaborated discussion of these metaphors and their interrelations.

I have used the following criterion for distinguishing metaphor from non-metaphorical but figurative transfers of meaning: can we distinguish two content planes as simultaneously operative? This criterion is valid regardless of the novelty of the particular use of a given expression. An active metaphor, be it novel or standard, has two distinct and distinguishable content levels, each from distinguishable

---

[18] These naturalized citizens may have children who are then simply normal citizens (natives) but are second-generation (of immigrant parentage)—e.g. a chair *stands* on its legs.

[19] Harnish via personal communication with Adrienne Lehrer.

(though not necessarily *completely* disjoint) conceptual fields. A novel metaphor employs two fields rarely brought together, or rarely brought together in such a way as to effect the particular transfer of relations we find in that distinct case. Thus while habit and use can diminish the potency of a metaphor, they do not *necessarily* vitiate its status as metaphor. With age and use a metaphor may indeed die[20] or become standard. However, given the proper context, the metaphor may be revived. This would be true of a context in which terms from the original semantic field of the vehicle were present in the linguistic environment, or when the non-linguistic situation could easily be rendered in terms of that content domain.

Among metaphors one can distinguish active ones from dead ones and novel ones from standard ones. The two distinctions are fairly independent. Although a novel metaphor will be active as long as it is novel, if it remains in the language it may become standard like, for example, 'river-*beds*', and many technical terms, for example, 'force' in physics. An interesting question for diachronic semantics and psycholinguistics to answer is why a metaphor stays in the language and, if it does, why it becomes either dead or standard.[21]

APPENDIX: EXTRACTS FROM PLATO'S THEAETETUS

THEAETETUS: . . . I can neither persuade myself that I have a satisfactory answer to give, nor hear of any one who answers as you would have him; and I cannot shake off a feeling of anxiety.

SOCRATES: These are the pangs of labour, my dear Theaetetus; you have something within you which you are bringing to the birth . . . I am the son of a midwife . . . and I myself practise midwifery.

Midwives know better than others who is pregnant and who is not . . . And by the use of potions and incantations they are able to arouse the pangs and to soothe them at will; they can make those bear who have a difficulty in bearing, and if they think fit they can smother the embryo in the womb. . . . Did you ever remark that they are also most cunning matchmakers and have a thorough knowledge of what unions are likely to produce a brave brood? . . . The true midwife is also the true and only matchmaker . . . Such are the midwives,

---

[20] This is in contrast to views such as those expressed by Hervey that '*a metaphor is the first and novel creation of a "homonym" from a sign already established in a given language*', (1978, 36). Indeed Hervey takes the above to be a *definition* of metaphor.

[21] There are also cases in which a usage is considered metaphorical in one language community or dialect but literal in another.

whose task is a very important one, but not so important as mine; for women do not bring into the world at one time real children and at another time counterfeits which are with difficulty distinguished from them; if they did, then the discernment of the true and false birth would be the crowning achievement of the art of midwifery. Well, my art of midwifery is in most respects like theirs but differs, in that I attend men and not women, and I look after their souls when they are in labour and not after their bodies; and the triumph of my art is in thoroughly examining whether the thought which the mind of the young men brings forth is a false idol or a noble and true birth. And like the midwives, I am barren, and the reproach which is often made against me, that I ask questions of others and have not the wit to answer them myself, is very just . . . And therefore I am not myself at all wise, nor have I anything to show which is the invention or birth of my own soul, but those who converse with me profit. Some of them appear dull enough at first, but afterwards, as our acquaintance ripens . . . they all make astonishing progress . . . The many fine discoveries to which they cling are of their own making. But to me and the god they owe their delivery. And the proof of my words is, that many of them in their ignorance . . . have gone away too soon; and have not only lost the children of whom I had previously delivered them by an ill bringing up, but have stifled whatever else they had in them. . . .

Dire are the pangs which my art is able to arouse and to allay in those who consort with me, just like the pangs of women in childbirth . . . I tell you this long story, friend Theaetetus, because I suspect, as indeed you seem to think yourself, that you are in labour—great with some conception. Come then to me, who am a midwife's son and myself a midwife, and do your best to answer the questions which I will ask you. And if I abstract and expose your first-born because I discover upon inspection that the conception which you have formed is a vain shadow, do not quarrel with me on that account, as the manner of women is when their first children are taken from them. (Plato, *Theaetetus*, 148 E 3–151 C 6, trans. B. Jowett.)

8

Concluding Remarks: Reference and Truth in Metaphor

IN the opening chapter I claimed to be putting forward a perspectival theory of metaphor. The perspectival shift achieved by metaphor has been explicated in terms of a theory of metaphorical meaning in which metaphor is not readily paraphrasable into literal language. The meaning of metaphor, unlike the meaning of most literal language, is a second-order affair. Understanding a metaphor involves understanding the literal meaning called upon in the metaphor and understanding the vehicle's contrastive and affinitive relations which are transferred to a new domain. Finally, it involves the ability to find an interpretation based on that analogous transference of relations which orders a conceptual or semantic domain distinct from the one to which the metaphorically used term applies in its literal-conventional application. The interpretation need not be a unique sentence—indeed, it rarely is. By the reordering of the topic domain, indefinitely many interpretations are made possible. To the extent to which these possible interpretive explications are useful to the understanding of the subject of the metaphor and to the extent that there are explanatory, predictive, and prescriptive resonances, the metaphor is cognitively significant. It receives the cognitive content through a perspectival move captured in the reordering of one content domain in accordance with the relations governing another semantic field. In this way I have given the perspectival theory of metaphor its linguistic coin.

To the extent that the speaker has no other linguistic resources to achieve these ends, the metaphor is cognitively irreplaceable. Note, for the moment, that the fact that a speaker may not have certain linguistic resources available need not mean that these are not available in another language, in the speaker's language now, or in a future development of the speaker's language. Later in this chapter, I shall insist that the cognitive irreducibility of metaphor has to do with our grasp of a language as it incorporates a given conceptual scheme. Our own understanding of the conceptual scheme may alter—as appears to be the case in the maturation of linguistic capacity[1]—or the language may change to accommodate changes in our conceptual scheme.[2] The resources available to a speaker thus alter, and a metaphor once irreducible may no longer be so, although it may still be conveniently paraphrasable. Before pursuing this point, I need to raise a different question relating to the cognitive significance of metaphor.

However enlightening an account of metaphorical meaning may be, it still fails to inform us about a key factor in the cognitive significance of any linguistic phenomenon, namely its relation to the things of the world, that is, its reference. To speak of a metaphorical referent which is distinct from the literal referent appears to invoke a rather mysterious, and no doubt superfluous, entity. Therefore all but the most intrepid thinkers have maintained a silence on, or given a negative response to, the question: do metaphors refer?[3] Let us say that if the literal referent is the referent of an expression understood literally, then the metaphorical referent is the referent of the expression understood metaphorically. I maintain that the referent of a metaphorical expression—or, more precisely, of the *focus* of the metaphorical expression—when that expression takes the form of a singular referring term, is the literal referent that would be specified by an appropriate term from the topic domain. Such a term may or may not exist. The metaphor permits us to locate the position in the topic domain that such a term would need to occupy in order to refer to the extralinguistic reality. But we need multiply no extralinguistic entities when granting the possibility of metaphorical reference. Metaphor achieves its cognitive aims not by positing new existents but by forcing a reconceptualization of what is already given. Such a reconceptualization may alter the boundaries and the shape of a referent, or even what may count as a referent. But it need not. Metaphorical reference, that is the reference of the expression when the expression is understood metaphorically, as I shall try to show in Section 1 of this chapter, follows a

---

[1] See Carey 1985.

[2] Cf. Boyd's (1979) discussion of a dynamic and dialectical conception of reference that permits the accommodation of our language to our increasing understanding of the causal structure of the world.

[3] Among those who have claimed that metaphor refers, we can include Goodman (1968; 1978*b*), Ricœur (1978*b*), and Binkley (1974). Most recently, Stern (1985) has maintained the thesis that metaphors behave essentially like demonstratives and thus have a referential function. His paper appeared too late for a thorough consideration in this volume.

quite pedestrian route—namely, that of anaphoric reference. But by the action of metaphorical meaning, what we find at the end of the road is a different landscape in which our referent is now located. My claim, then, is that in the Wordsworth poem discussed in Chapter 7, the definite description 'the eldest child of liberty' refers metaphorically to the city of Venice. Similarly, when Socrates speaks of 'my art of midwifery' he refers to his philosophical and educational activities. It is *that* city that people refer to as 'Venice' that Wordsworth refers to when he speaks of the noblewoman that is Venice; again, it is *those* activities practised by Socrates, which are generally termed 'educating' and 'philosophizing', that Socrates refers to when he speaks of his 'art of midwifery'. But in both cases we have a particular epistemic access to the referents that we lack without the metaphors.

In Section 2 of this chapter, I wish to suggest, using an extended metaphor, how metaphor provides a distinctive epistemic access to a referent, and in what sense we can speak of metaphorical truth.

I METAPHORICAL REFERENCE AS ANAPHORA

In a provocative paper Brandom (1984) claims that we can explain away reference using the notion of anaphora, that there is no distinctive relation of reference between word and the world, but rather that all reference is an inter-linguistic matter. This is not the place to take up this radical proposal; instead I want to adopt a proposal in the spirit of Brandom's thesis, namely, that metaphorical reference can be explained away as anaphoric reference, in which some member of an antecedent chain refers literally. However one then decides the issue of how literal language hooks up to the world, one applies that analysis to the anaphoric antecedent of the metaphorical referring expression. The metaphorical expression inherits its antecedent's referent.

Crucial to this position is the notion of an *anaphoric chain* developed by Charles Chastain in his seminal work on anaphora and reference.[4] To locate an anaphoric chain, we look at a context and determine the referring expressions that form a sequence such that 'if one of them refers to something then all of the others also refer to it' (Chastain 1975, 205.) Among referring expressions we may include proper names, definite descriptions, pronouns, and demonstratives. Chastain

---

[4] Chastain is concerned only with singular referring expressions—but a similar analysis may be worked out for general terms. For simplicity, I shall follow Chastain in speaking only of singular expressions.

argues that we need to include indefinite descriptions, such as 'a young prisoner', 'a woman walking down the street', etc. when these begin an anaphoric chain.[5]

Let us look once more at the opening lines of Wordsworth's poem:

8.1 Once did She hold the gorgeous East in fee,
   And was the safeguard of the West: the worth
   Of Venice did not fall below her birth,
   Venice, the eldest child of liberty.

In 8.1 we find the anaphoric chain:

8.2 She[6] . . . Venice . . . her . . . Venice . . . the eldest child of liberty.

'She' in the first line of the poem is the *anaphoric antecedent* of 'Venice', which in turn is the anaphoric antecedent of 'her', etc. The last element in the chain, 'the eldest child of liberty', is a definite description, and while it cannot be taken as referring literally to Venice— liberty is not something that literally bears children and Venice, being a city, cannot literally be said to have had a childhood—its anaphorical antecedent is clearly 'Venice'. Here the anaphoric antecedent is determined by the grammatical relation that identifies the two appositional terms 'Venice' and 'the eldest child of liberty'. I have said that an ana-

---

[5] Definite descriptions, proper names, pronouns, and demonstratives are said to *purport to refer*. Chastain argues that whether or not a singular expression refers depends not on form but on context: 'An expression is a singular term *in* or *relative* to a given context' (1975, 203). But if a proper name or definite description occurs in a discourse that is explicitly fictive, then it cannot be the case that it *purports* to refer since the making of its fictive character explicit also explicitly cancels any purported reference. More precisely, 'It is only when a singular expression is *introduced* within the scope of a fiction-indicating device that its purported singular reference is cancelled' (1975, 204). On the other hand, a context can make it apparent that an indefinite description, a form of description usually excluded from the class of referring expressions because the indefinite article does not demand that one and only one thing be specified by the description, is being used referentially. In the context 'A man was sitting underneath a tree eating peanuts. A squirrel came along, and the man fed it some peanuts' the indefinite description 'a man' heads a chain continued by the definite description 'the man'. Both refer to one specific individual, if they refer to anything at all. But unlike the definite description, the indefinite description cannot replace all occurrences of referring descriptions in a chain. It has to head a chain. A repeated occurrence begins a new chain. Compare: 'A man was sitting underneath a tree eating peanuts. A squirrel came along, and a man fed it some peanuts.'

[6] While the pronoun may be said to begin the anaphoric chain, if we move from the context of the text to that which also includes the title, we can say that the chain begins with 'the Venetian Republic' mentioned in the title: 'On the Extinction of the Venetian Republic'.

phoric chain is such that if any term in the sequence refers to an object then all the terms in the sequence refer to it. The metaphorical phrase, then, refers in just the same way as 'She' and 'her' refer in 8.1, namely, through their anaphoric link with the proper name 'Venice'. This account, of course, leaves open the question of how 'Venice' refers to the actual city. But my point here is, simply, that however this question is decided, we can say that 'the eldest child of liberty', as the phrase is anaphorically linked in Wordsworth's poem, refers to the actual city *through* its anaphoric link with the term that does so refer.

Similarly, consider the text (4.14) we looked at in Chapter 4:

8.3 (i) The corporate existence was becoming too much for Mr S, who many thought was the ultimate corporation man.

(ii) He was constantly on display, trotted out before prospective clients, a performing seal who knew all the requisite tricks needed for success in the corporation.

(iii) The endless meetings and the tedious details of his job left Mr S bored and weary at the end of the day.

(iv) At last, it was five o'clock.

(v) The seal dragged himself out of the office.

In 8.3, we find the anaphoric chain:

8.4 Mr S . . . the ultimate corporation man . . . He . . . a performing seal . . . who . . . his . . . Mr S . . . The seal.

It includes the indefinite description 'a performing seal' which is also a metaphorical description of Mr S. In 8.3, as in 8.1, the metaphorical expression is in grammatical apposition to a referring term which either may be said to refer literally itself or is linked to an expression which may be said to refer literally. And because what is attributed to 'a performing seal' is also attributed to Mr S (through the anaphoric use of the pronoun), the sentence 8.3(ii) would fail grammatically unless we interpreted 'He' as the antecedent of 'a performing seal' and 'Mr S' as a still earlier antecedent of 'He'. Although the grammatical coherence is bought at the expense of a conceptual incongruity, the anaphoric linkage is clear.[7] As in our first example, if 'Mr

---

7 What of the fact that 'a performing seal' is an indefinite description? If it is the case that indefinite descriptions refer only when they begin an anaphoric chain (see n. 5 above), then it may seem that we have a second referential chain that begins with this indefinite description. But I think that we can see that an indefinite description, while not substitutable throughout a text as are definite descriptions (see Chastain 1975, 206; and Brandom 1984, 472–3), can exist within an anaphoric chain that has been

S' refers, then, whatever it refers to, all the other elements in the chain
will refer to that entity.

If disposing of metaphorical reference in this way seems too easy,
too cavalier, it may so appear because of the sense that the descriptive
nature of the definite or indefinite description must have something to
do with reference, and the metaphorical content of 'the eldest child of
liberty' in 8.1 and of 'a performing seal' in 8.3 directs us to a wrong or
impossible referent. One may object that passing the descriptive content through an anaphoric sieve does not dispose of the problematical
nature of metaphorical reference. One might further object that we
can use a metaphorical description not embedded in a linguistic discourse to refer. I might look at Mr S and mutter in a contemptuous
tone: 'A performing seal'. A like-minded person sharing my visual and
auditory space would have little difficulty identifying the object of my
scorn. But where is the anaphoric chain linking the metaphorical utterance to 'Mr S' or some other referring expression used literally?

Both problems can be disposed of by drawing the distinction
between reference and denotation. Chastain (1975) points to the
difficulties faced by *denotationism*, the view that when we refer by
means of a singular expression, we refer to whatever is uniquely
denoted by the words of that expression. Thus 'the author of the
poem "On the Extinction of the Venetian Republic" ' uniquely
refers to William Wordsworth. Similarly 'the ultimate corporation
man' refers to that individual who is the ultimate corporation man.
But the distinction drawn by Donnellan between the attributive and
referential uses of the definite description[8] undermines denota-

---

introduced by another singular expression, if it is set in apposition to a proper name,
pronoun, or definite description that is anaphorically linked to the originating term. To
illustrate with a variant of an example of Chastain, consider the following text:

> At eleven o'clock that morning an ARVN officer stood Brown, bound and
> blindfolded, up against a wall. The officer asked the prisoner, a man in his early
> twenties, several questions, and when he failed to answer, beat the young pris-
> oner repeatedly.

It does not seem that that 'Brown' and 'a man in his early twenties' initiate two different
anaphoric chains.

   [8] Since this distinction is now so well known I do not discuss it in the body of the text.
For those unfamiliar, or in need of a reminder, I quote the following passage in which
the distinction is clearly laid out: 'To illustrate this distinction, in the case of a single
sentence, consider the sentence, "Smith's murderer is insane." Suppose first that we
come upon poor Smith foully murdered. From the brutal manner of the killing and the
fact that Smith was the most lovable person in the world, we might exclaim, "Smith's
murderer is insane." I will assume, to make it a simpler case, that in a quite ordinary

tionism, at least with regard to definite descriptions.[9]

In Donnellan's example

8.5 Smith's murderer is insane,

'Smith's murderer' is used *attributively* to speak of whoever it is that has committed the brutal murder of Smith, a murder so horrid that one can only assume that the murderer is insane. The phrase is used *referentially* to speak of the man on trial, Jones, who is acting in a most peculiar manner and is thus judged by the speaker to be insane, whether or not it turns out that Jones is in fact the murderer. In the referential use, the speaker and hearer cannot be said to refer via the descriptive content of the phrase, since it may well be that Jones did not commit the murder—and indeed that Smith did not have a murderer but, in a mad frenzy, mutilated himself and then committed suicide. Even if the denotation is empty, the phrase has still succeeded in its referential use.

Using the attributive–referential distinction, we can say that just as the reference of a definite or indefinite description can be different from its denotation, so the reference of a metaphorical expression may be different from the (literal) denotation of the words composing the utterance. This point pertains especially to the referential use of a metaphorical utterance where there is no linguistic anaphoric antecedent. Were denotationism correct, then literal definite or indefinite descriptions would denote via the content of what was denoted. But if reference is severed from denotation then the same problem that arises for an unconnected metaphorical expression will arise for literal expressions. If I am in the courtroom in which Jones is on trial for Smith's murder, and I look straight at Jones and say to my neighbour, 'Smith's murderer is insane', the expression appears to have no

---

sense we do not know who murdered Smith . . . This, I shall say, is an attributive use of the definite description.

'The contrast with such a use of the sentence is one of those situations in which we expect and intend our audience to realize whom we have in mind when we speak of Smith's murderer and, more importantly, to know that it is this person about whom we are going to say something.

'For example, suppose that Jones had been charged with Smith's murder and has been placed on trial. Imagine that there is a discussion of Jones's odd behaviour at his trial. We might sum up our impressions of his behaviour by saying, "Smith's murderer is insane." If someone asks to whom we are referring, by using this description, the answer here is "Jones." This, I shall say, is a referential use of the definite description (Donnellan 1971, 102–3).'

[9] Kripke (1972*a*) undercuts denotationism in regard to proper names.

anaphoric links that can connect it with Jones or with any descriptive phrase used attributively. How, then, does the phrase refer?

Kripke (1972*b*) has argued that what Donnellan has called the referential use of definite descriptions pertains not to sentence reference but to speaker reference, so that Donnellan's distinction is essentially a pragmatic one. If Kripke is correct, then the reference of a definite or indefinite metaphorical description, where there is no linguistic anaphoric antecedent that refers literally, is similarly a matter of speaker reference. That is, when I remark, 'A performing seal,' casting my gaze at Mr S, the description refers because of a pragmatic feature of the utterance, namely, the fact that I have in mind Mr S in using the expression 'a performing seal' referentially. Therefore we can acknowledge that some metaphorical reference is a matter of pragmatics rather than semantics. Notice, however, that this does nothing to undermine my claim that an understanding of metaphor requires a semantic account, since my claim is *not* that it requires *only* a semantic account. As we saw in the discussion of the identification of metaphor in Chapter 2 above, some conditions for an utterance to be metaphorical are semantic, while others are pragmatic.

Chastain, however, offers an account of the referential use of a singular expression that attempts to assimilate the referential use of an expression that is uttered without a linguistic context to anaphoric reference, and reference ultimately to an *epistemic* connection between the speaker and the object. According to Chastain (1975), there is an implicit context, a 'covert context', which connects the use of the term with that object that the speaker meant to pick out by the term. He suggests the following contexts, one covert, the other overt. While

8.5 'Smith's murderer is insane'

is the overt context, it is preceded by the covert context:

8.6 'Jones is on trial here for the murder of Smith. He sure looks
    like a criminal. He's got beady eyes. He must be guilty. He
    murdered Smith. He's behaving very strangely. He's staring
    like a madman. Smith's murderer is insane. That's why Smith's
    body was so horribly mutilated.' (Chastain, 1975, 235)

According to Chastain, 8.5 'is what the speaker says, . . . [8.6] is what he thinks.' (1975, 235) What he thinks is similarly a discourse, and there is an anaphoric link *across* contexts such that 'Smith's murderer' is linked to 'Jones', so that the former refers to whatever the latter refers to.

Chastain's strategy of employing a covert context is similar to the strategy I employed in Chapter 2 when expanding the linguistic context of an utterance to include non-linguistic elements of the context by means of the expressibility principle. We could adapt the latter strategy to the present case as well. How we proceed is a matter of indifference here, for the point is simply that the phrase or sentence refers in virtue of its connection to a larger (or adjacent) context and not in virtue of what is denoted by the expression. Chastain's claim that the connection between the referential term and the object in the world is not a linguistic one but an epistemic (and to some degree a causal) one means that the speaker must have some sort of knowledge or acquaintance with the object to which she or he refers, if she or he refers at all.[10]

Chastain's theory depends on interesting but controversial notions both of context and of what may count as 'having knowledge of an object'. Context includes 'anything that has *meaning* or *sense* . . . Anything which *expresses* something or *represents* something' (Chastain 1975, 195). Contexts include not only discourses, texts, maps, paintings, statues, scale models, etc. but also mental states such as memory, imagination, and perception. To deal with metaphorical language, I have found it useful to translate the salient features of non-linguistic contexts into linguistic terms. Chastain's 'covert contexts' are a similar, though implicit, evocation of an expressibility principle.

[10] Of course, one might say that the effect of Chastain's strategy is to make all referential uses of a referring description that are not also attributive uses a matter of speaker reference and hence of pragmatics. In that case, the fact that metaphorical reference turns out to be pragmatic rather than semantic in nature makes it no less a matter of pragmatics than literal reference. However these issues are sorted out, it seems clear that metaphor is in the same situation as literal language in regard to the semantic–pragmatic issue: some aspects of both literal and metaphorical language are semantic, others are pragmatic.

Beyond this, the reader should note that Chastain's is a very rich and subtle account of reference. I cannot do justice to it here. Generalizations such as the above are importantly qualified in his discussion. First, the epistemic connection holds true for cases of *primary* reference but not *secondary* reference. For the latter one would have to maintain a causal chain of the sort Kripke suggests (see Chastain 1975, 229; and Kripke 1972*a*). Secondly, Chastain acknowledges that in certain contexts definite descriptions can refer without the speaker having any knowledge of the referent. If I say, 'The first person to walk through the yellow door receives the prize', then I refer to whosoever walks through the door, regardless of whether or not I have any acquaintance with that individual.

Either Chastain's strategy, or my own, or some similar framework is useful if we are to form a unified conception of the reference of a metaphor as dependent on anaphoric reference. Rather than say that metaphorical reference is sometimes got from the literal reference of the appropriate anaphoric antecedents and sometimes through speaker reference, we can say that metaphorical reference is always achieved through anaphora—anaphoric antecedents given in either the explicit or implicit context. Whether we adopt and adapt Chastain's strategy or Kripke's, it is clear that a denotationist account of the reference of a metaphorical expression will yield only the referent of the expression understood literally. As such, it directs us to the wrong object, and hence the wrong truth conditions for the sentence as it is understood metaphorically. Using anaphora, we can provide an account that tells us how it is that the expression can be understood as speaking about the right object, that is, the referent of the expression understood metaphorically.

However, Chastain's account of how a term finally does hook up to the world, an account dependent on his notion of what counts as knowledge of an object, is not crucial to my account of metaphorical reference. As long as one is not wedded to a form of denotationism, one can construe the world–word connection in a number of different ways and still hold that metaphorical reference depends on an anaphoric link with a term that refers *directly*. (Yet my hunch is that, in the end, reference depends on a recognition of contrasts and affinities perceived between things, just as meaning depends on the contrasts and affinities between the terms available in a language. If so, then all reference is mediated by a sorting process—even the directly referential 'this' refers by virtue of a contrast with some 'that'.

I have now answered both the objections I raised above. One objection was to the idea of anaphoric linkage as the source and explanation of metaphorical reference—I posed the example of a metaphorical singular referring expression used without an accompanying linguistic discourse. Using Chastain's apparatus, we can see how the utterance of the isolated expression 'a performing seal' directed at Mr S can refer to Mr S. We can posit a covert context such that 'a performing seal', is anaphorically linked to some element of the covert context which is in turn linked to a term by which the speaker refers to Mr S.

The other objection was that the descriptive content of a definite or indefinite description has something to do with locating the referent and that the move through anaphoric reference does not cancel the oddity of employing the descriptive content of a metaphorical description to fix the referent. This objection is directly answered by drawing the distinction between denotation and reference. A metaphorical description may denote (literally) one thing, but it can be used to refer (*simpliciter*) to another—just as 'Smith's murderer' can be used to refer to Jones even when Jones is not the murderer of Smith, in the appropriate contextual setting. Do we not now want to ask: what then is the point of using a referring expression metaphorically? The answer to this question will occupy much of the remainder of the chapter.

2 EPISTEMIC ACCESS AND METAPHORICAL TRUTH

Justifying the Claim to Cognitive Content

When a descriptive singular term *denotes*, its denotation satisfies its descriptive content. This occurs when we use a term attributively—that is, in the case that the individual referred to as 'Smith's murderer' is Smith's murderer. In 8.3, the descriptive content of 'Mr S' includes all the information we get about Mr S: that he works for a corporation, that he knows 'all the requisite tricks needed for success in the corporation', that he has 'endless meetings', is made 'bored and weary' by the 'tedious details' of his employment, etc. Included in this passage is also content—namely, that he is a 'performing seal'—which we take to be metaphorical (once we have concluded, as through the discussion in Chapter 2 above, that the text concerns a man and not a seal).[11]

It is in terms of the descriptive content of a context that the conceptual interest of a metaphorical referring expression comes into play. As Chastain points out a referring term 'not only purports to refer but purports to refer to a thing of a specified kind' (1975, 230). While denotationism may not be a correct theory of reference, it is not entirely wrong either. While the descriptive content may not supply the 'hook' by which the singular expression refers to the world, it does guide us through the sorting of the objects in the world such that we have access to the referent. The distinction between the attributive and referential use of a term is possible because attribution can fail while reference succeeds. Reference can succeed, while attribution fails because we have more than one route to a referent: we can describe it,

---

[11] My use of 'descriptive content' diverges somewhat from that of Chastain: cf. Chastain 1975, 230.

we can see it, we can smell, taste, hear, or touch it, or we can learn about it through another's description. Literal description reflects a conceptual scheme, a sorting grid, which organizes much of our experience according to certain principles and for certain purposes. Through the descriptive content of a context we know *the thing of the specified kind* to which we want to refer. We may have been in error in thinking that the thing to which we wanted to refer was of *that* specified kind. Or we may have had no more than a perceptual experience of the referent, and, except in a rather minimal sense of knowing the object to be of some perceptual kind, we may not have known the kind of specified thing it was. We would then be reduced to pointing or using the demonstrative.

Sometimes we need to direct a hearer to a referent through whatever means we find available. And sometimes that involves relying on our capacity to make and understand metaphor. A vignette of a young child with an earache makes the point well. A two-year-old child who has suffered from earaches but has not yet learned the term 'earache' awakes one night and comes into his mother's room, holding his ear and crying. He says:

8.7 Mummy. An elephant stepped on my ear.

Evidently there is no elephant to serve as a referent. Instead we should say that the entire sentence 'An elephant stepped on my ear' refers to that sensation which the boy is experiencing and which he does not know how to name otherwise.[12] Using a Chastain-like analysis, we can say that the anaphoric antecedent of the sentence *cum* singular term is an element in an imaginative context, namely, the boy's imaginative portrayal of what his ear would feel like if it had been stepped on by an elephant. That imaginative element in turn refers to the sensation that is known, indeed painfully experienced, by the child. We can say that this sensation is 'known' to the boy, in that the boy experiences it. But he does not know it as an 'earache'. How is he to communicate his pain and its source to his mother? A less inventive child might simply point and cry. But this child does more than communicate the pain. He tries to make sense of it. He tries to know it *as something*. Within his emerging conceptualizations, we can reconstruct his thought as follows:

---

[12] Cf. Danto 1983, in which he suggests that entire works of art should be regarded as metaphors. Also cf. the discussion in Chapter 3 Section 1 above concerning Eliot's poem 'The Hippopotamus'. We can say now that the poem as a whole functions as a metaphor referring to the Church.

when big things step on you, pain results (and perhaps, more specifically, a certain sort of pain results);[13]—*ergo* something very big (an elephant) just stepped on my ear. Metaphors that are of conceptual interest do just what the elephant achieves for the little boy. They allow us to know a referent *as something*, more particularly *as something which serves some conceptual end*. Metaphors provide for us *epistemic access* to the referent.

This account puts the conceptual importance right back in the sphere of meaning rather than in the sphere of reference. And that, I believe, is how it should be, if the role of metaphor is not to tell us *of something new*, but of something new about what we already know. In the process of the (re)description, we may be guided to discover some new object or phenomenon. In that case, metaphor serves as a generator of hypotheses. But we have to know our way around the subject matter to know which sort of hypotheses generated by a metaphor are worthy to pursue and which are not. The shift to a distinct semantic field, and the use of its descriptive resources, its relations of contrast and affinity, provides epistemic access to the referent not otherwise available. It provides epistemic access to the referent through a different conceptual organization from the one through which we normally have access—if we have such literal descriptive access—to the referent.

I have argued here that metaphorical expressions can be used to refer metaphorically. If we can speak of metaphors referring, can we speak of the sentences in which these singular terms occur as metaphorically true or false? In the pages that follow, I want to make the point that truth and falsity are relative to a conceptual scheme, and that metaphorical truth and falsity must be understood in these terms. Relative to a scheme in which cities are thought of as women, 'The Venice of the Renaissance was a noblewoman' would be true while 'The Venice of the Renaissance was a washerwoman' would be false. But while metaphorical reference can be understood by appeal to anaphora, metaphorical truth must be understood through the conceptual detour provided by the second-order meaning specific to metaphor.

The detour through a semantic field that normally applies to another domain is the distinctive metaphorical move—the perspectival shift in which the projection of the structure of the vehicle field on to the topic

---

[13] It is intriguing to think what this example could do to Wittgenstein's (1953) private language argument.

domain can force a reconceptualization of the referent, or the subject (when there is no referent), of the metaphor. It is such a reconceptualization that makes metaphor, when it is cognitively significant, irreducibly so. But why irreducibly so? This is the sceptical and powerful criticism that Donald Davidson aims at Black's theory of metaphorical meaning. He writes:

> If a metaphor has a special cognitive content, why should it be so difficult or impossible to set it out? If . . . a metaphor 'says one thing and means another', why should it be that when we try to get explicit about what it means, the effect is so much weaker . . . Why inevitably? Can't we, if we are clever enough, come as close as we please? (Davidson 1981, 215.)

In order to make the case for the irreducibility of the cognitive content of metaphor and to demonstrate the relationship between meaning and truth in metaphor, this treatise on metaphor will, appropriately, conclude with a self-reflective figure: 'rearranging the furniture of our minds' as a metaphor for metaphor. To do so requires an appeal to conceptual schemes, the 'very idea' of which Davidson (1974c) so skilfully criticized. Therefore I must precede the metaphor with a brief consideration of Davidson's critique.

Davidson argues that conceptual relativity is incoherent, whether understood as the wholesale incommensurability of two entire conceptual schemes or of portions of such conceptual schemes. He takes to task 'the very idea of a conceptual scheme' for it posits what he takes to be an untenable dualism, the 'dualism of scheme and uninterpreted content' or 'scheme and reality' (1974c, 9). The particular version of this dualism which Davidson attempts to discredit, and which is pertinent to the metaphor below, is that a conceptual scheme in some sense organizes our experience of our world. Davidson's critique of this particular view involves arguing against the coherence of the notion that we can organize something unitary such as 'experience' or reality. He argues that we can only organize something that is itself plural:

> Someone who sets out to organize a closet arranges the things in it. If you are told not to organize the shoes and shirts, but the closet itself you would be bewildered. How would you organize the Pacific Ocean? Straighten out its shores perhaps or relocate its islands or destroy its fish. (1974c, 14.)

I find Davidson's position odd, since it is not clear to me that experience or reality is unitary, and, in the figure I set forth below, reality is a plurality. But what if we were somehow to construe reality or experience, prior to the application of a conceptual scheme, as an undifferentiated whole? Is Davidson right in his insistence that the notion is incoherent? I fail to see the force of Davidson's argument. *Of course* it is possible to imagine organizing 'the closet itself': we could build or install shelves, a shoe platform, etc. Department stores are full of clever devices for organizing a closet, or wardrobe, and these do not include instructions for straightening out and ordering the contents of the wardrobe. Similarly, though without building or installing anything, we could make perfectly good sense of the idea of organizing the Pacific Ocean. If the purpose of the 'organization' was to chart the ocean so that a sailor could locate her position on the ocean, we might draw a map and impose a grid, like that of the lines of longitude and latitude. We might want to 'organize' the ocean according to thermal differences at different depths, or according to the habitations of sharks, etc. Different organizations will serve different purposes, but they are all organizations of the unitary thing that is the Pacific Ocean.

And in just the same sense, experience can be organized—and organized differently according to different purposes. It is in this sense that I conceive of the relation between experience and conceptual schemes. The different ways of organizing the Pacific Ocean are just so many different conceptual schemes. Similarly, if the wardrobe to be organized were our experience, then the positioning of the shelves and shoe racks would represent one of many possible conceptual schemes by which to organize our experience. For our purposes, at least, Davidson's argument against the coherence of the notion that a conceptual scheme can organize experience does not carry weight.

Davidson directs other arguments against the thesis of the incommensurability, in part or whole, of alternative conceptual schemes. In my example, I shall be concerned with conceptual schemes that may be incommensurable in part. But to take the view that two languages, taken at a distinct synchronic moment (or two different synchronic states of the same language, or two dialectical variants of the same language within a synchronic moment) are incommensurable in part, does not commit one to the view that these languages (along with their conceptual organization) cannot be gradually, but sufficiently, altered so that the formerly incommensurate statements become translatable in the modified versions of these two languages.

Significantly, natural languages are in a constant state of flux—one slow enough to permit speakers to adjust to shifts in meaning. Some local shifts may be abrupt, as in the case of the paradigm shift that

Kuhn (1970) has described. But these can be explicated in part metalinguistically in the language in which both variants are embedded and in part in that practice essential to the understanding of any craft-bound discourse. Furthermore, the possibility of non-denotational reference allows us to talk about the same thing (more or less—see below) although our conceptual schemes change over time (see Boyd 1979, 382). If one looks at actual usage, there need be no more paradox about the way we communicate, in spite of a certain incommensurability between languages or between synchronic language states, than there is about the fact that we move from place to place. Like Zeno's clever paradoxes, Davidson's conundrums point to questions we need to consider, but just as we would not consider dispensing with the idea of motion in physics, we ought not to be compelled to dispense with the idea of a conceptual scheme in the theory of language.

Metaphor as Rearranging the Furniture of the Mind

Imagine that we enter a room fully furnished. The room has the usual set of windows, cupboards, doors. Its furniture is arranged in a fashion familiar to the Western eye, with items placed around the room in certain conventional or traditional groupings. Upon occupying the room, we make a few changes—we move a comfortable chair closer to a reading light and retire the television to an inconspicuous corner, etc. Still, we respect certain implicit rules for ordering furniture: chairs go next to tables, desks, or reading lights; the dining-room table is surrounded by chairs; night lights and night tables are placed within reach of the bed; etc. We declare that everything is in order.

As we live in the room, a variety of friends and acquaintances pass through, many with particular needs and habits which require some temporary and some permanent changes in our furniture arrangement. One suffers from a back problem and, finding only soft, upholstered chairs in the living-room area, she moves a hard-backed chair from the dining area over to the sofa where we are seated. Generally, after she leaves, we shall put the chair back into its 'proper place'. Why, we may ask, is its former place and not its new situation its 'proper place'? We may have a variety of answers: it belongs with the other dining-room chairs; it serves another important function in its original position; it meets certain aesthetic demands better; it creates a clutter in the new position; we are simply used to it in the old place. If our friend visits often enough, we may just leave the chair there. Now the chair, in its new position, will be in its 'proper place', although its design may betray its borrowed origins.[14]

Another acquaintance, who has lived in the East for several years and comes to use the typewriter, chooses a low sofa to do her damage. She removes the sofa cushion, places it on the floor, so that she can sit cross-legged on the cushion while using the de-cushioned sofa as a typewriter stand. To avoid tripping over the cushion, to make the sofa serviceable again, and to get the typewriter back to its suitable position, we have to replace these each time she leaves. Yet another friend, who calls himself an artist, denounces the excessive functionalism of our room. Insisting that one ought to create new meaning through anti-functionalism, he stands our sofa on its side and places it right in front of a window. While this arrangement gives a 'new look' to the room, under no conditions would we assent to it as a permanent state of affairs—we return the sofa to its former position.

Working through the analogy we can say that the room, with the walls, windows, and doors intact, as well as the material of which the furniture is composed is the world we humans encounter, prior to our activity of structuring and creating our environment. The furniture, the relation the pieces bear to one another, and the rules we follow for placing and using the furnishings represent our creation and arrangement of the world we inhabit.

The sentences in the language of our room world refer to the furniture, its relation to the room and to other pieces of furniture, and its relation to our needs, desires, aspirations, *vis-à-vis* what happens in the room. The meaning of a piece of furniture has to do with its form and material, its placement in the room relative both to the room's fixed and movable elements and to its serviceability as regards our needs, desires, aspirations, etc. As we find and arrange the furniture of the room, we set and define the order among things which we assume, given our knowledge, beliefs, and desires at that time, to be the best (or the only, or the only conceivable) way of arranging our world. To speak correctly is to utilize the furniture according to current conventions reflected in its correct placement or to make changes governed only by the rules of furniture arrangement—for example, while chairs go near tables, dining-room chairs go *under* a dining-room table and armchairs go *next to* side tables. To speak correctly is also to assent to the correct

---

[14] Though we can imagine that one day we replace the dining-room chairs with another set and then only a historical record can inform us of its origins; it will no longer be evident from the present furnishings and arrangements.

placement of a piece or pieces; we can assent or dissent either by responding to questions or by utilizing the furniture as it is correctly or incorrectly placed. To assent to the proper placement of a piece of furniture is to speak the truth. To sit down at a table where there is no chair is effectively to utter a falsehood. To assent to a misplaced chair would be to assent to a falsehood. To assent to a bureau placed against the door leading to the bath would be to speak nonsense. To assent to all the furniture clumped in the middle of the room would be to speak of possible, but improbable worlds. To assent to the proper placement of a piece of furniture is, again, to speak the truth. Truth, then, is relative to what is the proper order. What is designated the proper order is the preferred or privileged conceptual scheme.

Our friends, who habitually disrupt our arrangement by moving chairs, cushions, typewriters, and sofas 'out of their proper places', take furniture which has a certain material form and placement suited to a given purpose or sense and adopt it for another use in a different furniture arrangement. Where this second sense and placement in some way reflects and retains the previous one, the rearrangements are 'metaphorical placements'. By replacing the chair (or cushion or typewriter or sofa), we effectively confirm that theirs is a false utterance, given the proper order.

Let us stay, for the moment, with the least disruptive displacement—the moved dining-room chair. The context of its literal use is to seat someone at the dining-room table. In the context of a person with lumbago in need of a chair, the displaced object still has a 'meaning', that is, it serves a reasonable and intelligible purpose (one of the several things furniture may do). Straight-backed dining chairs are well-suited to reflecting the relative cultural formality of dining in Western societies—we do not eat reclining or seated on the floor, and only in haste do we eat standing up. But that straight-backed structure is also well-suited to seating persons with back problems. Once our friend leaves, the chair is just 'out of place'—it is no longer in a context which provides for it the sort of meaning possible for furniture-in-place to have.

The move is metaphorical in that it disrupts a given order and utilizes a feature of the old order in the creation of a new one: while the straight-backed chair may have been created to serve a posture suitable for formal dining, amid a cluster of soft-upholstered furniture it provides a weakened back with all the comfort required for conversing. We could say that some of the 'conceptual content' of the dining situation is retained in its new placement. Similarly the cushion of the sofa, when converted to a seat for a typewriter stand, retains its service as something upon which we sit, although the mode of sitting is distinctive.

Notice that in the rearrangement by our first visitor, the reordering in the room creates no radical change in the concepts utilized—the chair is still used as a chair, though of a different sort, and there is no change in fundamental rules of furniture ordering—chairs get clustered together to permit conversation.[15] Converting the sofa into a typewriter stand and seat respects certain required relationships between a seat and a typewriter stand but significantly violates rules for what to do with sofas. Having a sofa in the manner of the anti-functionalist breaks all the rules—but that is just the point.

Notice also that once someone has discovered that the dining-room chairs can be used in this new clustering, other dining-room chairs may be dislocated for the same purpose. The metaphorical use of the sofa can be adapted to other purposes as well—decushioned, it can serve as a dining surface or as a writing table (if it is firm enough), etc. Once a metaphorical usage has been introduced, it is not unusual for other terms associated with the metaphorical term to be used in a similar metaphorical fashion. This is the productive power of metaphor.

Alterations may be more radical, more systematic, and more productive of far-reaching rearrangements. We may switch around whole areas of the room and replace movable with built-in furniture. (In which case we should not merely organize the *multiple* things in the room but organize the *unitary* room itself.) Many pieces of furniture would be 'out of place' and altered—but systematically so. In virtue of the disorienting new arrangements, we find ourselves putting books back on refrigerator shelves rather than in their familiar book cases. The reorderings are, at first, metaphorical. We can imagine a great commotion in our model world as furniture is moved back and forth in a trial and error fashion. These displacements are metaphorical and

[15] As with an unfamiliar metaphor, we might, at first, be charmed by a new arrangement. But if we found that we continually tripped over the displaced chair and missed it in its former place, we should return it to its former place—it would be a transient metaphor. If our friend became a habitual visitor, the move would be repeated so frequently that it would become a conventional metaphor—useful for serving our friend's special needs and ready at hand for any similar future need. If it could conveniently serve its old function in the dislocated place, or if it were no longer needed in its former place, it could become a dead metaphor: Americans will use the phrase 'burned up', with little discomfort of mind, for consigning (or being consigned) to flames and for being very angry. A phrase such as '*the head of* the table' has virtually no use in literal sense—that displaced chair can sit in its new position without much bother at all.

'false' or 'nonsensical' statements, if you will. The experienced superiority of a new ordering (or perhaps something more random and less rational, such as laziness, special interests, or new habits) allows it to become entrenched and to replace the old ordering. As it takes hold, we forget that the furniture was ever differently ordered. To the extent that the change is systematic and widespread, it leaves only the slightest trace of its metaphorical origin. (And unless we have carefully recorded such things, the tenant who takes the room after us will assume that the dining area was always by the sunniest window—after all, why would anyone ever place a bed in such a place?) It is now the literal truth.

Notice that a Japanese visitor would find it an odd truth, since for him furniture placed against walls violates all aesthetic and pragmatic rules for furniture arrangement. An African friend accustomed to living in a long house would find even the configuration of our room odd. She would be amused at the bed (regardless of its placement) and appalled by the lack of hammocks. However both would come to see this arrangement as serviceable, given the conditions of Western living. (And, most likely, neither would see any merit in the sofa on its side.)

Truth in our analogue world, then, has something to do with given realities such as gravity, the solidity of walls, the construction of doors and windows, etc. (read laws of nature, natural climatic and environmental conditions, societal regularities, and restrictions of a more fundamental sort), much to do with the furniture (read objects and concepts of objects) which we have found, constructed, arranged, and rearranged, and something to do with what we need, want, desire, and believe about the furniture and its arrangement. Meaning has to do with the serviceability of the objects and their arrangement—where utilization includes satisfying not only needs but desires, aesthetic considerations, or any reasonable or intelligible goals. Reference has to do with those objects that are placed about the room and utilized according to the 'meaning'. A conceptual scheme is a chosen ordering which will both reflect and shape what we take as true and meaningful, although the fact of alternate schemes need not be precluded by a given arrangement.

While meaning is closely tied to use, and we could say that a furniture's standard (and literal) meaning is its standard use, its meaning still does not change by virtue of an occasional non-standard use. A book placed under the leg of a table does not change its meaning from something to be read to something to support a table. But it is not a metaphor either. The non-standard use which is metaphorical does not change the meaning of the standard use either, but it results in a second-order meaning which depends on and reflects the standard use. Since use is closely related to both the position and the form of the article, if its position or shape is systematically altered and becomes a new standard use, then surely its meaning changes as well—though its former form may encode within itself an entire order now lost in the new meaning. (If we all forgot how to read, then books might serve only as supports and never as reading material, but it would remain possible for some clever archaeologist to rediscover their former meaning.)

A Davidsonian in our model world might say that if we knew when to assent to a piece being in its proper place, then we should know the meaning of the sentence asserting that the piece was in its place. And if we utilized the piece in a fashion commensurate with its form and its positioning, then we should understand how to make meaningful and true sentences with the object. In that case assenting to a piece of misplaced furniture would be assenting to a false statement—the displacement would have no extraordinary meaning, no metaphorical meaning—it would just be a displacement which called our attention to something, for example, the need for a hard-backed chair along with the cluster of sofa chairs.

The point of the furniture metaphor is to indicate what the Davidsonian neglects, that the room, *per se*, can tolerate a large variety of furniture arrangements just as our world can tolerate varied conceptual schemes. We need not counter the conundrum of incommensurability, however, for in our room as in our lives, there will be certain fixed elements and certain fixed needs. Both our shelters and our language respond to fixed needs and conditions. Since responses to constancies vary, sometimes systematically, locating the fixed points is often not a trivial problem. Often we will need to learn our way about the unfamiliar arrangement in order to determine the points of coincidence with our own scheme. From these, the intelligibility and serviceability of varied schemes can be deciphered and delineated.

In the case of metaphor, we generally encounter alterations and conflicts in localized parts of general schemes. We introduce a new partial reordering which is in conflict with the order as it currently coheres with the general scheme. Some (re)orderings serve a need which is transient, easily accomplished by a temporary rearrangement, and are disorder only relative to a chosen order which was established relative to some fixed and some alterable constraints. Others are more global. The most significant changes force us to reorder permanently parts of our conceptual system, as we do in cases of important social, economic, or scientific upheavals. These, in turn, become literal truth. But we assent to a new use as literal only when it fits in with other established uses and without creating a conceptual incongruity.

If what is meaningful and true has to do with proper arrangements then meaning and truth are mediated by what we take as proper. What we take as proper is, in turn, determined by those considerations which are pertinent to truth. How we specify these considerations will define one among many possible orders or conceptual schemes. If we take the perspective of those who live in a world richer than our room, we can see that, apart from the sort of considerations I have mentioned in recounting the allegory of the room, there is no 'proper place' for a chair. There may in fact be good reason to place a chair on top of a table on occasion—perhaps to examine a crack in the ceiling (especially if no one has yet conceived of a ladder). Even the sofa turned on its side and placed against the window may have a purpose, aesthetic, practical or jovial. For example, it may serve as a fortification in a shoot-out with the FBI à la Bonnie and Clyde (who move mattresses against the window to shield themselves from bullets); or in the case of passionate Bonnie and Clyde fans, it may serve as an allusion to their outlaw heroes. In such cases, an overzealous housekeeper, placing the sofa on its feet and against a wall in a more conventional fashion, would be disrupting the room.

Once we settle on a furniture arrangement, a privileged conceptual scheme, we can indeed claim that there is a proper place for each piece—though some may be designated as highly movable or transient items, for example, coasters, ashtrays, books,[16] just as commonly used adjectives or the word 'good' are not firmly in a semantic field. Given a chosen arrangement, with allowances for minor variants, displace-

---

[16] Although we have a bookshelf, a book lying on a bedside table is not necessarily out of order. A book remains serviceable as a book and not out of place in almost any location, except perhaps in the refrigerator or under the leg of a table (where it may be serviceable as a wedge to level the table), just as the word 'good' can be placed in front of almost any sort of word, except perhaps prepositions and articles. Also, just as a book would generally not be serviceable as a chair and never as a bed, so 'good' does poorly as a verb. Precisely because it can so easily occupy different positions meaningfully, a book's location rarely constitutes a metaphorical utterance. Analogously, 'good' is almost never used metaphorically (though it can be used ironically). Note that a book used to support the leg of a table is more like a code word than like a metaphor. It is a new use but one not connected with the original use.

ments are either metaphors, mistakes or jokes or artful or useful innovations. A metaphor presupposes that the arrangement is relatively transient; what is displaced goes back to its proper place as soon as the new use and the special contextual considerations which have given rise to it are no longer operative. It also presupposes that the new use is related to its former use, and that it is only a displacement relative to the given (and still serviceable) established order.

The given arrangement yields what I have called a first-order meaning. Alterations which at once respect that order but answer to different constraints—constraints that call for a different sense of order— are species of second-order meaning, metaphor, in particular. If, as I have suggested, this sense of order is what we call a conceptual scheme, then metaphors introduce partial reorderings of our conceptual scheme. As long as the established scheme is the basis for first-order meaning, metaphors cannot be paraphrased in literal first-order language, since they come into being and exist as such in virtue of a different ordering. If the displacement is indeed a metaphor, it cannot be accommodated in the old system without altering that scheme. If the altered scheme is accepted and becomes the 'proper ordering' then, what was once a metaphor can now be represented literally in the new scheme. When light was reconceived as a wave phenomenon, the term 'light wave' became a literal expression and could be fully explicated in literal terms—that is, until quantum theory demonstrated the limitations of such a literal order. But as long as the old order remains serviceable, we can keep switching back and forth—just as we keep moving the hard-backed chair back to the dining table when our lumbago sufferer leaves.

Notice that we can always choose to find a new word (or new piece of furniture) to serve a newly emerged purpose. And some language and furniture are 'made to order'. But there are limits—of space and economy in our room-world, of conceptual economy in the linguistic one—and we decide when to invest in made-to-order furniture, or cultivate a 'made-to-order' vocabulary, and when to improvise through metaphor. We also balance losses in heuristic power against gains in definitive precision. But only when a metaphor serves an identified need can it be so replaced by language made to order. When it is the work of metaphor itself to fashion or give voice to conceptual needs, it is not replaceable prior to that identification. And the conceptual order from which the metaphor originates will serve to model further rearrangements in the furniture of our mind.

With regard to reference, the issue with which I began this chapter, we may ask the following question: when our Eastern-inspired friend, who uses the de-cushioned sofa as a typewriter stand, refers to 'the typewriter stand', and when I refer (ruefully) to my (now cushion-less) sofa, ought we to say that we are referring to the *same* thing? The answer evidently is yes *and* no. We can both see and touch the same object. But while my furniture ontology includes sofas, not cushionless sofas (they are not the sort of things sold in furniture shops, for example), hers does—only they are now typewriter stands. Perhaps both ontologies include sofa cushions (at least I have a name for such things), but in my ontology they are a part of another item, while in hers they need not be part of anything else. When my friend points to an integral object in her furniture arrangement she points to a cushionless sofa; when I point to an integral object in my furniture arrangement, I point to the sofa with the cushions in place. The alteration in the conceptual organization of my room has altered the *boundaries* of the objects referred to. This is sometimes, but not always, a consequence of a metaphorically descriptive reference. Speaking of Venice as a 'noblewoman' in no way alters the *boundaries* of Venice. But when Socrates speaks of his as the art of midwifery, he conceives of the actual practice of philosophizing and educating as different from that practised by the sophists. In this case, conceiving of the referent (the activity of philosophy) differently does alter the boundaries of the activity.

I have used the room metaphor to suggest that truth is relative to an accepted system of concepts and beliefs which reflects a given set of relations a language community has to the world it occupies. What language expresses, means, and refers to at once shapes and, dialectically, is shaped by such a conceptual frame—one which is itself in a dialectical relation to language. It is a frame which must be adaptable both to our world's temporary, imaginary, and permanent alterations and to our understanding of that world; it must be a frame which will allow us to adapt our lives and our circumstances to change. As such, language is not primarily a conveyer of truth and falsity but exists as an expressive form in a dialectical relation to our purposes, our conceptual system, and what (to use a Davidsonian phrase) 'we hold to be true'.[17]

---

[17] Davidson (1986) recognizes that such a dialectic functions in our understanding of malapropisms, but the consequences for his treatment of metaphor and for his adherence to a truth-conditional semantics remain to be worked out.

Reference, Conceptual Schemes, and Epistemic Access

Richard Boyd speaks of some metaphors as 'constitutive of the theories they express'. These are metaphorical expressions that 'constitute, at least for a time, an irreplaceable part of the linguistic machinery of a scientific theory: cases in which there are metaphors which scientists use in expressing theoretical claims for which no adequate literal paraphrase is known' (1979, 360). Boyd uses the metaphor of the brain as computer as illustrative of a constitutive metaphor. His discussion of the utility of the constitutive metaphor is very much in the spirit of the discussion in earlier sections of this book. Using his brain example, he writes:

Part of the function of this metaphor as a theoretical statement is to suggest strategies for future research by asserting that, as investigations of men and machines progress, additional, or, perhaps entirely different, important respects of similarity and analogy will be discovered . . . the function of such metaphors is to put us on the track of these respects of similarity or analogy. (1979, 363.)

This is the conception of metaphor which I have tried to explicate in terms of the induction of the structure of a semantic field of the vehicle in the domain of the topic. But the research programme thus initiated is not fixed in advance. Which relations are fruitful to explore? Which will fail to uncover interesting insights? How are the fruitful analogies to be explicated? Boyd writes: 'Thus, it is hardly surprising that, at least for a time, it is not known exactly what the relevant respects of similarity or analogy are: many have yet to be discovered or understood' (1979, 364).

In that case, metaphors are not reducible to literal paraphrase, not only because metaphors depend on the introduction of alternative conceptual schemes but also because it is not clear (at least for the moment) *what it is* that is to be paraphrased. Here the cognitive importance of the referential use of metaphor re-emerges:

[Theory-constitutive metaphors] do share with literary metaphors the important property that their utility does not depend on the (even tacit) availability of such an explication [that is, a literal paraphrase]. Indeed, the utility of theory-constitutive metaphors seems to lie largely in the fact that they provide a way to introduce terminology for features of the world whose existence seems probable, but many of whose fundamental properties have yet to be discovered. (1979, 364.)

In particular, Boyd suggests, constitutive metaphors are useful for fixing the referent, when the referent is a property that is relational in character.

In this discussion Boyd's notion of reference allies itself with the epistemic view we have already encountered in Chastain. However, Boyd, following Putnam's discussion of the causal theory of reference as applied to natural kinds,[18] extends reference to general as well as singular terms. Boyd attempts to defend the view that reference involves epistemic access with regard to information gathering. The epistemic access in the case of metaphor is indirect, through a distinctive conceptual organization, and relational—not properties but relations between properties are accessed.[19]

To explicate fully the way in which metaphor provides epistemic access requires giving an account of metaphor's role in *establishing* concepts and categories. That part of the story of the cognitive force of metaphor will remain untold in this book. That is a direction for further research.[20] This book has detailed a theory of metaphorical meaning. A full account of the cognitive significance of metaphor requires a comparably detailed discussion of metaphorical thought. When the results are in, I believe that we shall find metaphorical thought to be as fundamental as inductive and deductive reasoning in formulating hypotheses, providing explanations, forming categories, generating predictions, and guiding behaviour. That metaphor is pervasive in language is an aspect of its prominent place in the structure of thought itself. The first step in establishing the importance of metaphorical thought has been to provide a careful dissection of the microstructure of linguistic metaphor.[21] Within this detailed examination, we can see the elements that will figure in the more grandiose speculations: conceptual incongruity and restructuring; the relationality and

[18] See Putnam 1975a.

[19] One could say that only relational properties were accessed as long as one understood that with different relata, the properties are only analogically related. See the discussion on analogy in Chapters 3 and 4 above.

[20] I begin this project in Kittay 1982.

[21] I do not mean to suggest that no one has as yet attacked the question of metaphorical thought. The studies of the role of metaphor in science (see e.g. Hesse 1966; 1980; Leatherdale 1974; Boyd 1979; Gentner 1980a; 1980b; 1982; Gentner and Gentner 1982) have done much to give us an understanding of metaphorical thought as it functions in science. The work of Lakoff and Johnson and a number of their students has explored metaphorical thought in our everyday conceptual life. Numerous psychological studies explore the topic as well. In a future work I intend to review this literature and work towards establishing a theory of metaphorical thought based in part on these studies and in part on the groundwork provided in the present book through its analysis of metaphorical language.

contextuality of language generally and of metaphor particularly; the transference of relations across domains and the subsequent induction of the structure of one field on to another; and the interplay of semantics and pragmatics in the creation of second-order meaning.

Conclusion

> The drive towards the formation of metaphors is the fundamental human drive, which one cannot for a single instance dispense with in thought, for one would thereby dispense with man himself. This drive is not truly vanquished and scarcely subdued by the fact that a regular and rigid new world is constructed as its prison from its own ephemeral products, the concepts. . . . This drive continually confuses the conceptual categories and cells by bringing forward new transferences, metaphors and metonymies. It continually manifests an ardent desire to refashion the world which presents itself to waking man, so that it will be as colourful, irregular, lacking in results and coherence, charming, and eternally new as the world of dreams. (Nietzsche, 'On Truth and Lies in the Nonmoral Sense' in *Philosophy and Truth: Selections from Nietzsche's Notebooks of the early 1870's*, trans. and ed. by D. Breazeale, 1979, 89.)

Language and our concepts, in their 'proper' and metaphorical arrangements, like the room and its furnishing in our metaphor, are things we live among. They change with time, need, desire, and whim. They both reflect and shape our beliefs and desires. They are rarely as tidy as we might like, although we can glory in the disorder—knowing that our room and our language have a lived-in character. Some order, at least one intelligible to ourselves and to those with whom we share our space and our words, none the less remains crucial. And a systematic tolerance of a 'disorder' that can be shown to be purposeful and intelligible is equally essential, if we are to remain in touch with the well-springs of our creativity and to keep our surroundings and our minds adaptable to the changing circumstances of our lives and our world. Understanding the workings and the meaning of this latter 'disorder' is as much a part of understanding meaning and language as is understanding the 'proper order'. It is within a carefully conceived 'chaos' that metaphors attain an irreducible cognitive content and their special meaning.

BIBLIOGRAPHY

Adler, J. E. (1984), 'Abstraction is Uncooperative', *Journal for the Theory of Social Behaviour*, vol. 14, no. 2, pp. 165–81.

Alston, W. (1967), 'Meaning', in P. Edwards (ed.), *The Encyclopedia of Philosophy* (New York, Macmillan), vol. 1, pp. 233–41.

Anderson, R. C., and Ortony, A. (1975), 'On Putting Apples into Bottles: A Problem of Polysemy', *Cognitive Psychology*, vol. 7, pp. 167–80.

Asch, S. E. (1958), 'The Metaphor: A Psychological Inquiry', in R. Tagiuri and L. Petrullo (edd.), *Person Perception and Interpersonal Behavior* (Stanford, Calif., Stanford University Press), pp. 86–94.

—— and Nerlove, H. (1960), 'The Development of Double-Function Terms in Children: An Exploratory Study', in B. Kaplan and S. Wagner (edd.), *Perspectives in Psychological Theory* (New York, International Universities Press), 47–60.

Bain, A. (1888), *English Composition and Rhetoric* (New York, D. Appleton).

Bally, C. (1940), 'L'Arbitraire du sign: valeur et signification', *Le Français Moderne*, vol. 8, pp. 193–203.

Barfield, O. (1973), *Poetic Diction*, (Middleton Conn., Wesleyan).

Barthes, R. (1967), *Elements of Semiology* (London, Cape).

Basso, K. H. (1976), ' "Wise Words" of the Western Apache: Metaphor and Semantic Theory', in K. H. Basso and H. A. Selby (edd.), *Meaning in Anthropology* (Albequerque, NM, University of New Mexico Press), 93–121.

Beardsley, M. C. (1958), *Aesthetics: Problems in the Philosophy of Criticism* (New York, Harcourt Brace).

—— (1962), 'The Metaphorical Twist', *Philosophy and Phenomenological Research*, vol. 22, pp. 293–307.

—— (1967), 'Metaphor', in P. Edwards, (ed.), *The Encyclopedia of Philosophy*, (New York, Macmillan), vol. 5, pp. 284–9.

—— (1976), 'Metaphor and Falsity', *Journal of Aesthetics and Art Criticism*, vol. 35, pp. 218–22.

—— (1978), 'Metaphorical Senses', *Nous*, vol. 12, pp. 3–16.

Bendix, E. M. (1966), *Componential Analysis of General Vocabulary* (The Hague, Mouton).

Benveniste, E. (1939), 'Nature de signe linguistique', *Acta Linguistica*, vol. 1, pp. 23–9.

Berggren, D. (1962), 'The Use and Abuse of Metaphor', *Review of Metaphysics*, vol. 16, pp. 237–58, 450–72.

—— (1966), 'From Myth to Metaphor', *Monist*, vol. 50, pp. 530–52.

Bergmann, M. (1979), 'Metaphor and Formal Semantic Theory', *Poetics*, vol. 8, pp. 213–30.

—— (1982), 'Metaphorical Assertions', *Philosophical Review*, vol. 91, no. 2, pp. 229–45.

Berlin, B., and Kay, P. (1969), *Basic Color Terms* (Berkeley, Calif., University of California Press).

Bickerton, D. (1969), 'Prolegomena to a Linguistic Theory of Metaphor', *Foundations of Language*, vol. 5, pp. 34–52.

Bierwisch, M. (1970), 'Poetics and Linguistics', in D. Freeman (ed.), *Linguistics and Literary Style* (New York, Holt, Rinehart & Winston), 96–115.

—— (1971), 'On Classifying Semantic Features', in Steinberg and Jakobvitz (1971), 410–35.

Billow, R. M. (1975), 'A Cognitive Developmental Study of Metaphor Comprehension', *Developmental Psychology*, vol. 11, pp. 415–23.

—— (1977), 'Metaphor: A Review of the Psychological Literature', *Psychological Bulletin*, vol. 84, pp. 81–92.

Binkley, T. (1974), 'On the Truth and Probity of Metaphor', *Journal of Aesthetics and Art Criticism*, vol. 33, pp. 171–80; reprinted in Johnson (1981).

Black, M. (1962), 'Metaphor', in M. Black, *Models and Metaphors* (Ithaca, NY, Cornell University Press), pp. 25–47; originally published in *Proceedings from the Aristotelian Society*, 55 (1954); reprinted in Johnson (1981).

—— (1979), 'More about Metaphor', in Ortony (1979*a*); reprinted from *Dialectica*, 31 (1977).

Bloomfield, L. (1933), *Language* (New York, Holt, Rinehart & Winston).

Boyd, R. (1979), 'Metaphor and Theory Change: What is "Metaphor" a Metaphor For?', in Ortony (1979*a*), 356–408.

Brandom, R. (1984) 'Reference Explained Away', *Journal of Philosophy*, vol. 81, no. 9, pp. 469–92.

Breton, A. (1972), *Manifestes du surréalisme*, ed. Jean-Jaques Pauvert (Bordeaux and Paris, Delmas). Originally published 1924.

Brooke-Rose, C. (1958), *A Grammar of Metaphor* (London, Mercury Books).

Brown, S. J. M. (1927), *The World of Imagery* (London, Kegan Paul, Trench, Trubner).

Bruss, E. W. (1975), 'Formal Semantics and Poetic Meaning', *Poetics*, vol. 4, pp. 339–63.

Burke, K. (1941), 'Four Master Tropes', *Kenyon Review*, vol. 3, pp. 421–38.

—— (1969), *A Grammar of Motives* (Berkeley, Calif., University of California Press).

Carbonell J. G. (1981), 'Metaphor Comprehension', Carnegie Mellon University (unpublished manuscript).

Carey, S. (1985), *Conceptual Change in Childhood* (Cambridge, Mass., MIT Press).

Cassirer, E. (1946), *Language and Myth*. trans. S. K. Langer (New York, Dover).

—— (1955), *Symbolic Forms*, 1 (New Haven, Conn., Yale University Press).

Cavell, M. (1984), 'Commentary on Kittay's Reply to Davidson', delivered at the Conference to Honor Donald Davidson (Rutgers University, Rutgers, New Jersey).

Caws, P. (1974), 'Coherence, System, and Structure', *Idealistic Studies*, vol. 4, no. 1, pp. 1–17.

Chastain, C. (1975), 'Reference and Context', in Gunderson (1975), 194–269.

Chomsky, N. (1961), 'Some Methodological Remarks on Generative Grammar', *Word*, vol. 17, pp. 219–39.

—— (1964), 'Degrees of Grammaticality', in Fodor and Katz (1964), 384–9.

—— (1965), *Aspects of the Theory of Syntax* (Cambridge, Mass., MIT Press).

—— (1971*a*), 'Deep Structure, Surface Structure, and Semantic Interpretation', in Steinberg and Jakobovitz (1971) pp. 183–216.

—— (1971*b*), *Problems of Knowledge and Freedom:–The Russell Lectures* (New York, Random House).

Clark, H. (1970), 'Word Associations and Linguistic Theory', in J. Lyons (ed.), *New Horizons in Linguistics*, (Harmondsworth, Middx. Penguin) pp. 271–286.

Cohen, L. J. (1977), 'Can the Conversationalist Hypothesis Be Defended', *Philosophical Studies*, vol. 31, pp. 81–90.

—— (1979), 'The Semantics of Metaphor', in Ortony (1979*a*), 64–77.

—— (1981), 'Chess as a Model of Language', *Philosophia*, vol. 11, pp. 51–87.

—— (1985), 'A Problem about Ambiguity in Truth-Theoretic Semantics', *Analysis*, vol. 45, no. 3, pp. 129–75.

—— (1986), 'How is Conceptual Innovation Possible?', *Erkenntnis*, pp. 221–38.

—— and Margalit, A. (1972), 'The Role of Inductive Reasoning in the Interpretation of Metaphor', in D. Davidson and G. Harman (edd.), *Semantics of Natural Language*, (Dordrecht, D. Reidel), 722–40.

Cohen, M. R. (1965), 'The Logic of Metaphors: Figurative Truth', in M. R. Cohen, *Preface to Logic* (New York, Meridian Books), 95–9.

Cohen, T. (1975), 'Figurative Speech and Figurative Acts', *Journal of Philosophy*, vol. 72, pp. 669–84.

—— (1976), 'Notes on Metaphor', *Journal of Aesthetics and Art Criticism*, vol. 34, pp. 249–59.

Crane, H. (1965), 'The Dynamics of Metaphor', in R. Ellmann and C. Feidelson, (edd.), *The Modern Tradition* (New Haven, Conn., Yale University Press), 158–62.

Culler, J. (1975), *Structural Poetics* (Ithaca, NY, Cornell University Press).

Danto, A. (1984), 'Philosophy And/As/Of Literature', in *Proceedings and Addresses of the American Psychological Association*, vol. 58, no. 1 pp. 5–20.

Dascal, M., and Margalit, A. (1974), 'A New "Revolution" in Linguistics?:

"Text-Grammars" vs. "Sentence-Grammars" ', *Theoretical Linguistics*, vol. 1, pp. 195–213.

Davidson, D. (1965), 'Theories of Meaning and Learnable Languages', in Y. Bar-Hillel, (ed.), *Proceedings of the 1964 International Congress for Logic, Methodology, and Philosophy of Science* (Amsterdam, North-Holland), 383–93; reprinted in Davidson (1984).

—— (1967), 'Truth and Meaning', *Synthese*, vol. 17, pp. 304–323; reprinted in Davidson (1984).

—— (1968), 'On Saying That', in D. Davidson and J. Hintikka, *Words and Objections: Essays on the Work of W. V. Quine*, (New York, Humanities Press), 158–74; reprinted from *Synthese*, 19 (1968–9); reprinted in Davidson (1984).

—— (1969), 'True to the Facts', *Journal of Philosophy*, vol. 66, pp. 748–64; reprinted in Davidson (1984).

—— (1973), 'Radical Interpretation', *Dialectica*, vol. 27, pp. 313–28; reprinted in Davidson (1984).

—— (1974*a*), 'Belief and the Basis of Meaning', *Synthese*, vol. 27, pp. 309–23; reprinted in Davidson (1984).

—— (1974*b*), 'Semantics for Natural Languages', in G. Harman (ed.), *On Noam Chomsky: Critical Essays* (New York, Anchor Press) pp. 242–52; reprinted from *Linguaggi nella Società e nella Tecnica*, Edizioni di Comunità, Milan, 1970; reprinted in Davidson (1984).

—— (1974*c*), 'On the Very Idea of a Conceptual Scheme', *Proceedings and Addresses of the American Philosophical Association*, vol. 47 pp. 5–20; reprinted in Davidson (1984).

—— (1975), 'Thought and Talk', in S. Guttenplan (ed.), *Language and Mind* (Oxford, Clarendon Press), 7–23; reprinted in Davidson (1984).

—— (1977*a*), 'Reality Without Reference', *Dialectica*, vol. 31, pp. 248–58; reprinted in Davidson (1984).

—— (1977*b*), 'The Method of Truth in Metaphysics', in P. French *et al.* (edd.), *Midwest Studies in Philosophy*, vol. 2, pp. 244–54; reprinted in Davidson (1984).

—— (1979), 'The Inscrutability of Reference', *Southwestern Journal of Philosophy*, vol. 10, pp. 7–19; reprinted in Davidson (1984).

—— (1981), 'What Metaphors Mean', in Johnson (1981 pp. 200–27); reprinted from *Critical Inquiry*, 5, (1978); reprinted in Davidson (1984).

—— (1984), *Inquiries into Truth and Interpretation* (Oxford, Clarendon Press).

—— (1986), 'A Nice Derangement of Epitaphs', in R. Grandy and R. Warner (edd.), *Philosophical Grounds of Rationality: Intentions, Categories, Ends* (Oxford: Clarendon Press) pp. 157–75.

—— and Harman, G. (1972), edd., *The Semantics of Natural Language* (Dordrecht, D. Reidel).

Derrida, J. (1975), 'White Mythology: Metaphor in the Text of Philosophy', trans. F. T. C. Moore, *New Literary History*, vol. 6 pp. 5–73; originally published as 'La Mythologie blanche', *Poétique* vol. 5 (1971).

Dijk, T. A. van (1972), *Some Aspects of Text Grammars* (The Hague: Mouton).

—— (1975), 'Formal Semantics of Metaphorical Discourse', *Poetics*, vol. 4, pp. 173–98.

Donnellan, K. S. (1971), 'Reference and Definite Descriptions', in D. D. Steinberg and L. A. Jakobovitz (edd.), *Semantics*, (Cambridge University Press), pp. 100–40, also reprinted in S. P. Schwartz (ed.), *Naming, Necessity and Natural Kinds* (Ithaca, NY, Cornell University Press 1977).

—— (1979), 'Speaker Reference, Descriptions and Anaphora', in French et al. (1979) pp. 28–44.

Drange, T. (1966), *Type Crossings* (The Hague: Mouton).

Dretske, F. I. (1972), 'Contrastive Statements', *Philosophical Review*, vol. 81, no. 4, pp. 411–37.

—— (1983), *Knowledge and the Flow of Information* (Cambridge, Mass., MIT Press).

Dummett, M. (1976), 'What is a Theory of Meaning? (II)' in G. Evans and J. McDowell (edd.), *Truth and Meaning* (Oxford: Clarendon Press) pp. 67–137.

Eco, U. (1973), 'Sémantique de la métaphore', *Tel Quel*, vol. 55, pp. 25–46.

—— (1984), *Semiotics and the Philosophy of Language* (Bloomington, Ind., Indiana University Press).

Elgin, C. Z. (1983), *With Reference to Reference* (Indianapolis, Ind., Hackett Publishers).

Empson, W. (1951), *The Structure of Complex Words* (New York, New Directions).

—— (1966), *Seven Types of Ambiguity* (New York, New Directions).

Fillmore, C. J. (1968), 'The Case for Case', in E. Bach and R. T. Harms, (edd.), *Universals in Linguistic Theory* (New York, Holt, Rinehart & Winston), pp. 1–90.

—— (1971), 'Types of Lexical Information', in Steinberg and Jakobovitz (1971) pp. 370–92.

Fodor, J. A. (1975), *The Language of Thought* (New York, Crowell).

—— and Katz, J. J. (1964), edd. *The Structure of Language: Readings in a Philosophy of Language* (Englewood Cliffs, NJ, Prentice-Hall).

—— et al. (1975), 'The Psychological Unreality of Semantic Representations', *Linguistic Inquiry*, vol. 6, pp. 515–31.

Frege, G. (1970), *Translations from the Philosophical Writings of Gottlob Frege*, trans. and ed. P. Geach and M. Black (Oxford: Blackwell).

—— (1971), *Gottlob Frege: Schriften zur Logik und Sprachphilosophie: aus dem Nachlass*, ed. G. Gabriel, (Hamburg, Felix Meiner Verlag).

French, P. A., et al. (1979), *Contemporary Perspectives in the Philosophy of Language* (Minneapolis, Minn., University of Minnesota Press).

Freud, S. (1965), *The Interpretation of Dreams* (New York, Avon) 11th edition.

Furth, H. G. (1968), *Thinking Without Language: Psychological Implications of Deafness* (New York, Free Press).

Gentner, D. (1980*a*), 'The Structure of Analogical Models in Science' Research Report (Cambridge, Mass., Bolt Beranek & Newman).

—— (1980*b*), 'Studies of Metaphor and Complex Analogies', delivered at the American Psychological Association Symposium on Metaphor as Process (Montreal, Sept.).

—— (1982) 'Are Scientific Analogies Metaphors?', in D. S. Miall (ed.), *Metaphor: Problems and Perspectives.* (Brighton, Harvester Press) pp. 106–33.

—— and Gentner, D. (1982), 'Flowing Waters or Teeming Crowds: Mental Models of Electricity', in D. Gentner and A. Stevens (edd.), *Mental Models* (Hillsdale, NJ, Erlbaum) pp. 101–29.

Gildea, P., and Glucksberg, A. (1984) 'On Understanding Metaphor: The Role of Context' *Journal of Verbal Learning and Verbal Behavior*, vol. 22, pp. 577–90.

Gleitman, H. (1981), *Psychology*, (New York, W. W. Norton).

Glucksberg, A., *et al.* (1982), 'On Understanding Nonliteral Speech: Can People Ignore Metaphors?', *Journal of Verbal Learning and Verbal Behavior*, vol. 21, pp. 85–98.

Goodman, N. (1965), *Fact, Fiction and Forecast* (Indianapolis, Ind., Bobbs-Merrill).

—— (1966), *The Structure of Appearance* (2nd edn.; Indianapolis, Ind., Bobbs-Merrill).

—— (1968), *Languages of Art* (Indianapolis, Ind., Bobbs-Merrill).

—— (1978*a*), 'Realy to Beardsley', *Erkenntnis*, vol. 12, pp. 169–73.

—— (1978*b*), *Ways of Worldmaking* (Indianapolis, Ind., Hackett).

—— (1984), *Of Mind and Other Matters* (Cambridge, Mass., Harvard University Press).

Grandy, R.E. (1982), 'Semantic Intentions and Linguistic Structure,' *Notre Dame Journal of Formal Logic*, vol. 23, no. 3, pp. 327–32.

—— (1987*a*), 'In Defense of Semantic Fields', in E. Le Pore (ed.), *New Directions in Semantics* (London, Academic Press), pp. 259–80.

—— (1987*b*), 'Information-based Epistemology, Ecological Epistemology and Epistemology Naturalized', *Synthese*, vol. 70, pp. 191–203.

Grice, H. P. (1968), 'Utterer's Meaning, Sentence-Meaning, and Word-Meaning', *Foundations of Language*, vol. 4, pp. 225–42.

—— (1969), 'Utterer's Meaning and Intention', *Philosophical Review*, vol. 78, pp. 147–77.

—— (1975), 'Logic and Conversation', in D. Davidson and G. Harman (edd.), *The Logic of Grammar*, (Encino, NM, Dickenson), pp. 64–75.

Gunderson, K. (ed.) (1975), *Language, Mind and Knowledge* (Minnesota Studies in the Philosophy of Science, 7; Minneapolis, Minn., University of Minnesota Press).

Halliday, M. A. K., and Hasan, R. (1976), *Cohesion in English* (London, Longman).

Hawkes, T. (1972), *Metaphor* (London, Methuen).

Helmer, J. (1972), 'Metaphor', *Linguistics*, vol. 88, pp. 5–19.

Henle, P. (1965), 'Metaphor', in P. Henle (ed.), *Language, Thought, and Culture*, (Ann Arbor, Mich., Ann Arbor Paperbacks), 173–95.

Hervey, S. G. J. (1978), 'Notions in the Manipulation of Non-Denotative Meaning in Speech', *La Linguistique: revue internationale de linguistique générale*, vol. 7, no. 1, pp. 31–40.

Hesse, M. B. (1962), 'Review of Turbayne', *Foundations of Language*, vol. 2, pp. 282–4.

—— (1966), 'The Explanatory Function of Metaphors', in M. B. Hesse, *Models and Analogies in Science* (Notre Dame, Quebec, Notre Dame University Press), 157–77.

—— (1974), *The Structure of Scientific Inference* (Berkeley, Calif., University of California Press).

—— (1980), *Revolution and Reconstructions in the Philosophy of Science* (Bloomington, Ind., Indiana University Press).

Hjelmslev, L. (1961), *Prolegomena to a Theory of Language*, trans. F. J. Whitfield (Bloomington, Ind., Indiana University Press) 2nd revised edition.

Hofstadter, D. (1985), *Metamagical Thema*, (New York, Basic Books).

Ipsen, G. (1924), 'Der alte Orient und die Indogermanen', in *Stand und Aufgaben der Sprachwissenschaft: Festschrift für W. Streitburg*, C. Winter ed. (Heidelberg) pp. 200–37.

Itard, J. M. G. (1932), *The Wild Boy of Aveyron*, (New York, Appleton-Century-Crofts).

Jackendoff, R. S. (1972), *Semantic Interpretation in Generative Grammar* (Cambridge, Mass., MIT Press).

Jakobson, R. (1960), 'Closing Statement: Linguistics and Poetics', in T. A. Sebeok, (ed.), *Style in Language* (Cambridge, Mass., MIT Press), 350–77.

—— (1968), 'Poetry of Grammar and Grammar of Poetry', *Lingua*, vol. 21, pp. 597–609.

—— (1971), *Studies in Child Language and Aphasia* (Janua Linguarum, Studia Memoria, Series Minor, 114; The Hague, Mouton).

—— and Halle, M. (1956), *Fundamentals of Language* (The Hague, Mouton).

Johnson, M. (1981), ed., *Philosophical Perspectives on Metaphor* (Minneapolis, Minn., Minnesota University Press).

—— (forthcoming), *The Body in the Mind: The Bodily Basis of Reason and Imagination* (University of Chicago Press).

Kaplan, D. (1979a), 'Dthat', reprinted from P. Cole (ed.) *Syntax and Semantics*, vol. 9; (New York, Academic Press), 1975. In French *et al.* (1979), pp. 383–400.

—— (1979*b*); 'On the Logic of Demonstratives', in French *et al.* (1979), pp. 401–14.

Katz, J. J. (1964), 'Semi-sentences', in Fodor and Katz (1964) pp. 400–16.

—— (1966), *The Philosophy of Language* (New York, Harper & Row).

—— (1972), *Semantic Theory* (New York, Harper & Row).

—— (1977), *Propositional Structure: A Study of the Contribution of Semantic Meaning to Speech Acts* (New York, Crowell).

—— (1982), 'Common Sense in Semantics', *Notre Dame Journal of Formal Logic*, vol. 23, no. 2, pp. 174–218.

—— and Fodor, J. A. (1963), 'The Structure of a Semantic Theory', *Language*, vol. 39, pp. 170–210; reprinted in Fodor and Katz (1964).

—— and Langendoen, T. (1976), 'Pragmatics and Presupposition', *Language*, vol. 52, pp. 7–17.

—— and Postal, P. M. (1964), *An Integrated Theory of Linguistic Descriptions* (Cambridge, Mass., MIT Press).

Kintsch, W. (1974), *The Representation of Meaning in Memory* (Hillsdale, NJ, Erlbaum).

Kittay, E. F. (1978), 'The Cognitive Force of Metaphor' dissertation (Graduate School of the City University of New York).

—— (1982), 'The Creation of Similarity: A Discussion of Metaphor in Light of Tversky's Theory of Similarity', *PSA 1982*, vol. 1, pp. 394–405.

—— (1988) 'Woman as Metaphor', *Hypatia*, vol. 3, no. 2, pp. 63–86.

—— (1984), 'The Identification of Metaphor', *Synthese*, vol. 58, pp. 153–202.

—— (1984), 'The Identification of Metaphor', *Synthese*, vol. 58, pp. 153–202.

—— (forthcoming), 'A Reply to Davidson's "What Metaphors Mean"—or Rearranging the Furniture of Our Minds', in M. Freund, (ed.), *The Philosophy of Language* (Costa Rica, University of Costa Rica Press).

—— and Lehrer, A. (1981), 'Semantic Fields and the Structure of Metaphor', *Studies in Language*, vol. 5, pp. 31–63.

Kripke, S. A. (1972*a*), 'Naming and Necessity', in Davidson and Harman (1972) pp. 253–355.

—— (1972*b*), 'Speaker's Reference and Semantic Reference' in French *et al.* (1979), 6–27.

Kuhn, T. S. (1970), *The Structure of Scientific Revolutions* (2nd edn.; University of Chicago Press).

—— (1974), 'Second Thoughts on Paradigms', in F. Suppes (ed.), *The Structure of Scientific Theories* (Urbana, Ill., University of Illinois Press).

—— (1979), 'Metaphor in Science', in Ortony (1979*a*), pp. 409–19.

Lakoff, G. (1973), 'Hedges: A Study of Meaning Criteria and the Logic of Fuzzy Concepts', *Journal of Philosophical Logic*, vol. 2, pp. 458–508.

—— and Johnson, M. (1980), *Metaphors We Live By* (University of Chicago Press).

—— and Kövecses, Z. (1983), 'The Concept of Anger Inherent in

American English'. Berkeley Cognitive Reports, Institute for Cognitive Studies, University of California, Berkeley.

Langendoen, T. (1970), *Essentials of English Grammar* (New York, Holt, Rinehart & Winston).

Lanham, R. A. (1969), *A Handlist of Rhetorical Terms: A Guide for Students of English Literature* (Berkeley, Calif., University of California Press).

Lawler, J. M. (1983), 'Review of *Metaphors we live by*. By George Lakoff and Mark Johnson.', *Language*, vol. 59, no. 1, pp. 201–7.

Leatherdale, W. H. (1974), *The Role of Analogy, Models and Metaphors in Science* (Amsterdam, North-Holland).

Leech, G. N. (1969), *A Linguistic Guide to English Poetry*. (London, Longmans, Green).

Lehrer, A. (1970), 'Static and Dynamic Elements in Semantics, *Hot, Warm, Cool, Cold*', *Papers in Linguistics*, vol. 3 pp. 349–73.

—— (1974), *Semantic Fields and Lexical Structure* (Amsterdam, North-Holland).

—— (1983), *Wine and Conversation* (Bloomington, Ind., Indiana University Press).

—— and Lehrer, K. (1982), 'Antonymy', *Linguistics and Philosophy*, vol. 5, pp. 483–501.

Leondar, B. (1975), 'Metaphor and Infant Cognition', *Poetics*, vol. 4, pp. 273–87.

Lévi-Strauss, C. (1963), *Structural Anthropology*, trans. C. Jacobson and B. G. Schoepf (New York, Basic Books).

Levin, S. R. (1977), *The Semantics of Metaphor* (Baltimore, Md., Johns Hopkins University Press).

—— (1979), 'Standard Approaches to Metaphor and a Proposal for Literary Metaphor', in Ortony (1979*a*), 124–35.

Lewis, D. (1972), 'General Semantics', in Davidson and Harman (1972) pp. 169–218.

Loewenberg, I. (1973), 'Truth and Consequences of Metaphors', *Philosophy and Rhetoric*, vol. 6, pp. 30–46.

—— (1975*a*), 'Denying the Undeniable: Metaphors are *Not* Comparisons', *Mid American Linguistics Conference Papers*, pp. 305–16.

—— (1975*b*), 'Identifying Metaphors', *Foundations of Language*, vol. 12, pp. 315–38.

Lyons, J. (1963), *Structural Semantics* (Oxford, Blackwell).

—— (1968), *Introduction to Theoretical Linguistics* (London, Cambridge University Press).

—— (1977), *Semantics*, 1 (London, Cambridge University Press).

MacCormac, E. R. (1971), 'Meaning Variance and Metaphor', *British Journal for the Philosophy of Science*, vol. 22, pp. 145–59.

—— (1976), *Metaphor and Myth in Science and Religion* (Durham, NC, Duke University Press).

McCloskey, M. (1964), 'Metaphors', *Mind*, vol. 73, pp. 215–33.

McIntosh, A. (1961), 'Patterns and Ranges', *Language*, vol. 3, pp. 325–37.

Mack, D. (1975), 'Metaphoring as Speech Act: Some Happiness Conditions for Implicit Similes and Simple Metaphors', *Poetics*, vol. 4, pp. 221–56.

Man, P. de (1979), 'The Epistemology of Metaphor', in Sacks (1979), 11–29.

Margalit, A. (1978), 'The "Platitude" Principle of Semantics', *Erkenntnis*, vol. 13, pp. 377–95.

Matthews, R. J. (1971), 'Concerning a "Linguistic Theory" of Metaphor', *Foundations of Language*, vol. 7, pp. 413–25.

Miller, G. A. (1979), 'Images and Models, Similes and Metaphors', in Ortony (1979*a*), 202–53.

—— and Johnson-Laird, P. N. (1976), *Language and Perception* (Cambridge, Mass., Harvard University Press).

Mooij, J. J. A. (1975), 'Tenor, Vehicle, and Reference', *Poetics*, vol. 4, pp. 257–72.

—— (1976), *A Study of Metaphor* (Amsterdam, North-Holland).

Morris, C. (1938), *Foundations of the Theory of Signs* (Foundations of the Unity of Science: Toward an International Encyclopedia of Unified Science, vol. 1, no. 2; University of Chicago Press).

Motley, M. T. (1985), 'Slips of the Tongue' *Scientific American*, vol. 253 no. 3, pp. 116–27.

Mukarovsky, J. (1964), 'Standard Language and Poetic Language', in P. Garvin (ed.), *A Prague School Reader on Aesthetics, Literary Structure and Style* (Washington, DC, Georgetown University Press) pp. 17–30.

Myers, C. M. (1968) 'Metaphors and Mediatively Informative Expressions', *Southern Journal of Philosophy*, vol. 6, pp. 159–227.

Nietzsche (1979), 'On Truth and Lying in the Moral Sense', in D. Breazeale (trans. and ed.), *Philosophy and Truth: Selections from Nietzsche's Notebooks of the early 1870's* (Atlantic Highlands, NJ, Humanities Press) pp. 79–97.

Nunberg, G. (1979), 'The Non-Uniqueness of Semantic Solutions: Polysemy', *Linguistics and Philosophy*, vol. 3, pp. 143–84.

Ohmann, S. (1953), 'Theories of the Linguistic Field', *Word*, vol. 9 pp. 123–34.

O'Neill, B. J., and Paivio, A. (1978), 'Semantic Constraints in Encoding Judgments and Free Recall of Concrete and Abstract Sentences', *Canadian Journal of Psychology*, vol. 32, pp. 3–18.

Ortony, A. (1975), 'Why Metaphors are Necessary and Not Just Nice', *Educational Theory*, vol. 25, pp. 45–53.

—— (1976), 'On the Nature and Value of Metaphor: A Reply to My Critics', *Educational Theory*, vol. 26, pp. 395–8.

—— ed. (1979*a*), *Metaphor and Thought* (Cambridge University Press).

—— (1979*b*), 'Beyond Literal Similarity', *Psychological Review*, vol. 86, pp. 161–80.

—— (1979*c*), 'The Role of Similarity in Similes and Metaphors', in Ortony (1979*a*), pp. 186–201.

—— *et al.* (1978*a*), 'Metaphor: Theoretical and Empirical Research', *Psychological Bulletin*, vol. 85, pp. 919–43.

—— *et al.* (1978*b*), 'Interpreting Metaphors and Idioms: Some Effects of Context on Comprehension', *Journal of Verbal Learning and Verbal Behavior*, vol. 17, pp. 465–77.

Paivio, A. (1979), 'Psychological Processes in the Comprehension of Metaphor', in Ortony (1979*a*), 150–171.

Pederson-Krag, G. (1956), 'The Use of Metaphor in Analytic Thinking', *Psychoanalytic Quarterly*, vol. 25, pp. 66–71.

Peirce, C. S. (1931), *Collected Papers*, vols. 1–6 ed. C. Hartshorne and P. Weiss, (Cambridge, Mass., Harvard University Press).

—— (1940), *The Philosophy of Peirce, Selected Writings*, J. Buchler, ed. (New York and London).

Pepper, S. (1928), 'Philosophy and Metaphor', *Journal of Philosophy*, vol. 25, pp. 130–2.

—— (1935), 'The Root Metaphor Theory of Metaphysics', *Journal of Philosophy*, vol. 32, pp. 365–74.

—— (1961), *World Hypotheses* (Berkeley, Calif., University of California Press).

Percy, W. (1958), 'Metaphor as Mistake', *Sewanee Review*, vol. 66, pp. 79–99.

Porzig, W. (1950), *Das Wunder der Sprache* (Berne, Francke).

Putnam, H. (1975*a*), 'The Meaning of Meaning', in Gunderson (1975) pp. 131–93

—— (1975*b*), *Mind, Language and Reality: Philosophical Papers* (Cambridge University Press).

Pylyshyn, Z. W. (1979), 'Metaphorical Imprecision and the "Top-Down" Research Strategy', in Ortony (1979*a*), 420–38.

Quine, W. van O. (1948), 'On What There Is', *Review of Metaphysics*, vol. 2, pp. 21–38.

—— (1951), 'Two Dogmas of Empiricism', *Philosophical Review*, vol. 60, pp. 20–43.

—— (1960), *Word and Object*, (Cambridge, Mass., MIT Press).

—— (1963), *From a Logical Point of View* (New York, Harper & Row).

—— (1971), 'Reference and Modality', in L. Linsky (ed.), *Reference and Modality* (London, Oxford University Press).

—— (1972), 'Methodological Reflections on Current Linguistic Theory', in Davidson and Harman (1972), 442–53.

Quinn, N. (1985), 'The Understanding of Marriage in Our Culture', in

D. Holland and N. Quinn (edd.), *Cultural Models* (Cambridge University Press).

Reddy, M. J. (1969), 'A Semantic Approach to Metaphor', in R. I. Binnick *et al.* (edd.), *Papers from the Fifth Regional Meeting of the Chicago Linguistic Society*, (University of Chicago), 240–51.

—— (1979), 'The Conduit Metaphor', in Ortony (1979*a*) pp. 284–324.

Reynolds, R. E., and Ortony, A. (1980), 'Some Issues in the Measurement of Children's Comprehension of Metaphorical Language', *Child Development*, vol. 51, pp. 1110–19.

Richards, I. A. (1936), *The Philosophy of Rhetoric* (London, Oxford University Press).

Ricœur, P. (1974), 'Metaphor and the Main Problem of Hermeneutics', *New Literary History*, vol. 6, pp. 95–110.

—— (1976), *Interpretation Theory: Discourse and the Surplus of Meaning,* (Fort Worth, Texas, Texas Christian University Press).

—— (1978*a*), 'The Metaphorical Process as Cognition, Imagination, and Feeling', *Critical Inquiry*, vol. 5, pp. 143–59.

—— (1978*b*), *The Rule of Metaphor: Multidisciplinary Studies in the Creation of Meaning in Language* trans. R. Czerny (Toronto, University of Toronto Press); originally published as *La Métaphore vive* (Paris, Editions du Seuil, 1975).

Rieser, M. (1958), 'Metaphoric Expression in the Plastic Arts', *Journal of Aesthetics and Art Criticism*, vol. 17, pp. 194–200.

Rosch, E. H. (1975*a*), 'Cognitive Reference Points', *Cognitive Psychology*, vol. 7, pp. 532–47.

—— (1975*b*), 'Cognitive Representations in Semantic Categories', *Journal of Experimental Psychology: General*, vol. 104, pp. 192–233.

—— (1973), 'On the Internal Structure of Perceptual and Semantic Categories', in T. E. Moore (ed.), *Cognitive Development and the Acquisition of Language* (New York, Academic Press), 111–44.

—— (1978), 'Principles of Categorization', in E. H. Rosch and B. B. Lloyd (edd.), *Cognition and Categorization* (Hillsdale, NJ, Erlbaum).

—— and Mervis, C. B. (1975), 'Family Resemblances: Studies in the Internal Structure of Categories', *Cognitive Psychology*, vol. 7, pp. 573–605.

—— *et al.* (1976), 'Basic Objects in Natural Categories', *Cognitive Psychology*, vol. 8, pp. 382–439.

Ross, J. F. (1981), *Portraying Analogy* (Cambridge University Press).

Rumelhart, D. E. (1979), 'Some Problems with the Notion of Literal Meanings', in Ortony (1979*a*) pp. 78–90.

Ryle, G. (1949), *The Concept of Mind* (New York, Barnes & Noble).

Sacks, S. (1979), *On Metaphor* (University of Chicago Press).

Sadock, J. M. (1979), 'Figurative Speech and Linguistics', in Ortony (1979*a*), 46–63.

Sanders, R. E. (1973), 'Aspects of Figurative Language', *Linguistics*, vol. 96, pp. 56–100.

Sapir, J. D. (1977), 'The Anatomy of Metaphor', in J. D. Sapir and J. C. Crocker, (edd.), *The Social Use of Metaphor: Essays on the Anthropology of Rhetoric* (Philadelphia, Pa., University of Pennsylvania Press).

Saussure, F. de (1966), *Course in General Linguistics*, ed. C. Bally, A. Sechehaye, and A. Riedlinger, trans. W. Baskin (New York, Philosophical Library).

Scheffler, I. (1979), *Beyond the Letter: A Philosophical Inquiry into Ambiguity, Vagueness, and Metaphor in Language* (London, Routledge & Kegan Paul).

Schön, D. A. (1963), *The Displacement of Concepts* (London, Tavistock).

—— (1979), 'Generative Metaphor: A Perspective on Problem Setting in Social Policy', in Ortony (1979*a*) pp. 254–84.

Searle, J. R. (1979*a*), *Expression and Meaning* (Cambridge University Press).

—— (1979*b*), 'Indirect Speech Acts', in Searle (1979*a*) pp. 30–57.

—— (1979*c*), 'Metaphor', in Searle (1979*a*) pp. 76–116, and in Johnson (1981).

—— (1979*d*), 'Literal Meaning', in Searle (1979*a*), pp. 117–36.

Shannon, C. E., and Weaver, W. (1949), *The Mathematical Theory of Information* (Urbana, Ill., University of Illinois Press).

Shapiro, M. and Shapiro, M. 1976, *Hierarchy and the Structure of Tropes*. (Bloomington, Ind: Indiana University Press; Liss: P. de Ridder Press).

Shibles, W. A. (1971), *Metaphor: An Annotated Bibliography and History* (Whitewater, Wis., Language Press).

Skinner, B. F. (1947), *Verbal Behavior* (New York, Appleton-Century-Crofts).

Smith, E. E., et al. (1974), 'Structure and Process in Semantic Memory: A Featural Model for Semantic Decisions', *Psychological Review*, vol. 81, pp. 214–41.

Sommers, F. (1959), 'Ordinary Language Tree', *Mind*, vol. 68, pp. 160–85.

Sparshott, F. E. (1974), ' "As", or the Limits of Metaphor'. *New Literary History*, vol. 6, pp. 75–94.

Sperber, D. (1975), *Rethinking Symbolism*, trans. A. L. Morton (Cambridge University Press).

Srzednicki, J. (1969), 'On Metaphor', *Philosophical Quarterly*, vol. 10, pp. 228–37.

Stalnaker, R. C. (1972), 'Pragmatics', in Davidson and Harman (1972) pp. 330–39.

—— (1973), 'Presuppositions', *Journal of Philosophical Logic*, vol. 2, pp. 442–57.

—— (1974), 'Pragmatic Presuppositions', in M. K. Munitz and P. Unger (edd.), *Semantics and Philosophy* (New York University Press), pp. 197–214.

Stanford, W. B. (1972), *Greek Metaphor* (New York, Johnson Reprint).

Steinberg, D. D., and Jakobovitz, L. A. (1971), edd., *Semantics: An Interdis-*

ciplinary Reader in Philosophy, Linguistics and Psychology (London and New York, Cambridge University Press).

Stern, G. (1932), *Meaning and Change of Meaning* (Göteborg, Hogskolas Arsskrift).

Stern, J. (1983), 'Metaphor and Grammatical Deviance', *Nous*, vol. 17, no. 4, pp. 577–99.

—— (1985), 'Metaphor as Demonstrative', *Journal of Philosophy*, vol. 82, no. 12, pp. 677–710.

Sternberg, R. J. (1977*a*), 'Component Processes in Analogical Reasoning', *Psychological Review*, vol. 84, no. 353–78.

—— (1977*b*), *Intelligence, Information Processing, and Analogical Reasoning: The Componential Analysis of Human Abilities* (Hillsdale, NJ, Erlbaum).

—— and Gardner, M. K. (1978), 'A Unified Theory of Inductive Reasoning in Semantic Space', MS (New Haven, Conn., Yale University).

—— and Nigro, G. (1978), 'Component Processes in Metaphoric Comprehension and Appreciation', MS (New Haven, Conn., Yale University).

—— and Rifkin, B. (1979), 'The Development of Analogical Reasoning Processes', *Journal of Experimental Child Psychology*, vol. 27, 195–232.

—— and Tourangeau R. (1978), 'Understanding and Appreciating Metaphors', Technical Report, 11, Office of Naval Research, Personnel and Training Research Programs, Psychological Sciences Division (New Haven, Conn., Yale University).

—— and Tourangeau, R. (1981), 'Aptness in Metaphor', *Cognitive Psychology*, vol. 13, pp. 27–55.

—— *et al.* (1979), 'Metaphor Induction and Social Policy: The Convergence of Macroscopic and Microscopic Views', in Ortony (1979*a*), 325–55.

Suppes, P. (1983), 'Probability and Information', *Behavioral and Brain Sciences*, vol. 6, pp. 81–2.

Tarski, A. (1959), 'The Concept of Truth in Formalized Languages' in *Logic, Semantics, Metamathematics*, (Oxford University Press) pp. 152–278.

Todorov, T. (1974), 'On Linguistic Symbolism', *New Literary History*, vol. 6, pp. 111–34.

Tourangeau, R., and Sternberg, R. J. (1978), 'What Makes a Good Metaphor', MS (New Haven, Conn., Yale University).

Trier, J. (1931), *Der Deutsche Wortschatz im Sinnbezirk des Verstandes* (Heidelberg, Winter).

Tulving, E. (1972), 'Episodic and Semantic Memory', in E. Tulving and W. Donaldson (edd.), *Organization of Memory* (New York, Academic Press) pp. 355–403.

—— and Thomson, D. M. (1973), 'Encoding Specificity and Retrieval Processes in Episodic Memory', *Psychological Review*, vol. 80, pp. 352–73.

Turbayne, C. M. (1962), *The Myth of Metaphor* (New Haven, Conn., Yale

University Press); revised edition (Columbia, SC, University of South Carolina Press) 1970.

Tuve, R. (1947), *Elizabethan and Metaphysical Imagery* (University of Chicago Press).

Tversky, A. (1972), 'Elimination by Aspects: A Theory of Choice', *Psychological Review*, vol. 79, pp. 281–99.

—— (1977), 'Features of Similarity', *Psychological Review*, vol. 84, pp. 327–52.

—— and Gati, I. (1979), 'Studies of Similarity', *Psychological Review*, vol. 84, pp. 79–98.

Ullmann, S. (1957), *The Principles of Semantics* (2nd edn.; Oxford, Blackwell).

—— (1962), *Semantics: An Introduction to the Science of Meaning* (Oxford, Basil Blackwell & Mott).

—— (1975), 'Natural and Conventional Signs', in T. A. Sebeok (ed.), *The Tell-Tale Sign*, (Netherlands, Peter de Ridder), pp. 103–10.

Van Fraassen, B. (1980), *The Scientific Image* (Oxford, Clarendon Press).

Vesey, G. N. (1956), 'Seeing and Seeing-as', *Proceedings of the Aristotelian Society*, vol. 56, pp. 109–24.

Wartofsky, M. (1979), *Models, Representation and the Scientific Understanding*, (Boston, Reidel).

Weinreich, U. (1966), 'Explorations in Semantic Theory', in T. A. Sebeok (ed.), *Theoretical Foundations* (Current Trends in Linguistics, 3; The Hague, Mouton) pp. 395–477.

Wellek, R. and Warren, A. (1956), *Theory of Literature* (New York, Harcourt Brace & World).

Welsh, P. (1963), 'On Explicating Metaphors', *Journal of Philosophy*, vol. 60, pp. 622–3.

Whalley, G. (1974), 'Metaphor', in A. Preminger (ed.), *Encyclopedia of Poetry and Poetics*, (Princeton, NJ, Princeton University Press), pp. 490–5.

Whately, R. (1963), *Elements of Rhetoric*, ed. D. Enninger (Carbondale, Ill., Southern Illinois Press).

Wheelright, P. (1962), *Metaphor and Reality*, (Bloomington, Ind., Indiana University Press).

—— (1968), *The Burning Fountain* (Bloomington, Ind., Indiana University Press).

Whorf, B. L. (1956), *Language, Thought, and Reality*, ed. J. B. Carroll (Cambridge, Mass., MIT Press).

Wimsatt, W. K., Jr. (1954), *The Verbal Icon* (Lexington, Ky., University of Kentucky Press).

Winner, E. (1979), 'New Names for Old Things: The Emergence of Metaphoric Language', *Journal of Child Language*, vol. 6, pp. 469–91.

—— and Gardner, H. (1977a), 'The Comprehension of Metaphor in Brain-Damaged Patients', *Brain*, vol. 100, pp. 717–29.

—— —— (1980), 'Misunderstanding Metaphor: What's the Problem?', *Journal of Experimental Child Psychology*, vol. 3, pp. 22–32.

—— et al. (1976), 'The Development of Metaphoric Understanding', *Developmental Psychology*, vol. 12, pp. 289–97.

Wittgenstein, L. (1953), *Philosophical Investigations* (New York, Macmillan).

—— (1972), *On Certainty*, ed. G. E. M. Anscombe and G. H. von Wright (New York, Harper & Row).

Whorf, B. L. (1956), *Language, Thought and Reality*, ed. J. B. Carroll, (Cambridge, Mass: MIT Press).

Ziff, P. (1964), 'On Understanding "Understanding Utterances" ', in Fodor and Katz (1964), 390–9.

AUTHOR INDEX

SUBJECT INDEX

Subject Index